# PORCELAIN
## of the Nineteenth Century

Antoinette Faÿ-Hallé
Barbara Mundt

# PORCELAIN
## of the Nineteenth Century

*RIZZOLI*
NEW YORK

## List of Abbreviations Used in the Captions

| | | | | |
|---|---|---|---|---|
| Co. | county | | MfK | Museum für Kunsthandwerk, Frankfort |
| Coll. | collection | | MfKuG | Museum für Kunst und Gewerbe, Hamburg |
| D. | diameter | | MNC | Musée National de Céramique, Sèvres |
| H. | height | | MNCM | Musée National du Château de Malmaison, Rueil-Malmaison |
| L. | length | | | |
| Mus. | museum | | MPD | Museo delle porcellane di Doccia, Sesto Fiorentino |
| W. | width | | | |
| | | | NM | Naturhistorisk Museum, Frederiksberg |
| BN | Bayerisches Nationalmuseum, Munich | | NMW | National Museum of Wales, Cardiff |
| CM & AG | City Museum and Art Gallery, Derby or Stoke-on-Trent | | ÖMaK | Österreichisches Museum für angewandte Kunst, Vienna |
| DPM | Dyson Perrins Museum, Worcester | | RPF | Royal Porcelain Factory, Copenhagen |
| HL | Hessisches Landesmuseum, Darmstadt | | SMPK | Staatliche Museen Preussischer Kulturbesitz, Berlin |
| HSK | Ehemalige Hoftafel- und Silberkammer [Former Court Tableware and Silver Pantry], Vienna | | SP | Staatliche Porzellanmanufaktur, Meissen |
| | | | SSuG | Staatliche Schlösser und Gärten, Berlin |
| MA | Musée de l'Ariana, Geneva | | TM | Thüringer Museum, Eisenach |
| MAD | Musée National Adrien-Dubouché, Limoges | | V & A | Victoria and Albert Museum, London |
| MAN | Museo Arqueologico Nacional, Madrid | | VdSSGuS | Verwaltung der Staatlichen Schlösser, Gärten und Seen, Munich |
| MB | Museum Bellerive, Zurich | | | |
| MB-A | Musée des Beaux-Arts, Caen or Troyes | | VEB | (East German) State-owned company |
| MBG | Musée Baron-Gérard, Bayeux | | UM | Uméleckoprùmyslové Muzeum [Arts and Crafts Museum], Prague |
| MCM | Merseyside County Museum, Liverpool | | | |
| MdAd | Musée des Arts décoratifs, Paris | | WL | Württembergisches Landesmuseum, Stuttgart |

Note on the text: unless stated otherwise, the references in the margins refer to the plate numbers; the reference numbers in the captions refer to the numbers in the Catalogue of Porcelain Marks, pp. 278–87.

This book has been published with the generous cooperation of the Foundation 'Ceramica' in Basle, Switzerland.

French-language edition, *La porcelaine européenne au XIX<sup>e</sup> siècle*
Copyright © 1983 by Office du Livre S.A. Fribourg, Switzerland

English translation by AILEEN DAWSON and Office du Livre
Copyright © 1983 by Office du Livre S.A. Fribourg, Switzerland

Published in 1983 in the United States of America by:

## RIZZOLI INTERNATIONAL PUBLICATIONS, INC.
712 Fifth Avenue/New York 10019

**Library of Congress Cataloging in Publication Data**
Faÿ-Hallé, Antoinette.
    Porcelain of the nineteenth century.

    Translation of: La porcelaine européenne au XIX<sup>e</sup> siècle.
    Bibliography: p.
    Includes index.
    1. Porcelain, European.    2. Porcelain—19th century—Europe. — I. Mundt, Barbara.    II. Title.
NK 4483.H2813    1983      738.2'094       82-50108
ISBN 0-8478-0437-2

*Printed and bound in Switzerland*

# Contents

# Introduction

Porcelain has been a subject of fascination in Europe since the Renaissance. It reached a peak of popularity in the eighteenth century and was still much sought after in the nineteenth. At the time porcelain was discovered, the bourgeoisie were beginning to furnish their houses in a luxurious fashion which previously only the aristocracy had been able to afford. The artists concerned in the manufacture of porcelain used the material to express their own ideas, and the factory owners lowered manufacturing costs so that porcelain would be available to a larger number of people.

Most eighteenth-century porcelain factories were established by kings and princes for their own amusement. Shortly before 1800, and particularly after that date, there was a veritable explosion in the number of European porcelain factories. The 'secret' of making porcelain was now common property. In France the monopoly formerly enjoyed by the Sèvres porcelain factory had disappeared in the whirlwind of the Revolution. In England a heavy import duty had been imposed on Chinese porcelain. In Russia great landowners had realized that they could use their serfs as a labour force for the manufacture of a highly profitable product. Bohemia threw off Viennese domination, and Thuringia increased the prosperity of its own porcelain industry established in the eighteenth century. Almost everywhere favourable circumstances existed for anyone willing to take advantage of them. Naturally competition was fierce and many small concerns changed hands or rapidly went out of business. It is easy enough to calculate how many porcelain factories were in operation in Europe at the end of the eighteenth century, but it is almost impossible to know how many were in existence at the end of the nineteenth. In Germany and the Austro-Hungarian Empire there were about two hundred and fifty firms, not counting the minor ones, and their number was constantly increasing. The present work therefore makes no claim to be comprehensive. In any case, by the end of the century most factories had given up creating original models and were concentrating on mass-produced articles.

Most of the factories established in the eighteenth century were located in capitals or in large towns. The factories at St Petersburg and Copenhagen, at Sèvres in the vicinity of Paris and Meissen near Dresden, at Vienna, Berlin, and Munich all depended on the patronage of royal or princely courts. In contrast, privately owned factories of more recent date were established in the provinces close to the raw materials used in the manufacture of porcelain or near the fuel supply. Limoges, for instance, owed its growth to the presence of kaolin, while Staffordshire became a pottery centre because of its rich coal deposits. The advent of the railway during the nineteenth century greatly aided the transport of raw materials and contributed to the process of industrialization.

The increase in the number of factories established during the first half of the nineteenth century did not, however, take place in a period of economic optimism. The whole of Europe had been affected by the Napoleonic wars and the ensuing economic hardship. Competition from English creamwares worsened the situation. From 1830 there was a distinct economic recovery, and new factories were set up. The quality of their wares continued to improve, thanks to technical progress, and the rising middle classes, with their increasing desire for luxury, provided a ready market. What happened to the Paris porcelain manufacturing industry in the periods 1800 to 1820 and 1820 to 1850 is worth noting as this individual case is indicative of the development of the industry as a whole. There were neither raw materials nor fuel in the Paris region, and the railway was not yet established to solve the problem of transporting them from elsewhere. Besides, lack of space prevented expansion, so that factories could operate only on a small scale. Labour, affected by the numerous popular revolutions (especially by those of 1830 and 1848), was increasingly ill-disciplined and costly. All these factors meant that manufacturers who wished to survive left Paris and set up in the provinces. Thus Honoré moved his factory for the production of undecorated wares to Champroux in 1824. Success was dependent on the very ingredients that were not available in Paris.

There were periods of crisis in the latter part of the century as well. The years around 1860 and 1870 were difficult for most European countries. In France there was a crisis shortly after the Franco-Prussian War of 1870–1871. A number of porcelain factories closed down or changed hands at this time. In general terms, this crisis, which was partly attributable to a proliferation of factories operating in competition with each other, was satisfactorily resolved.

Not one porcelain factory proved able to survive solely by making individually hand-painted pieces. Sooner or later they all had to switch to mass-production of domestic wares in order to make a profit. All the expanding industrialized nations found a multitude of new uses for porcelain. The most

successful concerns in financial terms were those manufacturing pipes of all kinds, as well as laboratory and sanitary wares, cylinders, mills, sieves, components for weaving equipment, and insulators for the electrical industry. Porcelain is almost always acid-resistant, does not conduct electricity, and withstands extremes of heat and cold. It was thus destined to become a popular material in modern times. A clever businessman like Jules Richard of Milan was conscious of its future. In 1896, his firm took over the Doccia factory where art porcelain was still being made by the Ginori family. The two factories merged to trade under the name Società Ceramica Richard-Ginori. This line of development is typical of the history of European porcelain factories since the nineteenth century. They have become mass-production units, although some of the better firms have managed to preserve a branch that continues to make pieces of artistic merit in the craft tradition.

Exhibitions, which were held nationally before 1850 and became international following the success of the famous Crystal Palace Exhibition held in London in 1851, necessarily influenced the ambitions of nineteenth-century porcelain manufacturers. The numerous contemporary exhibition reports provide us with a wealth of information, even though they were often written from a thoroughly nationalistic point of view, thus giving contemporary readers a distorted picture. For example, there are numerous discussions centering around the fierce competition between the English and the French porcelain industries, one party claiming to uphold 'good taste', while the other claimed superiority in producing pieces for every need. In Ralph Nicholson Wornum's essay entitled 'The Exhibition as a Lesson in Taste', which was an appendix to the 1851 Exhibition catalogue, we read: 'The influence of France is paramount in the European productions' [p. V***], followed by 'First, generally, the English side does not betray that great inferiority of taste which has been so long prognosticated of it' [p. VII***], and finally, 'Though the Sèvres porcelain takes the lead in point of pretension, it is not superior in taste, and is certainly inferior in matters of utility, to the specimens of Alderman Copeland in Stoke-on-Trent' [p. XVIII***]. We readily agree with that last statement, although at the time it probably shocked French sensibilities. However it is more in the nature of a piece of quasi-chauvinistic propaganda than a valid aesthetic judgement. In any case, international exhibitions were held at ever more frequent intervals between 1851 and 1900 and constituted a series of challenges for the manufacturers. Time after time, they had to prove that they could do at least as well as their competitors and could match the productions of their rivals. For instance, at the end of the century most of them produced *sang-de-bœuf,* or ox-blood, and crystalline glazes in imitation of the Chinese glazes. A certain uniformity of taste became inevitable and tended to blur national characteristics.

At the beginning of the nineteenth century, there was a relative diversity of taste in Europe, which was then under Napoleonic domination. For example in England Japanese influence was still strongly felt, although it had disappeared elsewhere. Italian porcelain still relied heavily on the beauty of the white body to set off decorative schemes conceived in a Neo-Pompeian style. Yet since about 1760 there had been a recognizable European style in porcelain, which can be called Neo-Classical or Empire. The style relies on the use of fairly severe shapes as a basis for the painted decoration, which was considered highly important. Even the big English porcelain factories, especially Derby and Worcester, adhered to the prevailing style. The whiteness of the porcelain body was carefully disguised by delicately executed miniature paintings, generally of excellent quality. Gilding was abundantly used, often constituting a 'frame' for the 'picture' on the porcelain. At this period oil-painters working on canvas were producing work in a style identical to the porcelain painters. All oil-painters were seeking a glossy and scrupulously worked effect. The treatment of their subjects is often described in France as *porcelainée* ('china-like'). Given this state of affairs, it is hardly surprising that paintings by artists like François Gérard were copied on porcelain, and from there it was but a short step to copying all kinds of paintings. Only English painters managed to preserve a free painterly style, and the growth of the English water-colour technique has its parallel in the large number of landscape scenes painted *en camaïeu* on countless contemporary porcelain services.

Between 1820 and 1830, the bourgeoisie were demanding more variety and gaiety in every artistic sphere. Signs of industrialization appeared at the porcelain factories, which tried to avoid the exorbitant cost of detailed hand-painted decoration by producing ever more complex shapes that were in themselves decorative. Neo-Rococo was born, closely followed by Neo-Gothic. From the 1820s, under the inspiration of German eighteenth-century porcelain, firms like John Rose's Coalport factory created pieces that seemed to represent the very height of sumptuousness with their pierced work, gilt-scroll ornament, and their naturalistically painted flowers in relief. In fact, these pieces signalled a retrograde step in relation to the porcelain made early in the century: they represent an economic way of producing decorated porcelain. Naturalism was taking hold everywhere, especially in Russia.

Constant harking-back to historicist styles led naturally to the eclecticism that is such a feature of the middle of the nineteenth century. After 1850 eclecticism was the reigning mode and was encouraged by the cultural exchanges resulting from the international exhibitions. The most varied sources of inspiration existed side by side or were combined. In the case of the better factories, this led to the production of pieces of high quality. We are sometimes shocked by eclecticism, since nowadays we tend to admire only original works of art; the nineteenth-century viewpoint was not as purist as ours. In England especially, the intellectual élite wanted to find ways of making beautiful things available to all. William Morris tried to convert his contemporaries to the ideal of craftsmanship but had little success, whereas Henry Cole's ambition of supplying industry with good designs for manufacture at low cost was much more realistic. The success of Parian or 'statuary' porcelain in Great Britain, where it was used to make huge numbers of reproductions of famous pieces of sculpture proves that Cole's idea was practicable. The outlook which condoned, and even encouraged, the making of reproductions led to the growth of concerns that made self-confessed pastiches and 'fakes' of earlier works. Some of these firms, such as Coalport in England and Samson of Paris, were remarkable, but most were, of course, totally mediocre and are only known today for their unhappy reproductions of the work of others. Although today the term 'forger' is highly pejorative, the factories under discussion were enormously successful and received official sanction. The largest factories, including Minton, Meissen, and Sèvres, produced new editions of eighteenth-century pieces. From time to time the Sèvres factory supplied both English and French factories with moulds of their old pieces so that new examples of them could be manufactured.

However, there was no lack of original pieces during the period from 1850 to 1900. Many of these were only possible thanks to new decorative processes, such as the *pâte-sur-pâte* technique of decorating porcelain in relief, invented in the middle of the nineteenth century at Sèvres and in use at least until the end of the century in England as well as in France.

Yet constant looking back to the past was likely to affect the artists' imaginative powers. These were renewed by contact with oriental art, which provided the inspiration for innovation and creativity. The origins of the new spirit can be traced back to the International Exhibition held in Paris in 1867. Félix Bracquemond, among others, was strongly affected by Japanese art, which was to inspire the English Aesthetic Movement. This time Europeans were not impressed by Kakiemon or Imari porcelains but by unexpectedly asymmetrical decorative schemes and particularly by Japanese stonewares. From the 1880s, potters working outside the factory system were to turn increasingly to stoneware, but porcelain manufacturers too were open to oriental inspiration; the triumph of Art Nouveau, or Jugendstil, provided them with a rare opportunity. Architects and interior designers were creating unified and entirely modern decorative schemes. Porcelain, even when it was used for domestic wares, had to fit into these schemes. The Rozenburg factory in the Netherlands was unquestionably the most successful producer of pieces in the Art Nouveau style. It is clear that the fascination of porcelain did not fade in the nineteenth century, even though the nature of its charm altered with time.

The twentieth century is the age of severity. Decoration has been banished from buildings. Figurative representation has disappeared from the painter's repertoire, and consumer articles are used and thrown away. Porcelain, which initially appealed to a sense of the exotic and then revelled in sumptuousness, has lost its attraction. We hope that, through this book, our contemporaries may come to see with a new eye their forebears' audacious flights of imagination.

# I  The Techniques of Nineteenth-Century Porcelain

## FRANCE

Porcelain manufacturers have always been scholarly as well as practical men. Earthenware can be made by a good craftsman, but the manufacture of porcelain demands precise knowledge at a high level of the practical and technical aspects of chemistry and physics. At the beginning of the nineteenth century working conditions in the different French factories making porcelain varied widely, from those at Sèvres, a State enterprise, which largely sacrificed productivity to quality, to those of the privately owned factories where profits were of prime importance. In view of this situation it is extremely difficult to present an overall picture of the main manufacturing and decorating techniques in use in the nineteenth century in France. However, despite their differences, all these factories had one thing in common: they were fascinated by techniques and became increasingly spellbound by technical questions as the century wore on. The world exhibitions were largely responsible for this. Manufacturers were led to compare their wares with those produced by their competitors and, so as not to seem old-fashioned, they were forced to be constantly innovatory, aesthetically as well as technically.

The key word governing the interaction between these factories was, undeniably, competition. Year by year it became fiercer. Jean d'Albis and Céleste Romanet stress its importance in connection with the difficulties experienced by Charles Haviland around 1880, quoting his own words: 'At this time German and French competition was making itself keenly felt. "When undecorated porcelain was in fashion, the French product had the advantage over English china, but today fashion favours decorated tablewares and English underglaze decorated wares are very cheap. I am not relying on wares with high-temperature decoration to get us out of trouble, since this type of decoration is the most expensive to produce...." The creation of new shapes was necessary, which even in the white would attract the customer, supplanting the English products: "the more complicated and difficult we make our production, the less we shall have to fear competition." (December, 1882)'[1]

This last phrase of Charles Haviland's is indicative of the problem: in a highly competitive context the manufacturers could gain customers by virtue of technical improvements to their product, but they could also lower the cost price of their wares, even if it meant lowering to some extent the quality of

their product. The use of relief gold was part of the second, sometimes disastrous, expedient.

### The Technical Treatises of the Nineteenth Century

Interest in technical questions relating to porcelain manufacture is also expressed in some remarkable publications. One dates from the end of the first half of the nineteenth century and is the foundation of every study of ceramic technique. It is Alexandre Brongniart's *Traité des arts* cf. p. 24 *céramiques ou des poteries.*[2] As director of the Sèvres porcelain factory Brongniart was, of course, acquainted with the techniques in use at that time at what was without doubt the most sophisticated porcelain factory in Europe—but was also the most resistant to mechanization. Furthermore in 1809, he asked each *préfet,* or chief administrator, of the various French *départements* to submit a report on the ceramics made in his area, with explanations of the processes used and examples of the wares manufactured. When preparing his book he accumulated a vast amount of documentation. His travels put him in contact with a large number of Continental factories, whose production methods—often far more mechanized than those in use at Sèvres—he studied from the point of view of a specialist. His correspondents gave him a great deal of information about contemporary porcelain production. It is to Brongniart that we owe the classification of porcelains into the categories of 'soft-pastes' and 'hard-pastes'. Leaving aside Alphonse Salvetat's 'notes and additions' in the 1877 edition, Brongniart's text is especially valuable as a source of information about techniques in use during the first half of the nineteenth century.

As a source for the second half of the century, one can consult the *Nouveau manuel complet du porcelainier, faïencier, potier de terre...* (1898) by M. D. Magnier, revised by H. Bertran, and published as part of the Manuels Roret series.[3] In addition, there is the chapter 'Technique' in R. de Plinval de Guillebon's *Paris Porcelain 1770–1850* (1972),[4] together with that entitled 'The Evolution of Technique' in J. d'Albis and C. Romanet's *La Porcelaine de Limoges* (1980).[5] As the first deals with the first half of the century and the second is principally concerned with its latter part, it is not difficult to trace the change in outlook that developed during these two periods. In the early part of the century efforts were

concentrated on improving standards of quality and only incidentally on better methods of production, while during the second half of the century manufacturers actively sought to lower costs by using mass-production methods while at the same time trying to maintain standards of quality, which were to be cheerfully sacrificed in the twentieth century.

cf. p. 12 In a few pages it is impossible to give a full account of the extraordinary variety of porcelain manufacturing techniques, and especially of the wealth of decorating processes, in use in the nineteenth century; therefore, the detailed explanation of technical terms will be restricted to those that the reader will encounter in the course of this work.

## The Composition of Porcelain

The porcelain body in current use in nineteenth-century France was hard-paste porcelain. This term simply indicates a porcelain body with a glaze that cannot be scratched, as soft-paste porcelain can, by steel. In short, hard-paste porcelain is refractory, while soft-paste is more fusible. All porcelain is translucent and can be made in several different ways.

Brongniart, in his *Traité des arts céramiques,* sets out the indispensable ingredients for the making of hard-paste porcelain: 'Essentially, the body is made of two principal elements: the first is kaolin, an infusible clay, which can be used on its own or in association either with plastic clay or with magnesite; the second, which must be fusible, is felspar, or other calcareous minerals such as siliceous sand, gypsum, or chalk, either alone or in different combinations.

The glaze *[couverte]* is composed of felspathic quartz, alone or in combination with gypsum, but always without lead or tin.'[6]

What is often referred to as the 'bones' of the porcelain body is, therefore, constituted by infusible kaolinic clay, which is refractory and white-firing, giving porcelain its characteristic colour. The siliceous element that endows the material with its translucency and glassy nature is quartz. Felspar is the 'flesh' of porcelain, giving it plasticity and making it less greasy. The enamel, a glassy covering, gives it a shiny appearance.[7]

During the nineteenth century in France, kaolin supplies were mostly provided by deposits at Saint-Yrieix in the Limousin region. The discovery of kaolin in this area gave birth to large-scale porcelain production at Limoges. Sèvres and Paris also obtained their kaolin from this source. Other deposits of kaolin were discovered at the beginning of the nineteenth century in the western Pyrenees, in the Cotentin region and later in the Allier district. These discoveries each led to the establishment of small factories close to the supply.

The body most commonly used at Sèvres (called the *pâte de service*) is chemically constituted of the following ingredients, cf. p. 17 according to Brongniart:[8]

| | |
|---|---|
| Silica | 58 % |
| Alumina | 34.5% |
| Limestone | 4.5% |
| Potassium | 3 % |
| | 100 % |

The glaze has the same ingredients but has a higher proportion of silica (about 74%).

In 1880 the chemists Charles Lauth and Georges Vogt perfected the formula for their 'new porcelain', which is composed of:[9]

| | |
|---|---|
| Silica | 64.03% |
| Alumina | 28.92% |
| Potassium, Soda, Lime | 7.05% |

It is fired at a slightly lower temperature than the *pâte de service,* i.e. 1280 to 1310°C. The 'new porcelain' is more siliceous than the original Sèvres hard-paste body but less so than Chinese porcelain. It answered the need for a porcelain better suited to cf. p. 17 a more varied type of decoration that would be more colourful, since the pigments used could now be incorporated in the glaze itself. The revival of figure-making at Sèvres at the very end of the nineteenth century and in the twentieth, was largely due cf. p. 230 to the invention of this new paste.

From the beginning of the Second Empire (1852–1870), there were constant attempts by chemists and others at Sèvres with an academic interest in the history of the factory to reintroduce the production of soft-paste porcelain. Théodore Deck, for example, was one of those who conducted experiments on the soft-paste formula from 1887 to 1891, but although all the enthusiasts were successful experimentally, none of them managed to produce the material on an industrial scale.

It should also be noted that at least two French factories made English bone china: Creil and Bordeaux during the first half of the nineteenth century.

From the beginning of the nineteenth century, porcelain manufacturers such as Alluaud, who came from the Limoges area, specialized in the preparation and sale of clays, supplying the Paris factories among others. However, at many factories the clays were prepared on site. Several attempts were made to simplify this procedure. In 1833 the Parisians Grouvelle and Honoré published a method which 'consisted in drying the clay, which had been suspended in water so that it was in a liquid state, in bags made of tightly woven cloth. These were allowed to drip and drain before being pressed. A second method was based on actual filtration reinforced by atmospheric pressure'.[10]

## Manufacturing Methods

When the constituents of the porcelain body have been prepared, that is washed, filtered and 'wedged', or kneaded to remove air, then the clay can be worked. 'Throwing' is the most common way of forming pieces other than flat items such as plates. The potter's wheel, foot-operated at the beginning of the century, had been mechanized by its close. After the thrown piece has been dried to a semi-hard condition, it is 'turned' by being placed on the wheel again. The operative then uses a sharp tool to improve the profile and sharpen the contours.

Another method, which is almost indispensable for the making of square shapes involves the use of moulds. The procedure consists in placing wet clay in a porous mould, which is usually made of plaster of Paris. As it dries the clay takes the shape of the mould, and water is absorbed from it by the mould. Since the clay contracts as it drys, it can then easily be removed from the mould.

Using this basic principle, moulding can be done in several different ways. Balls of clay can be placed in moulds and shaped by a method known as *moulage à la balle.* Alternatively, slabs of paste can be pressed into each half of the mould *(moulage à la croûte)* or a rough shape can be thrown on the wheel and then finished in a mould *(moulage à la housse;* the rough shape

is called a *housse*). We have already mentioned that mechanization affected every aspect of porcelain manufacture during the nineteenth century. It was particularly marked at Sèvres and at Limoges where 'jiggering' began to be used to make plates and other circular pieces in 1844 and after 1870 respectively.[11] Moulding and turning were used in conjunction with each other in this process, and three machines were needed: for making the 'slabs' of paste, for positioning them, and for moulding and 'jiggering' them.[12]

The third method of making shapes, which was extensively used from about 1820 onwards and which became the most common technique in the twentieth century, is casting. Technicians at the Sèvres factory were responsible for improving this process in the first half of the nineteenth century. Instead of the clay being pressed into the mould, liquid clay, or slip, was now poured into it. As in the conventional method, the mould absorbs the water content of the slip, which contracts and can be easily removed from the mould when dry. Casting techniques were first evolved at Sèvres for the production of technical *tours de force*. Large plaques or, at the other end of the scale, ultra-fine porcelain of the type known as 'egg-shell', which was based on extremely fine Chinese and Japanese porcelains, were made using this process. Only at the end of the nineteenth century could slip-casting be used on an industrial scale with the discovery of deflocculants, which allowed reduction of the water content of the slip while maintaining its fluidity. Previously the amount of water in the slip, which had to be absorbed by the mould, spoilt it and reduced its working life so that the method was uneconomic.[13]

### *'Fettling' and Finishing*

In the porcelain factories worthy of the old eighteenth-century term 'manufactories' the piece is 'fettled' after being made. When it is dry, but has not yet been fired ('leather-hard'), all traces of the making process are removed from the surface of the pot. Thrown pieces are turned on a lathe, the operative cleaning up the contours and improving the profile of the piece with a sharp 'towing' tool. Moulded pieces, especially the 'biscuit' or unglazed porcelains mostly used for statuettes, are 'repaired' or 'fettled' using a knife, and the seam marks are sponged over and disguised with slip. At this stage pierced decoration can be carried out; it is, of course, an extremely delicate operation. Decoration in relief or in intaglio is done when the clay is leather-hard, sometimes using a metal roller to which oil has been applied. Nast used one of these 'even before he was granted a patent for it in 1810'.[14] It is at this stage that handles, spouts and knobs, made in moulds, are attached by means of slip.

### *Kilns and Firing*

When pieces have attained their final form, the soft, or biscuit, firing (called the *dégourdi* firing) takes place. It hardens the ware, though leaving it porous enough to absorb decoration. During this initial firing of hard-paste porcelain the temperature reaches about 1000 °C.

In the nineteenth century, pieces were glazed by being dipped into a vessel containing water in which the powdered glaze ingredients had been dissolved.

Decoration can be done either under or over the glaze, that is before or after the initial firing. In a fairly large number of cases, the piece is fired for the first time after being glazed but before being decorated.

1–8 *Vase*. National Porcelain factory, 1876–1877. Coloured hard-paste ▷ porcelain. H. 97 cm. Mark: inaccessible. MNC, Sèvres (9265)
This vase was made to commemorate the opening of the factory's new premises (cf. Pl. 395) and was decorated with vignettes showing the techniques involved in porcelain manufacture.
1   The preparation of the clay ('blunging')
2   The method of casting the vase
3   The vase being thrown and painted (under the glaze)
4   The pots being placed in the kiln
5   Unloading the kiln
6   The method of decorating fired porcelain
7   How porcelain is mounted in bronze
8   An exhibition of finished pieces

Kilns and firing methods changed radically during the course of the nineteenth century. In the early years wood was the universal fuel, but by the end of the century it had been replaced almost everywhere by coal, or in some places by gas. Coal-fired kilns were introduced around the mid-nineteenth century, at the time when the forests were disappearing and the construction of railways made possible rapid access to coal supplies. Nowadays, Sèvres hard-paste porcelain is fired at a temperature of 1410 °C. Pieces are placed in 'saggars', or fire-clay boxes, to protect the porcelain from the flame during firing. The system of placing pieces in saggars, and the saggars themselves, underwent considerable improvement throughout the century. Next the various 'chambers' of the kiln were [4, 5] loaded with porcelain. Kiln construction in France was completely transformed during this period. Circular or square kilns with one chamber only, dating from the beginning of the century, were succeeded by a circular kiln with two chambers, one above the other. The latter was introduced by Brongniart [cf. p. 17] at Sèvres in 1842. The upper chamber is used for the biscuit *(dégourdi)* firing, while the lower is used to fire glazed pieces. The use of coal led to further improvements, such as Gendarme's porcelain kiln.[15] The next development was the down-draught kiln, which ensured better distribution of heat. Continuous firing was the ensuing great step forward; clearly this method made possible great savings on fuel, since the kiln did not now need to be heated from cold at each firing. In the nineteenth century there were two quite different types of continuous kiln in use. The first relied on moving the pieces in the kiln, while in the second the heat source itself was moved. Eventually gas kilns, in which the temperature could be much more effectively controlled, came into use.

### Decoration

Even more profound changes took place in decorating processes than in manufacturing techniques. With regard to the latter, the great goal was to replicate mechanically processes that had formerly been carried out manually. However, with decoration, the aim was quite different, since the search was for [6] an increasingly wide variety of decorative effects, whatever means were employed. The French porcelain manufacturers lagged behind their English counterparts throughout the whole of the century in the mechanization of decorative processes.

### *Copperplate Engraving*

In France decoration was hand-painted throughout the first half of the century. Here, transfer-printing, developed in England about 1753, was in practice only used on

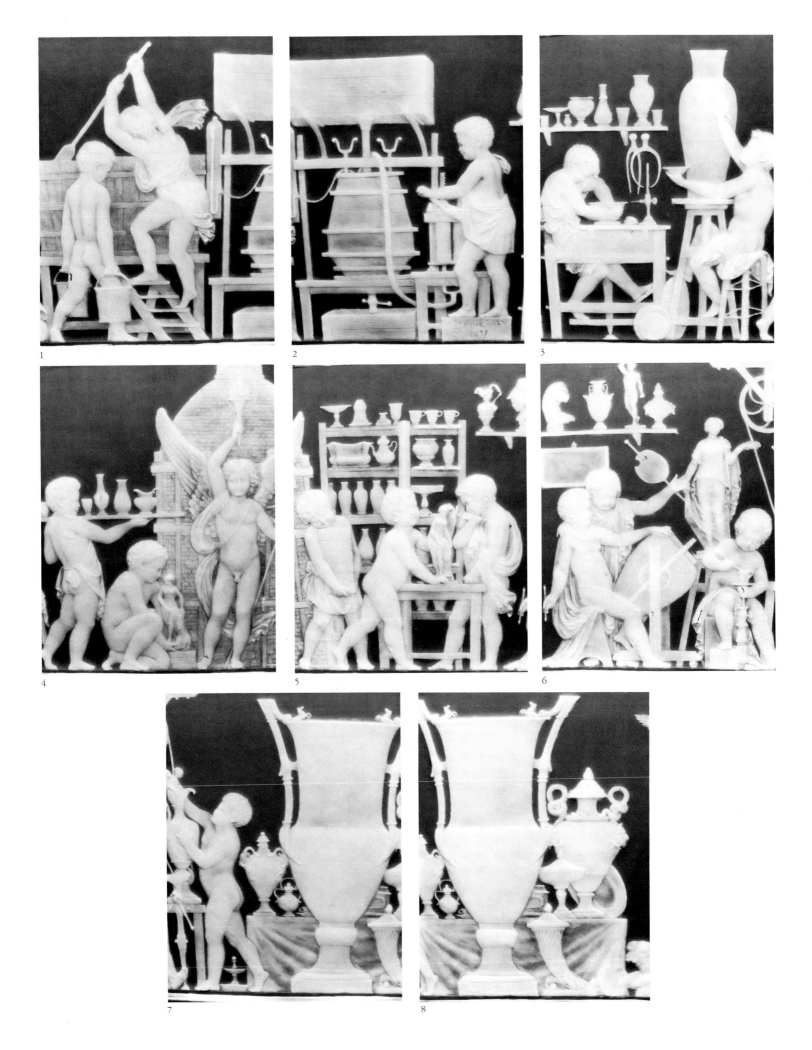

1

2

3

4

5

6

7

8

earthenwares. However, there were specialists who studied the process and were using it on porcelain after 1800. They included Potter, Gonord, Neppel, and Legros d'Anizy. D'Anizy printed a large number of outline designs, monograms and friezes in gold on Sèvres porcelain during the First Empire period (1804–1815), though Alexandre Brongniart barely mentions this. At his Paris factory, Legros d'Anizy carried out colour printing on porcelain. Visually the effect is very similar to hand-painting, and the process was possibly just as laborious. At Limoges, Pierre Tharaud carried out *grisaille* decoration by means of a method using sized-down transfers *(décor collé)*; he exhibited the results in Paris in 1839. All the decoration so far mentioned was produced as follows: the design was engraved in intaglio on a copperplate with a burin, or engraving tool. It was then filled in with ceramic colour mixed with a fluxing agent and printer's oil and transferred to a piece of paper (Gonord's method was slightly more complicated than Legros d'Anizy's since it used a bat of soft glue). When the print was placed on the piece of porcelain it left behind a coloured design. Sometimes outlines alone were printed on the ware, a method especially popular at Limoges, and were filled in by hand, thus avoiding the traditional process of 'pouncing', or stencilling, on the design. Between 1873 and 1876, Félix Bracquemond improved the printing process by using three techniques in conjunction with each other. He used lithography for the ground colour, etching for the outlines, and finally touched up the design by painting in details by hand.[16] This accounts for the high quality of decoration on Haviland products late in the century.

*Chromolithography*

Chromolithography was a mechanical process of colour printing used to produce polychrome decorated wares. The French had not lost their taste for colour on porcelain. Lithography, discovered in about 1796, was greatly improved in 1837 when colour images were first produced by the technique that came to be known as chromolithography.

Lithography makes use of the property of certain porous stones that absorb grease. The outline of the design to be reproduced is traced on to the stone and its surface dabbed over with grease. The stone is then pressed against a specially prepared paper which absorbs the grease. A ceramic colour is dusted on to the surface of the oily paper which is then applied face down to the porcelain that has been prepared, in turn, so that the mixture of grease and colour will adhere to it. Finally the paper is dampened and removed. Using a series of lithographic stones several different sheets can be impregnated with colour to obtain polychrome decoration. The principal difficulty encountered is the correct registration, or alignment, of the different colours.

A Parisian porcelain manufacturer, Macé, adapted the process to the decoration of porcelain. It was in use at Limoges in 1859, but the results were of indifferent quality. Bracquemond made some improvements to the technique, which was used in 1880 to decorate the *service du président Hayes* ('President Hayes Service'), which was, however, finished by hand. At the end of the nineteenth century, this process was the best mechanical means of achieving coloured decoration of up to eighteen different tones.[17]

*Colours*

Until about 1770 only soft-paste porcelain was made in France. Not until the nineteenth century was hard-paste procelain

systematically adopted. The manufacturers had to extend and adjust their range of colours to suit this relatively new ceramic body, using various metallic oxides that changed during firing to give a wide range of tones of colour. These technical problems, which were of particular concern in the first half of the nineteenth century, were tackled at the Sèvres and Paris factories. Distinctions are made between high-temperature colours, which can be fired up to about 1400 °C, low-temperature colours and enamel colours, which are fired in the muffle kiln. Metallic oxides can be used to colour the body itself or be incorporated into the glaze; alternatively, they can be applied under or over the glaze. Coloured bodies were popular at the beginning of the century when attempts were made to imitate the black and pale-blue fine stonewares developed by Wedgwood. Later they were used to imitate Chinese celadons or for black or pink porcelains in the Second Empire taste. To make these bodies, metallic oxides are mixed with the clay: chrome being used for green, cobalt for blue, iron for brown, manganese for violet, and titanium for yellow.[18]

During the first half of the nineteenth century, there was a considerable increase in the number of high-temperature colours available. In 1797 Vauquelin isolated chrome, which was used as a ceramic colour in 1802; Nast was almost certainly the first manufacturer to adopt it. For the French, chrome-green grounds are almost synonymous with the colour known as *vert empire*. At Sèvres it was used for the border decoration of the *service de l'Empereur* ('Emperor's Service'), dating from 1807–1810. Dark blue and a pale blue called *agate* are both obtained from cobalt oxide. The dark blue was achieved by the application of three layers of colour, while the pale blue needed only one.[19] This underglaze dark blue is the renowned *bleu de Sèvres*. Brongniart himself admitted that the Vienna factory produced a particularly fine version of this blue by using five separately applied layers of colour, and Limoges also made extensive use of it. Despite its excellent facilities, the Sèvres factory did not invent all the high-temperature underglaze colours. Honoré in 1822, Discry and Talmours in about 1836, and Fouque and Arnoux of Toulouse in 1844 also made additions to the range of colours.

Overglaze decoration is even more difficult to do than its underglaze counterpart, as Brongniart points out.[20] New overglaze colours were discovered, which have been listed by Régine de Plinval de Guillebon:

ultramarine blue by Mortelèque, in imitation of Vienna's (1808),
turquoise blue as a ground colour on hard-paste porcelain, by Mortelèque,
meadow green and blue-green, by Pau, a chemist in Paris (1833),
reds, by Pannetier,
light yellow, invented in 1819 by J.F. Robert, a landscapist at Sèvres,
platinum grey, prepared for the first time at Sèvres (it was being used there by 1814),
the 'pink colour' [lustre], a British invention studied in 1836 by the chemist at Sèvres, Malaguti.[21]

The so-called *demi-grand feu* colours are low-temperature colours, usually hardened by the addition of zinc carbonate, and were discovered in 1839 by Eugène Rousseau.[22]

Aside from the purely technical aspect, it should be stressed that the choice of certain colours and their method of

9 *Saucers with colour samples.* Vienna, 1806 and 1837. Overglaze colours, silver, gold, platinum. D. 18.6 cm. Marks: a) 107 b) 108 and year stamp. MNC, Sèvres (2517[4], 470[20]).
Proud of its particularly wide range of 'muffle,' or enamel, colours, Vienna produced these 'sample cards' from the early 19th century onwards.

application can often be an indication of the taste of the period. For instance, during the First Empire, the surface of fashionable porcelains was entirely covered with strong colour and highlighted with gold, or imitations of semi-precious stones, or was decorated with matt colours obtained by reducing the amount of flux.[23] The Restoration period (1814–1830) witnessed a taste for nankin ('salmon' yellow) grounds and also saw the revival of white grounds. In the second half of the nineteenth century, decorative processes rather than special colours were appreciated, for example the use of *pâte-sur-pâte* techniques and ox-blood and crystalline glazes. It should be pointed out that just as there were merchants specializing in the sale of prepared clays, there were also colour merchants, Mortelèque in Paris being one of the most famous.

## Gilding

We shall often have occasion to stress, when discussing the various factories, that the quality of their product is dependent upon the quality of its gilded decoration, which gives the pieces their character. The high cost of this type of decoration encouraged extensive research in this field from the eighteenth century onwards.

At the beginning of the nineteenth century gilding was applied using vitriol: 'gold leaf, dissolved in aqua regia, is precipitated with ferrous sulphate. The washed precipitate is mixed with a flux containing bismuth and melted borax together with oil of turpentine to make it flow more easily'.[24]

When the gold had been prepared in this manner, it was applied by means of a brush, not without a certain amount of difficulty, according to Brongniart. After being fired it is burnished with a hardstone to bring out its full brilliance.

Mercury gilding was another method in use: instead of using ferrous sulphate to obtain a precipitate, nitrate of mercury was employed, which naturally had a deleterious effect on the health of the operative involved with this process. In 1844, to make the gold more durable, Rousseau of Paris devised a technique of applying it over a platinum base. Finally gold can be coloured by various means. It can be lightened by the addition of silver and platinum, and given a red or a green appearance, using mercuric oxide or chrome respectively.[25]  cf. p. 19

Silvery highlights were obtained using silver following a method perfected by Rousseau in 1844. Platinum can also be used to great advantage since it does not tarnish.[26]

Metallic lustres were rarely used on porcelains in France, except for 'bismuth lustre' obtained according to a process patented by the porcelain manufacturer Jules-Joseph-Henri Brianchon. In the second half of the nineteenth century the technique was adopted in Ireland.[27]  cf. pp. 19, 21

391

## 'Pâte-sur-pâte' Decoration

During the second half of the nineteenth century porcelain manufacturers were more interested in the techniques of decoration than in perfecting the colours themselves. The most important of these techniques was *pâte-sur-pâte* decoration, which took its inspiration from Chinese porcelain. Its use goes back to the patent taken out in 1820 by Dodé and Frin of Paris for the application of specially prepared clay to the unfired pot by means of a brush.[28] In the collection of the Musée National de Céramique, Sèvres, are two vases from the Discry factory  203
decorated with white *pâte-sur-pâte* reliefs on a celadon ground.[29]

As they were acquired in 1851, they must have been made some time before this date. However, it was when the Sèvres factory adopted the technique that it acquired immense prestige. The Minton factory in Great Britain owes part of its reputation to the work of Marc-Louis Solon, a Frenchman trained at Sèvres who became established at Stoke-on-Trent after the Franco-Prussian War of 1870–1871. In England the technique was used on Parian porcelain rather than on hard-paste porcelain; the former proved to be an ideal material for the purpose since its low firing temperature meant that a wider range of colours was available. Solon himself explained his technique in the *Art Journal* of March, 1901:[30] on the unfired piece an outline of the design is traced by the artist, who then builds up the desired number of layers of slip, allowing one layer to dry before applying the next. The biscuit firing, glazing and glost firing then take place. Occasionally, at least at Sèvres, glazing was omitted. *Pâte-sur-pâte* decoration (also known in France as decoration *en pâte rapportée* or *à la barbotine*) often took the form of white reliefs on a pink ground. Sometimes at Sèvres it was applied to a type of ground called *pâte changeante* ('changing paste'), which had the property of passing from celadon colour to grey and then to pink according to the quality of the light.[31]

To a great extent the decorative process studied by Auguste Rodin when he worked at Sèvres (1879–1882 and 1888) was related to the technique of *pâte-sur-pâte* decoration, and in the finest of his pieces he attains a subtlety not hitherto achieved, only adding the smallest amounts of slip and preferring to pare away the surface to achieve the required sharpness of detail.

*Flamed Glazes*

The 'flamed' or flambé glazes are also known as 'ox-blood' or *sang de boeuf* glazes when they are dark red. Seven pieces by Alphonse Salvetat with this type of decoration are in the Sèvres museum and are dated 1848.[32] Production of wares with these glazes took place mainly in the decade 1883–1893 and was connected with the use of the new porcelain *(pâte nouvelle)* mentioned earlier, perfected by Lauth and Vogt to answer the need for more varied decorative effects. The two men explained the process as follows: 'We obtain *flambé* glazes by firing at a high temperature pieces of new porcelain with a fritted glaze containing copper. The fire is controlled so that there is a reducing atmosphere during most of the firing.'[33]

At Sèvres, the end of the nineteenth century saw the birth of new decorative techniques. The most famous of these are the crystalline glazes, which were in fact copied from the Copenhagen factory. The other innovation was the development of a new range of high-temperature colours, which did not prove especially successful in France as they were too pale.

To conclude this brief outline, it must be emphasized that, at the end of the nineteenth century, Sèvres followed in the footsteps of the artist potters: porcelain was replaced by stoneware as the creative medium. The great days of porcelain were over.

## ITALY

The Doccia factory tried to use Italian raw materials in the manufacture of its porcelain. Kaolin from the island of Elba and from Tretto in the province of Vicenza was employed but, wrote Brongniart, 'these are clays which resemble talc, rather than being true kaolin'.[34] Clay from Monzone, quartz from Saravezza, and glaze material containing pegmatite from Calabria were also used. A sort of hybrid porcelain called *masso bastardo* was produced from these inferior raw materials. For higher quality pieces, kaolin and felspar were imported from Saint-Yrieix.[35]

The most important contribution made by Italy to the technique of porcelain in the nineteenth century was the construction of a new type of kiln with four chambers arranged vertically. It was perfected in 1822 by Marchese Lorenzo Ginori, who immediately published his invention, much to everyone's surprise, and to the admiration of Brongniart.[36] The kiln made possible simultaneous firing of several ceramic materials and was, therefore, much more economic.

Brongniart studied the Vinovo porcelain made under Vittorio Amadeo Gioanetti with great attention.[37] The body of this porcelain is not composed of kaolin but is made of magnesite. Since it was hardly translucent and was somewhat yellowish in colour, its production was discontinued, though Brongniart voiced his regret for this, as the material could have been the basis of a good-quality porcelain body which would have been economic to manufacture because of its low firing temperature.

The porcelain made at Milan does not seem to have been made according to any special technique.

## CENTRAL EUROPE, RUSSIA, AND SCANDINAVIA

Alexandre Brongniart, who has been mentioned as having been the first to write a technological handbook on nineteenth-century porcelain, can be read to advantage by students of central European porcelain as well. Brongniart made two major trips to the centres of porcelain manufacture in the German-speaking world and gave a first-hand account of the production methods and paste formulae of the Sèvres factory's competitors in his *Traité* of 1844,[38] a work for which no parallel exists in German. The publications by nineteenth-century factory managers (given in the bibliography) are all confined to describing conditions in the writer's own firm, as for example Kolbe's *History of the Berlin Porcelain Manufactory* (1863). The first book to go beyond the information supplied by Brongniart is one on which the following text draws heavily, Bruno Kerl's *Handbook of the Pottery Industry*,[39] the first edition of which (1871) was several times expanded. All editions deal with the nineteenth century, and, in a systematic classification of pottery types, contain all the key facts about pastes, firing techniques, methods of decoration and so on. Gone were the days when a factory's employees faced heavy penalties if they allowed the 'arcanum' of porcelain to leak out, although Brongniart reported from Meissen as late as 1812 that he had had the greatest difficulty in getting into the factory and that his travelling companion, Friedrich Georg Frick from Berlin, had been refused admission.[40] Before long, however, the chemists were in a position to analyse rival products, and in the latter part of the nineteenth century a properly scientific exchange of information took place. The theory of porcelain manufacture appeared on the syllabuses of institutes of technology in the 1830s,[41] the first technical handbooks were published around 1870, and from 1876 onwards there were two important specialist journals in which new knowledge was discussed and new methods and discoveries were, so to speak, patented by publication.[42]

296

375

cf. p. 17

435

cf. p. 19

414
cf. p. 19

## Pastes

All the porcelains used in the German-speaking world, in Russia, and in Scandinavia until after 1880, were hard-paste porcelains derived from Johann Friedrich Böttger's basic 'arcanum' of 1709. In what follows they are referred to simply as 'porcelains'. Nineteenth-century German and Austrian porcelains employed the finest kaolins, which were either used pure or mixed with a quartz-sand flux, and were extracted in Saxony and Thuringia, the Upper Palatinate of Bavaria, and Bohemia—that is, from a large and loosely articulated region at the heart of the German-speaking world, which was also where most of the smaller porcelain factories were established during this period. The kaolin had to be mixed with quartz and felspar in proportions that varied according to the work to be done. Tough industrial or sanitary porcelain calls for a different mixture from that used for modelling statuettes, which needs to be more workable; a different paste again is required for biscuit figures or lithophanes, where a high degree of transparency is desirable. And occasionally, for reasons of economy, less carefully refined clays were resorted to, for example for utility ware in Meissen after the Napoleonic wars.

Kerl gives comparative statistics for all kinds of porcelain and associated glaze pastes from the year 1878. These show the German and Bohemian porcelains to have differed from the French in that they contained less felspar than the finer Limoges porcelains, which are more transparent but also more fragile, and less clay than Brongniart's hard-paste porcelain. The Berlin service paste, for example, contained 54.9% clay as against 66% in Sèvres and 40–56% in Limoges. But the proportions also varied from factory to factory, whereas today all European porcelain manufacturers use a few standard pastes. This diversity in the pastes employed contributed greatly to the enormous variety of porcelains. Every factory tried to produce as white, hard, resonant, and at the same time transparent a porcelain as possible. It is interesting to compare some typical paste compositions with the figures for Sèvres:

cf. p. 11

| | Silica | Alumina | Limestone | Potassium |
|---|---|---|---|---|
| Berlin | 64.3% | 29.0% | 0.3% | 3.6% |
| Meissen | 58.5–60% | 35.1–35.5% | 0.3–0.6% | 5.0–2.3% |
| Vienna | 59.6% | 34.2% | 1.7% | 2.0% |
| Nymphen-burg | 72.8% | 18.4% | 3.3% | 0.6% |
| Bohemia | 71.5% | 23.4% | 0.1% | 3.1% |
| Thuringia | 72.8% | 24.5% | | 0.1% |

plus traces of, for example, magnesium and soda.[43]

Even the kaolins used were of very varied composition, which affected the mixture as a whole. The particularly fine Sennewitz kaolin from the Halle region, which the Berlin factory was using around 1875, contained 64.87% silica to 23.83% alumina and trace elements, whereas Zettlitz earth from the Karlsbad (Karlovy Vary) region of Bohemia contains 46.87% silica to 38.56% alumina, which makes it much more workable.

The composition of the raw materials and of the paste is not all that determines the quality of the porcelain body. Further modifications may be effected during firing. For example, a high degree of transparency in the finished product may be achieved either by means of a large proportion of flux and quartz or by a high firing temperature. The colourless glazes, too, which were always necessary except on biscuit porcelain

(for statuettes), varied in their composition, although all European factories used felspathic glazes whereas in the Far East fully transparent calcareous glazes were the rule. Chinese and—in Germany—Japanese porcelain with a high proportion of silica (c. 70%) and less alumina (c. 22%), which can be fired at comparatively low temperatures, became the model for European decorative porcelain from 1880 onwards. Mention has already been made of the new Sèvres pastes. In Germany Hermann Seger of Berlin was the first to produce a new soft-paste porcelain containing only 25% clay to 45% quartz and 30% felspar (or 78.8% silica, 16% alumina, and 5.3% potassium).[44] Firing at 1250° to 1300 °C, this porcelain offered an outstanding vehicle for coloured glazes in which part of the limestone of the colourless glaze was replaced by a staining metallic oxide. A dark blue glaze, for example, contained 42% felspar, 27.2% quartz sand, 13% kaolin, 14% marble, and 3% cobalt oxide. For the most sensational of all the coloured glazes, the so-called 'ox-blood' red, Seger used between 0.5 and 1% copper oxide.

For the coloured, 'flow', crystalline, and crackle glazes that sold so well at the end of the century, all the other manufacturers making artistic porcelain—from Meissen to Copenhagen and St Petersburg—developed pastes that could be fired at a low temperature. They all contain only a small proportion of tough clay body and are therefore—like all soft-paste porcelains—very fragile and suitable only for ornamental pieces. An experiment in the same direction but with other means took place in Rozenburg, near The Hague, where shortly before 1900 the only modern soft-paste porcelain was made that contained no kaolin and was consequently more of a glass-like frit.

Biscuit porcelain, too, repeatedly had a role to play in the nineteenth century—in the Neo-Classical period for statuettes, in the Biedermeier period for lithophanes. In both cases a delicate yellow tinge in the white body was preferred to blue, which called for reduction during firing. To give the required degree of transparency the paste contained a high proportion of felspar. In the case of lithophanes it usually carried a thin, almost imperceptible glaze.

## Firing and Kilns

The firing process finally determines what the finished porcelain will look like. Painting with metallic oxide colours often went wrong as a result of fluctuating kiln temperatures, sooty flames, and other factors. The coloured, 'flow', and flambé glazes of the last two decades of the nineteenth century were largely dependent upon processes inside the kiln (such as the admission or extraction of air), which could by then be precisely observed and controlled. For keeping an eye on the temperature the pyrometer (in regular use since Wedgwood's day) became increasingly important and was much experimented with; but it was not until Seger cones came on to the market in 1886 that reliable readings were available.[45]

Economic considerations had led to experiments in Germany at the beginning of the nineteenth century aimed at replacing wood as a fuel. For a long time these were unsuccessful, and it was not until 1839 that Meissen, the first firm to do so, succeeded in going over to firing with brown and mineral coal. The steadily rising price of fire-wood made other factories follow suit. In France, attempts at coal-firing are said to have been made from 1845 onwards and to have been

adopted at Sèvres from 1849. Even after 1900, however, wood was still regarded as the superior fuel, and for certain tasks, such as baking sensitive colours, it was indispensable. In 1848, very soon after these experiments with coal and after initial trials in the brick industry,[46] engineers began to think about going over to gas-firing. Venier reported good results in Klösterle (Bohemia) in 1860, and on the strength of these Meissen fired with gas generators from 1863 to 1867. The results were superb, but the hoped-for cut in costs failed to materialize; in fact, of course, more rather than less coal was being used because coal was employed to generate the gas in the first place. In 1868 Berlin began to record satisfactory results with this kind of 'semi-gas-firing'. The great advantage of gas-firing was that it was very clean—soot in the kiln having always been a major problem. Electric firing, which has the same advantage of being soot-free as well as maintaining a constant temperature, did not become important until the twentieth century.

Besides thinking about fuel, the physicists and engineers of the nineteenth century devoted much attention to modifying and improving kiln construction. Here too, as in the use of new fuels, Germany was ahead of Sèvres. While Sèvres went on using the old horizontal tunnel-kiln until 1842, Berlin introduced an upright round kiln with several storeys as early as 1797 (Meissen 1815, Vienna 1830).[47] The round kiln, which underwent constant improvements in the decades that followed, systematically exploited the different 'layers' of temperature present in every kiln. Porcelains for high-firing were placed on the bottom rack, while on the upper racks the heat was still sufficient for biscuit-firing. In three-storeyed kilns the middle rack was used for firing muffle colours and similar jobs. There were attempts to use an additional firing to produce an even temperature on all racks (St Petersburg, 1806; Ginori, Doccia, 1822) as well as all kinds of other experiments. In Bohemia—for example in Altrohlau—particularly large three-storeyed round kilns were built on the pattern of English stoneware kilns from 1850 onwards. They had eleven firing inlets and were capable of baking 30,000 plates on the high-firing rack alone in a single twenty-seven-hour firing. Such kilns were of course only suitable for very large factories. The so-called 'down-draught' kilns, in which a complex system of ducts and chimneys enabled better use to be made of the available heat, were usually somewhat smaller.[48] The largest Bohemian rack-type kilns had a capacity of $c.$ 57 m$^3$ for high-firing; the down-draught kiln in general use in Berlin in the 1890s had a capacity of $c.$ 38 m$^3$. Large kilns like these were filled with industrial wares: mass-produced tableware, petticoat insulators, vessels for chemical and sanitary purposes, pipes, loom components, and so on. For the rational exploitation of large kilns, manual placing was no longer viable; the mechanization of many operations, the construction and acquisition of many auxiliary appliances and machines followed as a matter of course. Particularly the preparation of the raw materials, from the breaking and crushing of the felspathic rock and the quartz sand to the pugging and washing of the clay, was gradually mechanized. The first steam-engine ever installed in Prussia was put into the Berlin porcelain manufactory from 1793 to prepare the paste.

For the shaping of plates, bowls, pots, jars, cups, and so on, increasing use was made of the moulding processes developed in England for the manufacture of stoneware.[49] Simple ornamentation too, such as borders, friezes, and later gilt rims, was done by machine.

The modelling of the finer porcelains, discussed in the present volume, nevertheless remained largely unaffected by industrial production methods. Even the firing of the finer wares was done in small muffle kilns with a capacity of only $c.$ 1 m$^3$. This was to permit more careful and individual handling of their delicate overglaze painting, coloured glazes or bodies.[50] Painting and gilding, like the modelling and application of sculpted elements, were done by hand.

## Decoration

Connected with developments in paste and kiln technology were developments in decoration. Until 1888 the prime concern was with refining the muffle colours that in the case cf. p. 60 of the leading factories of Vienna, St Petersburg, Berlin, and Meissen had in the first two decades of the century already approached the richness of the water-colourist's or oil-painter's palette. The colours, derived from metallic oxides, increased in variety and the painters' skill at mixing them and modifying them by multiple firings became ever greater. Exact copies of oil-paintings and deceptive imitations of semi-precious stones were already within the capabilities of Vienna, St Petersburg, Meissen, and Berlin in the first quarter of the century. They represented extraordinary achievements on the part of not only the artists who executed them but also by all the technicians involved. Many porcelain paintings had to go into the kiln several times because particularly delicate intermediate tones could not be baked in one firing. Yet even the final firing could jeopardize the entire work, possibly representing months of labour. Writers since the late nineteenth century have philosophized about the point of such heroic feats;[51] what is clear is that they indicate a level of technological and artistic skill far above that achieved anywhere today.

'Muffle' colours (better known as overglaze or enamel colours) are painted on the glazed and already vitrified porcelain body and fired at 710° to 770 °C.[52] Intermediate shades often require several applications with firing in-between. The basis of every muffle colour is a colourless or slightly tinted flux (lead glaze) with which coloured oxides are mixed. Every chemist with every firm was constantly experimenting to increase the luminosity or delicacy of his colours and the number of shades he could obtain. The colours cited in the section on France are offered purely as an example.[53] cf. p. 14 Vienna and Berlin had particularly good laboratories at the beginning of the century, but even a small out-of-the-way factory like Popov's at Gorbunovo had its own colour laboratory as early as 1806 (the first one in Russia). Some factories sold their colours to smaller firms, and many of the younger establishments, such as those in Thuringia and Russia, took advantage of this.

In the period up to 1888, fire-proof or underglaze colours played a part only for utility or otherwise unpretentious tableware, partly because they were restricted to two colours, blue and (from 1815 in Germany) green. In Thuringia, Saxony, and Copenhagen, cobalt-blue was used very extensively to decorate services with the 'strawflower pattern'. Around 1820 Meissen revived its own eighteenth-century Chinese-influenced 'onion pattern', and from around 1870 this was produced in enormous quantities. Chrome-green in the popular vine-tendril pattern also had a part to play, particularly at Meissen from 1817. It was known in Vienna and Berlin from 1815 onwards, and at Sèvres, where it had also been used to

decorate plate flanges, several years earlier (*c.* 1808). For pictorial decoration, underglaze colours were not suitable—until the Copenhagen factory managed to invest them with the requisite quality of differentiation in 1885. Cobalt-blue was then used in an atomizer for pictorial work in delicate pastel shades. This marked the beginning of a predilection for painting in underglaze colours that characterized all Danish and German manufacturers until beyond the turn of the century. At last new colours were developed for underglaze painting too that were proof against high-temperature firing (*c.* 1400 °C); these were based on iron for brown, manganese for yellow and pink, nickel for brownish-green, uranium for yellow and grey and so on.[54] The colourfulness of underglaze painting, in which the metallic oxide colours fuse completely with the porcelain body and appear to lie in or beneath the glaze, is of a quite different order from that of muffle colours painted on top of the glaze. Their soft, hazy appearance had an enormous influence on European Art Nouveau porcelain.

*Gilding*
Metals were used as a painting medium in a quite different way. Gold in particular invariably accompanied painting in muffle colours—sometimes, in the first third of the century, to excess. The splendour and delicacy of Neo-Classical Viennese porcelain is largely due to its 'gilt pattern' painting, finely gilded relief ornamentation on plate flanges and the like. For this the drawing was done in a flux mixed with crushed porcelain body or a refractory enamel and then gilded as usual. The addition of silver, platinum, or enamel colours produced gold *à trois couleurs,* while sand-polishing gave a matt finish and polishing with agate a high gloss. Besides gold we also find silver and platinum on the colour-sample plates of the Vienna factory. Platinum oxide brought to red heat produces a silver colour that does not blacken like real silver, which needs to be glazed, gilded, or given some other form of additional treatment.[55] The large areas of gilding so popular in the early decades of the nineteenth century, when the outsides and particularly the insides of fine porcelain wares were gilded all over, was doubly expensive: on one hand because of the quantity of metal required, on the other because of the lengthy and laborious process of polishing. Consequently every possibility of making the gilding process cheaper was welcomed—a branch of research in which the Meissen laboratory particularly distinguished itself. Its first success was in applying the gold in a more diluted and therefore more economical form with the aid of red mercuric oxide, which burned away in the kiln. Even less actual gold was required in the process known as *Glanzgold* ('shiny' or 'gloss gilding'), adopted at Meissen in 1827 and the object of universal envy; this had the additional advantage that on glazed porcelain it came out of the kiln already shiny.[56] Gloss gilding was as much disparaged as it was imitated, with varying degrees of success, and improvements continued to be made to it throughout the century. Its discovery was linked to another made by Kühn at Meissen in 1837, that of lustre or 'iridescent' colours, which were also applied under gloss-gilding. Bismuth, copper, lead, gold, silver, or uranium, mixed with essential oils, came out of the kiln as lustrous colour coatings that enjoyed enormous success.[57] It was not until 1858 that Brianchon applied for a patent for lustre colours in Paris, and in the 1860s they were much used at Belleek in Ireland.

But there were undoubtedly nobler decorative possibilities than lustre colours, which in fact were only used for a short

cf. p. 15

time at Meissen before being taken over by factories with a less demanding clientèle. One of the most beautiful is *pâte-sur-pâte* decoration, discovered at Sèvres in 1848 and adopted in England on bone china in 1870, and which was even slower in reaching Germany. Not until 1879 did Meissen take up *pâte-sur-pâte* decoration, though applying it to hard-paste porcelain and using coloured pastes from the outset.[58] In Berlin and St Petersburg it was in use for a few years from around 1890. At about the same time Berlin paid greater attention to another relief technique, that of bead glazing or jewelled porcelain, often combining it with gold edging to obtain a kind of cloisonné enamel effect.[59]

cf. p. 15
cf. p. 22

All these decorative processes emerged gradually from older types, whereas the adoption of coloured glazes, which at the end of the century dispensed entirely with representational decoration, constituted a revolutionary departure. Once again the initial influence came from Far Eastern porcelain, which this time led Sèvres and Berlin to develop new porcelain pastes that vitrified at lower temperatures than hard-paste porcelain. At these temperatures it was possible to fire glazes in radiant colours that had eluded manufacturers hitherto and that resembled those of the universally admired Chinese porcelain of the Ming dynasty.

The most difficult and sought-after of all these, the deep red ox-blood glaze, was achieved in Berlin in 1881 and at other factories shortly afterwards. In 1882 Hermann Seger presented some eighty other coloured glazes for his porcelain, fired at 1280 °C.[60] Further experiments were conducted with the ox-blood copper-oxide glaze: the introduction of air at the reduction stage of firing produced blue, violet, and green 'flamed' glazes; coating the red (or blue, brown, yellow, pink, or celadon-coloured) ground glaze with a fondant that melted easily producing a merging of colours. The Sèvres laboratory was the first to report 'misfiring' of coloured glazes having crystals in the coloured cover as a result of the accidental presence of zinc silicate or titanium salts. Arising out of these, the chemists of the Copenhagen factory developed the crystalline glazes that are among the most beautiful of Art Nouveau techniques. Even the crazing effect so often cursed as the 'hereditary defect' of porcelain manufacture was now exploited with what came to be known as crackle glazes.[61]

cf. p. 17
cf. p. 17

All these last-mentioned decorative processes were applied to individual pieces. Of far greater economic importance were certain quite different processes such as the various printing techniques. In the depression during and after the Napoleonic wars nearly all European manufacturers introduced the transfer-printing processes used so successfully on English stoneware in an attempt to cut their production costs for decorated porcelain—not least in order to be able to compete with stoneware imported from England. The original attempts were invariably short-lived. Systematic use of transfer-printing was made only for rims, friezes, and borders in Meissen soon after 1814. Not until the 1840s did it replace hand-painting for pictorial work as well and was first applied in the larger factories of Bohemia (e.g. Schlaggenwald). A generation later a whole range of such techniques was already in use. Kerl lists the following as common methods: rubber stamps, bat printing, flexographic printing plates, copperplate printing, lithography and chromolithography, photolithography, photo-printing, and transfer-printing.[62] By such means monochrome and polychrome pictures could be transferred to porcelain relatively easily and cheaply, but they were never regarded as artistic techniques.

cf. pp. 12, 21

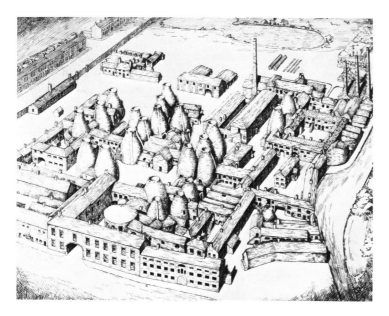

10 *Spode factory.* Stoke-on-Trent (Staffordshire), *c.*1834. Spode Ltd, Archives, Stoke-on-Trent.
The factory was in the centre of the town; the road in front of the main entrance (leading off to the left) led to the Newcastle to London road and (to the right) to Uttoxeter and Derby. A branch of the Trent and Mersey Canal formed the southern limit of the factory premises (at the right of the illustration). Numerous bottle-neck kilns can be seen.

## ENGLAND

### Bodies and Glazes

*Bone China*

In England in the eighteenth century soft-paste porcelain, a glassy composition that does not contain kaolin, was made. It was first manufactured in about 1745 at the Chelsea factory, then soon after, in about 1747, at Bow. English potters began to use calcined bone ash, obtained from ox bones, which contributes calcium phosphate to the composition of the paste. Like French potters, English potters were carrying out research into methods of making hard-paste porcelain and were not unsuccessful: hard-paste was still being made at New Hall around 1812–1814. However, at the end of the eighteenth century, bone china (soft-paste porcelain) was perfected, and it was in production at Spode in about 1799. The recipe for this body varies according to regional factors such as the cost of transport, the availability of raw materials, and the quality of ware required.[63] Some factories actually had several different formulae in use at any one time. The composition of bone china was also affected by new research into the chemistry of the porcelain body. For example, in 1820 at the Coalport factory John Rose substituted a felspathic glaze for the lead glaze used up to this time.

It is necessary at this point to clarify the differences between the British porcelain industry, manufacturing bone china, and the Continental industry, which has continued to produce hard-paste porcelain. Alexandre Brongniart explained this phenomenon in his usual succinct manner: 'English soft-paste porcelain is easier and more economical to make and also has a lower failure rate than the French soft-paste porcelain made at one time. It has no harmful effects on the workers' health. It represents a half-way house between hard-paste porcelain and creamware, having a more fusible body than hard-paste and a

lead glaze. It is superior to creamware as it is translucent and has a harder glaze. The raw materials used in the manufacture of English soft-paste porcelain are almost the same as those of creamware'.[64]

Brongniart continues in a later passage: 'Both the biscuit and the glost ovens are identical with those used to fire creamware'.[65] This rather summary statement explains a situation that the French certainly find puzzling: English nineteenth-century porcelain manufacturers often also made creamware, using the same materials—although in very different proportions to those used for the porcelain body. Kilns of similar, if not identical, design were used for both types of ware, and the same processes were employed to transfer-print decoration on the pieces. Creamware, which was cheap to make, subsidized the production of porcelain. The fuel used was invariably coal, which, in France, only slowly replaced wood. Staffordshire had become an important centre for the manufacture of ceramics by the eighteenth century because surface coal was readily available. The area is called the Potteries because of the numerous enterprises making pottery that existed, and still exist, there. Most of the raw materials are also plentiful in Cornwall: kaolin is in fact known as Cornish clay and pegmatite as Cornish stone.

As we have seen, there is more than one formula for bone china. The following recipe has been taken from L. Whiter's book, *Spode: A History of the Family, Factory and Wares from 1733 to 1833* (1970), and is a formula for high-quality china.[66] It dates from before 1821 when felspar came into use in glazes at the Spode factory:

| | |
|---|---|
| Bone or calcium phosphate | 50% |
| China clay or kaolin | 19% |
| Blue clay or plastic clay | 6% |
| China stone or pegmatite (felspar and quartz) | 19% |
| Flint | 6% |
| | 100% |

*Glazes*

From 1820 John Rose abandoned the use of lead glazes, which were known to be injurious to health. In addition, these glazes were of low quality and subject to crazing. The Spode factory gave up using lead in glazes in 1821, and many other factories followed suit. Rose's glaze formula is quoted by Magnier:[67]

| | |
|---|---|
| Felspar | 44% |
| Sand | 8% |
| Kaolin | 5% |
| Borax | 28% |
| Potash | 10% |
| | 95% |

Today all English glazes contain borax.

Magnier goes on to explain how the body was fashioned and fired: 'When the clay has been weathered, it is put either into a heated "slip kiln" or into a filter press to remove impurities. Being fairly plastic it is easily worked, either by throwing, moulding, or casting, a method used for small hollow items. There is no biscuit firing. Once the piece has been made it is fired at a high temperature, too high for the glaze but lower than the vitrification point of hard-paste porcelain (about 1240 °C rather than 1410 °C). Printed decoration can be applied either under or over the glaze. Pieces are then dipped

in glaze and fired again, this time at a lower temperature.'[68] This is a glaze in the strict sense of the term [called *glaçure* in French]. The relatively low firing temperature means that a wide range of colours is available to the potter. The glost firing is done in smaller kilns, which are nevertheless of similar shape to the high-fire kilns. The characteristic shape of these so-called 'bottle-neck kilns' was for a long time a feature of the Staffordshire countryside.

*Parian Ware*

In 1844 the Copeland factory started making a new type of porcelain body, which has been known by various names, all of which emphasize the similarity of the material to marble. It is commonly known to posterity as Parian ware. An argillo-felspathic body, it takes on a slightly yellowish tone after being fired when unglazed. Like bone china, it can be made using various different formulae. In 1854 specimens of Parian ware supplied by Copeland were analysed by A. Salvetat, chemist at Sèvres.[69]

| | |
|---|---|
| Loss in firing | 6.40% |
| Silica | 58.51% |
| Alumina | 21.00% |
| Iron oxide | 1.00% |
| Limestone | 0.14% |
| Magnesia | 0.05% |
| Potassium | 11.40% |
| Soda | 5.08% |
| | 103.58% |

The 'ivory porcelain' made at the Worcester factory from the middle of the nineteenth century was a glazed Parian body.

Casting was the usual method employed in the manufacture of figures. Thomas Battam, artistic director at the Copeland factory, gave a written account of figure-making in 1849.[70] Iron oxide, which occurs naturally in the clay or felspar, was responsible for the creamy colour of the body that was fired in an oxidizing atmosphere[71] at a temperature of about 1100 °C. The body proved ideally suited to the technique of *pâte-sur-pâte* decoration, since its low firing temperature made possible the use of subtle or vivid shades of many colours.

## Decoration

Bone china and Parian ware provided English potters with two porcelain bodies that could be decorated with varied and scintillating scenes. The high temperatures, which the metallic oxides used as colouring agents could not withstand, were not necessary for the firing of bone china and Parian ware. The extensive mechanization of English industry in the nineteenth century is well known, and had been a feature of the preceding period, when it affected mainly the manufacture of creamware, but had also characterized many porcelain factories.

When pieces were decorated by hand the methods used were essentially the same as those applied on the Continent, except for the low firing temperature which ensured attractive colours. This was to the advantage of the English porcelain industry, which now uses a colour printing method closely related to transfer-printing. On hard-paste porcelain the colours seem to float on top of the glaze, while the colours on bone china attractively merge with the glaze, seeming to melt into it.

*Transfer-Printing*

The design is engraved on to a copperplate, or alternatively, if greater durability is desired, on to a steel plate. Next the colours are made ready in the form of printer's ink. The oil base is prepared using linseed or nut oil which is heated, then metallic oxides are added to it as colouring agents and lamp-black as a binding agent. The mixed colour is rubbed into the engraved copperplate and any surplus colour is cleaned off. The printed design can be applied either under or over the glaze.

A piece of tissue-paper is then put on to the copperplate, and when the design has been transferred to it, it is left in a bath of water. If the printed decoration is to be applied to a piece already glazed, the glaze is prepared with a thin film of size thinned with turpentine. This coating is then dried and the inked paper placed on to the glazed piece, where the ink is deposited. Then the piece is fired.

When the decoration is applied to the biscuit, or unglazed, porcelain the paper used for the transfer-print must be of a special quality. The surface of the paper (printed with the transfer) can be applied directly to the biscuit. In order to detach the transfer-paper, the piece is plunged into a bath of water. The damp pot is then fired so that the greasy base burns away and disappears, leaving behind the printed impression. The piece is then glazed and fired once more.

*Bat Printing*

Printing processes were refined in the eighteenth century by English potters using the bat-printing technique (using 'bats' of soft glue), which gives a more subtle effect than the process discussed above. First the gelatin (or glue) is heated to a syrupy consistency. It is then formed into a plaque or 'bat' about 2 to 3 millimetres thick.

An engraved copperplate is then covered with nut oil mixed with turpentine and cleaned off in the manner already described for transfer-printing.

When the 'bat' of glue is applied to the copperplate it absorbs the oil. The bat is then applied to the piece which is to be decorated, transferring the design in the form of oil to the piece. Then colour in the form of fine powder is sprinkled over the oil to which it adheres. The operative cleans up the powder that has fallen outside the oiled zones with a brush. Then the piece is fired. This technique was used for single-colour, polychrome, or gilt decoration. Peter Warburton of the New Hall factory took out a patent for printing gold using the bat-printing technique in 1810.[72]

*Gilding*

In the nineteenth century mercury gilding was that normally used in Great Britain. Probably because of the extremely soft glazes used, English gilding has a flat appearance when compared with gilding on Continental porcelain. It was perhaps in an effort to remedy this that 'raised gold' was so frequently used at the end of the nineteenth century. The process had been in use for a long time, having been invented by Henry Daniel, a decorator at Spode.[73] It consisted of drawing the outline of the parts to be gilded, then applying, by means of a brush, the first layer of decoration composed of a metallic oxide for the ground colour, together with a flux and a fritted glaze, all suspended in a turpentine base. A second layer of this mixture can be used if necessary, either before or after firing the first. The relief was then finally gilded.[74] Gilding done in this way is dull in appearance and regrettably can also be rather brownish in tone.

11 *Cup and saucer and pattern-book.* Stoke-on-Trent (Staffordshire), Minton, *c.* 1802. Bone china. D. (cup) 6 cm; (saucer) 13.5 cm. Mark: 206. Minton Mus., Royal Doulton Tableware Ltd, Stoke-on-Trent.
On the right-hand page is the number '85', which is also found on the cup and saucer. If a piece bears a number, it can sometimes be identified by consulting factory pattern-books, even in the absence of any factory marks.

At the beginning of the nineteenth century several Staffordshire manufacturers, including the large ones like Spode,[75] as well as smaller concerns, used metallic lustres to decorate their pieces. Pink lustres were used on rather charming pieces with rustic scenes. Silver lustres, obtained from 176 platinum, were used at Spode and have almost the same colour as lead; they can also be obtained using silver. Gold lustres, 173 which fired to pink, purple, or gold, were also perfected.[76] The 391 pearlized glaze on Belleek porcelain is a bismuth lustre.

To obtain a variety of effects with gilding, the technique used on the Continent since the eighteenth century was also used in England. It involved exploiting the different textures of gold by burnishing parts of the design with a hardstone and polishing the rest with a soft cloth and fine sand.

These contrasting effects enabled the production of modelled designs on a gilded surface, a process that was necessarily laborious and costly. In 1863 the Minton factory led the way by substituting acid-gilding for the hand-finishing 371 method,[77] and other factories quickly adopted this new process. An acid-resistant material was applied to the areas to be gilded and burnished in the normal way, then the areas to be left matt were coated with acid. This and the resist were removed before

the piece was gilded. After the piece had been fired and parts of the design had been burnished, the full effect of the contrasting matt and burnished gilding became visible.

*'Pâte-sur-Pâte' Decoration and Other Methods*
During the second half of the nineteenth century, as in France cf. p. 15 and following the lead given by the Sèvres factory, the English factories, headed by Minton, began to use the *pâte-sur-pâte* technique of decoration. As with the method used in France, the decorator first traced the outline of his design on the porous unfired piece. Various layers of white or coloured slip were then applied, each layer being allowed to dry before the next was painted on. The contours were then sharpened with a metal tool, which removed excess slip, or they could be emphasized by applying a thicker slip. The piece was then glazed and fired. We have already remarked that Parian ware was especially 372 suited to this technique, since its low firing temperature enhances the subtle tones produced by the metallic oxides used as colouring agents but which cannot stand great heat. James 475 Hadley seems to have decorated his pieces with slip coloured by means of metallic oxides and by adding accents of thicker slip.

Small drops of enamel were applied to pieces and fused over gold or silver foil to produce a type of relief decoration imitating small pearls, a technique known as 'jewelling'. It had 380 been used at the Sèvres factory by Cotteau at the end of the eighteenth century and was revived by various English factories in the second half of the nineteenth. The Countess of Dudley Service (Worcester, 1865) is the most famous example.

Certain firms such as Worcester in the second half of the nineteenth century and Doulton at the end of the nineteenth century and beginning of the twentieth, systematically developed new styles and techniques. Henry Sandon, in his book *Royal Worcester Porcelain from 1862 to the Present Day* (1973), found it necessary to begin with a glossary of styles. In fact in several cases Worcester employed well-known techniques for certain decorative schemes. The 'Raphaelesque' 386 wares had relief decoration consisting of Renaissance motifs 222 directly inspired by Doccia porcelain made in the early years of the nineteenth century, attributed at the time Worcester was producing it not to Doccia but to Capodimonte. In other cases, however, a special, newly developed technique was used. 'Sabrina' ware, for instance, was made in the following way.[78] A piece of Parian ware was given a biscuit firing, then areas to be kept blank were covered with a protective coating. The piece was then impregnated with a mixture of metallic oxides, cobalt, chrome-green, sulphuric acid and water. After drying, it was hard-fired. During the firing crystalline effects in the glaze, as well as luminous areas and shadowy patches developed. The turn-of-the-century taste for glaze effects, often achieved by chance rather than design, is evident in this type of ware.

## Pattern-Books and Marks

In nineteenth-century England, decoration was frequently partly printed, using a variety of different processes, and partly hand finished. Gilding was often applied by hand. This method of work has proved useful to later generations of collectors and historians, since English factories gave a number to each hand-painted pattern. Each factory had a pattern-book, a copy of which was held by the London wholesalers and retailers. Every hand-painted pattern was shown in water-colour in the book next to a number, which also appeared on the pieces themselves. Some of these nineteenth-century pattern-books 11 have survived, providing an invaluable means of attributing numbered pieces. Even unnumbered pieces can often be attributed to specific factories thanks to the enormous amount of work done by specialists in English nineteenth-century porcelain, who have studied the shapes used by many factories. The study of handle shapes has proved most useful in this respect in deciding the origin of unmarked pieces.

Apart from pattern numbers, which occur on some objects, many pieces bear factory marks in the same way as the products of other European factories, although they are rarely dated. From 1843 the Patent Office in London began to register new designs, which were then protected by copyright. The lozenge-marks with the Patent Office date-code are a good way of establishing the date of objects, though they only indicate the date when the design was registered. The Patent Office records reveal the name of the factory or workshop responsible for a shape or decorative scheme on an unmarked piece. Both English and Continental firms registered designs in this way.

The amount of information available ensures that the history of the English factories is currently the most well researched of all the nineteenth-century porcelain factories.

# II 1800–1830: The Triumph of Painting

## FRANCE

### Sèvres Porcelain

On 14 May 1800 (25 *Floréal an* VIII), Lucien Bonaparte, Minister of the Interior, appointed Alexandre Brongniart (1770–1847) director of the Sèvres porcelain factory. Thus he gave this prestigious institution a director whose qualities remained dazzling from every point of view for almost half a century. Thanks to Brongniart the Sèvres factory did not cease to wield a profound influence in Europe throughout the nineteenth century.

Alexandre Brongniart,[1] whose portrait bust modelled in the eighteenth century by Simon-Louis Boizot remains famous, was the son of the architect Théodore Brongniart, who designed the Paris Bourse which was completed in 1808. Alexandre's education was intended to make him a man of taste. His training was as a scientist: he was a mining engineer and wrote on mineralogy, zoology, and geology. In 1822 he was created Professor of Mineralogy at the Muséum national d'histoire naturelle and rigorously divided his time between the Muséum in the south-east of Paris, Sèvres in the suburbs at the south-west of the city, and the rue Saint-Dominique in Paris itself where he lived.

Since his mind had been cast in the intellectual mould of the eighteenth century, Alexandre Brongniart had encyclopaedic knowledge that was both broadly cultivated and extremely precise in scope. Apart from his activity at the factory, Brongniart carried out various, and very diverse, projects that led to the establishment of the Musée céramique et vitrique ('Museum of Ceramics and Glass')[2] in 1812 and culminated in cf. p. 10 the publication of his *Traité des arts céramiques,* published 1844, which is still the basis of our knowledge of the ceramic techniques of his times.

### *Finance*

When Brongniart was appointed director of the Sèvres factory, he found it in a state of total financial collapse. Under the *Ancien Régime* the factory had been the personal property of the king, but the Revolutionary era that followed was a critical period, which could have easily condemned the factory, as it did the monarch, to death. The budget was strained by the payment of wages to workers too old to do their jobs. Costaz,

12

12, 13  *Vase fuseau* ('spindle vase'), largest size. Sèvres, Imperial Porcelain factory, 1813. Hard-paste porcelain. H. 108 cm. Mark: inaccessible. S.A. Prince Murat Coll., Paris.

Napoleon gave this vase to his mother in 1813 on the occasion of the baptism of his son, the King of Rome, one of whose godmothers she was. The scene representing Napoleon Crossing the Alps is after a painting by David and is signed by Georget.

14  *Vase d'Austerlitz.* Sèvres, Imperial Porcelain factory, 1806. Hard-paste porcelain. H. 133 cm. Mark: inaccessible. MNCM, Rueil-Malmaison (MM 40-47-8408).

Bergeret designed and decorated this baluster vase *(vase à bandeau),* which has a black ground in imitation of Greek vases (thought at that time to be Etruscan), and the aim was to identify Napoleon I with the emperors of Antiquity.

13

14

who was in charge of the Department of Arts and Manufactures at the Ministry of the Interior, dismissed 159 of the 220 workers. In this respect, at least, Brongniart found himself in an unambiguous situation. In order to increase cash-flow he sold off stock both abroad, to Russia and England, and at home, which brought in large sums. However, these were insufficient to enable him to reorganize the factory's finances, which were not to be restored to a healthy state until the Sèvres factory was put on the First Consul's Civil List in 1802 (1ᵉʳ *Vendémiaire an* XIII) and its debts paid by the Sinking Fund.

In practical terms, the placing of the factory on the Emperor Napoleon's Civil List restored it to its pre-Revolutionary status and to financial independence, but henceforth, contrary to eighteenth-century practice, it was obliged to balance its budget. In 1815, at the fall of the First Empire, the factory underwent another serious crisis. It was occupied by Prussian officers who imposed their own rules on the factory. They appropriated pieces and ordered the destruction of any alluding to the Napoleonic era. In fact, Brongniart saved a large number of pieces by hiding them.

From then until 1870, various monarchs succeeded each other in France and kept the factory on their Civil List; they all had the future of the factory at heart, assuring it the necessary sums for the production of pieces that would be worthy of the nation. As high-ranking servants of the State, Brongniart and his successors were to demonstrate with ease their loyalty to each consecutive government.

15   *Figurine: L'Insomnie* or *La chercheuse de puce*. Sèvres, Imperial Porcelain factory, 1809. Hard-paste porcelain, tinted blue. L. 27 cm. Incised on base: 'Sevres/9/11/B/1B/18/V'. MNC, Sèvres (17 829).
The model was created by Boizot and has been interpreted in two-colour porcelain in imitation of Wedgwood's jasper ware.

*Sales of Undecorated Wares.* Under these conditions it is surprising to learn that between 1816 and 1819, in 1826, and again in 1840 Brongniart allowed large loss-making sales of glazed white pieces, often of inferior or reject quality. Both in France and abroad (frequently, it seems, in England) these were decorated, or 'clobbered', sometimes with the intent to deceive the future purchasers, in a fashion quite unworthy of the Imperial, later Royal, factory. This explains why so many pieces can be found that are quite clearly made of Sèvres porcelain but have decoration that was evidently not done at the factory. In fact, the larger porcelain factories have traditionally disposed of undecorated pieces at reduced rates. Brongniart used these sales both to improve cash-flow and to acquire in exchange pieces destined to enrich the collections of the Musée céramique et vitrique.[3]

*Techniques*
*Hard-Paste Porcelain.* A particularly important aspect of the subject, since it was of such overwhelming importance during the period, was that Brongniart, as a scientist, on taking over the administration of the factory, made a major decision about the technical side of the factory's activities: that is, he ordered that soft-paste porcelain, which had been made concurrently with hard-paste at the end of the eighteenth century, should no longer be manufactured, so that from 1804 production was concentrated on hard-paste wares. In order to justify this decision, Brongniart continually denigrated soft-paste wares, attributing to them all sorts of defects. He wrote: 'the old artificial porcelain was difficult to work, and the processes were harmful to health, since the ceramic body was insufficiently plastic for direct modelling and had to be moulded and then lathe-turned when dry, releasing a glassy alkaline dust, injurious to the pulmonary organs....[4] The firing of this soft-paste porcelain takes appreciably longer than the time required

for hard-paste.[5] In 1804, when its production at Sèvres ceased, it had to be fired five times in the kiln we call the *grand feu*, or high-temperature, kiln in order to attain perfection....[6] Burnishing of this gold [that is on soft-paste porcelain] was more difficult and the result was always less brilliant than with gold on hard-paste porcelain.'[7]

All these assertions were, of course, designed to prove that the hard-paste formula, newly discovered by Brongniart, was vastly superior to the old body.

Apart from the ceramic body that bears his name, Brongniart attempted or encouraged the creation of other innovations that have already been referred to (see page 10): the 'bronze body', which was sombre in colour; porcelain lace;[8] a blue body inspired by Wedgwood's blue jasper ware; cameo encrustation, originally conceived in the eighteenth century for a service made for Catherine the Great and taken up again by Boudon of Saint-Amans in 1821.[9]

Brongniart also improved manufacturing methods, introducing casting (used from 1819), installing a rose-engine turning lathe (in 1819) and a two-chamber kiln (1842).[10]

*The Decorator's Palette.* Because of the change to a different ceramic body and the evolution of taste, the creation of a new range of colours for decorating wares was needed. This new palette included, for example, such ground colours as dark blue, a pale blue called 'agate', and chrome green. These high-temperature overglaze colours were most frequently used during the First Empire (1804–1815). The range of low-temperature colours, fired in the muffle-kiln, which were applied either as ground colours or used as an element of painted decoration, was extremely wide. It was only the development of these colours that made possible the faithful reproduction of oil-paintings on porcelain which were particularly numerous from the 1820s onward.

16 *Medici vases.* Sèvres, Imperial Porcelain factory, 1808–1809. Hard-paste porcelain. H. 44 cm. Marks: 54, 55. Grand Trianon, Versailles, ([1835] T 1376, 4710).
Both vases have blue grounds. One, which is one of a pair, is decorated with profiles of Roman emperors by Delafosse and dates from 1808. The other was painted by Swebach and gilded by Boullemier. An imperial hunt is depicted in worked gold. At the time of the Restoration, the *concierge* at Versailles tried to remove Napoleon's unmistakable profile (Ledoux-Lebard 1975, p. 121).

17 *Breakfast service: Femmes célèbres de l'Antiquité.* Sèvres, Imperial Porcelain factory, 1813–1815. Hard-paste porcelain. L. (oval plate) 44 cm; H. (teapot) 15.6 cm. Mark: (oval plate) 59; (other pieces) 60. MNC, Sèvres (23 582).
The cloudy blue ground with its gold flecks imitating lapis lazuli, the gilt and platinum friezes, and the pseudo-cameo decoration are all typical of the products of the Sèvres factory during the First Empire. Classical iconography was only one of many sources of inspiration at Sèvres at this time but is extremely well suited to these pieces. The portraits were painted by Degault after Visconti, while the scene on the oval plate, representing Penelope Surprised by the Suitors, is by the same porcelain painter after Flaxman.

Gilding was a highly important element of decoration during this period.[11] It achieved the maximum brilliance applied over the glaze—during the First Empire and Restoration cups were generally *doublées d'or,* that is their inner surface was entirely covered with gold. When the gold was applied directly to the unglazed, or biscuit, porcelain, it appeared relatively matt even after burnishing.

*Transfer-Printed Decoration.* The Sèvres factory commissioned some transfer-printed decoration by Legros d'Anizy.[12] A plate in the Sèvres museum, painted with a naturalistic rose in the centre and with a border of fruit alternating with animals, surrounded by decorative motifs in gold, has on the reverse a label in the handwriting of the first curator of the museum, D. Riocreux, which reads: 'Colour printing on Sèvres porcelain by Mr Legros d'Anizy 1830'.[13] The rather carelessly executed appearance of the decoration in the centre, which is highly unusual for this period, leads one to think that this piece was experimental, despite its relatively late date. Later on, transfer-printed decoration was in common use and was adopted at the

Sèvres factory itself, as Brongniart took care to point out.[14] It was, in fact, used for the *service forestier* ('Woodlands' Service') made in 1834, as well as for the services with gilt decoration on a white ground destined for Louis-Philippe's residences.[15]

Brongniart's technical innovations ensured the production of porcelain of the highest quality. This consistent perfection is without doubt one of the factors that assured the Sèvres factory its leading role, whether in the manufacture of smaller pieces for domestic use or in the production of special items.

*Style*
It is certainly a matter of taste whether one appreciates a particular style or not, and the style prevalent at the Sèvres porcelain factory during the first half of the nineteenth century has not always met with universal approval. In this context the words of George Lechevallier-Chevignard can be quoted: 'As for the pieces produced at the factory during the long period between 1800 and 1847, it must be recognized that the remarkable technical perfection achieved through the scientific skill of Brongniart only served, generally speaking, to

manufacture works of doubtful artistic worth and never led to the creation of a characteristic style comparable with that of Vincennes and Sèvres during the preceding century. While pieces made in the Louis XV and Louis XVI periods exhibit an infinite diversity, the majority of pieces of this period can, on the contrary, be classified according to a few formulae, hardly modified during the course of half a century'.[16]

Lechevallier-Chevignard denied the wares any artistic value, even though he was obliged to recognize that they displayed some sort of unity, if not an instantly recognizable style. His point of view becomes more understandable when one takes into account that he was writing at the very time (1908) when the factory was boldly concentrating on the production of extremely white porcelain, which had been totally despised by Brongniart a century earlier. His contempt for it is somewhat surprising in view of the trouble invariably taken by ceramists to make porcelain with the whiteness and translucency characteristic of Chinese wares. Alexandre Brongniart, as the servant of the emperor, was anxious to please his master by supplying him with pieces made in contemporary taste, that is in the Neo-Classical idiom, which is, in principle, strongly influenced by the arts of Antiquity. However, apart from certain shapes deriving from the antique ('Medici' vases, *vases fuseaux,* especially of the *service égyptien*) and certain decorative themes (such as those found on the *service Olympique,* on the *cabaret* painted with famous women of Antiquity, and on the *vase d'Austerlitz*), porcelain, by its very nature, escaped the dominance of the canons of Antiquity. The potters of the Classical era never produced ceramics of such high quality. Moreover, the production achieved by Brongniart was the culmination of research carried out at Sèvres since at least 1770, when hard-paste was first in use.

Since the mid-eighteenth century European earthenware and porcelain manufacturers had been making an increasing number of trompe-l'oeil objects, especially pieces in the shape of flowers, fruit, and vegetables. At Sèvres in the eighteenth century this tradition was continued in hard-paste porcelain, which was decorated in imitation of wood, tortoise-shell, lacquer, silk, goldsmiths' work, jewellery, cameos and so on.

The idea of a 'painting on a porcelain plaque' reproducing an oil-painting or a fresco and destined to be mounted in furniture or in panelling is even older: 'they seem to have begun in 1761 and 1762 with portraits of Louis XV'.[17] Brongniart took this eighteenth-century tradition of trompe-l'oeil to an extreme point, although he did limit the number of materials imitated. During the time he was director only the following were imitated: hardstones, bronzes (patinated bronze was copied using the 'bronze composition', and gilt bronze achieved by applying gold directly to biscuit porcelain so that it appeared relatively matt), goldsmiths' work (by using gold as a ground colour and *en doublure,* inside cups), marble (by using hard-paste biscuit porcelain, which had already been in use in the eighteenth century for such a purpose), and especially oil-paintings.

*Painters*

Even the smallest First Empire plate is in many ways an imitation on a reduced scale of an easel painting, its border entirely covered with a coloured ground, richly gilt. The border took the place of a frame surrounding the central well of the plate, which was decorated with a miniature painting. Oil-painting was at this period carried out using techniques similar to those of painting on porcelain and Brongniart employed

18　*Flared cup of the shape known as jasmin à pied cannelé, and saucer.* Sèvres, Imperial Porcelain factory, 1810. Hard-paste porcelain. H. (cup) 9 cm; D. (saucer) 10.5 cm. Mark: 56. MNC, Sèvres (2008).
These pieces show just how richly decorated Sèvres porcelain could be in the First Empire period. Porcelain has been used to imitate goldsmith's work. The portrait of the Empress Josephine was painted by Madame Jaquotot.

painters such as Martin Drolling, Jean-Baptiste Isabey and Ambroise Louis Garneray to execute these miniatures on porcelain. The talents of the specialist porcelain painters were not inferior to those of artist-painters. The factory artists who deserve mention in this connection are Antoine Béranger, who was responsible, with others, for The Arrival at the Louvre of the Italian Masterpieces on a *vase étrusque à rouleaux* painted in 1813,[18] Marie Victoire Jaquotot, who painted numerous portraits on cups (including the Empress Josephine, and Marie Louise)[19] and Abraham Constantin, who went to Rome in 1830 and in 1842 to copy Raphael's frescoes in the Vatican.

Brongniart set out to prove that porcelain can be a vehicle for high art. The pieces he manufactured were often of monumental proportions and were decorated in a manner intended to be, as it were, the reflection of great painting.

*Modellers*

If Alexandre Brongniart took great care to choose painters of high calibre, he took similar pains to ensure that the shapes of his pieces were designed by leading artists. One of the most famous of them was his father, the architect Théodore Brongniart who collaborated with others to create the *vase fuseau* of 1800, the *vase coupe B* of 1806 and the 'Medici vase' of 1806. He also designed decorative motifs such as the scheme for the *guéridon des saisons* ('pedestal-table of the Seasons') for Fontainebleau Palace (1806–1807) and above all the border of the *service particulier de l'Empereur,* which is embellished with swords, laurel leaves and gold stars on a green ground.

Another famous architect who modelled shapes during the First Empire was Charles Percier. In 1813 he designed a famous pendulum clock-case in biscuit porcelain. Its massive yet harmonious proportions are lightened by figures modelled in low relief and by the presence of an elegant bowl which surmounts the whole.[20] The same idea of decoration in low

relief, this time on a gold ground, is found on the so-called *déjeuner Régnier à reliefs* ('Régnier breakfast service with reliefs'), modelled by Régnier in 1813.[21] Another version of the same *déjeuner* has painted rather than relief decoration.[22]

*Shapes*

Under the First Empire there was a constant search for purity of form. It can be seen in the shapes of vases such as the spindle *(fuseau)* vase or even the *vase à bandeau* but is even more evident in cup shapes. Naturally eighteenth-century shapes were still made in Brongniart's time. The *tasse à café litron* ('cylindrical coffee cup') with its straight sides had an inherent appeal to imperial taste, but perhaps the cup most typical of the period is the shape called *jasmin,* or jasmine. The profile is flared; it has either a simple or fluted foot and the handle is either porcelain or silver-gilt. Equally elegant are the cups that go under the name *coupe,* referring to their bowl-like form. The cups in the Régnier *déjeuner* have finely formed bases, while the coffee cups of the shape known as *calice à volute* ('scrolled chalice') have much bigger bases.

The most popular cup shape in the Restoration period (1814–1830) was the *tasse à chocolat AB* ('AB chocolate cup'), created in 1813, probably by A. Brachard. In comparison with the *jasmin* cup, its profile is heavy, and from now on, elegance and purity of outline gave way to 'imposing' forms. Several fantasies were created, notably by Alexandre-Evariste Fragonard, the son of the well-known painter, and himself a painter of figures and decorative subjects. He was also responsible for designs for furniture, baskets, utility wares and even for biscuit figures, which all show a feeling for the picturesque sometimes seen in the decorative schemes of the First Empire, but never in its shapes.

19  *Cup and saucer 'AB 1813'.* Sèvres, Royal Porcelain factory. 1829. Hard-paste porcelain. H. (cup) 9 cm; D. (saucer) 16 cm. Marks: (cup) 64; (saucer) 65. MNC, Sèvres (2628).
During the First Empire period the flared or trumpet-shaped *tasse jasmin* was the most fashionable cup shape. The Restoration period favoured this heavier shape. The portrait of Charles X on the cup is by Moriot.

20  *Breakfast service.* Sèvres, Imperial Porcelain factory, 1809. Hard-paste porcelain. H. (cup) 5.3 cm; D. (saucer) 9.7 cm. Mark: 53. Grand Trianon, Versailles ([1839] 6294–[1852] T 5651).
The elegant shape of the hemispherical cups, so-called *tasses coupes,* is typical of First Empire taste. Less suited to painted decoration than the flared *(jasmin)* cups, their purple ground has been transfer-printed with gilt motifs.

## Special Pieces

Sèvres's products between 1800 and 1830 can be divided into several categories: 'special pieces', plaques, vases of different sorts, table services and sculpture. 'Special pieces' earned their name mainly on account of their size. We have already referred to the *vase d'Austerlitz* (in the Musée national du Château de Malmaison, Rueil-Malmaison), which was completed in 1806 for the chateau of Saint-Cloud. This *vase à bandeau,* or baluster vase, is no less than 133 centimetres high; the red decoration on a black ground is copied from antique red-figure vases and so serves to identify the victorious sovereign of Austerlitz with the Roman emperors, an historical analogy perfectly attuned to the mentality of the period. The design, drawn by Bergeret, has all the stiffness so much appreciated in the imperial era. The largest *vase étrusque à rouleaux* measures 120 centimetres in height and the example in the Sèvres museum is dated 1813. The decoration on the body, painted by Béranger, depicts the arrival at the Louvre of the masterpieces sent from the Cisalpine region after Napoleon's Italian Campaign. The scene is characterized by the quality of painting mastered by David's pupils, combining precision with poetry. The painting is surrounded by rich gilding covering the base, shoulder, and neck of the vase itself, and continued on the gilt bronze handles.

The footed bowl called the *coupe des sens* is also in the Sèvres museum.[23] Its shape, recorded as *coupe B,* was designed in 1806 by Théodore Brongniart. It was painted in 1825 by Madame Ducluzeau after Alexandre-Evariste Fragonard and is a characteristic example of the evolution of taste, which was now tending towards the picturesque. The miniature paintings decorating the outer surface of this piece represent allegories of the Five Senses with the figures shown in sixteenth-century dress.

The few pieces of furniture produced during the First Empire also come into the category of 'special pieces'. Examples of this type of object are large *guéridons,* or pedestal-tables, the most famous of which is *La Table des Maréchaux* ('Marshals' Table'),[24] made in 1810 and now in the Malmaison museum. It was painted by Isabey and has, in the centre, a portrait of Napoleon I surrounded by a sunburst; the leading officers of the *Grande Armée* are shown in medallions. The foot is decorated with low-relief figures after Baron François-Joseph Bosio representing Abundance, Fame, History, and Victory in biscuit porcelain and were modelled by Brachard. The gilding was done by Philippine and Boullemier, and the burnishing by Moreau. As so often during this period, Thomire was responsible for the gilt bronzes. The 'Marshals' Table' was delivered to the Tuileries Palace in 1810.

A rectangular console table dating from 1819, its shape and decoration designed by A. E. Fragonard, is part of the *Mobilier national.* Intended to be placed against a wall, and lighter in shape than the other pieces so far mentioned, it is supported on four pilasters at the back and four columns at the front. Gilt bronze is still an important element of the design, but the painted decoration by Zwinger, based on plant life, is very graceful.[25]

All idea of grace was quite forgotten in 1827 at the time of manufacture of a *bureau-secrétaire,* a type of writing desk, now in the Sèvres museum, composed of porcelain plaques over a scarcely visible, stout, wooden structure. Gilt bronze has been used in this piece merely as a frame for the plaques. The central plaque represents the Muses on Pindarus. It is signed 'E. C. Le Guay 1827', and its polychrome decoration does not

21 *Plaque painted with Saint Teresa.* Sèvres, Royal Porcelain factory, 1829. Hard-paste porcelain. H. 73 cm; L. 45 cm. Mark: inaccessible, signed at lower left: 'Mme Ducluzeau 1829 d'après Gérard'. MNC, Sèvres (7660).
The technique of early 19th-century oil-painting lent itself to reproduction on porcelain.

harmonize with the other plaques covering the piece of furniture, which imitate cameos. Whatever one may think of the overall effect of the piece, the quality of the painting on these plaques is astoundingly high.[26] Another *bureau-secrétaire* exhibited in 1830 at the Louvre and now at the château of Versailles has a central plaque decorated with a view of this royal palace that is far better integrated into the overall scheme of the design.

Other objects, such as pendulum clocks and caskets, also belong to this group of 'special pieces' and are all extremely well painted.

## Plaques

Quality of execution had to be perfect when it came to porcelain plaques imitating oil-paintings or frescoes. They were made between 1818 and 1848—this is at least true for the plaques in the Sèvres museum, which houses a remarkable collection containing around forty of these 'pictures'. The earliest plaques in the Sèvres museum are small (about 14 × 11 cm), date from 1818 and are painted with a portrait of Louis XVIII by Georget after M. Robert, or with the Comte d'Artois, the future King Charles X, by Madame Rogeard after

Gérard.[27] It has already been mentioned that Brongniart introduced the technique of casting at Sèvres in 1819, and this innovation enabled the factory to make much larger plaques that were flat and evenly formed. The 'Diogenes plaque', painted in 1829 by Langlacé after Poussin,[28] measures no less than 68 centimetres in height by 99 centimetres in length, and is by no means exceptional in size. Twelve of the collection of around forty plaques in the Sèvres museum reproduce paintings by Raphael or his followers, from the frescoes in the Vatican such as the *School of Athens,* the *Mass at Bolsena* and the *Deliverance of Saint Peter.*[29] Others are reproductions of very well-known paintings of the French and Italian schools, and a third group consists of copies of French nineteenth-century paintings in the Neo-Classical style such as *Cupid and Psyche,* painted in 1824 by Marie Victoire Jaquotot after Gérard,[30] or works of the Romantic school, for example *Saint Teresa* by Madame Ducluzeau after Gérard. By the time of the Second Empire (1852–1870) the fashion for these plaques had died out, and the Sèvres museum has only one example bearing a date after 1850. It is a copy of the *Embarkation for Cythera* painted in 1872 by A. Schilt after Watteau,[31] and the misty atmosphere of the original proved impossible to capture on painted porcelain. As tastes changed and 'porcelain-like' finishes were no longer in demand, the attempt to reproduce oil-paintings on porcelain was abandoned.

*Vases*

Besides monumental special pieces and plaques, some original and varied vase forms were created during the First Empire and Restoration periods. We have already drawn attention to vases decorated in imitation of hardstones. Equally worthy of mention are other pieces in the Neo-Classical style imitating cameos. Very early in the century, pieces in the styles of earlier periods were created at Sèvres in a precocious historicist style. Two *vases étrusques carafe* in the Sèvres museum belong to this group; they were painted by Huart with views of Florence on a ground imitating 'Florentine mosaic'.

*Table Services*

Table services were also of high quality. Napoleon revived the tradition of ordering large services either for his own use or as diplomatic presents. Each service contained a considerable number of pieces, easily between 100 and 140 separate items, as well as a large biscuit porcelain centrepiece. Besides the Emperor's own service, which had a chrome-green border, and which is now dispersed, others were created such as the *service égyptien* ordered as a present from Napoleon I to Josephine in 1812, but which she refused. It remained at the Sèvres factory until offered in 1818 as a present by Louis XVIII to the Duke of Wellington, then British ambassador at Paris:[32]

Paris, 20 March 1818

I have heard, my dear Duke, that a few days ago at a dinner at your house you expressed a preference for antique rather than modern porcelain. Allow me to appeal against this judgement, and, in order to enable you to decide whether I am correct to do so, I beg you to accept several plates which may perhaps bear comparison with those of an earlier period. I am encouraged to take this step by an old proverb that I will try to render in your language. *Do [sic] little gifts—keep friendship alive.*

With continued assurances, my dear Duke, of my friendship and good wishes towards you.

Louis

22  *Carafe vase in the Etruscan style ('vase étrusque carafe').* Sèvres, Imperial Porcelain factory, 1813. Hard-paste porcelain. H. 40.5 cm. Mark: inaccessible. MNC, Sèvres (5250).
The view on the front of this vase is of the cupola of Santa Maria dei Fiori, Florence; on the reverse is a Classical scene. The vase has a companion piece, painted with the Ducal Palace and the Palace of the Princes, Florence. Both vases are decorated by Huart with a 'Florentine-mosaic' ground imitating Renaissance motifs. The use of this iconography and the juxtaposition of Florentine views with Classical scenes reveals that eclecticism had already taken hold at Sèvres by the early 19th century.

23

24

25

This service is now in the Victoria and Albert Museum, London.

23     The *service à marli d'or* ('Service with a Gold Border') was made in an unusual fashion. It was part of a *commande perpétuelle,* that is to say the number of plates wanted was not specified at the time it was ordered. It was in fact composed of pieces made from 1805 until the beginning of the Restoration period by artists not occupied with any particular project. The pieces all went to different destinations. Some were used as presents, others were sent to the imperial, later royal, residences. Eighteen plates can be found in the Sèvres museum. Apart from the dominating presence of the gold border, their subjects are extremely varied and show the precocious eclecticism prevailing at the Sèvres factory, as well as a taste for the picturesque. For instance in 1806 one subject was Don Pedro Killing Himself with Henri IV's Sword,[33] in 1812 there was An Egyptian Barber,[34] and in the same year Her Imperial Majesty leaving the Flower-Garden in the Park of Saint-Cloud on Horseback.[35] Floral decoration was also common.

During the Restoration period the manufacture of large table services continued, though their iconography changed completely. The post-Revolution monarchs, more modest than the Emperor Napoleon I, hardly dared to demand outright that *they* should be glorified by the Arts, so from now on France itself was glorified. The skills of her inhabitants were
24  celebrated in the *service des arts industriels* ('Service of the Industrial Arts'), made between 1823–1836, which was still in the manner of the table services of the preceding period and included on some plates precious representations of work at the Sèvres factory painted by Develly. This service was presented to Metternich by Louis-Philippe in 1836. The desire to glorify France and the French people is even more evident in the case
25  of the *service des Départements* ('*Départements* Service'), made between 1824 and 1829. Not only is the centre of each plate painted with a landscape scene evoking a certain region of France, but on the back of each plate is an inscription giving a list of famous people, as well as the distinctions gained by and the 'attributes' of that region. The decorative scheme itself is conceived in a more modern idiom comprising a border painted with garlands, emblems and medallions that contain inscriptions or portraits all on a nankin (yellow) ground. The impression of a gold 'frame' created by the use of a gilt border has been completely abandoned.

Although seemingly more modest than the large services, the *cabarets* or *déjeuners,* coffee or tea-services or breakfast

23  *Plate from the Marli d'or Service.* Sèvres, Imperial Porcelain factory, 1808. Hard-paste porcelain. D. 24 cm. Mark: 52, signed 'Sauvage' on the base. MNC, Sèvres (1794).
This typically Neo-Classical scene symbolizes Spring. It is painted in *grisaille* on a ground imitating semi-precious stone. Sauvage was responsible for the decoration.

24  *Plate from the service des Arts industriels.* Sèvres, Royal Porcelain factory, 1823. Hard-paste porcelain. D. 23.8 cm. Mark: 61. MNC, Sèvres (2872¹).
The service, which consists of 112 plates, 2 ice-pails, 2 sugar bowls, 4 comports, was painted by Develly between 1823 and 1835. It was presented by Louis-Philippe to Metternich, the Austrian diplomat, in 1836, with the exception of six plates now preserved in the Musée National de Céramique. Three of the six plates depict the work of the Sèvres factory itself. The plate illustrated shows Sculptors and Trimmers. Another illustrates the Preparation of the Clay, and the third depicts Painters and Gilders.

25  *Plate from the service des Départements.* Sèvres, Royal Porcelain factory, 1827. Hard-paste porcelain. D. 23.6 cm. Mark: 63, inscribed (rim): '*Département de la Corse*'; (central well): '*Vue d'Ajaccio*'; signed on the reverse: 'A. Poupart 1827'. MNC, Sèvres (12 863).
The decoration of this service shows the stylistic development which took place at Sèvres during the Restoration period, since the border of each plate is no longer designed merely as a gold frame surrounding the painting in the centre. The 'nankin' colour of the border is characteristic of this period.

services, were often exceptionally sumptuous in the years between 1800 and 1830. Examples include the *déjeuner Régnier à reliefs* made in 1813 (Sèvres museum), which has biscuit porcelain reliefs on a matt gold ground (the matt effect is achieved by applying the gold directly to the biscuit porcelain), with shiny gold (applied over glazed porcelain) for the handles and interior surface of each cup. Another such service, produced between 1817 and 1818 and recently acquired by the Museum of the Château de Pau, is known as the *cabaret de l'Apothéose d'Henri IV* ('Apotheois of Henry IV' Breakfast Service). The abundance of its decoration is only equalled by the richness of effect.

## Sculpture
Surprisingly, sculpture in porcelain is the poor relation among the Sèvres pieces made during the period under discussion. One would have expected to see the Neo-Classical taste expressed in figures in biscuit porcelain, since it is the ideal substitute for marble, which is itself the perfect vehicle for this style. It is all the more surprising in view of the fact that Brongniart perfected a body that was more siliceous than the one in general use and which had been specially developed for sculpture. Just

26 *Sugar bowls from the service égyptien.* Sèvres, Imperial Porcelain factory, 1812. Hard-paste porcelain. H. 32 cm; 32.5 cm. Marks: 57, 58. V & A, London (127$^{α A}$. 1979).
Egyptian motifs became fashionable in France after Napoleon's return from the Egyptian Campaign in 1799. He had taken with him several scientists, including Champollion, as well as artists who brought back important information on Egyptian art.

27 *Chinese teapot designed by Leloy ('à côtes Leloy').* Sèvres, Royal Porcelain factory, 1827. Hard-paste porcelain. H. 13.5 cm. Mark: 62, MNC, Sèvres (24 784).
This piece is in the fanciful style generally associated with Paris factories rather than with the French State factory.

28 *Equestrian statuette of Napoleon Bonaparte as First Consul.* Sèvres, Porcelain factory, 1801. Hard-paste porcelain. H. 35 cm. Mark (plinth): incised 'SEVRES'. MNCM, Rueil-Malmaison (556¹).
Modelled by Leriche after Carle Vernet, this figure inaugurated the production of official portraits at Sèvres in the 19th century. Later, generally only busts or medallions were made, although during the Restoration some of these busts were of monumental size.

as academic sculpture in the early nineteenth century lacked inspiration, so biscuit porcelain at Sèvres was only considered of interest as a means of introducing technical innovations, such as a bronze body, a blue-tinted composition imitating Wedgwood's jasper wares, and for the production of large-scale pieces such as certain busts of rulers, including one at the Sèvres museum of Louis XVIII, which measures no less than 92 centimetres in height.[36] The factory was, as will become apparent, using biscuit porcelain for much the same purpose as in the eighteenth century, that is for the production of figures and busts of the king and the royal family, as well as for table-centres. The most famous of these is the one from the *service égyptien* which is made up of seventeen pieces and consists of temples, pylons, colonnades, and obelisks. The idea of making table-centres using architectural elements was not new. At the time of the wedding of the Dauphin and Marie-Antoinette in 1770, the factory had modelled the royal palace at Rheims in porcelain. Once again it is clear that the modernity of the pieces resides in the *way they are made* rather than in their conception.

Around 1830 the Sèvres factory was, therefore, in a quite unique position. It was not trying to assert itself by adopting modern styles and ideas at any price, because, as we have seen, some ideas were retained or re-used which would have seemed quite out-moded in Paris, for example. However, this is not to say that the factory did not, with many of its pieces, join the ranks of the avant-garde who were progressing towards the eclecticism of the Second Empire period (1852–1870). Finally,

the most important thing was that the factory had equipped itself with the means to make pieces of such remarkably high quality that for decades it was, with very good reason, to be an object of fascination to the most diverse and distant factories, from Naples to St Petersburg. Its excellent technical record explains the survival through several centuries of the Sèvres mystique.

## Paris

The manufacture of Paris porcelain commenced in the late eighteenth century, in the 1770s when clay from the Limoges region became commercially obtainable and the monopoly held by the royal factory at Sèvres for the manufacture of porcelain was first broken. In the eighteenth century Paris porcelain was characterized by the quality of its craftsmanship (numerous workers laid off by the Sèvres factory were employed at the Paris factories), by its simplicity (necessitated by economic factors) and by its faithful adherence to fashion in obedience to the whims of taste of its clientele. Decoration *aux barbeaux,* which consisted of scattered cornflowers, is typical of Paris porcelain during the reign of Louis XVI (1774–1793). The white ground showed the porcelain to its full advantage, tiny flowers were placed on the piece in a regular fashion calculated to please a clientele tired of Rococo fantasy, and the decoration enhanced objects whose forms were sober in outline.

The French Revolution (1789–1795) caused severe upheavals in the Paris porcelain industry, as at Sèvres, because of the removal of their patrons, the rich aristocracy. However, the Revolution did help to increase the number of factories now fully liberated from the Sèvres monopoly though most of these factories were in operation for a short time only. They fell victim to the economic crises of 1805–1806 and 1810–1813 resulting from the Napoleonic wars and were also threatened by competition from the so-called *chambrelans,* or outside decorators. There were, according to Madame Dihl, more than four thousand of these independent painters in Paris in 1806, who obtained white porcelain, painted it, and then resold it.[37]

Despite these setbacks the Paris porcelain manufacturers enjoyed their period of greatest prosperity in the 1820s. After this time their number declined continuously when it was found that great fortunes could not be made from the production of porcelain. Labour was expensive and unreliable and expansion in the very heart of Paris proved impossible. These factors led to the closure of several factories, such as the Dihl concern, which closed before 1828, and the Nast factory, which ceased production in 1835, or their removal to the provinces. Thus in 1824 Honoré established a factory at Champroux in the Allier district where he made white porcelain according to his requirements; only the decoration was still done in Paris. By 1850 there were few Paris factories

29 *Plaque.* Paris, Dihl and Guérhard factory, 1797. Hard-paste porcelain, H. 48 cm. Signed and inscribed on the base at the left: 'Le Guay 1797; Mᵗᵘʳᵉ de Dihl et Guérhard'. MNC, Sèvres, (2931).
The painter Le Guay worked for Dihl and Guérhard at Paris as well as at the Sèvres factory. This portrait of Dihl showing him holding a paintbrush, his palette beside him, and jars of colour and examples of his porcelain on his desk calls attention to his work on the firing of colours. Dihl was particularly interested in colours designed for the decoration of porcelain and stained glass.

30

31

32

30 *Plate*. Paris, Dihl and Guérhard factory, *c.* 1800. Hard-paste porcelain, D. 24.5 cm. Mark: 27. MNC, Sèvres (13 919).
The white ground is delicately painted in a green, imitating bronze, and in gilt with motifs inspired by Pompeian wall-paintings.

31 *Cup and saucer*. Paris, Dihl and Guérhard factory, *c.* 1800–1805. Hard-paste porcelain, H. (cup) 9 cm; D. (saucer) 14 cm. Mark: 28. MNC, Sèvres, (10 962).
These two pieces, which do not belong together, are decorated with an 'agate' ground and gilt. They demonstrate that Paris factories, like Sèvres, were trying to imitate hardstones.

32 *Ink-well with the Empress Josephine's monogram*. Paris, Dihl and Guérhard factory, *c.* 1805–1810. Hard-paste porcelain, H. 20 cm. Mark: 29. MNCM, Rueil-Malmaison (76-4-1).
The 'worked gold' scale pattern that almost completely covers this piece gives it the appearance of goldsmith's work.

in existence and those that remained were of minor importance: 'there are only seventeen porcelain makers left in Paris; of these only four have more than ten employees, and eight work by themselves or have only one employee'.[38] This fact explains why it is quite sensible to designate all unmarked hard-paste porcelains which are firmly datable on stylistic grounds to the first half of the nineteenth century 'Paris porcelain' (known familiarly in France as *vieux Paris*). Pieces appearing to date from the second half of the nineteenth century are with good reason often attributed to Limoges for the same reason.

In fact throughout the nineteenth century a great deal of Limoges-made porcelain was decorated in Paris, a practice which has never entirely died out.

The history of even the most important Paris factories is complex. Comte X. de Chavagnac and the Marquis de Grollier in their *Histoire des manufactures françaises de porcelaine* (Paris, 1906) more or less unravelled the thread connecting the movements, sales, purchases, marriages and re-marriages of the various porcelain factory owners. It is at times difficult to distinguish the actual potters from the painters and even from the wholesalers who were also in the habit of marking wares.

### The Dihl and Guérhard Factory

This factory was known in the eighteenth century by the name of its titled patron, the Duc d'Angoulême. It was established in 1781 in the rue de Bondy under the management of two partners, the porcelain maker Dihl, and Guérhard, who acted as administrator. In 1789 the factory moved to vast premises in the rue du Temple. Guérhard died in 1793, but the partnership remained in existence as Madame Guérhard took her husband's place, and later married Dihl.

The factory weathered the Revolution extremely well by selling porcelain to Flight in London from 1789 onwards. During the Napoleonic period its situation was less happy as competition became fiercer following the economic recovery of the early years of the nineteenth century. The ageing Dihls did not adapt to the changing times, and the doors of the factory closed in 1829.

In 1797 the artist Charles-Etienne Le Guay (1762–1846) painted a portrait of Christophe Dihl on a porcelain plaque.[39] 29 To show his keen interest in problems relating to ceramic colours, he is portrayed in front of a palette with a brush in his hand. The high-point of his factory corresponds with the apogee of Neo-Classical taste; the simplest of shapes were used for his pieces.

The Paris porcelain factories specialized in adapting the creations of Sèvres to bourgeois tastes, but it is difficult to concede

33

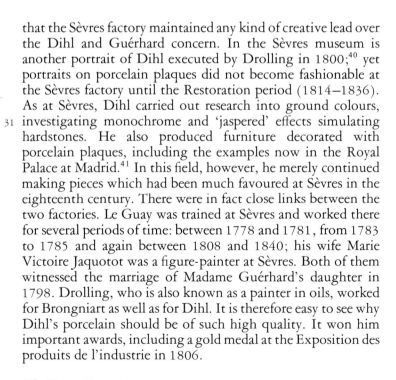

34

35

that the Sèvres factory maintained any kind of creative lead over the Dihl and Guérhard concern. In the Sèvres museum is another portrait of Dihl executed by Drolling in 1800;[40] yet portraits on porcelain plaques did not become fashionable at the Sèvres factory until the Restoration period (1814–1836). As at Sèvres, Dihl carried out research into ground colours, investigating monochrome and 'jaspered' effects simulating hardstones. He also produced furniture decorated with porcelain plaques, including the examples now in the Royal Palace at Madrid.[41] In this field, however, he merely continued making pieces which had been much favoured at Sèvres in the eighteenth century. There were in fact close links between the two factories. Le Guay was trained at Sèvres and worked there for several periods of time: between 1778 and 1781, from 1783 to 1785 and again between 1808 and 1840; his wife Marie Victoire Jaquotot was a figure-painter at Sèvres. Both of them witnessed the marriage of Madame Guérhard's daughter in 1798. Drolling, who is also known as a painter in oils, worked for Brongniart as well as for Dihl. It is therefore easy to see why Dihl's porcelain should be of such high quality. It won him important awards, including a gold medal at the Exposition des produits de l'industrie in 1806.

*The Darte Factories*

These factories exhibit the complexity of the network of family links between factory owners and illustrate their successive removals from place to place.

33 *Cup and saucer.* Paris, Darte factory, *c.* 1830. Hard-paste porcelain, H. (cup) 12.6 cm; D. (saucer) 16.2 cm. Mark: 23. MdAd, Paris (13 558).
Paris factories copied the flared *(jasmin)* cup created at Sèvres. The gilt decoration illustrates the Romantic taste for 'Gothic' motifs. On the cup is a portrait of the Comte de Chambord.

34 *Tripod cup.* Paris, Darte *frères* factory, *c.* 1810. Hard-paste porcelain, D. 20 cm. Unmarked but inscribed: 'Manufacture de Porcelaine des Frères Darte'. MNC, Sèvres, (22 331).
The decoration shows three views of the Darte brothers' factory at Paris. Illustrated here is the View of the Porcelain Salesrooms from the Garden.

35 *Vase.* Paris, made at the Nast factory, decorated at the Darte factory, 1819. Hard-paste porcelain. H. 40 cm. Mark: 24, signed: 'Moriot'. MNC, Sèvres (9090).
There are four vases of identical shape in the collections of the Sèvres museum. Although known to have been made by Nast, three bear the Darte factory mark. Two of them were included in the 1819 Exhibition. They are decorated in differing styles, inspired either by Dutch or Italian paintings.

Régine de Plinval de Guillebon[42] described three factories bearing this name. The first, in which three brothers, Joseph, Louis-Joseph, and Jean-François Darte, were partners, lasted from 1795 until 1804.

The second, known as Darte *aîné,* belonged to the eldest brother, Joseph, and was in production between 1813 and 1823 when it was bought by Discry. Its porcelain was described as mediocre at the Exhibition of 1823.

The third factory, known as Darte *frères* was officially established in 1808 at the rue de la Roquette by the two

36 *Cream jug.* Paris, Nast factory, *c.* 1805–1810. Hard-paste porcelain, H. 16 cm. Mark: 33. MNC, Sèvres (8495).
The foot, neck, and handle have been decorated with motifs in relief and gilt. Some of the reliefs were produced by means of a roulette. Matt gold applied over the unglazed porcelain imitates the appearance of gilt bronze perfectly.

37 *Clock-case.* Paris, Nast factory, *c.* 1810. Hard-paste porcelain, H. 51 cm. Mark: 34. MNC, Sèvres (15 600).
Nast used his porcelain-manufacturing ability to make biscuit-porcelain clock-cases. This piece is of blue and white biscuit porcelain in imitation of Wedgwood's jasper ware.

brothers Louis-Joseph and Jean-François in partnership. In 1824 Louis-Joseph took his son Auguste Rémi into the partnership, which was dissolved in 1825. Despite financial problems Louis-Joseph carried on making porcelain until about 1833. He died in 1843. Other members of the Darte family were also involved either in the decoration or sale of the porcelain produced by the concern.

34    A tripod bowl in the Sèvres museum is decorated with three views of the Darte factory in the rue de la Roquette. The piece is highly typical of the production of Darte *frères* in its originality of shape (it has a central depression and its feet are surmounted by relief masks) and in the quality of its meticulously painted and gilded decoration. The same originality and high quality of workmanship can be found in the later products of the Darte *frères* factory such as the pendulum clock in the shape of a two-handled vase which is now in the Palacio National in Ajuda.[43] Its gold ground is decorated with burnished flowers.

35    In the Sèvres museum are four vases, two of which are decorated with a religious scene after Raphael and on the reverse with a peasant scene after Paulus Potter; the other two vases are each painted with a scene of figures in a landscape; these four vases were made at the Nast factory. Three bear the mark of the Darte *frères* factory, where they were decorated, and the scenes after Potter and Raphael are signed 'Moriot', standing for Nicolas Marie Moriot, a figure-painter at Sèvres between 1828 and 1848. There is clearly a great deal of

overlapping between the various factories. In a private collection in Paris are two vases of the same shape as the pieces just mentioned, which must therefore be of Nast porcelain, yet they bear Darte marks. They are decorated with miniature portraits of the opera singers Malibran and Mademoiselle Sontag by Sophie Girard. It should be remembered in this connection that Nast sold a great deal of undecorated porcelain. The dating of these vases is tricky: two of this shape were exhibited in 1819, but the ones showing Malibran and Mademoiselle Sontag cannot have been made, or at least cannot have been decorated, before the 1830s, since one of the ladies was born in 1808 and the other in 1806. The decoration could perfectly well have been carried out long after the vases were made.

Services made at the Darte factory with flower or fruit decoration in a trompe-l'oeil style on a blue ground heightened with gilding are not uncommon. They correspond to the service produced at Sèvres and known as *le service des productions de la nature* ('the Productions of Nature Service').

*The Nast Factory*
In 1783 Jean Nepomucène Hermann Nast, of German extraction like so many other Paris porcelain manufacturers, bought a small factory in the rue Popincourt. He survived the Revolution and on his death in 1817 his two sons took over the factory, which had become one of the most prosperous in Paris. From 1831, one of them, Henri, carried on the business

38 *Sugar bowl and cover.* Paris, Nast factory, *c.* 1810–1820. Hard-paste porcelain, H. 19.5 cm. Mark: 35. MAD, Limoges (ADL 3122).
The bluish ground with painted decoration in the Pompeian style is as richly coloured and as well executed as any piece made at Sèvres.

39 *One of a pair of trumpet-shaped vases.* Paris, attributed to the Nast factory, *c.* 1810. Hard-paste porcelain, H. 15 cm. Unmarked. MNC, Sèvres (6800).
The matt colours used on this piece are proof that this type of polychrome enamel decoration, which is documented, was successfully produced.

40 *Centrepiece.* Paris, Nast factory, *c.* 1820. Hard-paste porcelain, H. 67 cm. Unmarked. MAD, Limoges (ADL 3706).
The plastic quality of Nast's sculptural creations can be clearly seen in this piece. Nast and his sons were awarded numerous gold medals at the industrial exhibitions held in the first half of the 19th century.

41 *Cup and saucer.* Paris, Nast factory, decorated at an unidentified workshop, *c.* 1820–1830. Hard-paste porcelain, H. (cup) 13.2 cm; D. (saucer) 17.3 cm. Mark: 33. MAD, Limoges (ADL 3151).
The portrait of Henri IV and the way in which the surface is completely covered are typical of the First Empire period, but the royal iconography and Neo-Gothic motifs are Romantic in feeling.

42 *Cylindrical cup (tasse litron) and saucer.* Paris, Dagoty factory, *c.* 1810. Hard-paste porcelain. H. (cup) 6.1 cm; D. (saucer) 13 cm. Mark: 19. MNCM, Rueil-Malmaison (MN 47-2934/2935).
The 'salmon'-coloured 'nankin' ground–very pale here–is generally characteristic of the 1830s, but here it has been used much earlier, since the 'Classical' decoration is typical of the early years of the 19th century.

alone but in 1835 he was obliged to close it down, having abandoned the idea of moving to the provinces.

At the exhibitions of the products of French industry the juries regularly gave the highest awards to Nast and his sons in recognition of the excellent quality of their wares and of their technical innovations. One of these was the invention of a roller to produce relief decoration for the borders of plates for which Nast took out a patent in 1810. Using this method he obtained fine decorative effects with sharp reliefs usually only achieved by the use of metal dies. By gilding the reliefs he produced a simulated bronze effect; when the gilding was applied to glazed porcelain it imitated gilt bronze, while when it was applied to biscuit porcelain it simulated patinated bronze. Nast was carrying out his own research into the trompe-l'oeil effects of the eighteenth century contemporaneously with Brongniart. Like Sèvres he occasionally tinted his biscuit porcelain blue in imitation of Wedgwood.

Vauquelin, chemist at the Nast factory, who died in 1828, experimented with colours, and the discovery of chrome-green 39 is attributed to him. He also created matt colours.

As to the style of Nast's porcelain, it is an accurate reflection 36, 41 of contemporary taste. Around 1815–1820 it was influenced by the Neo-Classical movement, while later on it became 'Romantic' in feeling. However, it has one outstanding characteristic—the abundance of relief motifs. Nast evidently owed a large part of his success to the high quality of these reliefs. He could therefore sell a large part of his production undecorated 'in the white', including the vases already mentioned.

### The Dagoty and Honoré Factories

The history of these factories is the most complicated of all.

François Maurice Honoré was a porcelain manufacturer in Paris from 1806. The Dagoty factory was run by three brothers, who had been pupils of Dihl and Guérhard and who went into porcelain manufacturing during the Revolutionary period. In 1804 Pierre Louis Dagoty became the sole proprietor of the

45  *Cylindrical cup (tasse litron) and saucer.* Paris, Dagoty factory, c. 1810. ▷ Hard-paste porcelain. H. (cup) 6.2 cm; D. (saucer) 12.7 cm. Mark: 20. MNCM, Rueil-Malmaison (MN 47-2930/2931).
Tulips often appeared on 18th-century French earthenware but became less common later. Here Dagoty included a tulip motif in a typically First Empire decorative scheme.

46  *Pair of pots-pourris.* Paris, Schoelcher factory, c. 1810. Hard-paste ▷ porcelain, H. 22 cm. Mark: 46. MNC, Sèvres (24 987).
Like Sèvres at the same period, Paris porcelain factories often tried to copy different materials. These pots-pourris imitate painted *tôle* ('sheet metal') in use at that time for many domestic utensils.

47  *Bowl on pedestal stand.* Paris, Caron and Lefèbvre factory, c. 1805. Hard- ▷▷ paste porcelain. H. 25 cm. Mark: 17. MNC, Sèvres (6799).
Biscuit figures ornament this piece, which is painted in matt enamel colours. Technical research into colours has been employed here to add a note of charm to a very simply designed object.

48  *Water jug and basin.* Paris, Pouyat factory, c. 1820. Hard-paste porcelain. ▷ H. (water jug) 26.5 cm; L. (basin) 32 cm. Mark: 42. Michel Bloit Coll., Paris. Both are decorated with an unusual scene, treated in a rather free style for the Classical motif, of a procession of Roman soldiers. The white ground is embellished with large gilt scrolls.

43  *Seated cupid in biscuit porcelain.* Paris, Dagoty factory, c. 1810. Hard-paste porcelain, H. 16 cm. Mark: 21. MNC, Sèvres (13 791).
The album of models in the Musée des Arts décoratifs, Paris, features many cupids, which usually form the foot of ink-wells or egg-cups.

44  *Cylindrical cup (tasse litron) and saucer.* Paris, Dagoty factory, c. 1820. Hard-paste porcelain. H. (cup) 6 cm; D. (saucer) 12 cm. Mark: 19. MNCM, Rueil-Malmaison (MN 47-2928/2929).
Snow scenes were unusual subjects in the early 19th century. The melancholic mood sometimes aroused by the bareness of the winter landscape constituted an early manifestation of Romanticism—as did the Gothic style of the building on the cup.

49 *Pair of vases.* Paris, Honoré factory, *c.* 1820. Hard-paste porcelain, H. 35.4 cm. Mark: 31. Madeleine Castaing Coll., Paris.
Paris pieces painted with Classical subjects are rare, since customers were used to more light-hearted subjects. The ground colour of these vases is the so-called 'nankin' yellow, which has a pinkish cast here, and was favoured during the decade 1820 to 1830.

50 *Page from a pattern-book.* Paris, Dagoty and Honoré factory, pattern-book used by the factory. Cabinet des dessins, MdAd, Paris (CD. 3857).
The illustration shows that after about 1800–1815, when streamlined forms were favoured, the Paris factories, like Sèvres, began to make more squat shapes.

51 *Coffee-pot.* Paris, Russinger or Russinger-Pouyat factory, *c.* 1800–1810. Hard-paste porcelain, H. 22 cm. Mark: 45. Michel Bloit Coll., Paris.
The elaborate relief decoration and rich gilding gives the piece a rather strange appearance; many Paris factories were mainly interested in producing pieces remarkable for their novelty.

52 *Vase.* Paris, Pouyat factory, *c.* 1810–1820. Hard-paste porcelain. H. 31 cm. Mark: 41. MAD, Limoges (2457).
The handles, shaped like small angels on this vase, are done with much less attention to detail than the relief decoration on contemporary porcelains, for example from Sèvres or the Nast factory.

53 *Ink-well.* Paris, Pouyat factory, decoration attributed to an unknown English painter(?), *c.* 1810. Hard-paste porcelain. L. 18.5 cm. Mark: 43. Michel Bloit Coll., Paris.
Although the piece is clearly marked by the Paris factory operating from premises in La Courtille, rue de la Fontaine-au-Roi, its heavy floral decoration is uncharacteristic of Paris porcelain painters, and it is tempting to attribute it to an English pupil of the flower painter William Billingsley.

factory, which expanded considerably under his direction. It was supported by loans from the state and by his imperial clientele. On 1 January 1816 François Maurice Honoré, acting as a sleeping partner on behalf of his son Edouard, merged his business with that of Pierre Louis Dagoty. Honoré contributed his factories, one of which was in Saint-Yrieix, the other being situated in Paris, where his showrooms were also located. Dagoty brought into the partnership his factory in the boulevard du Montparnasse and his showrooms in the boulevard Poissonnière. In 1820, when the company ceased trading, Edouard Honoré retained the Paris operations, while Dagoty kept the factories in Saint-Yrieix. In 1824 Honoré ceased making porcelain in Paris as wages were too high and space was at a premium. From this date, production was carried out at Champroux in the Allier district where kaolin supplies were available. Only the decoration was done in Paris either on Honoré's own premises or by outside decorators.[44] Edouard Honoré died in 1855, and his son Oscar sold the Champroux

factory in 1865. Thus, the heyday of the Dagoty factory was the First Empire period, and the Honoré factory was at its most successful during the Restoration; pieces can therefore be dated on stylistic grounds as well as by their factory marks.

A miscellaneous collection of fifty-nine gouaches and a lithograph showing pieces made at the Dagoty and Honoré factories at different dates between the First Empire period and the middle of the century represents a unique survival of such records in France.[45] This collection is in the Cabinet des dessins at the Musée des Arts décoratifs in Paris.[46] Besides their painterly qualities, the variety and originality of the shapes shown is striking. This applies especially to the small pieces, such as inkwells and egg-cups, which are in the form of snails, seated, kneeling or standing cupids, water-carriers, and figures taken from mythology or from the Bible. Another surprising feature is that the modelled relief decoration of a piece is often more remarkable than its painted decoration, for example there are cups in the form of flowers, shells, swans, and so on. If these

50, 199

illustrations are dated to the 1820s (the dating can only be surmised since the sheets are undated) they can be seen as the forerunners of the Neo-Rococo style of Jacob Petit.

*The Locré-Russinger-Pouyat Factory*

The factory was established in 1773 by Jean-Baptiste Locré who, in 1777, went into partnership with Laurent Russinger. The premises were at La Courtille in the rue Fontaine-au-Roi. In 1797 Russinger took the porcelain wholesaler François Pouyat into partnership. The association was terminated in 1808 and in 1810 Pouyat's three sons acquired the factory. In 1816, together with a new partner, Guillaume Le Bourgeois, they transferred the business which manufactured white porcelain to Fours in the Nièvre region where it continued under successive owners until about 1865.

The slow artistic development which took place at the end of the eighteenth century and the beginning of the nineteenth can be especially well traced from a study of pieces in a private collection in Paris. The products of the La Courtille enterprise, marked with two crossed torches in imitation of the Meissen factory mark, are easily recognizable, although they are not dated. The shapes of the eighteenth-century pieces made at this factory, set up in the year preceding the commencement of Louis XV's reign, reflect the sobriety of the late years of the century combined with the slightly undulating outlines inherited from an earlier period. Lobed borders are common, and ewers are found in the shape of fluted shells. In the early nineteenth century simpler forms were preferred, at least the contours of pieces were less fussy, even though they often had applied decoration in relief. Water jugs were the most widely made item, and one model was decorated with a relief mask of Napoleon Bonaparte under the spout. In the eighteenth century swags of flowers or single scattered flowers were the dominant decorative motif, but the nineteenth century saw the introduction of more varied decoration, either painted *en grisaille* or polychrome. Landscape scenes, either with or without figures, mythological, religious and floral subjects are all commonly found. As usual on Paris porcelain dating from the first half of the nineteenth century, the gilding is of extremely high quality.

53 Like Nast and the other Paris firms, this factory sold undecorated pieces. Illustrated above is an ink-well, which, if one were judging by the style of its heavy floral decoration, could easily be English.

*The Schoelcher Factory*

Like Russinger and Nast, Marc Schoelcher (1766–1832) was of German extraction. He came from the Rhineland, arriving in France in 1789 where he met Russinger, Locré's partner at La Courtille. Initially he sold earthenwares, then bought the so-called Comte d'Artois factory in the Faubourg Saint-Denis in 1798, and later purchased a showroom for the sale of porcelain in the boulevard des Italiens. In 1828 he took his son Victor into partnership; he is more famous for his successful fight against slavery than for his porcelain manufacturing activities. It seems that production had already ceased at this time and only the shop in the boulevard des Italiens was still trading. Victor Schoelcher closed it down in 1834.

Marc Schoelcher's porcelain was designed for wealthy customers. It was well made, finely decorated and magnificently gilded, reflecting the taste of the time without losing an element of fantasy. There are pots-pourris in the

46 Sèvres museum that imitate pieces in *tôle* ('sheet metal') with

54 *Tea urn.* Paris, Caron and Lefèbvre factory, 1812. Hard-paste porcelain. H. 81 cm. Unmarked. Grand Trianon, Versailles (T. 641).
Delivered to the Garde-Meuble, the agency in charge of government furniture, in 1812 by Lefèbvre and Caron in settlement of a government loan made in 1807. This is a specially executed piece, inspired by a design by Percier and Fontaine (Ledoux–Lebard, 1975, p. 92).

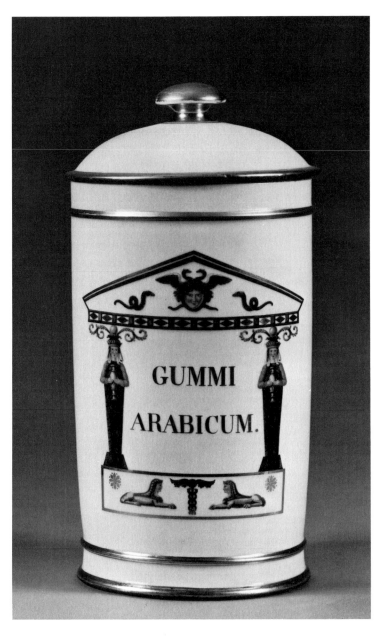

55 *Apothecary jar and cover.* Paris, decorated at the Deroche workshop, *c.* 1815. Hard-paste porcelain, H. 40 cm. Mark: 26. MNC, Sèvres (4596). Until the end of the *Ancien Régime* apothecary jars had concave sides; 19th-century examples, however, are straight-sided.

56 *Cup and saucer.* Paris, Denuelle factory, *c.* 1820. Hard-paste porcelain. H. (cup) 11.6 cm; D. (saucer) 16.4 cm. Mark: 25. MNC, Sèvres (14622). In 1819 Cadet de Vaux and Denuelle were awarded a silver medal at the Industrial Exhibition. This enchanting cup shows that Paris factories were capable of producing porcelain equal in quality to that made at Sèvres. A Sèvres shape, 'AB 1813', has been copied here. Like Sèvres pieces, the cup has been gilded on its inner surface *(doublée d'or)*. The decoration on the outer surface includes 'worked gold'. The element of fantasy noticeable in the decoration is characteristic of Paris porcelain.

57 *Bowl.* Paris, unidentified decorating workshop, first quarter of the 19th century. Hard-paste porcelain, D. 19 cm. Mark: 48. MNC, Sèvres (13705). The identity of the Paris decorator 'D.T.' is still unknown. However, the gilt decoration on a black ground is no less beautiful for the lack of an attribution.

58 *Cup.* Paris, Stone-Coquerel factory, decorated by Legros d'Anizy, *c.* 1810–1820. Hard-paste porcelain, H. 6 cm. Mark: 47. MNC, Sèvres (14608).
The straight sides of the cylindrical cup shape termed *litron* are ideally suited to transfer-printed decoration, the quality of which equals that of hand-painted pieces.

59 *Plate.* Paris, Stone-Coquerel factory, decorated by Legros d'Anizy, *c.* 1810–1820. Hard-paste porcelain, D. 23.5 cm. Unmarked. MNC, Sèvres (10464).
Although unmarked (it is inscribed on the reverse 'Jeux séculaires/An de Rome 515'), this piece was certainly decorated by Legros d'Anizy since it is printed. Its iconography is similar to that of numerous creamware plates printed in monochrome brown by d'Anizy.

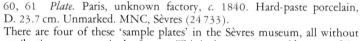

60, 61 *Plate.* Paris, unknown factory, *c.* 1840. Hard-paste porcelain, D. 23.7 cm. Unmarked. MNC, Sèvres (24733).
There are four of these 'sample plates' in the Sèvres museum, all without attribution to any particular factory. This is the most unusual because of the decoration on the reverse. Clients could choose the motif they wanted from the selection on the sample plate before placing their order.

62 *Cabaret.* Sèvres, Royal Porcelain factory, and Paris (plate with blue ground), 18th century, decorated by the Irlande, Perez, and Jamard Workshop, 1816–1818. Soft-paste porcelain. L. (tray) 43 cm; H. (teapot) 12 cm. Mark: 95. MNC, Sèvres (1892).
This piece has been 'clobbered'. Brongniart sold porcelain 'in the white' or painted with a blue ground, which was then decorated in Paris or abroad. This cabaret was painted by Soiron with a rather ambitious decorative scheme: on the tray is a portrait of Louis XIV, on the teapot are depicted Madame de Grignan and Madame de Sévigné; Mademoiselle de Montpensier is shown on the milk jug, and on the cups are Madame de Montespan and Queen Henrietta Maria of England. Portraits of members of the French royal family or their retinue are often found on fake Sèvres, but rarely on 18th-century pieces made and decorated at the factory itself.

flowers in relief foreshadowing the Rococo productions of Jacob Petit. The craftsmanship is superb.

*Decorators and Unattributed Pieces*

A detailed discussion of individual Paris factories will not be given since Régine de Plinval de Guillebon in her *Paris Porcelain, 1770–1850* has already provided a wealth of specialist information that need not be duplicated in this work. However it is worthwhile discussing the importance of independent decorators in the early nineteenth century and examining some aspects of Paris porcelain illustrated by unmarked pieces that cannot be attributed to any particular factory or decorator.

In 1806 Madame Dihl stated that there were thirty-three factories and more than four thousand outside decorators in Paris.[47] In 1850 there were seventeen porcelain factories and one hundred and fifty-eight outside decorators,[48] by which time Limoges and the provinces had overtaken Paris. Between these two dates painters of porcelain were extremely important, some of whom such as Feuillet, Legros d'Anizy, and Gonord signed their work. Feuillet was particularly active during the Restoration period. Both Gonord and Legros d'Anizy specialized in transfer-printed decoration, though France lagged well behind England in the use of this technique, which had been extensively employed there since the eighteenth century. Gonord's particular skill consisted in reproducing the same motif in various sizes using the bat-printing process. In the Sèvres museum is a series of Sèvres porcelain plaques dating from 1812[49] and printed with the same medallion in three different sizes, ranging in diameter from 14, 9, 3 and 6 centimetres. Gonord received official recognition in the form of silver and gold medals at the exhibitions of industrial arts of 1806 and 1819; however, because of the complexity of his process, he did not attract customers.[50] His successor, Perrenot-Gonord, made the invention profitable but his wares were more notable for their quantity than for their quality.[51]

58   François Antoine Legros d'Anizy achieved success much more rapidly. He has already been mentioned in connection with his work at Sèvres, where he was employed from 1803. In 1808, 1809, and 1812 he took out patents on his processes with his partners Stone and Coquerel and exploited his inventions at their premises in the rue du Cadran. From 1818 he worked alone, changing location several times. He subsidized his efforts by decorating *en grisaille* an enormous amount of cream-coloured earthenware. Porcelain decorated

59   by him is, however, very rare. Subjects similar to the ones he used on earthenwares can be found on plates in the collection at the Sèvres museum, which are decorated with Classical scenes. The quality of the colour printing is astounding.

Paris porcelain was characterized by the production of pieces with a strong element of fantasy. Such objects were to be the speciality of Jacob Petit a short time later. The style is difficult to define but can be illustrated by various pieces such as the

60, 61   plate recently presented to the Sèvres museum; it is a sample plate painted with bands of decoration showing different schemes produced by the factory, which so far, unfortunately, remains unidentified. Other examples of plates of this type are known,[52] but this piece has on the reverse a most unusual decorative scheme comprising the sun, the Signs of the Zodiac, and flowers.

62   Another surprising creation is a porcelain *déjeuner,* which is to our knowledge the earliest 'fake Sèvres' made in the nineteenth century. The *déjeuner* is composed of pieces of

63   *Vase.* Limoges, attributed to the Baignol factory, *c.* 1806–1810. Hard-paste porcelain, H. 22.5 cm. Unmarked. MAD, Limoges (ADL 2516).
The decoration, a Bacchante painted *en grisaille,* is typical of the early 19th century. According to a partly effaced inscription on the base of the piece, it was made at Etienne Baignol's factory around 1806 with decoration by his son, François Baignol.

Sèvres soft-paste porcelain of eighteenth-century manufacture sold by Brongniart as rejects in 1816 to Messieurs Irlande, Perez, and Jamar. Between 1817 and 1818 they were decorated by the painter Soiron and gilded. The tray is painted with no less than a portrait of Louis XIV. The pieces are marked with the interlaced LLs. The forgers even suggested to Louis XVIII that he should buy the *déjeuner,* passing it off as having been in the possession of Louis XV. When the deception was uncovered the *déjeuner* was retained at the Sèvres factory and passed into the Sèvres museum.[53] It is interesting to speculate how many undiscovered fakes exist besides this one piece that we know about.

## Limoges

Like Paris porcelain the porcelain made at Limoges[54] was born of the discovery of kaolin at Saint-Yrieix in 1768. From this date entrepreneurs were keen to make use of this highly prized raw material at its place of origin. Massié with his partner and financier Grellet, who were already active locally in the making of earthenware, were the first to manufacture porcelain at Limoges. Under the protection of the Comte d'Artois (brother

of Louis XVI), and later under royal protection in association with the Sèvres factory, this firm launched an industry that was to take on huge proportions in the nineteenth century. In the beginning it was merely a business, the profitability of which was uncertain. Another factory was established at La Seynie in 1774; it too was on a small scale and closed down in 1785. From this time onwards these factories assumed the role they were to maintain in the first half of the nineteenth century: they manufactured principally white porcelain for sale to the Sèvres or Paris factories where the pieces were decorated. Sales of clay subsidized the product which was expensive even when undecorated. This procedure was adopted by the two leading figures, François Alluaud and Etienne Baignol, who were active in the early part of the nineteenth century.

Etienne Baignol (c. 1750–1821) had in fact been employed as a thrower at the Royal Sèvres Factory; between 1789 and 1794 he attempted to run the factory at La Seynie and in 1794 set up his own business at Limoges itself in part of the Augustine convent there. Exhibited at the Musée national Adrien Dubouché are a number of pieces which, when studied in conjunction with the descriptions of the wares he sent to the Paris exhibitions of 1804 and 1806, give a fairly clear idea of the style of his products.

After the Revolution, factories were no longer obliged to mark their wares, and the Limoges factories gave up using any marks on the base of their pieces. This made it easier for them to sell white porcelain to decorators and more difficult for us to attribute pieces to specific factories in Limoges or Paris.

Baignol was not the only one in Limoges and the surrounding area to derive profit from the liberalism of the Revolution. In 1795 Léonard Monnerie bought the Augustine convent and occupied it with the intention of making porcelain there. Initially he was quite successful, but in the nineteenth century he found himself up against stiff competition and was forced to rent his buildings to François Alluaud in 1813. Alluaud (1788–1866) was the son of the former director of the royal factory at Limoges. In 1799 on the death of his father he inherited the new factory built by him in the rue des Anglais in Limoges. As the owner of kaolin deposits and of forests, he sold clay on extremely profitable terms. Of course he also sold wares made at his factory thanks to his outlets in Paris and Toulouse, as well as through his representative in south-western France. He was assisted by his brother Jean-Baptiste-Clément, and in 1814 they set up a company called Alluaud *frères*. In 1813 François Alluaud rented Monnerie's factory, as his own in the rue des Anglais was too small for his needs. In 1817 he concentrated his production in a new factory in the faubourg des Casseaux.

The two brothers continued to be successful despite economic crises and political upheavals, although Jean-Baptiste-Clément ceased to be associated with François in 1825. From 1830 the latter progressively handed over the running of his business to other members of his family.

Pierre Tharaud (1783–1843) began making porcelain at Limoges slightly later than Baignol and Alluaud. Trained by Baignol and employed by Alluaud and possibly also at Sèvres, he had been in charge of the Darte factories in Paris. After being recruited by the Alluaud brothers he returned to Limoges in 1815 but left them in 1817 to set up his own porcelain factory, which he established in the buildings of the old royal factory. In 1821 he gained the protection of the Comte d'Artois and decided to build new premises. He declared in 1823: 'My present establishment has only been in existence for

64    *Part of a coffee service.* Limoges, Pierre Tharaud factory, 1824 (?). Hard-paste porcelain. H. 25.5 cm. Unmarked. MAD, Limoges (ADL 2514). Although unmarked these pieces all bear a label attributing them to Pierre Tharaud in 1824. However, Tharaud only mentions this kind of sized-down transfer *(décors collés)* in 1839. Transfer-printing was rarely used at Limoges.

a year. It is capable of great expansion. Its location and size would allow me to quadruple my production. At present I employ seventy to eighty workers. My outlets are in the Midi and the north of France, but principally in Paris'.[55] In 1827 he employed one hundred and fifty people, the same number as Alluaud had been employing since 1819.

By the beginning of the nineteenth century, therefore, Limoges was the site of an important porcelain manufacturing industry. The way the industry was constituted was in a certain sense the reflection of the Paris industry, which it frequently served.

Several other small factories were established between 1800 and 1830 such as the Magnac-Bourg and Bourganeuf concern founded in 1819, the Solignac factory established in 1824, the Saint-Brice factory set up in 1825 by François Baignol, the son of Etienne, and the Bonneval factory, active between 1819 and 1825.

*Technical Developments*

Most innovations introduced in the Paris factories were designed to improve production methods or to enable a greater variety of wares to be made. At Limoges the sole aim was to lower the cost of production. During the nineteenth century there was a constant need to maintain and adapt premises (one of the reasons for the progressive decline of the Paris factories was the impossibility of expansion within the city itself). Alluaud and Tharaud quickly perceived this situation. The sale of white porcelain, which avoided the need to employ painters, counteracted the effect of the extremely high cost of labour. The problems of obtaining fuel to fire the kilns were also considerable. Alluaud sited his Casseaux factory near the port

of Naveix where raft wood was landed. From 1816 his brother Jean-Baptiste-Clément had in mind a scheme for using coal as fuel, which however came to nothing because of the high cost of transportation. However, he did acquire the first mill for crushing the heat-resistant materials designed to improve the saggars that protected the wares during firing, while Tharaud enlarged his kilns.

The body and glaze of Limoges porcelain remained largely the same as those used in the eighteenth century but were of a consistently higher quality in the later period. Tharaud was commended for the quality of his wares by the jury at the exhibitions of 1823 and 1829. Decorative motifs, either in relief or painted, were similar to those used in the Paris factories at the same period. Like Nast, Baignol favoured bands of relief decoration, which emphasized the shape of his pieces. On Baignol's wares these motifs usually took the form of rows of little white pearls. Since painted decoration was expensive, it was usually restricted to the simplest level on Alluaud's pieces: a painted or gilt line. Despite this he carried out research in conjunction with Brongniart into high-temperature blue, a project which was to prove unsuccessful. From 1813 he used chrome-green, invented by Vauquelin during the time he was working for Nast at the beginning of the century. In 1827 he succeeded in producing maroon grounds fired at a high temperature. Pierre Tharaud seems to have attempted to use a colour printing process in 1824 from the evidence of labels on the bases of vases and on a coffee service in the Adrien Dubouché museum at Limoges. This experiment had no immediate practical application.

*Style*
Of the three Limoges porcelain-makers active in the first third of the nineteenth century, it is to Baignol that the most typical 'Empire style' production is frequently attributed on the basis of C. Leymarie's work.[56] The shapes are uncluttered, even angular. Cups and teapots have straight sides, ewers and basins are streamlined and vases are trumpet-shaped. Painted decoration is normally found on a white ground, although reddish-brown, yellow, or pink grounds are known. Colours are used discreetly, and certain motifs were rendered in grey *en camaïeu*. The quality of the gilding is superb.

Following the guidelines laid down by Chavagnac and Grollier, biscuit porcelains have been attributed to the Baignol factory. They include figures in an eighteenth-century idiom and inkwells composed of small containers with gilt decoration in reserve with the addition of a winged cupid or a seated female figure in unglazed white porcelain in the Classical style.

Two apothecary vases now in the Adrien Dubouché museum are the only known examples from the Monnerie factory. One was exhibited in 1803 and was described in the exhibition catalogue: 'the vase, which is of remarkable size, is rather meanly formed, and the mask handles are in poor taste'.[57] We can only concur with the writer's opinion regarding the technical imperfection of the piece, but as for its 'poor taste', that merely reflects the ideas of the period.

Jean d'Albis and Céleste Romanet have analysed François Alluaud's account-book for the years 1810 to 1819.[58] The pieces sold are described, giving us a good general idea of Limoges production at this period. In outline, stylistic development evolved in much the same way as at Paris, although the pieces were less ambitious and lacked the element of fantasy evident in the Paris porcelain. The shapes resembled those of the First Empire period, occasionally in a debased

form: *vases fuseaux* of flattened shape with coiled handles are an example of the type made. Just as during the First Empire period, it was the handles that showed the greatest invention.

Changes in style are more marked when it comes to decorative schemes. Coloured grounds were again favoured, including a tortoise-shell effect, chrome-green and even black. These strong grounds were an excellent foil for floral motifs, landscapes and figures. The taste for motifs from nature, unfashionable during the First Empire, reappeared once more. In 1834 Alluaud produced an ambitious service that had a different flower painted on each piece. It was made for the marriage of his daughter Louise to a member of the Malevergne family. Instead of the circular form he normally used for plates, he created for this service a shape with a slightly lobed border decorated with gilt branches in relief and with the monogram AM within a garland of the moss roses that were later to be so widely used at the Limoges factories. The painter Müller introduced floral decoration at the Baignol factory, which was still in production during the Restoration period.

In the Adrien Dubouché museum is a *veilleuse* (small teapot and stand with warmer) marked 'Solignac' and dated 1825. This piece, with its decoration of pointed arches, shows the precocious influence of the Gothic revival, demonstrating just how quickly a small provincial factory could catch on to an evolution in style; 1825 is early for this type of decoration.

65  *Cache-pot (flower-pot case).* Caen (Calvados), Aigmont-Desmares factory, 1810. Hard-paste porcelain. H. 24.5 cm. Mark: 4. MB-A, Caen (78-11-1.1/2).
The Caen factory was established in 1797. In 1799 it ceased production of creamware in order to make porcelain, but in 1814 the shareholders decided to close it down. The pieces made were similar to contemporary Paris porcelain.

66 *Perfume 'fountain'.* Bayeux, *Veuve* Langlois's factory. 1845. Hard-paste porcelain. H. 34.5 cm. Mark: 1. MBG, Bayeux.
From 1830 the Bayeux factory specialized in Kakiemon-type decoration, which was little used in France.

67 *Medici vase.* Valentine (Haute Garonne), Fouque, Arnoux & Cie, 1834. Hard-paste porcelain. H. 19.2 cm. Unmarked. MNC, Sèvres (1638).
The Valentine factory is famous for its pieces decorated in relief as well as for its coloured grounds. This vase was shown at the 1834 Paris Exhibition and entered the Sèvres museum in the same year. Brongniart was interested in ceramics of all types, even when they were lacking in aesthetic appeal. He amassed a unique collection of contemporary pieces, especially for the first half of the 19th century, which enable us to date similar pieces using the acquisition date of the Sèvres museum items as a guide.

## French Provincial Factories

The liberation brought about by the Revolution was not only felt in the capital. Some of the provincial factories that appear to have been significant for various reasons will be briefly surveyed here, though no attempt will be made to give a comprehensive picture.

### Factories in Normandy
During the Revolutionary period two small factories were established in the Basse Normandie region. The first was founded in 1797 at Caen, and was forced to close in 1814, the second was set up at Valognes in 1792, moved to Bayeux in 1812, and only ceased production in 1951.

The Valognes factory began by making earthenware in small quantities but encountered competition from the English product. For both factories profitability seemed to lie only in making hard-paste porcelain, which was not manufactured in England. The Caen factory failed since successive directors lost too much shareholders' money. However, its artistic success is undeniable, and its products are not inferior to Paris porcelain.

The Valognes-Bayeux factory remained in existence much longer, as its proprietor-director Joachim Langlois (1759–1830) was lucky and astute enough to purchase kaolin deposits

at Les Pieux in the Cotentin area. The proximity of seaports also assisted the importation of raw materials and the exportation of finished wares. After an initial phase during the First Empire period, when Langlois imitated the style of Paris porcelain, he then specialized in the production of pieces decorated with oriental motifs, which were relatively original at the time. The greyish body obtained using local kaolin lent itself admirably to the creation of pieces painted predominantly blue, red, and gold with occasional touches of other colours. In Britain this style, loosely deriving from what the French call *vieux Japon,* which is itself based on Japanese Imari porcelain, enjoyed almost uninterrupted popularity during the first half of the nineteenth century. In France it had gone out of fashion under the First Empire and its revival foreshadowed the eclecticism of the Second Empire while echoing the eighteenth-century taste for orientalism. In short it was the glory of the Bayeux factory.

After Joachim Langlois's death his widow carried on the factory as long as possible, but when the type of decoration mentioned above lost its popularity she began to specialize in a range of products of a much more practical nature. These were white fireproof porcelains and laboratory wares. Bayeux porcelains were capable of withstanding much higher temperatures than the Limoges products. Langlois's widow

was awarded a bronze medal at the National Exhibition of 1844. She died in 1847. The factory, purchased by François Gosse in 1849, gained numerous awards for its laboratory porcelains at the international exhibitions held in the second half of the nineteenth century.

*Factories in South-Western France*
Like their counterparts in Normandy, the firms in south-west France took advantage of their distance from Paris to supply a mainly local market. In 1796 Joseph Fouque (1761–1829), the son of a famous Moustiers faience manufacturer, arrived in Toulouse.[59] There he bought a faience factory and went into partnership with his nephew, Antoine Arnoux, between about 1820 and 1822, making mostly creamwares. From 1824 he ran a porcelain-decorating workshop. In order to reduce production costs, which were high because of the expense of transporting wood, Fouque and Arnoux, who had already acquired kaolin and felspar deposits, decided to move their creamware factory to Saint-Gaudens in the 'Valentine valley', and also to make porcelain. Fouque died in 1829. The Valentine factory commenced production in 1832, while the headquarters of the firm Société Fouque-Arnoux et Cie (in which Fouque's sons took their father's place) remained in Toulouse as did some of the painters' workshops.

About 1840 Léon Arnoux (1816–1902), the son of Antoine, took over the running of the Valentine factory. He later went to Stoke-on-Trent, where he spent the greater part of his working life at the Minton factory.

Brongniart devoted a great deal of attention to the products of this remote factory. It interested him mainly for technical reasons. He carried on an extensive correspondence with its owners[60] and refers to the firm in his *Traité des arts céramiques.*[61] He mentions in particular its use of coloured grounds, especially their high-temperature cobalt-blue, black, and yellow, which 'gave to the pieces from this factory a range of colour that was brilliant and solid in tone'.

The style of the Valentine wares is typical of the Restoration period; pieces were decorated with reliefs, especially flowers, and had scrolling handles. The best known of their decorative schemes consists of chinoiseries, but other motifs were also used.

After Léon Arnoux left for England in 1849, the Valentine factory fell into an irreversible decline despite its purchase in 1864 by English interests who tried to rescue it. It closed down in 1890.

*The Niderviller Factory in Eastern France*
Besides the Paris and Limoges factories, a relatively important concern in eastern France also weathered the Revolutionary storms. This was Niderviller, initially an earthenware factory, which also began to make porcelain in 1765. It was acquired by the Comte de Custine in 1770–1771 and was taken over by his associate Claude-François Lanfrey on Custine's death in 1793. The factory was run by Lanfrey until his death in 1827. M. Dryander then purchased it, restricting its activity to the production of creamwares.

Claude-François Lanfrey made both creamware and porcelain. There was no marked stylistic development in the years between the end of the eighteenth century and about 1827, during which time the products exhibited a strongly Neo-Classical flavour. Pieces are generally attributed to the earlier period (1765–1827) even though in some cases they may have been made somewhat later.[62]

# BELGIUM

The porcelain industry in Belgium operated only on a small scale in the nineteenth century.

## Tournai

In the eighteenth century the Tournai factory had taken advantage of its geographical situation to escape the effects of the monopoly exercised by the Sèvres factory in France. By the nineteenth century the monopoly had disappeared, and all the French factories were profiting from this, even though the country was suffering the effects of the revolutionary and Napoleonic disturbances. Belgium only gained independence from the Netherlands in 1830.

In 1781 François-Joseph Peterinck, director of the Tournai factory, was granted privileged status as a porcelain manufacturer until 1808. He died in 1799 and his descendants succeeded him in troubled times. In 1781 he employed four hundred workers, a measure of the importance of this factory at the end of the eighteenth century. Its productions were either executed in the Rococo style or in the fashionable Neo-Classical idiom, serving customers both in the Low Countries and in northern France. Soft-paste porcelain was made at Tournai and later creamware began to be made, displacing porcelain during the nineteenth century.

Between 1808 and 1815 the Ragon and de Bettignies Company, set up by descendants of Peterinck, tried to keep the concern in production during these troubled years. Coffee and tea-services, with blue grounds, formed the basis of their production. The better artists such as the brothers Joseph and Adrien Hayer, Bastenaire Daudemaert and Piat Sauvage painted pieces with polychrome decoration. After the factory went bankrupt in 1815, Henri de Bettignies purchased it from his sister in 1817 and remained in control until 1850. Porcelain with a blue ground continued to be the most common product of this factory, although painted decoration was still sometimes executed. In 1850 the factory was purchased by Boch Brothers of Luxemburg and from that time produced almost nothing but felspathic creamwares.

Around 1800 François Peterinck's son, Charles François, established a second factory at Tournai that remained in operation until 1885 under the direction of the descendants of the founder. Little is known about this factory's production except that in 1835, it was considered by Brongniart to be of low quality.[63]

## The Brussels Factory and Decorating Workshops

At the end of the eighteenth century there was, besides Tournai, another porcelain-manufacturing centre in Belgium, in Brussels and its suburbs. It continued to exist, though on a smaller scale, in the nineteenth century. The Montplaisir factory, for example, was in production between 1787 and 1790, while the Etterbeck factory operated between 1787 and 1803. It is not clear whether Louis Cretté's factory, which is known to have been operative between 1791 and 1803, was actually making porcelain or whether it was merely a decorating workshop where pieces bought from Locré of Paris were painted in the Paris style. Charles van Marcke (active 1798 to 1810) and Joseph-Antoine Heeles (active 1798 to 1822) are 68

68  *Tea-service.* Brussels or Liège, Van Marcke decorating workshop, early 19th century. Hard-paste porcelain, H. (teapot) 17.8 cm. Mark: 98. MNC, Sèvres (18 180).
The landscape decoration painted *en grisaille* is in the same style as scenes on Paris porcelain of the same period. Belgian workshops often seem to have decorated porcelain manufactured at Limoges or Paris.

69  *Vase.* Nyon (Switzerland), Bonnard, Veret & Cie or Dortu & Cie, early 19th century. Hard-paste porcelain. H. 23 cm. Mark: 99. MA, Geneva (AR 5604).
Although the shape is Neo-Classical in style, some 18th-century decorative motifs have been used such as the rose garland and the genre scene. During the entire period it was in production there was virtually no stylistic development at the Nyon factory.

70  *Teapot.* Nyon (Switzerland), Dortu & Cie or Dortu Soulier, Veret & ▷ Cie, early 19th century. H. 14.5 cm. Mark: 99. MA, Geneva (AR 957).
According to E. Pelichet this teapot, decorated with a scene based on an engraving by Freudenberg, cannot have been painted at Geneva by P. Mülhauser (to whom it is traditionally attributed) as it is not signed. Moreover, the engraving has been copied with a freedom and liveliness often found in the work of painters working at Nyon. On the base of the teapot is the inscription: '*La petite fête imprévue*' ('The impromptu party').

71  *Teapot.* Madrid, Royal La Moncloa factory, *c.*1820. Hard-paste ▷ porcelain. H. 15 cm. Unmarked. MAN, Madrid.
The rather stiffly conceived design of this piece is typical of early 19th-century European porcelain.

known to have merely decorated pieces according to the current Paris fashion. Christophe Windish (1781–1842) was born at Niderviller of a family of porcelain manufacturers. After a period at Regensburg, where his marriage is recorded, he joined up with his parents again in Paris. They were making porcelain for the *chambrelans,* or outside decorators. At this time, during the period of Dutch supremacy in Belgium, the outside decorators were complaining that they were obliged to purchase their undecorated porcelain from France. In 1827 Christophe Windish went into partnership with a decorator named Frédéric Faber. They were to establish a factory at Ixelles while Faber was to decorate the pieces in his workshop in the rue de la Madeleine. In 1830, as the result of the revolution, Belgium gained its independance and Windish broke away from Faber. In 1832 he was joined by Jean-Jacques Coché-Mommens as a 'sleeping' partner. Windish was congratulated on the whiteness of his porcelain at the Brussels Industrial Exhibition in 1835. He died in 1843, but the factory continued in production under a Parisian, Michel-Antoine Caillet-Pouchelin. Descendants of Coché-Mommens inherited the business, which is still in existence. Between 1852 and 1869 Théodore Vermeren-Coché tried to manufacture decorated porcelains but after 1870 only domestic wares were made.[64]

In general the Belgian porcelain industry consisted of a few manufacturers and a number of decorators producing pieces in the Paris style.

## SWITZERLAND

### Nyon

In 1973 Edgar Pelichet, former Keeper at the Musée de l'Ariana in Geneva, published a book that traces the history of the Nyon factory.[65] It was established in 1781 by Ferdinand Charles Müller and Jacques Dortu. The latter, who had learned in his youth how to make and decorate porcelain at Berlin, was, like Müller, widely travelled. He had been at St Petersburg, Marseilles, Stralsund and Marieberg and at each of these places he had produced excellent porcelain. In 1787 Müller retired. Dortu had left Nyon in 1786 but returned there to direct his factory until 1813, when he was defeated by financial problems.

During its thirty-two years of existence the Nyon factory introduced few stylistic changes and kept in production every shape and decorative theme it had ever used. Although the pieces have their own character, they strongly reflect the Louis XVI style and represent a kind of continuation of late eighteenth-century Paris porcelain. The fine white body is enhanced by delicate decoration with a subtle palette highlighted by good quality gilding, which was more sumptuously applied during the First Empire period and when the pieces were more heavily painted. After 1809, however, gilding was more sparingly used. Yet Edgar Pelichet seems to have found the *mot juste* when he writes of 'the unity of spirit' common to all the pieces made at Nyon.

## ITALY

A number of Italian factories that had been established in the eighteenth century had their swan song in the first third of the nineteenth century. Unable to overcome the economic difficulties brought about by the Napoleonic invasions, they

72  *Plate.* Naples, Royal Naples factory: Ferdinand IV period, *c.* 1800–1805. Soft-paste porcelain. D. 23.5 cm. Mark: 103. MNC, Sèvres (2553²). Classical scenes, as well as views of Naples and its environs, often served the Neapolitan porcelain painters as sources of inspiration.

were generally speaking incapable of adapting to the rapid evolution of styles that marked this period and had to cease production.

### Naples

In southern Italy the Royal Naples Factory[66] fell victim to the factors described above. It had been founded by Ferdinand IV in 1771 to fill the gap left by the Capodimonte factory when that was transferred to Buen Retiro in Spain in 1759 and originally had premises in the Villa di Portici before removing to the Royal Palace in Naples itself in 1773. Domenico Venuti ran the factory between 1781 and 1807. In 1799 it was attacked by the Bonapartist forces, and from 1807, when the kingdom was handed over to Joseph Bonaparte, the factory was taken over by the French. It was then purchased by Giovanni Poulard Prad, who sold half of it in 1818 to Claude Guillard and Giovanni Tourné, and the other half to Francesco-Paolo Del Re in 1819. The factory closed in 1834.

The Royal Naples Factory established its own style at the end of the eighteenth century and hardly evolved at all stylistically during the early nineteenth century. The pieces produced there can be briefly described as Neo-Classical. The wares were made of a white body with a slightly yellowish tinge, and their shapes are strong and unfussy, enriched with relief motifs on the base, lip, and handle. Medallions or shield-shaped reserves generally enclose any figurative scenes, which are usually mythological in character. They resemble the motifs that were to be used at Sèvres for the *service olympique.* Many pieces are painted with views of Naples and its environs. Landscapes and urban scenes, the latter resembling those usually shown in printed decoration on early nineteenth-century creamwares, are customarily found

on Naples porcelain. Popular regional figures are also represented, anticipating the Romantic taste. The Royal Naples Factory was able to carry on using the same decorative schemes at the beginning of the nineteenth century only because during the preceding period these schemes had been somewhat advanced in taste. Some nineteenth-century pieces have richly painted ground colours and elaborate gilding in accordance with contemporary European taste.

The same holds true for figures made at the factory. The Neapolitan sculptors, led by Filippo Tagliolini easily adopted the Classical style, inspired by the antique works of art preserved in southern Italy. However, some of the productions are entirely Baroque in spirit, such as the *Fall of the Giants,* an enormous biscuit table centrepiece by Tagliolini. It was completed in 1787 and is now in the Capodimonte museum in Naples. The figures made at the factory also reflect the everyday life of all social classes. Charming little statuettes painted in coloured enamels were conceived and executed by various modellers: Giovanni Battista Polidora was responsible for figures of burghers shown chatting on benches, Simoni and Angelo Viva modelled figures representing the trades of Venice, and Ariello Ingaldi produced *Commedia dell'Arte* figures. Francesco Celebrano was capable of modelling biscuit figures in the grand Classical style as well as the more popular type of enamelled figure.

The ensuing period between 1807 to 1834 was far less brilliant. Lirri can be quoted on this subject: 'the body is not a porcelain body, the forms are not forms, and the porcelain that was produced was not porcelain'.[67] In short, although the traditions survived when Camillo Celebrano took over from his father, the porcelain body used was of such poor quality that it is no longer possible to classify the productions as great art.

The influence of the Naples factory was perhaps more strongly felt outside the factory itself. Painters trained at the Royal Naples Factory set up independently, often decorating porcelain made in France. Raffaele Giovine was one of these. He was active between 1826 and 1860 and produced over-decorated pieces that contrast strongly with the purity of the early nineteenth-century wares.

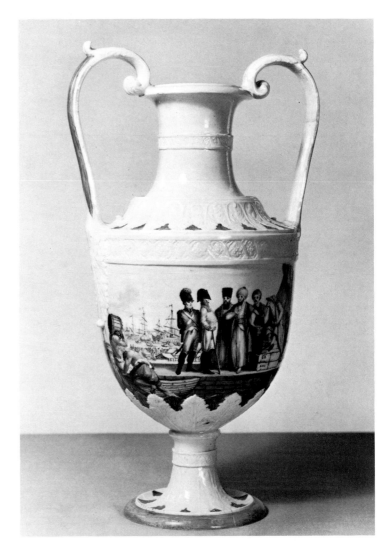

73   *Vase.* Le Nove (Veneto), Antonibon factory: G. Baroni period, *c.* 1810. Hard-paste porcelain. H. 34 cm. Mark: 104. V & A, London (C.18-1950). The Neo-Classical shape of this piece is decorated with a scene showing Levantine Merchants. In the 18th century this subject was frequently used; here it has been brought up-to-date by the painter, perhaps Giovanni Marcon, who worked at Le Nove and is known to have been responsible for similar scenes: the European figures are in contemporary costume.

## Rome

Giovanni Volpato's factory at Rome was given over to the reproduction in biscuit of statues on the Capitol and at the Vatican. Set up in 1785, this factory survived until 1818 despite Volpato's death in 1803. The quality of the porcelain body makes the pieces from this factory worthy of attention.

## Treviso

Another Italian factory which did not long survive the early part of the nineteenth century, was the Fontebasso factory at Treviso in the Veneto. It was in operation between 1759 and about 1840. The greater part of the Fontebasso pieces are made of a hybrid soft-paste porcelain, are of mediocre quality and lack inspiration. One painter worthy of the name, however, did sign several pieces made between 1830 and 1834. He was Gaetano Negrisolo, painter of scenes from the *Idylles* written by the Swiss poet Salomon Gessner. He was also responsible for flower decoration, which was typically Restoration in style, and for

amusing figures of Austrian soldiers based on those at the Treviso garrison.[68] Towards 1840 the Fontebasso factory concentrated on producing earthenware.

## Le Nove

In 1728 the Antoniboni established an earthenware factory at Le Nove, also in the Veneto, where they manufactured porcelain from 1752. They let their factory first to Giovanni Maria Bacin who started making creamware, and then in 1781 to Francesco Parolin who manufactured porcelain and employed a sculptor, Domenico Bosello, and a good painter, Giovanni Marcon. Between 1802 and 1825 the factory was let to Giovanni Baroni, who kept on Bosello and recruited foreign painters. The end of the eighteenth century and the beginning of the nineteenth century saw the factory troubled by political and military events, but at the same time it experienced a period of creativity during which its style developed from the Rococo to the Neo-Classical.

Curiously, between 1800 and 1810 in particular, *vases hollandais* were made in the style originating at Sèvres in the eighteenth century. These Le Nove pieces were painted with rather plain decoration negating their Rococo shape. Battle, port, and genre scenes exhibited originality in the placing of figures in space. These scenes were based on engravings issued by the printers Remondini of Bassano, and the pieces are sometimes signed by Giovanni Marcon. The production of figures evolved in a similar fashion. Around 1810 Domenico Bosello modelled figures and groups—there is a group symbolizing Prudence, Strength, and Humility in the Bassano museum and a female figure representing Venice in the Museum für Kunst und Gewerbe, Hamburg. These productions show a tendency towards Neo-Classicism, which is, however, loosely interpreted.

In the nineteenth century the production of creamware took on a much greater importance, and it is in this material that the creative works of this factory were conceived. However, it seems that the manufacture of porcelain continued until about 1835.

## Venice

Set up in 1765 by Geminiano Cozzi in Venice, near Le Nove, the factory closed down in 1812. It too generally used a hybrid porcelain of greyish tone for its wares, which were painted with chinoiseries, flowers and garlands and so on. As at Le Nove, it often made pieces strongly influenced by Sèvres, but these copies were, unfortunately, poorly realized. The factory also adopted the Neo-Classical style but less successfully than at Le Nove, despite some good attempts.

## Vinovo

The Vinovo factory, established in 1776 by Giovanni-Vittorio Brodel and Pierre-Antoine Hannong, passed into the hands of Dr Vittorio Amadeo Gioanetti in 1780 and was then taken over in 1815 by Giovanni Lamello. Any discussion of nineteenth-century Vinovo porcelain must rely on the evidence of the samples sent to Brongniart, director of the Sèvres factory, in 1809, since the wares are unmarked. He had requested that all the *préfets* of France and its occupied territories send him samples of local ceramic production. The pieces are preserved in the Sèvres museum.[69] They comprise on the one hand out-and-out fakes, copying Sèvres and Meissen and bearing false marks, and on the other tablewares and decorative pieces with modest decoration based on late eighteenth-century Paris porcelain, painted with, for example, scattered cornflower sprays.

Giovanni Lamello bought the concern in 1815, having worked there as a sculptor since 1790. The decoration of his biscuit porcelains was sometimes Neo-Classical in its iconography, although his styles of decoration remained influenced by those produced in the eighteenth century.

74 a, b *Soup tureen from an a vedute ('views') service.* Doccia (Tuscany), Ginori factory: Carlo-Leopoldo Ginori period, *c.* 1810–1820. Hard-paste porcelain. H. 32 cm. Unmarked. MPD, Sesto Fiorentino.
Like the Royal Naples factory, Doccia produced porcelain painted with architectural subjects. These themes were inspired by 16th-century Venetian majolica.

## Doccia

The Doccia factory in Tuscany continued to make porcelain of the highest quality under the direction of its original proprietors, the Ginori family, who had founded it in 1735. When Lorenzo Ginori died in 1791 his son Carlo Leopoldo (1788–1837) was too young to take over from his father but the succession was assured by his guardian and his mother. In 1792 the manufacture of creamware began in order to subsidize the production of porcelain. During the Napoleonic occupation a research laboratory was set up at Doccia while Marchese Carlo Leopoldo was preparing to run the factory. G. Morazzoni has described the vast amount of work accomplished by the Marchese between 1817 and 1822.[70] He obtained new clays from France and the Veneto, introduced greater mechanization, invented new types of kilns, supported two pupils at the *Accademia di Belle Arti* in Florence, bought the secret of a process for applying gilding and of another for 'changing colours', and established the Doccia museum. Like Brongniart at Sèvres, he was familiar with every aspect of the art and technique of porcelain. The first pieces of Doccia egg-shell porcelain with chinoiserie motifs, sometimes erroneously attributed to Le Nove, seem to date from his last years. The best collection of pieces from this factory is, naturally, at the Doccia porcelain museum, Sesto Fiorentino.[71]

The technical improvements introduced were most successful. The eighteenth-century pieces were made of a greyish body which, by the nineteenth century, had been replaced by a beautifully white composition. This led to the production of biscuit porcelains and improved enamelled pieces. Probably because he was influenced by the Royal Naples Factory, which he visited, Marchese Carlo Leopoldo made a large number of pieces decorated with urban scenes enclosed within shield-shaped reserves on a white ground. At times the inspiration of Classical art is evident in pieces with black grounds or with decoration *en camaïeu* in ochre. Some eighteenth-century decorative themes were retained such as animal subjects based on Buffon, used in friezes or enclosed within shield-shaped reserves. Chinoiseries, garlands and palms were among other types of decoration carried over from the eighteenth century. Doccia even employed grounds imitating wood-grain and enclosing pseudo-printed scenes *en camaïeu* in the manner of Niderviller, Sèvres, and Vienna.

For certain pieces, however, the Doccia factory adopted wholeheartedly the aesthetic of French porcelain of the First Empire period, as well as its special type of miniature painting. G. Fanciullacci learned from Constantin, a Sèvres painter, how to copy Renaissance paintings and frescoes, so numerous in Florence and an obvious source of decoration.

## SPAIN

The Spanish ceramic industry was, on the whole, extremely modest in scale in the nineteenth century. Wars and economic crises were responsible for this, as well as the difficulty in finding clays suitable for the manufacture of porcelain within Spain itself. The porcelain factories could only try and survive with the aid of financial contributions deriving from the manufacture of faience and cream-coloured earthenware.

## Madrid

*Buen Retiro*

The early years of this industry were marked by brilliance. In 1759 the Capodimonte factory, formerly in Naples, was installed in the outbuildings of the Buen Retiro Palace at Madrid. Between 1760–1765 it produced its masterpiece, the porcelain room in the palace of Aranjuez. But economic problems grew as the factory tried to adapt its production to the Neo-Classical taste. The beautiful Buen Retiro paste was both costly and outdated. One technical director was succeeded by another in the search for a suitable formula. Sebastian Schepers (1798–1802) was replaced by Felipe Gricci (1802–1803), followed by Bartolome Sureda (1803–1808) who was sent to France to study the Paris porcelain industry and is known to have been a competent technician. Like Brongniart at Sèvres, he tried to control the deficit incurred by the company. His chief achievement was to perfect a new body in

75  *Allegorical figure of History.* Madrid, Royal La Moncloa factory, *c.* 1825. Hard-paste porcelain. H. 19 cm. Unmarked. MNC, Sèvres (1078²).
In 1828 Sureda sent examples of La Moncloa porcelain to the Sèvres museum. This Neo-Classical piece was one of them.

which magnesite replaced kaolin so that the body was entirely composed of Spanish raw materials. The paste was somewhat lacking in homogeneity but its fineness ensured a new quality of production. He brought Frenchmen with him to Spain: Vivien, formerly employed at Sèvres, was in charge of the preparation of clays and of the making and firing of the wares; Jacques Victor Perche, who had worked in Paris, controlled the making of colours and decoration of the wares, while his wife was concerned with gilding.

Superb biscuit porcelains were made using the new body. Buen Retiro produced an important piece, the Parnassus centrepiece, during the years 1802 to 1804. It was composed of sixty figures designed by the painter Isidoro Velazquez and modelled by the sculptor Esteban de Agreda. A biscuit group known as *Time Discovering Truth* dating from 1804–1808 was also modelled by Esteban de Agreda, who was in charge of sculpture at the factory from 1797. The cold Neo-Classicism of the period is expressed in that Buen Retiro biscuit porcelain group. No large decorative piece or table decoration seems to have been made at this time at Buen Retiro, although tea- and coffee services conceived in the imperial style are known. Some are in the 'Etruscan' style with black figures in shield-shaped reserves coloured mauve with gilt ornamentation. Others are painted with garlands, drapery, and various figures. The improvement in the factory's situation did not last beyond 24 June 1808, when it was occupied by French soldiers and Sureda abandoned his post as director. In 1808 the factory buildings were destroyed by the English.

*La Moncloa Factory*
Queen Maria Isabel of Braganza wished to resuscitate the Royal factory, and on 8 July 1817 King Ferdinand VII decreed that it should be re-established in the buildings of la Granjilla de los Jerónimos, which were part of the royal palace of La Moncloa at Madrid.

The first director, Antonio Forni had formerly been employed at Buen Retiro. Production could only be carried out on a modest scale since there were only about twenty workers. However, the organization of the factory was completed in 1820 with the opening of a showroom in Madrid.

Although small, the factory proved too expensive to operate. In 1821 Sureda was recalled and the factory was reorganized with the loss of eight workers. It appears that the eight were in fact those responsible for making porcelain and that Sureda had decided to switch to the manufacture of earthenware, which was far more profitable. The situation did not improve, however, for a fire broke out in 1825 and in 1829 Sureda retired.

After 1844 there was a further attempt to manufacture porcelain. Between 1846 to 1848 a Frenchman, Jean Frédéric Langlois, who came from Isigny in Normandy, was called in to help but the factory was permanently closed in 1850.

Production as episodic as this cannot manifest any characteristic style, and it must be remembered that the La Moncloa wares are not often marked. The pieces reflect French taste and were strongly influenced by Neo-Classicism.

### Alcora (Valencia)

In 1751 the Count of Aranda initiated research into the manufacture of porcelain at his earthenware factory, and from 1787 porcelain was made under the guidance of a Frenchman,

Pierre Cloostermans. He and the Count of Aranda both died in 1798. The Duke of Hijar inherited the factory, but was plagued by internal dissensions within the factory in addition to the problems arising from the wars and economic crises. The various factory managers who succeeded each other were unable to impose any sense of unity on the enterprise, and each man in charge of a particular workshop pursued his own course. Pastor and Garcès were in turn entrusted with the task of improving the production of porcelain, but it still lagged behind the production of creamware.

### Santiago de Sargadela (Lugo)

In 1791 Don Antonio Ibañez, an Asturian, set up a creamware factory where porcelain was manufactured from 1812–1813. High quality pieces were produced, modestly decorated with lines or initials in gold or blue. A single more ambitiously conceived object is known. This is a bas-relief dating from 1814, the subject of which is the death of Daotz and Velarde on 2 May 1808.

## PORTUGAL

In the eighteenth century in Portugal, as elsewhere in Europe, they tried to find the kaolin necessary for the manufacture of porcelain on their native soil. In 1773 it seemed that they had indeed discovered it; however, no porcelain industry worthy of the name emerged at this time.

76   *Plate.* Vista Alegre (Aveiro, Portugal), Ferreira Pinto & Filhos, 1828. Hard-paste porcelain. D. 24 cm. Mark: 105. Museu da Fabrica, Vista Alegre. In addition to the factory mark, the piece bears the inscription: 'Fabrica da Vista Alegre, 1828'. It must therefore be one of the earliest pieces of Portuguese porcelain. The painted decoration is attributed to Manuel de Morais da Silva Ramos.

## Vista Alegre

In 1824 a porcelain industry seemed to be in the making. José Ferreira Pinto Basto set up a factory at Vista Alegre, near Aveiro. Its first two years of existence were taken up with perfecting the product rather than actually manufacturing it. The basis for future growth was established, however, with the foundation of the company known as Ferreira Pinto & Filhos. A mark was adopted, which consisted of the letters V and A beneath a crown encircled by palm branches. Creamware of the English type was manufactured under the name *pó de pedro* thanks to the recruitment of two young painters, João Maria Fabre (1805–1829) and Manuel de Morais da Silva Ramos (1806–1872); kaolin from the Porto and Aveiro regions was used in the creamware body.

Two cups and saucers[72] are known with inscriptions showing that they were fired in the very first kiln of ware produced at this factory. They are marked *Fabre Lusitano pinxit* and so must have been decorated before 1829, the year of Fabre's death. They can be dated to 1827 on the basis of comparison with a plate in the Vista Alegre factory museum. This is attributed to Manuel de Morais da Silva Ramos[73] and bears the factory mark and the date 1828. The cups and saucers by Fabre are obviously slightly earlier in date than this plate.

There is in fact a marked development in decorative style between these two dates. Fabre was still working in a style which owed a great deal to the late eighteenth century, while Régine de Plinval-Salgues has rightly compared the plate attributed to Manuel de Morais to a Schoelcher piece in the Palacio Nacional de Mafra in Portugal,[74] which is strongly influenced by the Neo-Classical movement.

In the Palacio das Necessidades in Lisbon is a group of six cups of slightly flared shape. Their profile is somewhat reminiscent of the flared *(jasmin)* cup so fashionable at that time at the Sèvres factory, but their elegant polychrome decoration of peasant figures painted on a white ground has little in common with the unnaturally rich decoration found on contemporary products from the latter factory.[75]

## AUSTRIA

In the early part of the nineteenth century it was the Vienna and Berlin factories that, together with Sèvres, took over the stylistic leadership as far as porcelain was concerned. Their products belong unequivocally to Neo-Classicism, the formal repertoire of which was already complete long before 1800 but continued in use, with variations, well into the second and even third decades of the century. The relatively unassuming shapes employed were enhanced by some extraordinarily varied, imaginative, and sometimes sumptuous painted decoration.

### Vienna

*Imperial Porcelain Manufactory*
As the century opened the Imperial Porcelain Manufactory in Vienna (est. 1744) was still under the successful management of Konrad Sörgel von Sorgenthal, who died in 1805.[76] The factory had been on the verge of bankruptcy when Emperor Joseph II came to the throne in 1765, and in 1784 he made an unsuccessful attempt to sell it at auction. Konrad Sörgel, the manager of the imperial wool mill, who had earlier been

77   *Covered cup with portrait miniature of the Austrian general Laudon and allegories of War and History.* Vienna, Georg Lamprecht, after 1889. Cobalt ground with ornaments in white and three-colour gold; muffle-colour painting. H. 17.7 cm. Marks: 107, year stamp, painter's signature. ÖMaK, Vienna (Ke 6902).
Viennese miniature painting was at its best under Konrad Sörgel von Sorgenthal, managing director from 1784 to 1805.

commissioned to analyse the causes of the porcelain factory's lack of success, was now put in charge of the latter. By getting rid of outmoded stocks and introducing improved methods of organization, business procedure, and sales promotion, he brought about a quite spectacular improvement in production within a very short time. His elevation to the peerage and subsequently to the baronage (as Freiherr von Sorgenthal) were just rewards for his achievements. In the choice and management of his staff Konrad Sörgel von Sorgenthal showed a degree of acumen that was to pay off handsomely. In his first year as manager he replaced master modeller Johann Joseph Niedermayer (1710–1784), who had worked at the factory for almost forty years, with the promising young sculptor Anton Grassi (1755–1807), who had been there since 1778. Grassi, a former pupil of the great Austrian sculptor Franz Xaver Messerschmidt, had his master to thank for a powerfully naturalistic style that was to prevent his Neo-Classical formal approach from degenerating into flaccidity. In 1892 the factory paid for Grassi to spend nine months in Rome, where as well as studying the works of Classical Antiquity he collected and drew patterns for the factory. His own artistic output during this period consisted of a series of Neo-Classical figures of Niobe. The staff structure of the factory was such that as master modeller Grassi was responsible for sculpture and for the shapes of the vessels; furthermore he was for a while sole artistic director, which meant that he was also in charge of the painting

78 *Déjeuner with polychrome landscape paintings on a pale green ground.* Vienna, *c.* 1802. Overglaze colours, relief gilt ornamentation. Tray 25.5 × 32.3 cm. Marks: 107, year stamp. ÖMaK, Vienna (Ke 4167).
An excellent example of the Neo-Classical shapes in fashion around 1800; the sugar bowl is a direct copy of a Classical model.

sections. His particular achievement was systematically to switch production away from a still partly Rococo allegiance and direct it along Neo-Classical lines. Anton Grassi was one of the most talented and influential figures in porcelain manufacturing during this period.

Where Grassi renewed the factory's formal repertoire, Joseph Leithner (retired 1829) began in 1785 to lay down fresh principles as far as decoration was concerned. In that year Sorgenthal released him from his contract with the flower-painting section in order to allow him to concentrate on his more important gifts in the field of colour technology. Coloured grounds, originally developed at Meissen and Sèvres, became under Leithner one of the glories of the Vienna factory in the early nineteenth century. 'Leithner blue', a brilliant cobalt-blue that could be employed as a ground and was a match for the Sèvres factory's *bleu roi,* was ready for use by 1792; it was followed soon afterwards by 'Leithner gold', which was destined to achieve equally rapid fame. In addition to these two developments particularly associated with his name, Leithner gave a new splendour to the whole gamut of muffle colours. Eventually this comprised thirty-six variable and intermixable muffle colours that were arranged on dishes (e.g. laid out as a colour circle) and submitted to other factories as proof of Vienna's expertise and efficiency. In addition to these colours there were gold, silver, and platinum, all of which could be further processed by means of etching or burnishing. Leithner's colours formed the basis for what was to constitute Vienna's glory: its painting.

Traditionally the porcelain factory comprised five painting sections; of these the 'blue painters' were responsible for the 'everyday' ware with blue rims or simple, commonplace patterns painted beneath the glaze. More interesting from our point of view were the four sections responsible for artistic decoration: the 'ornamentists', the 'pattern painters' (who included the separately managed 'gilt pattern painters'), the 'flower painters', and the 'historical and landscape painters'.

The widely renowned Johann Weixelbaum (1752–1840) was senior painter of the figure section from 1784, but a possibly even more gifted colleague was Georg Lamprecht, who had already worked at the factory from 1772–1779 but had afterwards, thanks to a travel grant from Prince Kaunitz, spent several years working in factories abroad, in particular at Sèvres. In 1788 he returned to the Vienna factory, where he produced some exquisite figure miniatures. From 1806 onwards senior painter Friedrich Reinhold was in charge of the 'pattern painters'. Under Sorgenthal's management the Vienna factory also became famous for its 'gilt pattern painting'. After repeated experiments during the eighteenth century, none of which had proved satisfactory, the dream of gilt relief decoration finally became a reality when it was found that 'Leithner gold' would adhere, without cracking or lifting, to the sometimes very delicate relief ornamentation that was so greatly sought after at the turn of the century. This art was brought to an unprecedented pitch of quality by Anton Kothgasser (1769–1851), a pupil of the Viennese miniature painter Heinrich Friedrich Füger. Kothgasser was employed at the factory as a gilt pattern painter from 1784 until about the time of the Congress of Vienna (1814–1815). He was subsequently to make a greater name for himself as a glass painter.[77] Other highly distinguished gilt pattern painters mentioned by W. Neuwirth[78] are Josef Geyer, active from 1806 until his death in 1836, and Josef Kürner (1789–1838); drawings by both still survive. These are just a few of the many names preserved on documents, and in some cases on pieces of porcelain, representing the gifted craftsmen who, under Konrad Sörgel von Sorgenthal's management, made the Vienna factory so famous. His death in 1805, followed by that of Anton Grassi in 1807, did not affect the factory's output stylistically. Sorgenthal's successor, Mathias Niedermayer, took over a commercially viable organization with an experienced staff and continued to run it until 1827 without any abrupt change of style.

## Shapes

From 1784 onwards Grassi systematically expanded a policy of adopting the occasional model from Sèvres and Meissen that

79 *Panoramateller.* Vienna, after 1804. Overglaze painting, relief gilt ornamentation (possibly by Anton Kothgasser). D. 25.5 cm. Marks: 107, year stamp. HSK, Vienna.
Landscape painting, always very popular, found particularly delightful expression in this set of plates.

80 *Ornamental plate with passion flower.* Vienna, Joseph Wundsam, 1821. Overglaze painting, gilt rims. D. 24.4 cm. Marks: 109, year stamp, painter's number, other impressed marks, and the description 'Passiflora'. HSK, Vienna.
These botanical plate sets, combining accuracy of depiction with great aesthetic charm, were painted for the Viennese court.

had been tentatively initiated a few years before his appointment. For tableware as well as for individual vases he let himself be guided entirely by the repertoire of the Classical potter, which for connoisseurs of Neo-Classicism constituted a familiar range of patterns thanks to the excavations going on at the time and the publications devoted to them.[79] Particular vase shapes could be adapted for contemporary use by a simple change of scale. His ice urns, sugar, confectionery, and dessert bowls, and vases all have direct Classical antecedents. Calathus, cyathus, and bell crater were turned into modern cups. Many other items were added, of which the simple shapes were derived from the Classical patterns that were so much admired. The most severely simple structures seemed adequate and did in fact last longest. Coffee and milk jugs were waisted with a slight rise above a tapering or cylindrical body, and the shallow dome of the lid was often crowned with a pine-cone knop following Classical models. No projections mar the vessel's clean lines; spouts and handles were kept as plain as possible, with the occasional use of little claw-and-ball feet to raise the vessel from the stand. Particularly with his cylindrical and egg-shaped ('campana') cups Grassi arrived at the same solutions as, for example, Sèvres and Berlin. Who invented a particular shape first cannot be established with any certainty. The earliest surviving cylindrical cup in the Neo-Classical style from Vienna is dated 1790; for Berlin, the date 1783 may possibly be admissible.[80] Cylindrical cups and jugs and saucers with straight rims and smooth edges were among the most popular shapes for tableware in the Neo-Classical period, offering as they did an ideally smooth and uninterrupted surface for any kind of decoration. Production in no way stagnated following the deaths of Sorgenthal and Grassi (in 1805 and 1807 respectively). On the contrary, the cup designs that found their

way into the Österreichisches Museum für angewandte Kunst when the factory was shut down in 1864–1866, and that were in some instances not rediscovered there until 1981, show an extraordinarily wide range of shapes.[81] Since cups sold particularly well as individual pieces and, especially when richly decorated, were much sought after by collectors and as gifts, they probably incorporated the greatest variety of shapes employed. In jugs and the different items of the table service, fewer variations of shape occur. In the first decade of the nineteenth century came the conical calathoi with slightly concave sides (examples exist from 1808 onwards) as well as the egg-shaped cyathi, also referred to as the 'campana' shape (from 1809), both kinds with and without an offset base. Cylindrical cups were varied at lip and base; the period 1807–1812 saw stepped cylindrical examples. As early as 1812 shallow, circular dishes with a foot offered a quite different range of possibilities, as did wide craters with a number of curved variants in tub, barrel, and bell shapes, the popularity of which probably increased towards 1820. Handles represented another area of possible formal modification. In addition to angular or simple looped handles every kind of distortion was used, whether upwards over the rim or away from the profile of the cup; as well as strap-shaped handles we find others that are twisted, doubled, intertwined, or even shaped like flower stems; both points of attachment feature not only Classical palmettes and rosettes but also bird, lion, snake, and fish heads as ornament.

*Decoration*
The wealth of decoration used defies description, nor can it even be classified in terms of distinct designs[82] and was executed by a large staff of pattern painters. The factory's policy

81 *Picture plate: Boreas entführt Oreithia ('The Rape of Oreithyia by Boreas').* Vienna, Johann Fiala, after 1816. Overglaze painting, relief gilt ornamentation on various coloured grounds. D. 24.4 cm. Marks: 108, impressed numerals, year stamp for 1816, painter's number. Kunstgewerbemuseum, Cologne (E 1195).
The picture is copied from a painting by Peter Paul Rubens in the Gemälde-Akademie, Vienna.

82 *Picture plate: Die verlassene Ariadne ('Ariadne* ▷ *Abandoned').* Vienna, after 1821. Overglaze painting, gilt ornamentation on a brown-red ground. D. 24.6 cm. Marks: 109, impressed numerals, year stamp. Hetjens-Museum, Düsseldorf (1940/150).
The paintings of Angelica Kauffmann became very popular as motifs for porcelain painting after 1800.

of employing only people who had completed a comprehensive course of training in a relevant discipline at the Academy of Arts and its insistence that employees go on attending evening classes at the Academy on a permanent basis account for the continuously high quality of its painted decoration. A capacity for independent invention was assumed and even demanded; each pattern painter had to decorate one cup to his own design every three months, and each figure painter had to produce one subject of his own half-yearly. Competitions and awards ensured that individual initiative was exercised over and above this minimum requirement. To ensure general production, the Vienna factory maintained, as all factories did, a continually expanding collection of models. The decoration of the turn-of-the-century period and the first third of the new century was only in part derived from Classical Antiquity. It certainly incorporated meanders, undulations, bead mouldings, acanthus and laurel leaves, griffins, pine-cones, and the like, but its vocabulary went a long way beyond that, using all types of geometrically constructed ornamentation incorporating lines and patterns, whether individually or symmetrically arranged, as well as naturalistic and stylized flower designs and later even the occasional historicist device. Other designs were developed that owed nothing to any known historical or naturalistic ornamental tradition, for example plain stripes or diamond lattice-work. A high degree of elegance was achieved in a series of French-inspired cups combining gilt relief ornamentation with a blue ground. Often cups and plates were divided into zones that were rhythmically articulated with 79, 81, 82 narrow friezes and bands and contained different decoration on differently coloured grounds. Variations could be achieved in

density of pattern, degree of colourfulness, and combination with gold. As a result of competition from ware imported from Paris, the management began around 1805 to instruct its painters to concentrate more on 'light decoration', which was cheaper and quicker to produce than the sumptuous and expensive gilt relief decoration, though of course it was for this that the Vienna factory was particularly famous.

Painted decoration that went beyond simple pattern painting for services and cups was executed by the figure, historical, and landscape painters, many of whom we know by name. Georg Lamprecht has already been mentioned; Moritz Daffinger, who left the factory in 1812, continued to make a 78 name for himself as a freelance miniaturist. On porcelain he painted portraits in the manner of Heinrich Füger and also scenes from Greek mythology, which retained their popularity for a long time. This style of painting was likewise practised by Leopold Lieb (active until 1836), by Claudius Herr, and by many others whose work has been tirelessly investigated in recent years by Waltraud Neuwirth, whose publications give what information is available on these artists.[83]

Portraits appear frequently, as do landscapes copied from engravings. A complete set of exceptionally charming examples is preserved in the *Panoramatellern* ('Panorama 79 Plates') in the former Hoftafel- und Silberkammer of the Viennese court. On the flanges of these smooth white plates are little glimpses of Swiss and Italian mountain landscapes or of the lovely valleys of the Forest of Vienna, painted by many different hands and assembled in a loose series; some have additional gilt patterns painted by, among others, Anton Kothgasser. In the early years of the century Egyptian-style

83 *Pieces from the Vergoldetes Service.* Vienna, 1813–1818. Polished and matt gilding. H. (tureen) 47 cm. Marks: 108, year stamp, impressed marks. HSK, Vienna.
Among the last major commissions from the court were several services in Empire shapes, ordered at the time of the Congress of Vienna (1815).

84 *Centrepiece from the Laxenburg Service.* Vienna, 1821–1824. Overglaze painting, gilding. H. 82 cm. Mark: inaccessible. HSK, Vienna.
Part of the state service made for Franzensburg, the Romantic Neo-Gothic palace Emperor Franz I had built near Vienna in 1798–1801.

decoration appears occasionally—as on Sèvres ware and probably following its example—as well as Classical decoration; miniature mosaic grounds and tiny mosaic pictures such as ruins and temples were imitated from 1802 onwards.[84] Around 1815 Lorenz Heer began imitating Classical cameos, his so-called 'onyx cameos', in monochrome painting, perhaps also inspired by Sèvres or Berlin.

Outdoing all other factories in both quality and quantity, these outstanding Viennese painters copied actual paintings on to porcelain plates, vases, and plaques, surrounding them with sumptuous gilt relief frames.[85] Among the copyists' favourite subjects were the elegant scenes of Angelica Kauffmann.[86] A further important field of Viennese porcelain painting emerges from the statistics: for the eleven figure painters recorded for the year 1809 there were forty-four flower painters. In other words, flowers, in every kind of arrangement and execution, played the principal decorative role—whether as a decorative element on edges and flanges, or as the main motif on service items or individual plates, cups, or vases, or as self-contained flower pictures.[87] Seventeenth-century Dutch flower paintings were copied or adapted on display vases, dishes, and framed plaques, while botanical works provided the basis for plate sets featuring plants that were depicted and captioned with scientific accuracy, one individual specimen occupying the bottom of each plate. Other factories had pioneered this kind of decoration (for example the *Flora Danica* Service produced in Copenhagen), but the Viennese plates are particularly beautiful with their flowers set off by a black background.[88]

The Congress of Vienna in 1814–1815, when foreign heads of state and diplomats filled the city for months on end, brought a unique succession of commissions for luxury articles. The Viennese court, too, ordered a number of extensive new services about this time. Parts of some large sets in Empire shapes are preserved in the former Hoftafel- und Silberkammer, featuring the same overall designs executed in three different patterns. The service with gilt lines and gilt vine tendrils dates from 1811; there is another simple gilt-rimmed service from 1815, and the magnificent all-gilt service with etched and polished decoration dates from the period 1813–1818. Novel in terms of shape and design was the service with matching centrepieces and cutlery ordered for Emperor Franz I to use in the Neo-Gothic palace of Franzensburg in Laxenburg Park and manufactured in 1821–1824. Echoing the architectural style of the palace, the centrepieces are in the form of fanciful edifices laden with Gothic tracery and bearing idealized portraits of the emperor's medieval ancestors. The sixty plates of the dining and dessert service are decorated with named views of Austrian castle ruins painted by Franz Sartory, who from 1799 to 1841 was one of the factory's best-known painters.

*Services*
In Vienna, however, unlike Sèvres, this kind of state tableware never accounted for more than a fraction of the factory's output. Figures issued in 1819 (and published many times)[89] give, for the immediate past, an annual output of *circa* 800 services for between twelve and sixty persons; of these, however, only fifty services were richly painted and gilded, while about 200 were lightly decorated. This source makes no mention of vases and the undoubtedly plentiful cups, coffee sets, and painted breakfast services, though it does speak of between fifty and sixty thousand simple blue-rimmed plates, which were important in terms of providing a stable economic foundation.

The Congress of Vienna represented the factory's heyday as far as large artistic commissions were concerned. It was followed by a period of stagnation, with slowly but steadily diminishing orders and sales. Production was curtailed, the staff had to accept wage cuts, and eventually there were redundancies. Competition from the Bohemian factories was beginning to make itself felt.

## BOHEMIA

In 1793 an event took place that was eventually to undermine the hitherto unchallenged position of the Vienna factory. One Gottlieb Sontag applied to the imperial chamber of commerce for a licence to manufacture porcelain at Rabensgrün in Bohemia. His application was turned down, but it created something of a stir and the manager of the Imperial Manufactory in Vienna was obliged to defend himself in a lengthy statement. The statement reveals that a number of similar applications had preceded Sontag's. Since, however, the Imperial Manufactory enjoyed the privilege of being the sole authorized manufacturer of porcelain in Austria, all previous 'intrusions' had been 'severely punished and prosecuted, their workshops destroyed, and their tools confiscated'.[90] Sorgenthal defended these measures on the grounds that the Imperial Manufactory was the only one in a position to match the major foreign manufacturers (Meissen, Berlin) in quality, that it also benefited the state as an exporter and in addition provided a not inconsiderable number of jobs. He further refused to allow ordinary domestic ware to be produced by other factories because the kilns of the period were constructed in such a way that even in Vienna three-quarters of the ware fired could only be of ordinary quality.

Sontag's unsuccessful application, which he had backed up by saying that his factory was the only one in Bohemia, aroused the wrath of a rival. Johann Georg Paulus of Schlaggenwald wrote to the district council in Elbogen, Bohemia, stating that he had built his own kiln in the Schlaggenwald area and since 1792 had been in a position—with the help of an expert recruited from Hildburghausen in Thuringia—to produce far better porcelain than Gottlieb Sontag could.

### Schlaggenwald

The 'Court Commercial Councellor' in Vienna thereupon issued a report recommending the licensing of factories in Bohemia on condition that their products were not too close to those of Vienna. At first this did not lead to much; the Rabensgrün factory was discontinued, and the Schlaggenwald works made so little progress that the aggressive Mr Paulus sold it in 1800 to the widow of a Thuringian porcelain manufacturer, Louise Sophie Greiner, who came from Gera. Very slowly things improved. When Alexandre Brongniart from Sèvres visited the porcelain factories of Germany and Austria in 1812,[91] the Schlaggenwald factory, which since 1808 had been owned by a surgeon called Georg Lippert and a mine-owner called Wenzel Haas, was producing ware with a body that Frick described as 'grey-blue and unpleasant', though the colours and painting struck him as 'sometimes very nice'.[92] In 1812 the Schlaggenwald factory received its coveted production licence, but there were still difficult years ahead.

85 *Cups and saucers with flower and putti decoration.* Schlaggenwald, *c.* 1825. Overglaze painting and gilding. H. (cups) 9.5 cm, 7.5 cm. Mark: 116. UM, Prague.
The Bohemian factories, which made steady progress after 1800, followed Vienna closely in terms of modelling and choice of motifs.

86 *Cup and saucer painted with views.* Schlaggenwald, 1831. Overglaze painting, etched and polished gilding. H. (cup) 14.2 cm. Mark: 117. UM, Prague.
Schlaggenwald was the first of the Bohemian factories to achieve something approaching Vienna's quality of painting.

87 *Amphora-shaped vase with landscape.* Schlaggenwald, *c.* 1825–1830. Overglaze painting, etched and polished gilding. H. 28.5 cm. Mark: 116. District Mus., Pilsen (Plzeň).
Bohemian factories deliberately chose subjects such as this view of Napoleon's tomb on St Helena to avoid the charge of provincialism.

From 1817 onwards, however, the Lippert and Haas factory went from strength to strength, its pipe bowls and coffee and dining services earning respect and recognition at trade fairs in the 1820s. Staff recruitment from abroad improved the factory's style; patterns were acquired from Vienna, Berlin, Meissen, Sèvres, and England. There was little investment in developing new shapes; instead the factory adopted designs that had already proved successful from Berlin, Meissen, and Vienna. As a result, 'campana' and calathus cups were in use here too around 1820, while the cylindrical Empire cups with their elaborate handles disappeared. Porcelain imported from France probably also provided a stimulus from time to time; for example a particular large chocolate-cup shape with a thickened base appears to have been taken from a Sèvres design. What primarily distinguished Schlaggenwald porcelain even in the 1820s was its painting. The emphasis was no longer on simple Thuringian-style strawflower (immortelle) and linear patterns painted in underglaze blue, as in the early years, but on tableware and individual cups painted with miniatures in muffle colours. As well as the 'blue painters' for everyday ware, the factory employed a sizeable contingent of polychrome painters. Coloured grounds are rare; the framed pictures, gilt lines, flowers, and arabesques usually occupy a white ground; matt gilt grounds with polished ornamentation are also relatively common. As far as colour technology was concerned, painters were able to draw on earlier developments at Vienna and Meissen; nothing, at any rate, is known of any original research carried out in this field at Schlaggenwald. The painters we know of from various sources came mostly from Bohemia itself.[93] There could be no question, either at Schlaggenwald or at any of the other factories in the backwoods of Bohemia, of the kind of conditions that were laid down in Vienna, where a painter was not employed unless he had studied, and continued to study, at the Academy. Original inventions are

88 *Pieces from a coffee service with scenes from mythology.* Giesshübel, *c.* 1815–1820. Overglaze decoration, gilt rims. H. (coffee-pot) 14.5 cm. Mark: 112. UM, Prague.
The many factories that sprang up in Bohemia after about 1810 initially adhered to the Neo-Classical repertory of shapes and motifs.

less frequent; the many pictorial representations were probably taken without exception from engravings, which by this time were available even in the provinces through magazines, picture-books, illustrations, and almanacs of all kinds. Scenes from mythology were still popular, but even more common were allegories (Love, Hope, Friendship) and illustrations based on the poetry of Ovid and Goethe as well as on contemporary novels, in so far as these were available through, for example, the sentimental engravings of Ramberg. Following the brilliant example of Vienna, the Schlaggenwald artists even ventured to copy paintings (from engravings)—for example Madonnas by Raphael and Carlo Dolci, Reni's *Ecce Homo,* and Dutch genre pictures of the Rembrandt era. They produced a great many cups decorated with views, and, beginning in 1820, large vases were also painted with views, exploiting for the purpose published prints of Vinzenz Morstadt's picturesque Prague *vedute* and Bohemian landscapes. Schlaggenwald's position at the heart of Bohemia's spas, which attracted visitors from all over the world, particularly helped sales of souvenir cups bearing views of Karlsbad (Karlovy Vary), Elbogen, Marienbad (Mariánské Lázně), and Teplitz (Teplice). To give a cosmopolitan impression, the occasional view from abroad was acquired and made use of (for example *Le Tombeau de Napoléon dessiné sur les lieux*). Also among the souvenir cups, which accounted for a large part of the factory's output, there are many surviving examples with mottoes and flower devices. Bouquets were often put together on the basis of the 'language of flowers' publicized in the almanacs, with painters selecting exactly the right flowers to represent fidelity, gentleness, devotion, and so on, and arranging them in sprays for gift cups. Acrostics, common on Viennese porcelain, occur less frequently on porcelain from Bohemia. Schlaggenwald, thanks to its sales at the spas, had discriminating customers—anybody who was anybody used to 'take the waters' in Bohemia—with the result that the factory was able to maintain a high level of quality. The awards it received at trade fairs from 1830 onwards were thoroughly justified. But by this time there was already competition for Schlaggenwald from the factories at Klösterle and Pirkenhammer.

## Klösterle

In 1793, following the discovery of kaolin on the Count of Thun's estate at Klösterle, a start was made in building up a porcelain factory with the help of Thuringian experts. Things were very difficult for the first few years, and it was not until the plant was leased to Gotthelf Greiner, the successful manager of the Volkstedt-Rudolstadt and Ilmenau porcelain factories in Thuringia, that Klösterle began steadily to develop in the period 1797–1803. From 1804 to 1820 the Klösterle factory operated under two local lessees, Melzer and Haberditzel. Nearly all the painters taken on at Klösterle in the early years came originally from Thuringia.[94] For a long time the factory produced mainly utility tableware in smooth or ribbed, bellied or cylindrical shapes based on Thuringian designs and decorated with strawflower and related patterns in underglaze blue or with red peonies painted on top of the glaze. This was, in other words, not court porcelain and it is of little artistic interest. Not until 1830 did the Klösterle factory start to become more interesting. Very much in the Schlaggenwald mould are the few noteworthy products of the early decades of the Giesshübel and Dallwitz porcelain factories (est. 1803–1804).[95]

## Pirkenhammer

The principal early competition to Schlaggenwald came from (Pirken-)Hammer, near Karlsbad (Karlovy Vary), with the establishment of a factory in 1803 by a member of the Thuringian porcelain dynasty of Greiner, Friedrich Hoecke. For the first few years he manufactured only very simple crockery. His pipe bowls evidently sold well, being exported in large quantities to Silesia. In 1811 the factory was purchased by Johann Martin Fischer, a businessman from Erfurt, and Christof Reichenbach of Pirkenhammer. A slow but steady improvement then commenced, which by the beginning of the 1820s had led to Pirkenhammer producing the best porcelain in Bohemia from the technological point of view. Fischer and

89  *Déjeuner with gilt dots.* Berlin, *c.* 1790. Gilt decoration. H. (coffee-pot) 14 cm. Mark: 121. MfK, Frankfort.
The typical tableware shapes of the first quarter of the century were fully developed at all the major factories well before 1800.

90  *Queen Louise cup.* Berlin, after 1810. Overglaze decoration, gilt inscriptions and rims, biscuit relief (after L. Posch). H. 11 cm. Marks: 123, painter's mark, and others. Kunstgewerbemuseum, East Berlin (Hz. 531). Cups in particular commemorated events in the Neo-Classical and Biedermeier periods, for example the death of the popular young Queen Louise.

91  *Cup commemorating the Battle of the Nations (Leipzig).* Berlin, after 1813. Dark blue ground, overglaze and gilt painting. H. 9 cm. Marks: 123, and painter's mark. Kunstgewerbemuseum, East Berlin (Hz. 540). The date on the campana-handled cup and the map on the saucer recall the famous victory by the Allies (Prussia, Russia and England) over Napoleon.

92  *Pieces from a service with mosaic decoration.* Berlin, after 1820. Overglaze ▷ painting, etched and polished gilding. H. (coffee-pot) 18.8 cm. Mark: 122 and painter's mark. SSuG, Belvedere, Berlin. Berlin began using 'mosaic' decoration after 1802; these jugs imitate both the Roman and Florentine types of stone inlay work.

93  *Coffee service for the Möhring family.* Berlin, 1813. Overglaze and gilt ▷ decoration. H. (coffee-pot) 25.5 cm. Mark: 122. Kunstgewerbemuseum, SMPK, Berlin (56,8). An unusual service with portraits of the Möhring family, views of their ancestral home, and local Berlin sights, and even, on one saucer, a map of the city.

to establish what, as late as 1821, was still calling itself the 'Viennese porcelain factory'. Its white ware found favour from the start; initially all the porcelain was taken to Vienna for painting. However, a formal connection with the Imperial Manufactory in Vienna, sought during the slump of 1816–1817, failed to materialize, despite the original plans; even in Vienna, post-war conditions made it necessary to introduce manpower cuts. Eventually, however, unlike its imperial forerunner, the privately owned Elbogen factory was able to improve its situation.

## GERMANY

### Berlin

Like the Empress Maria Theresa of Austria-Hungary, her great rival Frederick the Great of Prussia had also acquired a porcelain factory (in 1763).[97] The king ran the factory himself with enormous interest and would brook no interference. Not until his death in 1785 did it receive a board of management independent of the royal house and even so the board, which functioned on a collective responsibility basis, included two representatives of the Crown in addition to the factory management. The first royal commissioner was Baron Friedrich Anton von Heinitz, head of the state department in charge of mining and iron and steel, who subjected the factory to a thoroughgoing modernization programme that did much to secure its future. Von Heinitz reorganized the kiln and firing methods, and in 1793 he bought the factory its first steam-engine (it was even home-produced), which was used for preparing the clay. He also had the skill and foresight to foster improvements in the clay and colours used, and it is undoubtedly due first and foremost to him that the Berlin factory, like the one in Vienna, entered the nineteenth century as one of the most modern and technologically most efficient.

Reichenbach subsequently invested in luxury porcelain as well. A small number of talented painters decorated cups and services on the basis of patterns from Vienna and Schlaggenwald; the colours were bought from Höchst.[96]

### Elbogen

The Elbogen porcelain factory was established in 1815 as a subsidiary of the Imperial Manufactory in Vienna. Government officials had found kaolin deposits in the area in 1811, whereupon the manager of the Vienna factory, Mathias Niedermayer, instructed two friends of his, Eugen and Rudolf Haidinger, to prepare to set up a porcelain factory in the vicinity that would replace another subsidiary of the Vienna factory, Engelhardzell, which was destroyed in the Napoleonic wars. A three-year apprenticeship in the Vienna factory and an extended study trip abroad put the two brothers in a position

94 *Pieces from the Wellington Service*. Berlin, 1817–1819. Overglaze painting, etched and polished gilding. Marks: 123 and painter's marks. V & A (Apsley House), London.
This was the first of the large commissions that the Berlin factory received in the wake of the Napoleonic wars.

## Style

Frederick the Great had himself seen the first hesitant beginnings of the stylistic changeover from Rococo to Louis XVI, based on designs from Sèvres. The switch to the sober shapes of Neo-Classicism, discussed in connection with the Vienna factory, was complete long before 1800. Many of the profiles that were to remain valid for twenty years and more may have been achieved at Berlin earlier than at Vienna. The cylindrical cup known as 'antique smooth' with the angular, so-called *à la grecque* handle was certainly in production from 1786 at the latest, as were the matching jugs and the straight-rimmed plates and salvers with the conical flange. The smooth cylindrical shapes may have been derived from Classical cists, bronze receptacles with lids for holding cosmetic implements and the like, common from the fourth century onwards. In Berlin, at any rate, exact copies of cists with the typical handle attachments, pine-cone knobs on the lids, and other characteristic details appear for the first time in 1789.[98] All they needed to become cylindrical vessels of more simple shape was to be stripped of their decoration. The earliest evidence of the 'campana' cup, a shape based on the Classical Greek cyathus ladle, probably dates from 1805 (in Vienna they were making them in 1789); with its distinctive proportions it is regarded, along with the similar 'Etruscan' form (egg-shaped with a neck below the lip and a soaring handle), as one of the most successful shapes created by the Royal Porcelain Manufactory in Berlin. In the early years of the nineteenth century other shapes were evolved for coffee services and cups as well as a number of variants for display vases, based on the Classical crater. Berlin porcelain, like its Viennese counterpart, is distinguished by a wealth of painting of enormous variety and very high quality.[99] Coloured and gilt grounds with luxuriant floral and tendril decoration based on late Roman prototypes, but often also immaculate white grounds, are combined with friezes, ribbons, and medallions containing ornamental floral, landscape, and figure scenes. Allegories and scenes from mythology were popular even after 1800, as were heroic and later idyllic landscapes with figure decoration. The particularly charming decoration using flowers or strips of meadow called

*en terrace* occurs along with floral wreaths, bunches of flowers as separate motifs, and flowers and leaves used to form initials and garlands. Oak leaves were particularly popular at the time of the German Wars of Liberation, 1813–1815. The delicate technique of etching gold was mastered to perfection. Many examples of portraits on cups have survived, but above all there was one that was undoubtedly most frequently used: that of the popular Queen Louise, who died young in 1810. A variant of this was also produced with a relief portrait in biscuit based on a design by Leonhard Posch.

## Special Pieces

Special commissions tended to produce above-average results. In the opening years of the century, in the period 1801–1803, a number of large centrepieces were made for different courts; these followed the example of the *Reich der Natur* ('Realm of Nature') of 1791 in combining Classical-style biscuit statuettes with painted service pieces. The centrepiece for Tsar Alexander, in production at the Berlin factory from 1802, is preserved in the Hermitage, Leningrad, almost in its entirety.[100]

In 1806, in the tense situation following the French occupation, an exorbitantly magnificent gift had to be produced for Napoleon's wife,[101] a dining service comprising probably three or four hundred pieces that was one of the first so-called 'botanical' services, decorated with precise reproductions of plants. The models for the flower paintings were taken from, among other botanical publications, a collection of engravings entitled *Le Jardin de la Malmaison* that had been commissioned by the Empress Josephine herself, a passionate amateur botanist. The adaptation of these colour-point engravings based on water-colours by Pierre-Joseph Redouté is evidence of the high standard of quality achieved by the Berlin porcelain painters.[102]

## Shapes and Decoration

Even before 1800 the factory, following the example of Sèvres, made a speciality of painted imitations of hardstones. The bottoms or sides of cups, bases, socles, and plinths were painted to look like amethyst, lapis lazuli, porphyry, or marble. Colourful mosaic imitations, too, sometimes combined with copies of *pietra dura* works and painted in minute detail, possess a particular aesthetic charm. In Berlin there is evidence of these from 1802. A similar effect was represented by the imitation of Classical precious and semi-precious stones on porcelain, of which there is evidence at Sèvres and Vienna as well from about 1815 onwards. The bottoms of plates and vases are decorated in shades of brown, red, and black with very realistic imitations of banded agate, sardonyx, or cornelian carved into portraits. These appear to have come into fashion in Berlin after 1815, and they remained popular for a long time. A large display vase dating from as late as 1840 bears the portrait of King Frederick William IV of Prussia painted in this way.[103]

These stone imitations suited the Empire taste for bold colour, which swept away the insipid palette of the Louis XVI style. The bold ground colours, which were given either a high gloss or a deliberately matt finish, range from japan black and dark reddish-brown to a gay light blue and a deep green. This fondness for strong colour and large areas of gilding increased further towards the end of the war against Napoleon. The finest example of this is the magnificent table service that the grateful Prussians had made in 1817–1819 for the English commander and victor of Waterloo, the Duke of Wellington.[104] This was the largest and most expensive set

95 *Centrepiece for the Russian court.* Berlin, H.C. Genelli, J.G. Schadow, C.F. Riese, after 1802. Overglaze painting, various types of gilt decoration, biscuit figures, bronze mounts. H. 110 cm. Mark: inaccessible. Hermitage, Leningrad (3780–3782).
The figured centrepieces typical of Baroque table decoration continued to be commissioned by the Prussian court in the Empire style.

produced by the Berlin factory in the first half of the century. Two obelisks form the centrepiece; large candelabra, surrounded by twelve figures of Victory bearing wreaths, accompany them. Further biscuit statuettes represent Borussia, Britannia, and various rivers. The tableware itself bears elaborately etched gilt decoration and painted scenes. The Wellington Service again combines certain specialities that distinguish the Empire porcelain of the Berlin factory. The biscuit figures of the Victories, based on models by the leading Berlin sculptor, Gottfried Schadow, surmount columns that are painted to look like porphyry. The pictorial representations on the socles of the other statuettes are etched entirely in the gilt ground. The fruit bowls also have gilded sides with etched and polished ornamentation, harmonizing in the most luxurious way with the brilliant flower paintings on the inner surfaces and the imitation lapis-lazuli plinths. The large tureens are decorated with battle scenes while the plates feature other scenes and landscapes associated with the duke's life.

After 1814 services were also designed and specially made for 96 other deserving commanders, including Princes Augustus and

William of Prussia and Counts Tauenzien, Kleist von Nollendorf, and Yorck von Wartenburg. Laurel wreaths, dense oak wreaths, iron crosses, and black-and-white Prussian medal ribbons frame paintings of scenes from the war. In these services large areas of pure white, undecorated porcelain themselves play a decorative role. The court commissioned numerous variants of these magnificent services for family occasions, for example the weddings of Princess Charlotte and the Russian Crown Prince Nicholas (made 1817–1823)[105] and of Princess Louise and the King of the Netherlands (1825).[106] Crater- or amphora-shaped vases painted with views or portraits remained the official court presents. A further charming little speciality of the Berlin factory in the period when the Prussian and Russian courts were so closely related were its Easter eggs, also designed as gifts. Easter is the most 97 important festival in the Russian Church, and one of the customs associated with Easter is the giving of artistically painted eggs, usually made of wood. The Prussian court's answer was to give expensive porcelain Easter eggs produced by the Berlin factory: gilded and decorated with painted miniatures, these were designed either as purely decorative objects or for use as scent-bottles.[107]

The design of all new shapes, whether for Easter eggs, vases, services, individual items of tableware, or figures, was the responsibility of master modeller Johann Carl Friedrich Riese, who occupied this post from 1789 right through to 1834. All the monographs on the Berlin factory mention him as an artist

of little talent, and indeed for all exceptional commissions the management enlisted outside help from well-known sculptors. Although Riese was a qualified sculptor himself it was Gottfried Schadow who received the prestige commissions for the figurative parts of centrepieces ranging from the great *Reich der Natur* Service of 1791, for which Riese designed the additional socles, temples, and vases, to the Wellington Service of 1817. Often he was given the job of reducing Classical statuary to the scale of porcelain, or adapting designs by Schadow, Genelli, and later also Rauch for execution in porcelain. Only occasionnally was he given the opportunity of modelling figures or groups to his own design, and these were mostly portraits of the royal family.[108] Even here it was usually another artist who was given preference: Leonhard Posch, whose wax models for relief portraits were used both for ornamental iron castings and for porcelain.[109] Nevertheless it remains Riese's unquestioned achievement to have exerted an important influence, with innumerable designs for vessels ranging from the most tasteless to the most magnificent, on the overall picture of Neo-Classical Berlin porcelain for a period of forty years.

## Meissen

Europe's oldest porcelain factory at Meissen (est. 1710),[110] which had led the field in the eighteenth century, began the nineteenth century in the shadow of Sèvres, Vienna, and even Berlin. Between 1774 and 1814 the Royal Manufactory there was under the management of Count Camillo Marcolini, who

96 *Covered tureen from the Feldherrenservice.* Berlin, 1817–1822. Overglaze and gilt decoration. H. 29 cm. Marks: 123 and painter's mark. Grossherzogliche Sammlung, Darmstadt.
An elaborate base with lion supports lends a monumental air to this piece from a service commemorating the Wars of Liberation.

97 *Easter egg.* Berlin, after 1820 (probably 1850–1875). Lapis lazuli ground, overglaze painting, gilt rim, bronze mount. H. 4.2 cm. Unmarked. Berlin-Museum, Berlin.
It was in 1820 that Berlin began the long tradition of giving porcelain Easter eggs in return for the Russian court's painted wooden ones.

98 *Cup and saucer with decoration copied from paintings.* Meissen, c. 1806. ▷ Overglaze and gilt painting. H. 7 cm. Mark: 134. MNC, Sèvres (469⁹). Meissen began using paintings as a source of decoration as early as 1763— here a Titian *Venus* and *Cupid Drawing his Bow* by Anton Raffael Mengs.

99 *Plate from the Wellington Service.* Meissen, 1818–1820. Overglaze ▷ painting and gold rims. D. 23.8 cm. Marks: 135, impressed number, title. V & A (Apsley House), London.
Not only the allies Prussia and Austria, but Saxony too presented a service to the Duke of Wellington. This plate is decorated with a view of Dresden.

100 *Pedestal vase.* Fürstenberg, c. 1820. Overglaze and gilt painting. ▷▷ H. 37.5 cm. Mark: 130. Werksmuseum, Fürstenberg.
Neo-Classicism brought new life to the Duke of Brunswick's factory, where this vase type, in various sizes, enjoyed several decades of popularity.

101 *Covered cup with portrait miniature.* Meissen, *c.* 1790. Royal blue ground, overglaze and gilt decoration. H. 6.6 cm. Mark: 134. WL, Stuttgart (G 12,20).
Already in use at Meissen around 1740, the cylindrical cup shape became very much more important in the Neo-Classical era.

new style of the time, Neo-Classicism, and for this it found worthy artists. Biscuit body was apparently taken over from Sèvres in Kändler's lifetime, and before long unglazed and unpainted biscuit had come to seem the only possible material for modellers working in the spirit of Classical Antiquity. In the 1780s two of these began making a thorough study of the collection of Classical sculpture and plaster casts in Dresden: Johann Gottlieb Matthäi, who eventually became curator of the Dresden plaster-cast collection in 1795, and Christian Gottfried Jüchtzer, who, especially after his appointment as master modeller in 1781, directed Meissen along the strictest Neo-Classical lines. Under him a large number of figures and groups was produced in the style of Classical statuary, and up until 1795 Matthäi made numerous copies of Classical works. The factory had two other Neo-Classical modellers in Johann Daniel Schöne and Christian Karl Schiebel.[111] At the same time Meissen ventured into the field of blue-and-white relief ware in the Wedgwood manner.

Proof that the Classical style was adhered to in tableware shapes and painting too is provided by such surviving examples as the beautiful cylindrical cups with the portrait of Elector 101 Frederick Augustus III of Saxony in the Stuttgart Landesmuseum[112] or the piece purchased in 1808 for the 98, 102 specimen collection at Sèvres. Smooth-rimmed simple cylindrical and bowl shapes presumably were introduced around 1790, but seem to have taken longer to establish themselves than in Vienna or Berlin. It was probably due not least to the factory's foreign clientèle, which wanted *vieux Saxe* (as it does today) and associated the name Meissen with the style of Kändler and Höroldt, that there was a certain reluctance to go in for Neo-Classical shapes in tableware. Even the management may have felt in their hearts that they should hang on to their glorious past achievements and adapt to the new fashion only in so far as was absolutely necessary. Shortly before the Wars of Liberation the warehouses were still full of Rococo ware.

*Painting*
Certainly no particular attempt seems to have been made to promote the discovery and development of new types of tableware and new kinds of decoration. In this Meissen never achieved the variety of Vienna. Yet it would be wrong to speak of complete impoverishment because individual pieces of high quality in various collections, most of which have never been 98 made public, provide evidence to the contrary. The painting 98, 101–10 staff was relatively small at the beginning of the nineteenth century, but appears to have included some outstanding miniaturists. Walcha mentions a number of flower, animal ('wildfowl'), portrait, and battle painters who became well known.[113] There were gilt pattern painters, as in Vienna, though here their ornamentation was mainly derived from the 'gold lace' of the eighteenth century.

Meissen artists began early on to transfer the paintings in the famous Dresden gallery on to porcelain, a copy of Raphael's *Madonna della Sedia* by Johann Martin Heinrici being mentioned as early as 1763. Paintings by Angelica Kauffmann, Canaletto, and the best-loved Italian and Dutch artists were copied on to porcelain around 1800 and later. The factory's drawing master from 1796 onwards, Johann David Schubert, copied the gallery's most popular paintings. In 1795 Count Marcolini commissioned a bowl to be decorated with Correggio's *Magdalen.*

seems to have been unable to give it much artistic impetus. An inventory drawn up at the time when he took over showed that there was not much money to spare, and Marcolini began to introduce the economies that were to continue until his retirement, though they failed to revive the factory's fortunes. His endless and ever-increasing complaints have found an echo in the literature in that all authors speak unanimously of the tragic decline of the Meissen factory.

Economic problems there certainly were, largely due to the fact that in the late eighteenth century Austria and Prussia completely banned the import of Saxon porcelain and Russia, France, and England placed a tariff on it ranging from 40 per cent to 60 per cent. Even so, Russia and in second place Turkey continued to represent profitable markets.

The protagonists of Meissen's golden age, Johann Joachim Kändler and Johann Gregor Höroldt, lived on until 1775—the year after Marcolini took over. Meissen was slower and more reluctant than other factories to break away from the style that had made it internationally famous.

Even today Meissen is judged by the products of its heyday—the first half of the eighteenth century—with every subsequent achievement being regarded as an impoverishment and evidence of artistic decline. In order to remain competitive, however, even Meissen had, in Marcolini's day, to adapt to the

102 *Cup and saucer decorated with views.* Meissen, *c.* 1806. Overglaze painting, gilt rims. H. 7 cm. Marks: 134 and impressed marks. MNC, Sèvres (469[10]).
The saucer has a view of Dresden set in a brown ground, the cup is decorated with a view of Meissen itself.

103 *Cup and saucer with Neo-Renaissance ornamentation.* Meissen, *c.* 1806. Overglaze decoration; gold, silver, and platinum ornamentation. H. 7 cm. Mark: 134. MNC, Sèvres (469[11]).
Both the saucer and the campana-handled cup have broad friezes of brightly coloured late Roman grotesque ornamentation.

*Innovations*

Engravings and mezzotints also appear to have been copied on to porcelain even before 1800.[114] The factory's entire artistic output was concentrated on individual cups, plates, and small services; no more large centrepieces and display vases appear to have been commissioned. The last years of the Napoleonic wars brought production almost to a standstill. Marcolini retired a discouraged man and died in 1814. The new management were more fortunate. The managing director was Carl Wilhelm von Oppel, and from 1816 onwards he was assisted by Heinrich Gottlob Kühn (1788–1870) as his technical manager. Kühn's various innovations paved the way for the Meissen factory's subsequent economic recovery. One of his first moves in the direction of modernization was to install a round kiln of the type that had long proved its efficiency in Berlin. Other innovations of Kühn's with an important bearing on the future were the development of a new underglaze colour

104 *Egg-shaped cup with flower painting and saucer.* Meissen, 1816–1824. Overglaze painting, gold ground with etching. H. 8 cm. Mark: 135. Kunstgewerbemuseum, SMPK, Berlin (1981,1).
Flower still lifes on the Viennese model were introduced at Meissen by painters whom the factory had sent to study in Vienna.

105 *Coffee-pot.* Meissen, after 1817. Underglaze painting in chrome-green. H. *c.* 25 cm. VEB Staatliche Porzellanmanufaktur, Meissen.
The vine-leaf pattern was designed especially for chrome-green, which came into use in 1817 as the second fire-proof colour after cobalt-blue.

105 (chrome-green, in 1817) and of gloss gilding (1827/1830).

In 1818 the factory took on the well-known painter Georg Friedrich Kersting (1785–1847), a member of the group of Dresden Romantics that included Caspar David Friedrich, Carl Gustav Carus, and Gerhard von Kügelgen. Oddly enough, despite his having worked at the factory for almost thirty years, no designs for porcelain motifs can be attributed to his hand, though he seems to have established contacts and been a good general supervisor, capable of attracting skilful painters. In 1819 Meissen began work on its dessert service for the Duke of Wellington, for Meissen too, like Sèvres, Berlin and Vienna,

99 paid homage to the victor of Waterloo in porcelain—to be precise, in a 134-piece dessert service.[115] On vases, ice urns, dishes in various Classical shapes, and above all on plates we find delicate painting of a quality that probably matches anything produced in Berlin or Vienna at that period. The plates have views of Dresden and of the Saxon landscape, and their flanges are adorned with a wreath of dense foliage wound round with medal ribbons. The names of four painters are associated with the service, which was dispatched to London in 1820: Johann Samuel Arnhold, Johann Gottlieb Böhlig, Gottlieb Hottewitzsch, and Johann Friedrich Nagel.[116] Presumably the painting department received other large and prestigious commissions, for in 1827 it again had 121 painters in its employ. Admittedly this figure may have included the

105 underglaze painters, who, for example, were responsible for the vine-tendril pattern that was extraordinarily popular around this time and sold in vast quantities. It was designed by Johann Samuel Arnhold immediately after Kühn had developed his chrome-green; it has kept its popularity right up to the present day, together with the older onion pattern that was abandoned in the first quarter of the nineteenth century but was later reissued.

## Thuringia

In neighbouring Thuringia the successes of Meissen had encouraged private entrepreneurs to go in for porcelain manufacture back in the eighteenth century, rather as happened a generation later in Bohemia, following the example of Vienna. Glass and faience had long been produced in Thuringia, and the raw materials for porcelain manufacture were available in the region. The first trials succeeded in 1760, and it was not long before high-quality porcelain was being produced at Kloster Veilsdorf and subsequently at Gotha, Ilmenau, Grossbreitenbach, Gera, Rauenstein, and Wallendorf—and finally, still before 1800, at Blankenhain, Tettau, Eisenberg, and Pössneck. Thuringian manufacturers proved their skill abroad as well, for the first Bohemian factories actually to succeed (Rabensgrün and Schlaggenwald) owed their success to Thuringians, as did many later factories in Bavaria (Hohenberg, Selb, Arzberg) and Silesia (Waldenburg).[117]

Kloster Veilsdorf, Gotha, and Volkstedt supplied the local court households, but they could never have kept going on that basis; nor, certainly, could the many other firms operating in this relatively small area. They were all dependent on manufacturing articles that sold well, such as, primarily, pipe bowls, stick knobs, buttons, and writing utensils.

Often, however, they also made statuettes, in addition to coffee, chocolate, and tea-services. Many articles were expressly produced for the export market, such as small Turkish-style coffee cups for the East. Most articles were marketed at trade fairs in the local towns, but they also sold in Leipzig and Frankfurt and were to be found throughout Germany.

The Thuringian factories as a group share many points of similarity with the Bohemian group, such as their private-enterprise management, their dependence on a middle-class clientele, the quality of their products—which were usually quite coarse to start with and only became more refined after years of effort—and their stylistic dependence upon the big state-owned factories. Thuringia was of course producing porcelain as early as the last third of the eighteenth century and had its heyday during that period. The much-reduced importance of Meissen in the late Marcolini period (until 1814) and the Oppel period (1814–1833) appears to have had a depressing effect on the Thuringian factories as well. Their output at that time was in general less inspired and less up-to-date in terms of fashion than it had been in the eighteenth century. Most factories clung for too long to the tried and tested shapes and decorative motifs of the late eighteenth century. They began to lag behind the Bohemian factories, which were of course on the way to their first artistic successes in the 1820s. Enriched stylistically by the great art of Vienna's Sorgenthal period, the Bohemian factories summoned up all their skill and imagination in a bid to outgrow their provincial beginnings. The efforts of the Thuringian factories seem by comparison to have been less intensive and less successful. However, a great deal of work remains to be done—even the latest publication by the leading authority on the subject falls a long way short of answering all the questions about Thuringian porcelain production in the nineteenth century.[118]

### Gotha

Some beautiful porcelain was produced in the early nineteenth century in the Gotha factory,[119] which from 1802 to 1813 belonged to Prince Augustus of Gotha. This was probably its best period, in fact, although it continued to play a role in the later nineteenth century. All the ideas that Meissen, Vienna, or Berlin could supply were taken up here. Rectilinear vessel shapes with a wealth of representational painting predominated. The small court of Saxe-Gotha-Altenburg was a cultivated place and possessed a collection of Classical art that may have provided original patterns for the Neo-Classical ware popular at the Gotha factory in the 1790s, though the source of the types of decoration derived from Classical red-figure vase painting probably stemmed from earlier Viennese ware.[120] The products of the famous factories generally supplied the Thuringian modellers and painters of services, vases, and cups with their ideas: small flower pictures, sometimes in *en terrasse* form, birds, portraits, and *vedute,* often framed in gold, decorate cylindrical shapes; landscapes frequently use local, Thuringian, subjects or copy heroic or Romantic landscape paintings, such as, for example, a small framed picture based on Philipp Hackert in the Dresden porcelain collection (1832).[121] The quality of the painting on Gotha ware is regarded as the best of all Thuringian work in the first half of the century, so that unmarked but carefully painted pieces are usually attributed to this source, which clearly did not always apply its 'G'.

### Wallendorf

One of the earliest factories in Thuringia was that founded in 1764 by J.W. Hammann and J.G. and G. Greiner in

106 *Two pear-shaped jugs.* Rauenstein, *c.* 1800. Painting in underglaze blue.
H. (large jug) 25 cm. Mark: 139. TM, Eisenach.
The shape, ribbing, and 'Indian' flower decoration of these jugs represent a
far older tradition, and one that the Thuringian factories continued to use
until after 1850.

107 *Cocoa-pot.* Grossbreitenbach, *c.* 1800. Strawflower decoration in
underglaze blue. H. 11.2 cm. Mark: 132. Kunstgewerbemuseum, Cologne
(E 1223).
A further example of the traditionalism of the Thuringian factories; this was
the most popular form of decoration with their middle-class clientele.

Wallendorf in the duchy of Saxe-Coburg-Saalfeld.[122] Its
products are more typical of the majority of Thuringian firms
in the first third of the nineteenth century than those of Gotha.
Apart from shapes and painting styles that summarily follow
the lead of Neo-Classicism, late Rococo jug and tureen shapes
were retained and painted with the simple types of decoration
107 that were by then far from new: strawflower and onion patterns
in underglaze blue or 'Indian-style' purple flowers painted over
the glaze. Pear-shaped jugs and egg-shaped cups, often with
ribbed sides, were popular basic shapes. These same shapes and
types of decoration have been traced to the other factories
started by the Greiners at Grossbreitenbach in the principality

of Schwarzburg-Sondershausen (est. 1777–1778), Rauenstein
(est. 1783), and Ilmenau (est. 1777).[123] Evidence of the
popularity of the strawflower is provided by the flourishing    107
sales that the Thuringian factories achieved with this pattern
as far afield as Denmark and England. From England Ilmenau
adopted Wedgwood ware, and by 1798 at the latest it was
producing blue-and-white imitation jasper ware for medallions
and furniture inlays—apparently in larger quantities than
Meissen.[124] Rauenstein in Saxe-Meiningen (est. 1783), which
to begin with confined itself more to blue ware than the others
mentioned above, eventually fell in with these by adding
Indian purple flowers as well as a design, not unlike the
strawflower in composition, using slender flower sprays with    106
birds in them, most popularly in shades of blue-green. Here
such designs were carried on until the middle of the century.
Obviously the Thuringian factories were not entirely
unaffected by the Neo-Classical vessel shapes with gilt
decoration and miniature painting so typical of the period.
Nevertheless it is remarkable how steadfastly many of them
went on producing the conventional vessels fashionable in the
eighteenth century right up until the mid-nineteenth century
and painting them with simple ornamental decoration. With
their provincial, conservative clientele, only in exceptional
cases did Thuringian factories try to compete with state-
owned factories by introducing fashionable innovations.

## Regensburg

Thuringian white porcelain was also painted and treated
abroad. Regensburg, for example, is known to have been a
transhipment point for Thuringian porcelain destined for the
Eastern market. In 1803 a Regensburg porcelain painter made
a successful application for a licence to set up a porcelain factory
there, and in 1805 he began producing Turkish-style coffee
cups, pipe bowls, and tableware. The factory went through
repeated changes of ownership in the first twenty-four years,
but from 1829 to 1864 there was a period of continuous
production under the management of Johann Heinrich Anton
Schwerdtner. Documentary evidence shows that utility
porcelain accounted for the greater part of the factory's output.
The ware was unmarked, so that basically only a few pieces
painted with motifs from the Regensburg area can be
attributed with certainty. Style and quality resemble those of
the products of the less ambitious factories of Thuringia and
Bohemia.[125]

## Nymphenburg

There is also evidence of a porcelain factory in Passau in the
early nineteenth century, but of incomparably greater
importance in Bavaria was the factory established at
Nymphenburg near Munich by the Elector of Bavaria in 1757.
Its greatest claim to fame were the porcelain figures made by
its master modeller Franz Anton Bustelli (until 1763). The
appointment of Dominicus Auliczek and Johann Peter
Melchior as his successors continued the tradition of placing
special emphasis on porcelain figure work. Melchior (1742–
1825), who began his career at Höchst and Frankenthal as one
of the leading porcelain sculptors of the late Rococo period,
worked entirely in the Neo-Classical style at Nymphenburg    108
from 1797 onwards. His Classical gods and other similar

108 *Figure of Bavaria with Prince Maximilian of Bavaria and an Allegory of Joy.* Nymphenburg, J. P. Melchior, 1800. Biscuit porcelain. H. 46.3 cm. Unmarked. BN, Munich (Ker. 2267).
Sculpture played a minor role in the porcelain of the first half of the century, when marble-like biscuit body was its sole means of expression.

109 *Cups with portrait miniatures and saucers.* Nymphenburg, probably A. Auer, *c.* 1812. Royal blue ground, overglaze painting, gilt decoration. H. 9.7 cm. Marks: 137 and scratch signs. BN, Munich (Ker. 2249, 2238, 2241).
Portraits of members of the family of Maximilian I Joseph of Bavaria adorn these 'jasmine' cups, adapted from a Sèvres shape.

110 *Plate with decoration copied from a painting.* Nymphenburg, Louis Socrate Fouquet, 1821. Overglaze and etched gilt decoration. D. 23.5 cm. Marks: 137, various signs, and details of the original painting. Residenzmuseum, Munich (K II Ny 716).
Commissioned by Crown Prince Ludwig, Nymphenburg's porcelain painters had begun copying works in the royal collections on to plates in 1810.

three-dimensional sculptures, as well as his busts and relief portraits of members of the Bavarian royal family, are perhaps the most convincing examples of the kind of cultivated Neo-Classicism to which the Meissen, Berlin, and Fürstenberg factories were paying homage around the same time. From 1799 Bavaria was ruled by Maximilian IV Joseph, whom lengthy military service in France had predisposed to the culture of that country and who expected Melchior to switch to the French taste. So here too old stocks were auctioned off cheaply and the factory's output given a strictly contemporary appeal.

### Shapes and Decoration

Melchior's Neo-Classical tableware shapes possessed universal validity and were absolutely up to date. The painting, however, compared less well with that of such leading exponents as Vienna and Berlin. A source dating from 1804 names the not very numerous painters: Auer, who 'nearly always [did] portraits of the royal family', a flower painter, an arabesque painter, a general pattern painter, and finally one who painted bowls in the 'still sought-after wooden manner', in other words in the wood-grain imitations that belonged to the Louis XVI style.[126] The year 1801 saw the beginning of work on a

projected large service decorated with Bavarian landscapes, but it was symptomatic of the factory's limited potential that this never got beyond the early stages. Soon afterwards, however, the factory had an unexpected change of fortune when Crown Prince Ludwig (in 1825 he became King Ludwig I) began to take a personal interest in it. In 1810 the prince commissioned a large table service with plates to be painted with copies of the 'most outstanding' works in the royal gallery.[127] In Nymphenburg too this launched a trend that was to reduce porcelain more and more to a mere vehicle for pictorial decoration. The initial orientation towards porcelain sculpture, with which Nymphenburg had started so brilliantly in the days of Bustelli and Auliczek, was pursued no further. An outward

111 *Vase to commemorate the death of King Maximilian I Joseph of Bavaria.*
Nymphenburg, F. Gärtner and C. Adler, *c.* 1825. Overglaze painting and
etched gilt decoration. H. 44 cm. Marks: 137, other signs, artist's signature.
BN, Munich (R 6161).
The portrait is balanced on the reverse side of the vase by an unusual picture
of the apotheosis of the King enthroned in the clouds between angels of
death.

112 *Plate from the Onyx Service.* Nymphenburg, after 1835. Pompeian-red
ground, *grisaille,* gilt decoration. D. 23 cm. Mark: 137. Residenzmuseum,
Munich.
Under Friedrich Gärtner the Nymphenburg factory remained loyal to Neo-
Classicism right up until 1848.

sign of this development came when the factory's painting
department was given the title 'art institute'.

Anton Auer (b. 1777/1778), the best of the factory's
painters, began copying the paintings. After his death in 1814
the French artist Louis-Socrate Fouquet added another
twenty-seven plates up until 1820. Intensive work on the series
continued until 1826, but occasionally new plates were added
up until 1845 and even as late as 1883.[128] Following the death
of Johann Peter Melchior in 1822, Friedrich Gärtner (1792–
1847) was appointed artistic director. He was professor of
architecture at the Royal Academy of Arts and, like the crown
prince, a Neo-Classicist in his stylistic allegiance. He was
responsible for designs for ornamental vessels based closely on
the Classical crater and amphora shapes and offering a
magnificent vehicle for every kind of painting. A particular
type of vase related to the Classical hydria was adopted from
the Berlin factory as the *Münchner Vase* ('Munich vase') and
was still being produced around the middle of the century. In
1828 Gärtner gave up his supervisory job at the factory to
devote himself to his many architectural commissions, but he
continued to influence the style of its products. Painting as an
art was given every encouragement. Neither Gärtner nor the
crown prince had any interest in everyday, saleable tableware,
so that the factory very quickly ceased to be an economically
viable business. Dismissals of painters on the one hand
alternated continually with measures to create jobs on the
other. Among the latter was a commission from the king in
1827 to copy the most valuable paintings of his collection,
already preserved on plates, this time on to plaques. The
reasoning behind this seems slightly odd: these masterpieces of
painting were in this way to be preserved for posterity 'when
the ravages of time have finally destroyed the originals'.[129]
From the purely technical point of view these copies represent
a considerable achievement; many of the tablets are larger than
50 by 60 centimetres, and the colours match those of the
originals exactly, shade for shade. The early years of Gärtner's
period of office also saw the production of several large state
services. For Count Schönborn at Wiesentheid a service was
painted with Classical-style scenes taken from Flaxman
illustrations, and in 1835 work began on a similarly Neo-
Classical and extremely sumptuous service for Ludwig I, the
so-called Onyx Service. For this the painters took their models
from the royal 'Glyptothek' or sculpture gallery; Classical
sculptures in white stand out strikingly against a Pompeian-red
ground, framed with ornaments in gold or brick-red.[130]

## Fürstenberg

Finally, before concluding this section on the German
factories, mention must be made of the Duke of Brunswick-
Lüneburg's porcelain factory in Fürstenberg, which was
established in 1747 and was wholly given over to Neo-
Classicism long before the advent of the nineteenth century. A
speciality of the factory, in addition to copies of Classical
works, were busts and relief portraits of famous
contemporaries: scholars, writers, philosophers, poets, and

leading statesmen. All designed before 1800, they continued to be produced and sold until after the Napoleonic wars. In 1797 the reigning duke, Carl Wilhelm Ferdinand, appointed a well-known French ceramist to manage the factory, which for a while had been rather unsuccessful. Louis-Victor Gerverot (1747–1829)[131] fulfilled all the expectations placed in him by reorganizing and modernizing the entire operation. When under Napoleon Brunswick became part of the newly founded Kingdom of Westphalia, Gerverot managed after some initial difficulties to establish good relations with the court of Jérôme Bonaparte in Kassel, relations that resulted in some extensive commissions. This is the period of the 'vase-shaped' service with 'campana' cups and jugs derived from them—a service strongly reminiscent of earlier Viennese and Berlin ware—and of similar service pieces and vases in simple shapes. In 1814 Gerverot was dismissed because of his close connections with the court at Kassel, despite the fact that it was thanks to his efforts alone that the Fürstenberg factory was in a better state than most of its German competitors following the Napoleonic wars. No new service shapes were added to those introduced by Gerverot until the end of the 1820s, though more emphasis was placed on ornamental painting during this 100 period. In addition to the typical contemporary motifs in bright colours, sepia landscape drawings were particularly popular. The factory's painting shop was moved to the capital, Brunswick, where the artists had access to the Duke's art collections. In 1814 the painting staff had been expanded and new blood brought in, but in 1828 the entire department was suddenly closed down. One ex-employee continued on his own account, and it is thanks to him that Fürstenberg's Biedermeier porcelain too could be painted.

## DENMARK

### Copenhagen

The Duke of Brunswick's Master of the Hunt, Johann Georg von Langen (1699–1776), who had built up the Fürstenberg porcelain factory from 1747, had before that time been in the service of King Christian VI of Denmark, to which he returned in 1763. A few years later he was able to assist the chemist Franz Heinrich Müller in experiments that led in 1773 to the manufacture of the first hard-paste porcelain using Danish raw materials. From 1779 onwards Denmark too had its own Royal Porcelain Manufactory, which Müller managed until his death

113  *Covered tureen.* Copenhagen, *c.* 1800. Painting in underglaze blue. W. 39 cm. Mark: 146 with inverted crown and monogram. Kunstindustrimuseet, Copenhagen.
Still one of Copenhagen's biggest successes, strawflower decoration in underglaze blue was originally adopted from German ware.

114  *Piece from the Flora Danica Service.* Copenhagen, *c.* 1800. Overglaze decoration, gilt rims. H. 22 cm. Marks: 146 and impressed marks; also, in black writing, the botanical name of the flower depicted, *Ajuga genevensis.* MNC, Sèvres, (12 166).
For a long time this service was the factory's greatest independent achievement.

115  *Covered sugar bowl with painting of a view.* Copenhagen, Carl Martin Intz, 1826. Overglaze decoration and gilding. H. 14 cm. Marks: 146 and painter's monogram. NM, Frederiksberg (B 3100).
A delicate miniature of Rosenborg Palace on part of a coffee and tea-service that belonged to the court pharmacist, J.P. Groth.

in 1801. Owing to the fact that the master modeller, Anton Carl Luplau, had also been enticed away from Fürstenberg, Copenhagen's Empire porcelain was largely derived from German ware. The most enduring effect of this was the adoption of the strawflower pattern in underglaze blue, which became so popular as the nineteenth century wore on that today it has long enjoyed the status of a 'national' pattern.

The first wholly independent achievement of the Copenhagen porcelain factory was the *Flora Danica* Service, begun in 1790 but not completed until 1802. This was the first of the great tableware services with botanical decoration. One of the directors of the factory was the scientist Theodor Holmskjold, a pupil of Carl von Linné, and it was probably his idea to take as a basis for porcelain decoration the systematic work on the flora of Denmark that G. C. Oeder, director of the Copenhagen botanical gardens, had begun to publish in 1761. General views, details, and even in some cases sections through flower-buds and fruits were painted with scientific precision on more than 1,800 pieces comprising the hundred place settings, serving bowls, and so on, while the appropriate Latin name was inscribed on the underside.[132]

The rest of the Copenhagen factory's output is of pleasing quality but in formal terms follows the generally prevalent Neo-Classical types (as already described) stemming from the factories of Berlin—with which personal contacts were repeatedly renewed—Meissen, and Vienna. The painting likewise embraced all the current motifs from stone imitations and flowers to portraits, landscapes, and views.

The Neo-Classical trend received fresh impetus in 1821 when the services of the architect Gustav Friedrich Hetsch (1788–1864), a former colleague of Napoleon's court architect Charles Percier, were obtained as artistic advisor. Born in Stuttgart and trained in Rome and Paris, Hetsch had been in Copenhagen since 1815, working with C. F. Hansen on Christiansborg Palace. Here and as a teacher at the Academy of Arts he continued to hold a brief for Neo-Classicism in the applied arts until the middle of the century and beyond. His porcelain designs reflect the generally prevalent Neo-Classical vase types for which he had received inspiration at first hand during his Paris years from the study of Sèvres porcelain. On the advice of Hetsch, the managing director of the factory, Peter Johann Gottfried Garlieb (1787–1870) made a trip to Paris in 1823 and brought back some Neo-Classical engravings and a specimen collection of Sèvres porcelain.[133] The German factories, which had led the field artistically until then, subsequently lost this position to Sèvres.

## RUSSIA

### St Petersburg

The Russian empire, which in the eighteenth and nineteenth centuries was entirely Europe-oriented as far as culture was concerned, possessed its own Imperial Porcelain Manufactory in St Petersburg from 1763 onwards. Under Tsar Paul I this was managed by Prince Nikolay Borisovich Yusupov, a great enthusiast who directed it towards the contemporary Empire style. Antoine-Jacques Rachette (1744–1809), Professor of Sculpture at the St Petersburg Academy and a man who had worked for the factory under Catherine the Great, also provided the main artistic impetus under Yusupov. A Neo-Classical approach to shape and decoration, the introduction of

biscuit statuettes, and the inclusion of Neo-Classical figures in the composition of table services and centrepieces characterized his influence. But it was also Rachette who was responsible for the earliest painted biscuit statuettes of different Russian ethnic types that were to enjoy a steadily growing popularity in Russia throughout the nineteenth century. The models for these were taken originally from a book of prints by the German traveller Johann Gottlieb Georgi, *A Description of All the Nations of the Russian Empire* (1776–1780).[134]

In the first quarter of the nineteenth century this Neo-Classical approach was pursued with unbroken continuity. A year after his accession in 1801, Tsar Alexander I appointed Count D. A. Guryev to replace Prince Yusupov. At the same time the entire managerial structure of the imperial manufactories was reorganized and Guryev, as a member of the imperial cabinet, was placed in charge of the porcelain factory. Despite the fact that this possessed a large and extremely complex administration, all policy decisions appear to have stemmed from Guryev himself. He held auctions and sales to get rid of outmoded stocks and recruited skilled personnel from abroad to help modernize the factory both technically and artistically. Berlin provided three porcelain experts, of whom Seiffert in particular performed a major service in rebuilding the antiquated kilns. In 1806 he introduced the first rack-type kiln, and by 1814 the factory had four of them. As regards the composition of bodies and glazes there seems on the whole to have been no change, although in the 1820s the occasional colour was acquired from Paris and Berlin. France, on the other hand, provided mainly artistic personnel: in 1808 the porcelain painter G. Adam went to St Petersburg, in 1815 the technicians and moulders Pierre-Charles Landelle (until 1818) and Ferdinand Davignon, the pattern painter Denis-Joseph Moreau, and the battle, genre, and landscape painter Jacques François Joseph Swebach from Sèvres (until 1820).[135] Swebach in particular already had a reputation both as a freelance painter and in his capacity as head porcelain painter of the Sèvres factory under the First Empire. However, to the overall artistic style of the factory the Frenchmen had little to add; the Neo-Classical designs for figures, vases, and tableware were already well established and did not change before 1830, while the painting did not depart from current international practice. Far more influential as far as the style of design was concerned was the Russian sculptor Stepan Stepanovich Pimenov (1784–1833). He too was Professor of Sculpture at the St Petersburg Academy and one of the finest Russian sculptors of his day. For Pimenov, as for all his professional contemporaries, the study of the art of Classical Antiquity was the basis for all his work. The vase designs are derived from amphorae and craters, the most popular of which bear a striking resemblance to the *vase à rouleaux* that Charles Percier designed for Sèvres (1808), just as the slender spindle amphora added somewhat later resembles the *vase fuseau,* an Empire design from Sèvres.[136]

As far as utility vessels were concerned, the factory's repertoire was already complete around 1800 with smooth cylindrical, conical, and egg-shaped designs embellished with Neo-Classical reliefs. The painting was of exceptional quality and used as broad a range of motifs as the finest European factories did. Miniature and silhouette painting, the imitation of other materials, relief copying in the Wedgwood manner, gilding in several colours with etching, and the combination of coloured grounds with miniature painting and ornamentation were all mastered to perfection. Purple and yellow grounds for gilt ornamentation seem to have been

116 *Statuette of a milkmaid.* Kiselev factory (?), Gzhel' District, 19th century. Partly unglazed, painted porcelain. H. 28 cm. Mark: 150. M.M. Post Collection, Hillwood.
Originally modelled by Stepan Pimenov for the Imperial Manufactory, this figure was subsequently adopted by Gardner, Kiselev, and other factories.

117 *Plate decorated with soldiers.* St Petersburg, 1829. Overglaze painting, etched and polished gilding. D. 23.8 cm. Marks: 153, date and caption. MNC, Sèvres (19 683).
Military subjects—here two cavalry trumpeters—were popular in St Petersburg in the first half of the century.

particularly popular. Begun in 1800, two major services were manufactured to commissions by the court, one painted with bouquets of roses, the other with Italian landscapes—very much in the style of Vienna or Berlin.

*Exceptional Pieces*

One of the factory's greatest independent achievements in the early nineteenth century was the state service made for Count Guryev. Begun in 1809, it took several years to produce, eventually comprising some thousand pieces. The principal pieces of the service, which was designed for fifty persons, date from between 1809 and 1817.[137] Vases, bowls, and baskets, which form the actual centrepieces, are in many cases supported by figures. The biscuit colour of the figures, the dark red-brown ground colour of the vessels and the plate flanges, the sumptuous gilt decoration and the colourful miniatures in the white reserves of the vessels and in the centres of the plates add up to a charmingly elegant whole. The subject matter is unusual: in addition to views of St Petersburg and scenes from the life of its inhabitants, images were also included of Russian peasants and ordinary folk going about their daily business. In similar vein figures of men and women reaping support the fruit bowls and confectionery baskets, though admittedly Pimenov's fine Neo-Classical modelling made them so elegant that they would not have caused offence on any court banquet table. Besides Pimenov, other graduates and professors of the Academy worked for the St Petersburg factory. Consequently the painting too is often of exquisite quality. As in the other European porcelain centres, the large vases, sets of plates, and straight-sided cups constituted the ideal background for little framed paintings, of which the most popular in Russia depicted scenes from the lives of that vast country's many different ethnic groups as well as views of the major cities and scenes from the everyday life of the fashionable world, shown enjoying such pleasures as hunting, riding, sleigh-driving, and skating. Some of the most exquisite porcelain paintings of this type are those executed by the French artists Swebach and Adam shortly before 1820, though the miniatures painted by their Russian colleagues Voronchin, Golov, and others do not fall far short of them.[138] A feature of the Russian Imperial Manufactory was its heavy reliance on subjects from the war against Napoleon and military motifs in general.[139] Vases and cups are decorated with the portraits and uniformed figures of the victors of the battles of 1812; representatives of the different regiments and branches of the army parade on sets of

118

117

118 *Coffee service.* St Petersburg, *c.* 1816–1820. Overglaze and rich gilt decoration. H. (coffee-pot) 16.5 cm. Mark: inaccessible. Hermitage, Leningrad (2999–3003).
Smaller services from the St Petersburg factory also show a high standard of painting, as in these hunting scenes.

plates, surrounded by trophies and weapons: on horseback, on foot, resting or attacking, bivouacking, scouting, or in the thick of battle, always precisely coloured and in many instances accompanied by explanatory captions.[140]

### Private Factories

*Gardner*

The imperial manufactories department had granted a private individual permission to produce porcelain as early as 1766. Francis Gardner, a British entrepreneur who had probably been living in Russia for some time,[141] purchased land at Verbilki, near Moscow, and—quite illegally—also serfs from a Russian nobleman who had fallen on hard times. A factory was successfully founded with the help of experts from Meissen, and as early as 1777 Catherine the Great commissioned three display services from Gardner based on pieces from a Berlin and a Meissen service in her possession. In the early days it was again Meissen that provided the models for further tableware and for figure groups, but at the beginning of the nineteenth century Gardner began to adopt designs from the Imperial Manufactory. An important expansion of his repertoire of figures followed publication of the almanac *Laterna Magica, or Petersburg Tradesmen, Craftsmen, and Other Workers...* with drawings by Zelentsov. These statuettes became the Gardner factory's most successful line and were still being produced in the second third of the century. Russian peasant scenes and ethnic types and views of Russian towns also adorn Gardner's services, which in terms of shape are wholly indebted to the

119

116

119 *Coffee-pot with landscape decoration.* Gardner factory, Verbilki, first quarter of the 19th century. Overglaze painting, gilding. H. 35 cm. Mark: 156 and impressed Gardner in Latin letters. M. M. Post Collection, Hillwood.
Part of a large tea- and coffee service in Empire shapes with exceptionally fine paintings of various country games in landscape settings.

international style of the time. Gardner's products are distinguished by the elegance of their draughtsmanship and the high quality of their painting.

### Yusupov

Close to the perfection of Gardner's ware is the rare porcelain produced by Prince Yusupov. Having been managing director of the Imperial Manufactory from 1792 to 1802, in 1814 Yusupov founded a porcelain-painting workshop on his estate at Arkhangelskoye, near Moscow, which operated until his death in 1831 and manufactured porcelain for his personal use alone. White porcelain was not produced there but was purchased from Sèvres, Limoges, and Popov (see below). Shapes and painted decoration were deliberately kept within those traditional at court.[142]

### Batenin

Of a less luxurious nature were the products of the many other private factories established in Russia as the nineteenth century wore on, the imposition of protective tariffs in 1806 having brought the import of western European porcelain more or less to a standstill. One of the first was set up in St Petersburg in 1812 by a businessman called Sergey Batenin. Its porcelain was of a more robust kind with less sumptuous decoration, though considerable use was made of large areas of gilding and brightly coloured painting. Batenin's prices were much lower than Gardner's, with the result that it was he who opened up the urban middle-class market for porcelain cups and coffee services.[143] He prepared the ground on which, particularly in the second third of the century, a great many small manufacturers were at times able to do very well.

### Popov

While Batenin concentrated on tableware, the Popov factory specialized in figures for the same urban middle-class clientele. In 1811 Alexey Gavrilovich Popov, a merchant in the China trade, bought a small, ailing factory at Gorbunovo, near Moscow, from an ex-employee of Gardner's, the German Karl Melli. His statuettes of Russian craftsmen, tradesmen, peasants, and so on are more sought after by many collectors than those of Gardner. Popov's factory was thoroughly modern and appears to have been the only one of its kind in Russia with its own colour laboratory, which enabled it to produce particularly charming costumed figures as well as superbly painted tea-services, plates, and cups.[144]

## ENGLAND

There was no historical or artistic break in continuity in England between the late eighteenth and the early nineteenth centuries. However, there were far-reaching changes in economic conditions which affected porcelain production. The number of factories increased, and a growing proportion of creamware factories were now making porcelain. The main cause of this sudden expansion was the huge increase in import tax levied on Chinese porcelain. This had been coming into England in some quantity since the eighteenth century in the ships of the East India Company. In 1799 the duty was increased so that it equalled in value the cost of the porcelain itself. Miles Mason, a shrewd businessman, saw his chance and set up as a manufacturer in the late eighteenth century; however, from 1813 onwards, his sons, one of whom patented

120 *Ice-pail.* Derby, Duesbury & Kean factory, *c.* 1811. Bone china. H. 26 cm. Mark: 171, with inscription naming the landscape. Royal Crown Derby Mus., Derby.
The shape derives from Sèvres 18th-century ice-pails. The painted landscape, attributed to George Robertson, and the extremely flat gilding are both typical of the Derby factory.

121 *Shell-shaped dish.* Derby, Robert Bloor & Co, 1813–1815. Bone china. ▷ D. 23.3 cm. Mark: 171. Royal Crown Derby Mus., Derby.
This shape was created at Sèvres in the 18th century. The painted decoration of thistles was executed by 'Quaker' Pegg. Although botanical subjects were outmoded, Pegg instituted a revival of the genre thanks to his powerful style and elegant placing of the decorative elements. He worked from nature and did not base his work on engravings.

the stoneware known as 'stone china', controlled the business. Many of the porcelain factories established at the end of the eighteenth century or beginning of the nineteenth were to close down before 1850 or were to change hands repeatedly. Yet the English ceramic trade was in a period of extremely rapid growth in the first third of the nineteenth century. The catastrophic blockade of Continental trade (1806–1812) was succeeded by a series of economic crises, which preceded the boom of the Victorian era (1837–1901).

The flowering of the ceramic industry was a random process. Each individual manufacturer tried his luck and worked in the most varied of materials and styles. We shall discuss only the factories most typical of this rich period, and the reader is referred to the numerous specialized publications discussing individual factories in detail. An author's choice of factories is necessarily arbitrary. We shall look first at those concerns founded in the eighteenth century, all of which experienced their periods of maximum prosperity at different times. The Derby factory was at its zenith in the late eighteenth and early nineteenth centuries, while, in the period under discussion,

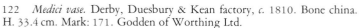

122 *Medici vase.* Derby, Duesbury & Kean factory, *c.* 1810. Bone china. H. 33.4 cm. Mark: 171. Godden of Worthing Ltd.
This vase, with its goats'-head handles in place of those usually found on Medici vases, has an unusual salmon-coloured ground and gilt decoration in typical Derby style. The Romantic landscape, doubtless the work of Robert Brewer, is described on the base of the piece in the usual fashion; the inscription reads: 'In Dudley Wood, Worcestershire'.

124

123 *Medici vase.* Derby, Robert Bloor & Co, *c.* 1815. Bone china. H. 17.4 cm. Mark: 171. CM & AG, Derby.
During the Bloor period numerous decorative vases were made at the Derby factory. The shape of these Medici vases was admirably suited to continuous decoration running round the body of the piece. This vase is painted with a landscape attributed to John Brewer.

124 *Cylindrical cup.* Derby, Robert Bloor & Co, 1811–1815. Bone china. H. 12.8 cm. Mark: 171. CM & AG, Derby.
The landscape is attributed to William Corden or Robert Brewer.

125 *Vase.* Derby, Robert Bloor & Co, *c.* 1820. Bone china. H. 22 cm. Mark: 172. V & A, London (312-1935).
The decoration on this piece is attributed to Thomas Steele, whose talent as a fruit painter was highly praised by John Haslem, who published a key work on the Derby factory.

126 *Medici vase.* Derby, Robert Bloor & Co, *c.* 1815–1820. Bone china. H. 20 cm. Mark: 171. CM & AG, Derby.
Most decorative pieces made at Derby have a white or blue ground ornamented in gold with palms, scrolls, or shells. This piece has a plain matt ground. The painted floral decoration cannot be attributed to any particular artist.

127 *Plate.* Derby, Robert Bloor & Co, 1815. Bone china. D. 21.6 cm. Mark: 171 and '75' in purple, '9' in red, '38' in grey. CM & AG, Derby.
The floral decoration on this piece has been attributed to Moses Webster or John Keys; the landscapes are the work of William Corden.

128 *Cup.* Derby, Robert Bloor & Co, 1820–1823. Bone china. H. 12.7 cm. Mark: 171. Royal Crown Derby Mus., Derby.
The decoration on pieces from this series was carried out by the painter William Dixon after John Haslem. Dixon worked at Derby between 1820 and 1823. The subjects were based on engravings by Tim Bobbins entitled *Human Passions Delineated* and published at Manchester at the end of the 18th century.

125

126

127

128

129 *Bowl.* Derby, Robert Bloor & Co, *c.* 1815–1820. Bone china.
D. 27.4 cm. Mark: 171. V & A, London (225-1938).
This large bowl with its gold ground painted with orange leaves and flowers
is an exceptional and successful piece.

130 *Figurine: The Magic Lantern.* Derby, Robert Bloor & Co, *c.* 1820. Bone china. H. 15.2 cm. Mark: 171 with '94' incised. CM & AG, Derby.
This group is based on work in biscuit made by Falconet at Sèvres in 1754. It should be stressed that, in the first quarter of the 19th century, the English porcelain factory that was the most directly inspired by 18th-century Sèvres porcelain was the Derby factory.

Worcester was especially successful during the years 1810 to 1830. We shall tell the story of William Billingsley's extraordinary peregrinations in the company of his son-in-law, Samuel Walker. These two, who had in a sense more in common with the eighteenth-century arcanists, embodied many of the endeavours of this period. Like many of their contemporaries they also came under the spell of Sèvres porcelains. We shall also describe the birth of the English porcelain industry as it took place at the various Staffordshire centres, before proceeding to examine its greatest period of prosperity, which belongs to the next chapter.

## Derby

Derby and Worcester were both founded in the mid-eighteenth century, and both were situated at some distance from Staffordshire, the traditional centre of ceramic production. From 1800 to 1830, there were gifted painters working at both centres. Derby, established around 1750, was owned by William Duesbury I between 1756 and 1786. Duesbury, who had run an enamelling establishment in London, initially began to manufacture porcelain in order to ensure supplies of undecorated ware for his London operation, but later the Derby factory set up its own decorating workshop. Under William Duesbury II the factory grew rapidly during the period 1786–1796, owing to the presence at the factory of talented painters such as Boreman. Michael Kean, Duesbury's partner, married Duesbury's widow and ran the factory until 1811. Although several painters left the Derby factory at this time, Kean managed to recruit others who maintained the high standard already achieved. Unfortunately the quality of the porcelain body in use at this time was inferior to that of the earlier period—it was now a felspathic composition. After 130–138 Kean's departure, when Robert Bloor took charge of the

factory, the quality of the ware deteriorated seriously. Bloor's rent was so high that he was obliged to sell warped pieces that should have been destroyed at the prices charged for first quality porcelain. Bloor succumbed to illness in 1828, but the factory carried on until 1848.

The painters at the Derby factory were responsible for its reputation at the end of the eighteenth century and beginning of the nineteenth. Zachariah Boreman was employed at Derby between 1784 and 1794 before going to London to work until his death in 1810 for John Sims.[145] He was a landscape painter and seems to have taught his friend William Billingsley his own technique of 'wiping out': after applying the pigments, the highlights were wiped out so that the white porcelain showed through and created effects of light and shade. Billingsley, who was an apprentice painter between 1774 and 1779, succeeded E. Withers as the chief flower painter at Derby in 1790. His famous 'apprentice plate' painted around 1794 and now in the Derby museum, is a dazzling example of his technique, which was to revive the art of flower painting on porcelain in England at the beginning of the nineteenth century. Billingsley left Derby in 1796, but Michael Kean secured new painters who carried on where their predecessors had left off. They included George Robertson, who painted 120 landscape and marine subjects at Derby between 1796 and 1820; Robert Brewer, a landscape painter who also treated 122, 124 marine and military themes from 1797 to about 1816; his brother John Brewer was taken on in 1795 to paint figurative 123 subjects, animals, landscapes, and flowers.

Landscape scenes on Derby porcelain of this period are unique in their lightness of execution. Before the changeover from soft-paste porcelain to a harder and whiter body, the colours sank into the glaze so that the fired enamel colours almost achieved the effect of water-colour painting. Landscape scenes were enhanced by border decoration in gold of the highest quality. Some pieces made at this time, such as the jewel-like cups forming part of luxurious services, shared with contemporary French porcelain an extreme simplicity of form and general conception, and are as subtly painted as English water-colours. After the changeover to the new body, landscapes on Derby porcelain took on the more familiar appearance of oil-paintings, in which a yellowish tinge was predominant. The decorator Daniel Lucas was employed during this phase of the factory's activity, arriving at Derby 136 around 1825.

After William Billingsley left the factory, John Brewer became the chief painter of botanical subjects which were copied from engravings. Another painter, William Pegg, known as 'Quaker Pegg', carried the art of botanical painting 121 on porcelain to its ultimate peak of perfection. A religious man, he interrupted his career at Derby because he was tortured by doubt. He was employed from the time of Billingsley's departure in 1796 until 1801, then again between 1813 and 1820. His decorative schemes consist of flowering branches or plants, such as the thistle, simply positioned in the centre of plates or dishes. They are painstakingly executed in a powerful painterly style that is quite unique. Pegg worked from nature and did not use engravings. Beside Pegg's work, Moses Webster's painting (1821–1825) lacks inspiration, although 127

131 *Soup plate.* Derby, Robert Bloor & Co, *c.* 1815. Bone china. D. 24.5 cm. Mark: 171. Royal Crown Derby Mus., Derby.
Numerous pieces decorated with 'Japan' patterns have been in production at Derby from the end of the 19th century up to the present day.

132 *Teapot.* Derby, Robert Bloor & Co, 1811–1815. Bone china. H. 15 cm. Mark: 171. Royal Crown Derby Mus., Derby.
Between 1805 and 1820 Derby used this somewhat heavy shape for their teapots. The illustration shows the brilliant but rather flat appearance of Derby gilding.

133 *Covered bowl on stand.* Derby, Duesbury & Kean factory, *c.* 1810. Bone china. H. 13.4 cm. Mark: 171 and '37'. V & A, London (306-1935).
Decorative schemes featuring playing-cards are among the most charming of all the types of decoration used in the early 19th century.

134 *Derby dwarfs.* Derby, Robert Bloor & Co, *c.* 1820. Bone china. H. 17.78 cm. Unmarked, incised '227'. CM & AG, Derby.
The model was already in existence in 1784 and was so successful that it has been in constant production throughout the 19th and 20th centuries. The figures were inspired by the Mansion House dwarfs (stationed in front of the Lord Mayor of London's house), whose hats bore advertising slogans.

135 *Figure of a peacock.* Derby, Robert Bloor & Co, *c.* 1830. Bone china. H. 16.51 cm. Unmarked. CM & AG, Derby.
In the 19th century, Derby carried on the local tradition of making porcelain figures and figure groups. Two brothers, Edward and Samuel Keys, played an important role in the production of figures. The peacock is the most famous piece made by Samuel Keys. Several editions of the figure have been made.

his naturalistically executed flowers are of high quality. Thomas Steele is generally credited with fruit subjects on 125 Derby porcelains, although during his period at the factory, which lasted from 1815 to 1848, he also painted flowers and insects. Animal subjects are also found fairly frequently on Derby porcelain and sometimes these are the work of John Brewer. Armorial pieces, the device either painted in the centre of a plate or on its border, were also used.

It was the painters who were responsible for the fame of the 129 Derby factory in the early years of the nineteenth century, though not all of them can be mentioned in this brief survey. Their work appeared to advantage on the simple shapes favoured by the factory which included plates and dishes with a plain or slightly lobed rim, cups and teapots with straight or 128, 132 slightly flaring sides and globular or Medici vases, their design 123, 126 usually based on Classical models. The authors have stressed the French influence on Derby porcelain because to anyone familiar with French porcelain this factory represents perhaps the only English concern, with the exception of Swansea and Nantgarw, which was faithful to the spirit of pieces made at Sèvres and at Paris. The shape and decoration of certain ice-pails 120, 121, 1 and shell-shaped comports is taken directly from Sèvres models

136  *Vase.* Derby, Robert Bloor & Co, *c.* 1830. Bone china. H. 53.34 cm.
Mark: 172. CM & AG, Derby.
The sombre decoration of this piece, copied from an oil-painting in need of
cleaning, is in the style of the painter Daniel Lucas, the last great artist at
the Derby factory.

137  *Vase with floral encrustation.* Derby, Robert Bloor & Co, *c.* 1835. Bone
china. H. 47 cm. Mark: 173. CM & AG, Derby.
Coalport is the porcelain factory best known for floral encrustation; however,
other factories also made products with this type of decoration. The flowers
on this vase, delicately highlighted with bright colours, stand out against a
blue ground. The overall effect of the colours is particularly well contrived.

138  *Plate.* Derby, Robert Bloor & Co, 1839. Bone china. D. 25.5 cm.
Mark: 174. CM & AG, Derby.
Decoration painted by John Haslem, known for his talents as a writer, in
1839 in the Rococo style of the period.

139 *Dish from the Duke of Clarence Service.*
Worcester, Flight factory, 1792. Bone china.
L. 52.7 cm. Mark: 229. DPM, Worcester.
The service was made in 1792 and painted by
Pennington. Each piece is decorated *en grisaille*
with a female figure of Hope, in different poses,
holding an anchor. The underglaze-blue border
has decorative motifs in gold.

of the eighteenth century. However these pieces can be distinguished from their French counterparts by their gilding. This is of extremely high quality, even though it is rather shiny and has a slightly 'flat' appearance.

The last years of the Derby factory were marked by a decline in quality. Too many pieces came out of the kiln warped because of under-firing. The shapes lost their purity, and the decoration became commonplace. One of the painters of this period should, however, be mentioned since he was responsible for handing down to us the history of the Derby factory and 138 its employees. John Haslem, who worked as a painter at Derby in its later years, published his book on the Derby factory in London in 1876.[146] The book is the fruit of careful study and observation during his working life at the factory. We shall discuss in a later chapter the revival of porcelain manufacture at Derby after 1848 when former factory workers once again occupied the premises at King Street.

## Worcester

### *The Flight Factory*

While the Derby factory experienced its greatest success at the end of the eighteenth century and the beginning of the nine-teenth, Worcester's high point occurred in the following decades. Established in 1751, the Worcester factory was the first to use the technique of transfer-printing on porcelain. In 1783 Thomas Flight bought the concern for his sons, John and Joseph, who experienced a number of problems in the early years. The kilns did not work properly, and the workman who was in charge of the composition of the porcelain body refused to reveal the secret of the Worcester formula. In 1788, however, the king conferred the title of 'Manufacturers to their Majesties' on the firm and in 1788–1789 a showroom was opened in London in connection with which John Flight went to Paris where he ordered porcelain from Dihl and Guérhard for sale in London. His visit probably explains why Worcester

porcelain of this period is so clearly influenced by its French counterparts. When John Flight died in 1792, Joseph Flight went into partnership with Martin Barr. The factory became known as Flight and Barr until 1804, at which date Martin Barr's son, of the same name, joined the partnership and it took the name Barr, Flight and Barr. Between 1792 and 1804 the firm experienced its first successes: the Hope Service, 139 commissioned by the Duke of Clarence and painted by Pennington, was completed and delivered. Improvements were made to the body, which was now harder. In 1804 the bat-printing process was adopted for the most commonly used decorative schemes, which could now be printed in colour. The Barr, Flight and Barr period lasted from 1804 to 1813. The factory continued to make improvements to every aspect of production. Research into bodies was carried out under the direction of William Billingsley and Samuel Walker, who claimed to possess the secret of making a more translucent body. New painters were taken on in order to introduce a note of variety into the classical, landscape or botanical scenes used to decorate the wares. On the death of Martin Barr in 1813, the partnership between Joseph Flight, Martin Barr junior, and George Barr was renewed, under the name Flight, Barr and Barr. It was to remain in existence until 1840 when the concern was taken over by the rival firm of Chamberlain.

140 *Fruit cooler and covered vase.* Worcester, Flight, Barr & Barr, c. 1815. ▷
Bone china. H. (vase) 29.84 cm; (fruit cooler) 29.40 cm. Marks: 230, 231.
DPM, Worcester.
These two pieces painted by Thomas Baxter show the variety of subjects he tackled. The reverse of the fruit cooler is painted with flowers. On the vase are scenes illustrating the works of Byron.

141 *Pierced dish for fish.* Worcester, Robert Chamberlain factory, c. 1800. ▷
Bone china. L. 36.2 cm. Unmarked. DPM, Worcester.
Decorated in a style inspired by the Chinese *famille verte* porcelains with a pattern called by the factory 'Dragon in Compartments' and numbered '75' in the pattern-book.

During the period 1800 to 1830, the Worcester factory experienced both its greatest success and its decline. At the outset its productions were conceived in an eighteenth-century style, typified by simple shapes and by the use of decoration on a white ground. Thomas Baxter, son of a London porcelain painter and a pupil at the Royal Academy, was largely responsible for the success of the firm. He only stayed at Worcester for two years, between 1814 and 1816, but created an extremely strong school of draughtsmanship there. In his book[147] Henry Sandon gives a list of Worcester painters who carried porcelain painting to the height of perfection in this period. He mentions Thomas Baxter, who specialized in painting figurative subjects and shells and was without doubt the most accomplished of all Worcester painters; T. Rogers, J. Barker, and J. Smith also depicted landscape subjects; W. Doe specialized in painting birds, feathers, and insects, while C. Stinton portrayed imaginary birds, T. C. Crowther, flowers, and G. Davis, birds. The list of painters gives some idea of the variety of subjects used as decoration on Worcester porcelain. Shapes were in the Etruscan style, simple in outline and well-suited to the type of motifs used. The uncluttered forms and outstandingly well-executed painting has much in common with French First Empire porcelain. That a feeling of rivalry with France existed at Worcester can be seen from a story quoted by Henry Sandon:[148] Mr Hope, a connoisseur, had shown to Thomas Baxter an admirably painted plate that he had purchased at Paris, saying that he was sorry he was unable to find anything comparable in England. Baxter replied that he had not only seen the plate before but had actually painted it himself.

There is therefore a clear link between Paris and Worcester porcelain. Both made porcelain characterized by a high degree of technical perfection. Pieces made by the Dihl and Guérhard factory are especially suited for comparison with Worcester products since both factories favoured a pictorial style of decoration. Both reproduced a wide range of materials found in nature, such as hardstones, which appear on Paris porcelain, and feathers and shells, which were painted on English porcelain. From 1820 Paris and Worcester porcelains began to move away from the pictorial tradition and to revert to the use of light colours on a white ground, while shapes became more elaborate. Worcester, however, still favoured painted decoration, but the shapes became heavier. Elaborate moulded feet, handles, and finials were used. Plates, which had been circular in shape around 1800–1810, now had lobed rims and were also ornamented with relief gadrooning on the border. Gilding was employed indiscriminately for grounds, as well as for banding and for decorative friezes, which were either Classical or Rococo in style. Gold was applied on both inner and outer surfaces. Around 1830 Worcester porcelain was so richly decorated that there was really no room for further development in this direction. There had to be a complete change of style, or else a choice had to be made between complex forms and elaborate decoration. However as no such choice was made, the factory found itself in a blind alley. The only pieces that had a white ground were those painted with armorial devices, but these were no less splendidly decorated since their borders were completely covered with gold friezes or reserves painted in colours and outlined with gilding.

At Worcester another quite different type of decoration was also in use, which could have been more effectively produced using printing techniques; this was the so-called 'Japan' decoration based on Imari porcelain (commonly known as

142   *Inkstand.* Worcester, Robert Chamberlain factory, early 19th century. Bone china. L. 23.5 cm. Mark: 226. V & A, London (C 541-1935). The rich Kakiemon-style decoration is used on a piece which is completely European in shape.

143   *Two cups with saucers.* Worcester, Robert Chamberlain factory, c. 1820. Bone china. H. (cups) 7 cm; D. (saucers) 15.5 cm. Mark: 228. Coll. of Her Majesty the Queen, Windsor Castle.
On the underside of the cups are inscriptions (below the factory mark) identifying the landscape scenes: 'Windsor new park' and 'Frogmore'; both are in Windsor Great Park.

144   *Pair of jugs.* Worcester, Robert Chamberlain factory, c. 1795. Bone ▷ china. H. 20.32 cm. Mark: 225. DPM, Worcester.
The curved flutes are alternately painted in blue and gilded with delicate garlands. The discreetly rendered portraits of Colonel Francis Hawley and his wife were perhaps painted by Humphrey Chamberlain. These jugs are typical of late 18th- and early 19th-century taste in England.

145   *Tureen, cover, and stand.* Worcester, Robert Chamberlain factory, early ▷ 19th century. Bone china. H. 28.5 cm. Mark: 227, printed in red on the base of the tureen, stand, and on the underside of the cover. Coll. of Her Majesty the Queen, Windsor Castle.
Although the shape is somewhat heavy in outline, the chinoiserie decoration is extremely delicately painted.

at the Worcester factory; extremely simple decoration gave way to a very elaborate style. Humphrey Chamberlain was himself an excellent figure painter. Thomas Baxter worked for Chamberlain as well as for Flight, Barr, and Barr from 1819. The firm also made biscuit porcelain figures. Grainger followed the same pattern and established a decorating workshop, which was active from 1801, and employed the painter John Wood. About 1805 he began making porcelain, but few marked pieces made before the 1830s are known.

## William Billingsley

The English porcelain market was dominated by Derby and Worcester products in the first third of the nineteenth century. The pieces were decorated in the English version of the pictorial style in use in all the European porcelain factories at this period. There was also another tributary of porcelain production that can be directly related to the eighteenth-century pieces made at Vincennes and Sèvres. This appeared in the work of William Billingsley who has already been mentioned as working at Derby and Worcester. Billingsley had his share of setbacks as well as some undeniable successes. He travelled from place to place accompanied by his daughters and his son-in-law Samuel Walker, much in the manner of the eighteenth-century arcanists. Born in 1758 in Derby, he was trained at the Derby factory as a flower painter where he contributed to the revival of the art of flower painting on porcelain. His method consisted in wiping out areas of colour, imitating the effect of water-colour technique. With his friend Zachariah Boreman he began experimenting with porcelain bodies between 1783 and 1793. His unlikely peregrinations started in 1796 when he moved to the Pinxton factory in Derbyshire. There he assisted John Coke in the manufacture of porcelain resembling that made at Derby in its body and glaze. Sober shapes, so beloved of the English in the late eighteenth century, and delicately 167

146 *Covered vase: The Taming of the Shrew.* Worcester, Robert Chamberlain factory, *c.* 1815. Bone china. H. 22.86 cm. Mark: 227. DPM, Worcester. Humphrey Chamberlain painted a scene taken from Shakespeare's *The Taming of the Shrew* on this vase. The inscription on the inside of the cover reads: 'Taming of Shrew. Pet. Tear not sweet wench, they shall not touch thee, Kate. I'll buckler thee against a million. Act III, sc. 2'. The 'pebbled' ground is painted in orange.

*vieux Japon* in France) or other oriental porcelain. Blue was the predominant colour and was applied under the glaze, while the other colours, mainly orangish-red and gold, were applied over the glaze. Worcester was only one of the many English factories to make large quantities of porcelain with this oriental-type decoration, which was no longer in production in France at this period. It was only around 1830 that the Bayeux factory, probably under English influence, began to use this type of decoration.

### The Chamberlain and Grainger Factories
There were two other factories in Worcester at this period. The Chamberlain factory was an offshoot of Flight, while the Grainger factory sprang from the Chamberlain concern. Robert Chamberlain set up a porcelain-decorating establishment in 1788. Around 1791 he began to manufacture 144–146 porcelain, helped by his son Humphrey. In general terms the stylistic evolution at this factory followed the same course as

147 *Cream jug.* Pinxton (Derbyshire), John Coke & Co, *c.* 1800. Bone china. H. 11.43 cm. Unmarked, pattern no. '312'. Godden of Worthing Ltd. William Billingsley worked at Pinxton between 1796 and 1799 before moving to Mansfield. The Pinxton factory changed hands several times between 1799 and its closure in 1813. Pieces made there are restrained in both form and decoration.

148 *Plate from the Garden Scenery Service.* Swansea (Wales), Dillwyn & Co, 1817. Duck-egg porcelain. D. 21.5 cm. Mark: 219. V & A, London (C. 3491-1901).

This service was painted by Thomas Baxter for L.W. Dillwyn. The decoration of flowers in a landscape on the pieces in this service is arranged in a fairly unusual fashion. Swansea's duck-egg porcelain is an exceedingly thin felspathic porcelain.

149 *Plate.* Nantgarw (Wales), Nantgarw China Works, 1817–1820. Soft-paste porcelain. D. *c.* 25 cm. Mark: 182. Schreiber Coll., V & A, London (Sch I 807).

The border decoration, imitating mid-18th-century Vincennes pieces, consists of scrolls and garlands of flowers in relief. The painting includes extraordinary tones of grey and was probably executed in London.

150 *Covered dish from the Burdett-Coutts Service.* Swansea (Wales), Dillwyn & Co, 1818. Duck-egg porcelain. D. 35.56 cm. Mark: 219. Coll. of Her Majesty the Queen, Windsor Castle.

The service was made in 1818 on the occasion of the second marriage of Thomas Coutts, the banker. It was decorated through Mortlocks, the London china dealers, probably at the John Sims workshops in Pimlico, London.

151

154

151   *Inkstand.* Nantgarw (Wales), Nantgarw China Works, 1817–1820. Soft-paste porcelain. L. 18 cm. Unmarked. NMW, Cardiff.
Billingsley and Walker, after leaving Swansea, produced their high-quality porcelain at Nantgarw. Billingsley specialized in flower painting.

152, 153   *Plates from the Mackintosh Service.* Nantgarw (Wales), Nantgarw China Works. 1817–1820. Soft-paste porcelain. D. 24.3 cm. Mark: 182. V & A, London (C. 588$^{aA}$-1935).
The extremely translucent Nantgarw porcelain body was very popular with London decorators, one of whom was doubtless responsible for the painting on these pieces.

154   *Covered bowl and stand.* Swansea (Wales), Dillwyn & Co, *c.* 1814–1822. Soft-paste porcelain. H. (bowl) 8 cm; D. (stand) 19.7 cm. Mark: 221. V & A, London, (C. 600 to b-1935).
Billingsley and Walker were obsessed with trying to make soft-paste porcelain in imitation of Vincennes and Sèvres porcelain. Billingsley was also influenced by decoration done at Sèvres in the 18th century and has recreated the 'partridge-eye' ground on this piece.

157   *Figure of a ram.* Swansea (Wales), Bevington & Co, *c.* 1820. Biscuit ▷ porcelain. H. 10.8 cm. Mark: 218. V & A, London (C. 3509-1901).
The sculptor Isaac Wood, who came from Nantgarw with Billingsley and Walker, stayed at Swansea after the departure of the two latter. He worked for the Bevingtons who bought the Swansea factory from L. W. Dillwyn. About a dozen of these curious pieces are known.

155 *Part of a tea-service.* Swansea (Wales), Dillwyn & Co, *c.* 1814–1822. Soft-paste porcelain. H. (cream jug) 11 cm; H. (cup) 10.8 cm. Unmarked. V & A, London (C. 107-1878).
Most Swansea porcelain is decorated with flowers. The painting on these pieces is attributed to William Pollard.

156 *Plate.* Nantgarw (Wales), Nantgarw China Works, 1817–1820. Soft-paste porcelain. D. 24.6 cm. Mark: 182. V & A, London (C. 3519-1901).
A richly conceived flower painting attributed to James Turner ornaments this piece of fine Nantgarw porcelain.

painted flower garlands and landscape scenes are characteristic of Pinxton porcelain. The factory closed down in 1813.

In 1799 Billingsley went to Mansfield, about six miles from Pinxton, to set up his own decorating workshop. Between 1802 and 1808 he was working at Torksey in Lincolnshire. In 1808 he took up employment in Worcester together with his daughters and son-in-law. Initially they were concerned with improvement of the enamel kilns, then around 1810 they attempted, with some success, to refine the porcelain body to make it more translucent. This was done by adding bone-ash. After their departure in 1813, Flight, Barr, and Barr tried in vain to obtain compensation from them for taking with them the secret of the paste they had perfected, which was supposed to remain the property of the Worcester firm. Walker and Billingsley now installed themselves at the Nantgarw factory in Wales where they were able to manufacture porcelain of a quite remarkable translucency. They soon exhausted their financial resources, as well as those of their sleeping partners, and applied for a government subsidy—with some temerity since England was at that time pursuing a rigorous policy of free trade. They were in fact bailed out by Lewis Weston Dillwyn, owner of the Cambrian Pottery at Swansea. Dillwyn's 168 aim was to produce the body developed by Billingsley and Walker on an industrial scale, despite the problems previously experienced in firing this body at Nantgarw—an enormous number of pieces had not survived the firing and were faulty. Some of the most translucent soft-paste ever seen was made between 1814 and 1815 at Swansea and later between 1817 and 1820 at Nantgarw. It was even finer and more translucent than French eighteenth-century porcelain, and many of the plates made have moulded decoration in low relief under the glaze on 149 the border like their eighteenth-century Vincennes counterparts. On others there are copies of wickerwork similar to that found on Meissen pieces. Decoration was often loosely based on Vincennes and Sèvres subjects, such as scattered 151–153 flowers, birds, 'partridge-eye' grounds, and so on, although the 154 oriental motifs commonly found on English porcelain were also used. The variety of painted decoration was partly the result of the practice of sending pieces to London for decoration. There was an outcry from the London merchants when Dillwyn proposed lowering the cost of production by reducing its quality.

Sadly, Walker and Billingsley were living in a bygone era. Financial support provided by the king of France had ensured the continuing production of soft-paste at Sèvres, and Brongniart had been forced to stop making it in the nineteenth century. In 1820 John Rose, owner of the Coalport factory, purchased Billingsley's formulae and his moulds. He also took on Walker and Billingsley. Billingsley died at Coalport in 1828. The improved Coalport body dates from about 1820, as does the production of 'fake Sèvres'. William Weston Young and Thomas Pardoe carried on painting porcelain in stock at Nantgarw until 1822 as did Bevington and Company, 157 Dillwyn's successors, at Swansea. This firm was making porcelain at Swansea in the 1820s.

## The Spode Factory

The experiments described above resulted in the manufacture of some outstandingly beautiful porcelain, but the methods used were unsuited to the times. Manufacturers making high quality bone china on an industrial scale were now coming to

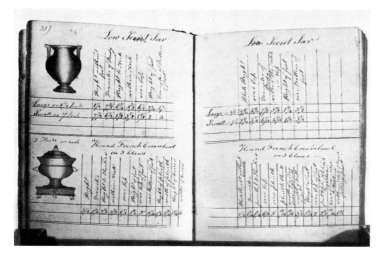

158 *Page from a shape-book.* Stoke-on-Trent (Staffordshire), Spode factory, 1820. Spode Ltd Archives, Stoke-on-Trent.
This remarkable pattern-book shows all the wheel-thrown shapes produced at Spode in 1820. The sizes given refer to the dimensions to which the thrower and turner worked.

159 *Vase.* Stoke-on-Trent (Staffordshire), Spode factory, 1820. Bone china. H. 24.8 cm. Unmarked. V & A, London (C. 311-1935).
This ornamented piece is based on an 18th-century Chelsea model known as the 'Eel-Basket Vase'.

the fore. Most of them, but not all, were working in Staffordshire. Although Minton was already enjoying some success at this time, it was to reach the peak of its activity rather later in the century. The Spode factory at Stoke-on-Trent (Staffordshire) was without doubt the most important factory in the early nineteenth century. Its history has been told in L. Whiter's comprehensive work,[149] although it has in part been superseded by more recent research. Josiah Spode I (1733–1799), the founder of a dynasty of potters, had established a soundly based business manufacturing creamware and fine stoneware. His son Josiah Spode II (1755–1827) carried on making these wares, marketing them as earthenware and stone china respectively. Like the French creamware the Spode pieces were not porcellaneous. In 1797 Josiah Spode II, who had been in London, returned to take over from his father. He soon started making porcelain, manufacturing bone china at an early date (which has not yet been accurately established). This characteristically English product has since become known the world over.

*Bone China*

L. Whiter has stated clearly: 'There is no such thing as *the* formula for bone china'.[150] Bone china can be made according to a number of different formulae, and one factory can use varying recipes according to its requirements, although the raw materials remain more or less the same. Kaolin (Cornish or china clay) and felspar (Cornish stone) from Cornwall and about 50 per cent bone-ash (phosphate) are the basic constituents. Porcelain made from these materials is white in colour, somewhat milky in tone, and although composed of two of the same basic ingredients as those used in European hard-paste porcelain, has more in common with French soft-paste. This was intentional. Whiter has emphasized this point: 'Spode II achieved his objective.... It was, quite simply, to produce a china as near as possible in appearance to Sèvres soft-paste, loveliest of all Western porcelains and then, as now, a standard of perfection'.[151] Spode managed to effect a perfect compromise between the aesthetic and practical considerations governing porcelain manufacture. In 1821 he began to use the felspathic glaze perfected at Coalport.

*Shapes*

A document existing in two versions and dated 1820[152] contains a collection of sketches of thrown pieces from this period with their dimensions before firing. It affords us unparalleled information on the large number of shapes made at the Spode factory. Apart from a few examples, the moulded pieces have been omitted from the list; we have no contemporary record of the complicated relief decoration used on pieces dating from this period. Most of the pieces seem much more judiciously designed than those shown in the album in the Cabinet des dessins at the Musée des Arts décoratifs in Paris, which are likely to have been made at the Dagoty and Honoré factory. The French album is contemporary, or virtually contemporary, with the Spode pattern-book. There was a remarkably large number of pieces in production: a total of 344, omitting variations.

160 'New French shape jar'. Stoke-on-Trent (Staffordshire), Spode factory, ▷ *c.* 1825. Bone china. H. 20.8 cm. Mark: 211, inscribed on the base: 'Merlin small, She held upon her Hande'. Spode Ltd Mus., Stoke-on-Trent.
Vases of this shape are usually painstakingly decorated. Spode porcelain is rarely painted with representations of the human figure.

161 *Dish.* Stoke-on-Trent (Staffordshire), Henry & Richard Daniel factory, 1827. Bone china. L. 36.2 cm. Mark: 204. Godden of Worthing Ltd.

In 1822 Henry Daniel ceased to be a partner in the Spode concern. In 1823 Daniel set up his own works in Stoke-on-Trent, expanding his factory premises at Shelton in 1827. Richard Daniel, Henry's son, became a partner in the firm in 1826. Their porcelain is of high quality. Armorials were a speciality, and the dish reproduced here bears the arms of the Earl of Shrewsbury under whose protection the Staffordshire potters worked.

162 *Oval dish.* Stoke-on-Trent (Staffordshire), Spode factory, *c.* 1802. Bone china. L. 31.3 cm. Unmarked, pattern no. '282' painted in red. Private coll.
Just at the time when Japanese motifs went out of style in France they became wildly fashionable in Britain. This piece is painted with Kakiemon-type decoration.

Surviving pieces show that most of the shapes made were indeed relatively well designed. In the 1820 pattern-book some of their names are given showing several different sources of inspiration, for example 'Antique Incense Burner', 'Dresden  160 Shape Jug', and 'French Shape Jar'. Some moulded pieces share  159 the love of fantasy evident in contemporary porcelain of Continental manufacture. A candlestick in the shape of an elephant and a cup formed as a flower are included among the designs. As time passed, the shapes became more complicated.[153]

*Decoration*

From about 1805 until 1822 the Spode factory's decorating workshop was run in a most unusual way. It was independent of the factory, although it was on the same premises, and was under the direction of one Henry Daniel. He combined the roles of artistic director, chief painter, colour-maker, and chemist. In 1822 he set up on his own account, establishing his own factory, so that Spode was obliged to create its own decorating workshop where the high standards set by Daniel would be maintained. None of the talented painters who worked for Daniel or Spode are known by name, since they were not allowed to sign their work.

The motifs used at Spode were mostly those popular at all the other contemporary factories. They included 'Japan' patterns derived from Kakiemon or Imari porcelains,  162, 163 armorials, landscapes, birds, and flowers. In comparison with  161–164, the painting on Worcester pieces, decoration at Spode was less  168, 169 ambitiously conceived. Figure painting was virtually unknown at Spode, and few naturalistic subjects, apart from flowers, were treated. The decoration was also less abundant, even though in some cases it is evident that the factory was trying to achieve the richness of French porcelains or of Worcester pieces. Underglaze-blue painted pieces with a gilt scale-pattern and  165 over-elaborate floral decoration in enamel colours are known. This rather unhappy type of decoration was probably the result of a misunderstanding of motifs on Sèvres porcelains. It is in fact unrepresentative of Spode decoration as a whole. Coloured grounds were frequently used, but these were often delicately tinted in shades like sea-green, sky-blue, and dark or pale  167–169 brown. The grounds never completely obscured the white body and complemented the painted motifs.

163 *Fruit dish.* Stoke-on-Trent (Staffordshire), Spode factory, *c.* 1809. Bone china. L. 37.1 cm. Unmarked, pattern no. '1250' painted in red. Spode Ltd Mus., Stoke-on-Trent.
Imari-type decoration was as fashionable as painting in the Kakiemon style.

164 *Plate from a service made for the Canton office of the East India Company.*
Stoke-on-Trent (Staffordshire), Spode factory, 1823. Bone china, felspathic
glaze. D. 25.7 cm. Mark: 212. Spode Ltd Mus., Stoke-on-Trent.
Spode was so famous for its porcelain that the East India Company in Canton,
the world's largest dealer in porcelain, ordered their own service from the
Staffordshire factory in 1823.

165 *Punch-bowl, cover, and ladle.* Stoke-on-Trent (Staffordshire), Spode
factory, first quarter of the 19th century. Bone china. H. 33 cm. Mark 214.
On loan to the Spode Ltd Mus., Stoke-on-Trent.
Pattern number 1166 dates from about 1806 and was used for several decades
(see Whiter, 1978, p. 84). The pattern consists of an underglaze-blue ground
with a decoration of gilt scales and naturalistically painted polychrome
flowers. It is faintly reminiscent of 18th-century Sèvres decorative schemes,
although its over-elaboration is unfortunate. The punch-bowl appears to
have been ordered by the Duke of Newcastle.

166 *Pot-pourri.* Stoke-on-Trent (Staffordshire), Spode factory, early 19th
century. Bone china. H. 19.7 cm. Mark: 213. V & A, London (Sch. I. 789).
This two-handled, ovoid pot-pourri vase is quite closely related to several
pieces shown in the 1820 pattern-book (Pl. 158). The quality of the painting
is remarkable.

167

168

167 *Sugar bowl and stand, dish and comport.* Stoke-on-Trent (Staffordshire), Spode factory, *c.* 1825. Bone china, felspathic glaze. L. (oval dish) 36.1 cm; D. (comport) 23.8 cm. Mark: 216; dish is unmarked. Spode Ltd Mus., Stoke-on-Trent.

Like other decorative schemes on Spode porcelain, botanical painting is remarkable for its harmonious blending with the colour of the ground. A discreet grey-beige has been used on these pieces and forms a perfect foil for the strong colours used for the flowers and fruit.

168 *Part of a tea-service.* Stoke-on-Trent (Staffordshire), *c.* 1804. Bone china. H. (teapot) 16.5 cm. Unmarked, pattern no. '557' on some pieces. Spode Ltd Mus., Stoke-on-Trent.

The black-printed decoration was achieved by the bat-printing process, which was usually used to depict delicate landscapes. The decor on these pieces is enhanced by garlands and bands in gold.

169 *Ice-pail.* Stoke-on-Trent (Staffordshire), Spode factory, *c.* 1815. Bone china. H. 29.6 cm. Mark: 215. Spode Ltd Mus., Stoke-on-Trent.
The apple-green ground gives an air of sophistication, and the painted decoration of the subject is known as the 'Tame Swan'.

170 *Oil-lamp.* Stoke-on-Trent (Staffordshire), Spode factory, *c.* 1815. Bone china. L. 24.5 cm. Mark: 217. V & A, London (378-1899).
Despite the Neo-Classical shape and decoration, this piece has been imaginatively designed.

171 *Cream bowl, cover and stand, and dessert plate.* Stoke-on-Trent (Staffordshire), Spode factory, *c.* 1812. Bone china. L. (cream bowl) 21.4 cm; D. (dessert plate) 21.5 cm. Unmarked. Spode Ltd Mus., Stoke-on-Trent.
The shapes were known as 'Dolphin Embossed Shapes', and the decoration can be identified with pattern '1696'. Gold bat-printed motifs on an underglaze-blue ground combine both richness and delicacy of effect.

172 *Part of a tea-service.* Stoke-on-Trent (Staffordshire), Spode factory, *c.* 1805. Bone china. H. (teapot) 15 cm. Unmarked, pattern nos. '822' and '527' painted and incised respectively beneath saucer. Spode Ltd Mus., Stoke-on-Trent.
According to L. B. Hunt the first platinum lustres were made at Spode around 1805. Gilding has been used as a ground and for garlands and friezes on these pieces.

Just as Spode succeeded in introducing a new porcelain body, so Daniel made certain innovations in decorative technique. The conventional method of brush-painting was of course still used, but Daniel also produced numerous pieces decorated by mechanical means that were, nevertheless, of extremely high quality. Some subjects were printed in blue either under or over the glaze. Pieces decorated in this way bear some resemblance to printed creamwares. In other cases printed outlines were filled in by hand. Spode also used the bat-printing process for delicate landscapes often found on tea-services of simple shape. These were not gilded. Leonard Whiter writes of these wares: 'there was thus a veritable conspiracy against ostentation'.[154] The same bat-printing technique was used for printing in gold according to a process patented by Peter Warburton in 1810. Decoration of this kind was invariably well executed.

Gilding at Spode was always of high quality. It was used for grounds, for banded decoration, or for various different friezes. Some tea-services have leaves and flowers in gold on a blue ground. 'Worked gold'[155] was popular in France but is not often found on English porcelain; however, it was fashionable at Spode around 1818. In 1822, either shortly before or shortly after his departure from Spode, Henry Daniel invented the 'raised gold' technique.[156]

Books written in the nineteenth century and pattern-books preserved at the Spode factory, which is still in production, suggest that lustres were in common use in the nineteenth century. There were three different types: silver lustre obtained from platinum, discovered by the painter John Hancock who had been taken on by Henry Daniel in 1805; gold lustre and pink lustre both obtained from gold. There are in fact few surviving lustred Spode pieces. Pink lustre was widely used by the smaller Staffordshire factories for charming rustic scenes. Lustre decoration was also used on earthenware.

## Other Staffordshire Factories

The Spode factory was so successful that it was imitated by nearly all the other English porcelain factories, even though most of these did preserve their own distinguishing characteristics. The Coalport and Minton factories will be discussed in the next chapter since their most significant pieces are in the revived Rococo style of the period 1830 to 1850. It should be remembered that Coalport was actually making pieces in this style in the 1820s. Wedgwood never specialized in making porcelain but concentrated on fine stonewares such as jasper ware and black basalt, and produced earthenware. Yet the firm was making bone china in the years 1812 to about 1820. Between 1790 to about 1810 certain factories seem to have had difficulty in deciding what type of porcelain to produce. John Davenport, whose factory at Longport (Burslem) was making creamware from about 1794,[157] was also manufacturing hard-paste as well as a hybrid type of porcelain. The Turners and Miles Mason of Lane Delph were producing these bodies too. Miles Mason is famous for his 'ironstone china' (incorrectly called in French *faïence fine*) but he is known to have made hybrid porcelain and bone china as well. Initially he was in partnership with several others but later, from 1804 until 1811, he worked alone at Lane Delph. The New Hall factory, established in 1781 by Staffordshire potters eager to make hard-paste porcelain of the Continental type, began to make bone china in 1814. It seems to have continued in production until 1835 when the factory closed. Tea-services of modest design rather than of the ambitiously conceived but non-utilitarian variety were the speciality of this factory. Although somewhat rigid in outline, the shapes of these pieces are well suited to the moulded ornamentation that characterizes them: the angular shapes were fluted and gadrooned. As time went on the shapes became clumsier but retained their tasteful simplicity. Delicately painted friezes, garlands, and scattered flowers were the favourite decorative motifs. Peter Warburton of New Hall patented his bat-printing process for gold in 1810. The technique was to be adopted at the Spode factory. New Hall represents the current of opposition to the large factories whose elaborate decorative schemes had reduced the pictorial tradition to absurdity.

Most of the other factories lay between the two extremes. Terry Lockett has defined the style of Staffordshire porcelain at

173 *Cup and saucer.* Staffordshire, unknown factory, c. 1820. Bone china. H. (cup) 5.7 cm; D. (saucer) 14.3 cm. Unmarked. V & A, London (1503-1924).
The pieces are decorated with a naive design on a pink lustre ground. This kind of porcelain, made for those who could not afford anything more costly, appeals to contemporary taste because of its simplicity.

174 *Teapot*. Etruria (Staffordshire), Josiah Wedgwood & Sons, *c*. 1815. Bone china. L. 24.77 cm. Mark: 176, and pattern no. '470' in red. Wedgwood Mus., Barlaston.
The Wedgwood factory, which is known for its creamware and fine stoneware, made comparatively little porcelain. This shape was originally made in creamware around 1770 and was fashionable at the beginning of the 19th century, when it was produced in bone china.

175 *Part of a tea-service*. Etruria (Staffordshire), Josiah Wedgwood & Sons, *c*. 1815. Bone china. L. (teapot) 27.94 cm. Unmarked, pattern no. '685' painted on several pieces. Wedgwood Mus., Barlaston.
Porcelain made at Wedgwood from 1812 is notable for its simplicity, a characteristic shared by most early 19th-century English porcelain. The landscapes, identified by inscriptions on the bases of the pieces, were painted by John Cutts (1772–1851) who worked at the Wedgwood factory between 1812 and about 1816.

176 *Bowl*. Etruria (Staffordshire), Josiah Wedgwood & Sons, *c*. 1815. Bone china. L. 25.72 cm. Mark: 176. Wedgwood Mus., Barlaston.
A few pieces of Wedgwood porcelain are painted with charming polychrome scenes. The decoration on this piece is attributed to John Cutts, after Pillement.

177

178

179

177 *Tureen, cover, and stand from a dessert service.* Longport-Burslem (Staffordshire), Davenport factory, *c.* 1810. Porcelain. H. 17 cm. Mark: 180. Coll. Geoffrey Godden, Worthing.
The pieces show the English porcelain-manufacturers' delight in extravagant forms, although the decoration is of the rather conventional chinoiserie type.

178 *Dish.* Longport-Burslem (Staffordshire), Davenport factory, *c.* 1815. Bone china. D. 20.6 cm. Mark: 181. V & A, London (2550-1901). Davenport porcelain often resembles Derby. It is likely that this dish was painted by Thomas Steele, a fruit painter who was a native of the Potteries and worked at the Derby factory between 1815 and about 1826.

179 *Cup and saucer.* Longport-Burslem (Staffordshire), Davenport factory, *c.* 1820–1825. Bone china. H. (cup) 7.5 cm; D. (saucer) 12.7 cm. Mark: 181. V & A, London (Sch. I. 788).
The *grisaille* decoration on a green ground with gilt enrichments on this cup and saucer is rather reminiscent of Paris porcelain of the First Empire.

180 *Cups and saucer of 'Bute' shape.* Shelton (Staffordshire), New Hall factory, *c.* 1815. Bone china. D. (saucer) 14 cm. Unmarked. Coll. Geoffrey Godden, Worthing.
These pieces are decorated with coloured-in printed designs and are more ambitious than most New Hall decoration, which is rarely figurative.

181 *Cups and saucer.* Shelton (Staffordshire), New Hall factory, *c.* 1810. Hybrid hard-paste porcelain. D. (saucer) 14 cm. Unmarked. Coll. Geoffrey Godden, Worthing.
In 1810 one of the owners of the factory, Warburton, patented a process for printing in gold or platinum. These pieces have been decorated by this method, often found in conjunction with a blue ground.

182 *Cream jug.* Shelton (Staffordshire), New Hall factory, 1814–*c.* 1831. Bone china. H. 8.2 cm. Unmarked, pattern no. '1161' in gold. CM & AG, Stoke-on-Trent.
New Hall made phosphatic porcelain between 1814 and 1831. The design of this piece is simple but the jug is richly decorated.

183 *Sugar bowl and cover.* Shelton (Staffordshire), New Hall factory, *c.* 1800. Hybrid hard-paste porcelain. H. 14.6 cm. Unmarked, painted pattern no. '89'. Coll. Geoffrey Godden, Worthing.
The extremely simple shape, with its elegant fluted decoration and almost rudimentary painted motifs, is typical of early 19th-century English taste, which was characterized by sobriety.

184 *Cup and saucer.* Shelton (Staffordshire), New Hall factory, *c.* 1820–1830. Bone china. H. (cup) 5.7 cm; D. (saucer) 14.3 cm. Mark: 183 and no. '88'. V & A, London (C. 676-1935).
In the first quarter of the 19th century vast numbers of small pieces were made in Staffordshire which have pleasing, if unsophisticated, decoration.

this time in the catalogue of the exhibition entitled 'Staffordshire Porcelain 1740–1851'.[158] He comments that, at the beginning of the nineteenth century, Staffordshire porcelain manufacturers had given up their pedantic adherence to the Neo-Classical idiom. The style had now been moderated by two 'enlivening forces'. The first came from the Continent: English manufacturers were doing their best to make porcelain that would equal in quality the productions of the Sèvres factory. The other influence was that of the school of English water-colourists. The typically British taste for delicately painted landscape scenes led to pieces both simple and poetic.

As time went by the number of Staffordshire potters continued to increase and there was an ever-greater demand for their wares. Twenty factories are listed in local directories for 1805, forty-seven appear in directories for 1835–1836, and these figures, even if only approximate, certainly indicate the scale of growth of the industry. Mechanization of manufacturing and decorating processes spread rapidly. Only the biggest factories could carry on using craft methods, and even they had to accept a large measure of mechanization.

180

181

183

182

184

185 *Cup and saucer.* Lane Delph (Staffordshire), Miles Mason factory, 1805. Bone china. H. (cup) 6.1 cm; D. (saucer) 13.7 cm. Mark: 177. V & A, London (C. 2662-1901).
Printed decoration was in use on English earthenware from the mid-18th century. Chinoiserie scenes were common and were sometimes printed on porcelain. Miles Mason made a large amount of earthenware, which he sold under the name 'ironstone china', as the name china conjured up porcelain. Mason also produced painted porcelain.

186 *Stand from a dessert service.* Shelton (Staffordshire), New Hall factory, c. 1815–1825. Bone china. L. 25 cm. Unmarked, painted pattern no. '1707'. Coll. Geoffrey Godden, Worthing.
The Rococo taste came back into fashion from about 1815–1820. It is expressed here in the use of elaborate decoration, some motifs being in relief.

186

187

188

189 *Sugar bowl and cover.* Lane Delph (Staffordshire), Miles Mason factory, *c.* 1805. Porcelain. H. 13 cm. Unmarked. Coll. Geoffrey Godden, Worthing.
Close analysis of shapes has enabled specialists to determine the precise origin of various pieces. This is a typical Miles Mason shape, decorated with a printed chinoiserie scene coloured by hand.

190 *Tureen, cover, and stand.* Shelton/Hanley (Staffordshire), John and William Ridgway factory, *c.* 1815. Bone china. H. 14 cm. Unmarked, painted pattern no. '565'. Coll. Geoffrey Godden, Worthing.
This high-quality piece has an elegant shape and charming painted decoration.

◁◁ 187 *Teapot.* Shelton/Hanley (Staffordshire), John and William Ridgway factory, Cauldon Place works, *c.* 1820. Bone china. H. 17.7 cm. Unmarked, painted pattern no. '2/1380'. Coll. Geoffrey Godden, Worthing.
Despite the high quality of execution, this piece from the 1820s is rather over-elaborate.

◁ 188 *Teapot.* Liverpool (Lancashire), Herculaneum Pottery Company, *c.* 1805–1810. Bone china. L. 25.4 cm. Mark: 179. MCM, Liverpool (1967.22).
At the beginning of the 19th century, the influence of Staffordshire pottery on Liverpool wares was considerable, as this teapot shows.

# III 1830–1850: From Art Institute to Industrial Manufactory

191 *Ovoid teapot with serpent handle and spout.* Sèvres, Imperial Porcelain factory, *c.* 1830 (?). Hard-paste porcelain. H. 14 cm. Unmarked. Pierre-Yves Guillemain Coll., Neuilly.
19th-century Sèvres porcelain is nearly always marked, except for pieces made at the beginning of the century. The bizarre shape of this piece was first modelled in 1808. The Musée des Arts décoratifs, Paris, has an example decorated in 1833.

192 *Chocolate service painted with Duguesclin et les plus fameux guerriers, ses contemporains.* Sèvres, Royal Porcelain factory, 1835. Hard-paste porcelain. L. (oval tray) 45 cm; H. (teapot) 14 cm; (cups) 8 cm. Marks: (tray) 67, (teapot) 68, (sugar bowl) 69. MNC, Sèvres (7547).
The decoration was devised by Leloy and carried out by Barbin, while Moriot was responsible for the portraits. On the tray is a scene representing Duguesclin and Clisson Pledging Themselves as Brothers-in-Arms at Pontorson on 20 October 1370. This scene after Bergeret had already been used on a breakfast service exhibited in 1819. Le Guay painted the tray,

Moriot the portraits. From 1819 Sèvres showed a marked interest in the Middle Ages. The shape of the milk jug stands out from the straight-sided forms of the other pieces in the *déjeuner*. Sèvres traditionally mixed shapes that were not designed to harmonize with each other.

193 *'Royal Family' Bowl.* Sèvres, Royal Porcelain factory, 1837. Hard-paste ▷ porcelain. H. (without handles) 43 cm. Mark: 70. Le Grand Trianon, Versailles (1939 V 1146).
This pattern was planned by Leloy; the portraits of the members of the Orléans family are by Moriot after Wintherhalter. The mount is by the bronze-founder Bouquet (Ledoux-Lebard, 1975, p.194). Although many patterns honouring the sovereign, his family, and heroic acts were produced during the First Empire by the Sèvres factory, in the Restoration period royal iconography was used much more sparsely.

Porcelain factories were invariably established and operated in the hope that they would earn their proprietors not only esteem as art connoisseurs but also tangible economic benefits. Never in the eighteenth century, however, was the economic consideration as important as it became in the second quarter of the nineteenth century, following the Neo-Classical period. With the exception of Sèvres, Nymphenburg, and St Petersburg, the prime concern of every factory was to avoid a deficit at all costs. Porcelain became just another product, its

artistic character now playing only a secondary role. In the interests of profitability and competitiveness and with a view to increasing productivity and sales, developments in kiln construction and firing methods and in the technology of paste preparation and decoration were pushed forward everywhere. Industrialization came in with a vengeance, and anyone who was not prepared to go along with it found himself—not inevitably before 1850 but certainly after that date—at a hopeless disadvantage *vis-à-vis* more 'progressive' competitors.

# FRANCE

## Sèvres

During the period 1830–1850 France experienced twenty years of relative peace during which the bourgeoisie grew increasingly wealthy. In the preceding period Alexandre Brongniart had worked under several different sovereigns without being greatly affected by the various changes. Louis-Philippe's reign (1830–1848) passed uneventfully as far as the Sèvres factory was concerned. The ageing Brongniart continued to work on according to the same principles as he had established at the very beginning of the century. The source of the eclecticism seen at Sèvres as early as the First Empire period had been exploited to the full, and in the search for new inspiration the taste for the Middle Ages was consciously pressed into service. It is evident, for instance, on a new edition of the chocolate service known as the *service Duguesclin et les plus fameux guerriers, ses contemporains* ('Duguesclin and His Famous Warrior Contemporaries' Service)[1] of 1835; the original model for the decoration on the tray is preserved at the Sèvres factory and dates from 1818, which is also the date of the first *déjeuner* with this type of decoration. At times this eclecticism led to the production of pieces that we find merely amusing. One of these is a 'Roman' pendulum clock[2] of fantastical shape bearing a central plaque which depicts Charlemagne Receiving a Superb Clepsydra (or Water-Clock) from Harun-ar-Rashid.

### The Reappearance of White Grounds

It would be unfair, however, to maintain that this period produced no new and original works. There were in particular two tendencies that serve to make the productions of the Louis-Philippe period at Sèvres readily identifiable. White grounds began to be visible once more as pieces were less heavily decorated. The decoration itself was almost invariably printed, especially when gilding was used.

Naturally plates destined for large expensive services were still decorated in the manner of small-scale easel paintings. The services produced were: the *service agronomique* ('Agronomic Service', 1831–1844), the *service forestier* (1834–1841), the *service historique* ('Historical Service of the Château of Fontainebleau', 1839–1844), which was designed to be hung on the walls of the Galerie des Assiettes at Fontainebleau.[3] The services termed *des productions de la nature* were composed according to the strict formula used at the beginning of the nineteenth century.

194 *'Roman' clock.* Sèvres, Royal Porcelain factory, 1845. Hard-paste porcelain. H. 90 cm. Unmarked. MNC, Sèvres (7557).
As its name indicates, this clock was inspired by Roman art, interpreted here in the most fanciful way. The sides, which imitate alabaster, are decorated with plaques painted *en camaïeu* with scenes symbolizing Mechanics and Astronomy. The plaque on the front was painted by M.F. Régnier with a scene entitled Charlemagne Receiving a Superb Clepsydre (or 'Water-Clock') from Harun-ar-Rashid.

195 *Plate from the service forestier.* Sèvres, Royal Porcelain factory, 1835. Hard-paste porcelain. D. 24 cm. Inscribed (front): 'L'If d'Andwerke pres Windsor', (reverse): 'Il a 32 pieds de circonférence/On lui attribue plus de 1000 ans/Entrevue d'Henry VIII et d'Ann de Boleyn/sous son ombrage'. [tiré de Sylvia Britannia], (border freize): 'Pin et Sapin'. Mark: 66. MNC, Sèvres (2630).
This Woodlands Service, made between 1834 and 1841, has a painting in the centre that is supposed to imitate an easel-painting. The border decoration acts as the picture frame. This plate was painted by Langlacé.

196   *Plaque painted with the Deliverance of St Peter.* Sèvres, Royal Porcelain factory, 1842. Hard-paste porcelain. L. 92 cm; H. 78 cm. Mark: inaccessible. Inscribed (lower border): 'La délivrance de St Pierre par Raphaël. Copiée à Rome par A. Constantin 1842'. MNC, Sèvres (7644).
Raphael's paintings were very much in vogue at the time when most of these 'paintings on porcelain' were done at Sèvres. Constantin also copied *The School of Athens* and *The Miracle at Bolsena* in 1833.

## Printed Decoration

It was in connection with the *service Louis-Philippe à Fontainebleau* ('Louis-Philippe at Fontainebleau Service')[4] that printing was first officially mentioned as being in use after 1845. A lithographic process was employed, allowing a considerable range of colours.[5] The decoration consisted of running animals within scrolls and was directly applied to the white porcelain. The services made for the château of Neuilly and the Trianon at Versailles have white grounds, while that made for the château d'Eu has a delicate green border overlaid with gold and polychrome decorative motifs.

Although it is difficult to prove that virtually all the gold decoration found on services made in this period is printed, it seems likely that this is the case. It is certainly true for each of the ordinary services made for the royal residences. Each residence was provided with a *service des Princes* ('Princely Service'), decorated with a border of ivy leaves and the royal monogram in gold, a *service des Officiers* ('Officers' Service'), which had a gilt monogram on a white ground, and a so-called *service d'Office* for the use of the staff, decorated with the royal monogram in blue on a white ground.[6] It is not known whether the printing of these services was done at the Sèvres factory by its own staff or by Legros d'Anizy. It seems likely that the Sèvres workers themselves were responsible for the decoration, even though Legros d'Anizy did occasionally carry out work for Sèvres up until 1848. In any case, Brongniart sought to conceal the fact that mechanical processes were employed to decorate the products of the royal factory. White grounds came back into use for everyday table services, and by the Restoration had become the accustomed decorative effect.

## Diversity of Decorative Themes

Like the services mentioned above, ornamental wares were either created in a style faithfully copying that of the preceding period, or they exhibited an exaggerated use of relief decoration. An example of the first type, based on the Neo-Classical idiom, is the *vase étrusque à rouleaux* of 1832.[7] It is decorated with scenes illustrating physical education in ancient Greece, painted by Béranger. In the second category can be counted the work of the ornamentalist Chenavard[8] as well as

a large part of Alexandre-Evariste Fragonard's work. The latter had been working at Sèvres since the time of the first restoration of the monarchy (1814) and was the designer of the *vase de la Renaissance*.[9] This piece is more pretentious than any product of the Paris factories and is in fact a copy of the type of relief-decorated pieces made by Jacob Petit.

Experiments made to imitate Limoges enamels on porcelain heralded the establishment of a workshop for enamelling on metal, which was set up in 1845. Some vases with decoration in the style of Limoges enamels are known. The enamelling workshop itself was closed in 1872.

197

198

198 *Vase.* Sèvres, Royal Porcelain factory, 1841. Hard-paste porcelain. H. 18 cm. Mark: 71. Inscribed (label in the handwriting of the museum Keeper, D. Riocreux): 'décor fait par Meyer Heine, peintre en émail de Paris, avec des procédés qui lui sont particuliers'. MNC, Sèvres (2937).
This piece was one of the first attempts made at Sèvres to imitate 16th-century Limoges enamels. The experimental work done at the factory led to the establishment in 1845 of a workshop for enamelling on copper which was in production until 1872.

197 *'Renaissance Vase' or 'François I Vase'.* Sèvres, Royal Porcelain factory, 1834–1835. Hard-paste porcelain. H. (without handles) 80 cm. Unmarked. MNC, Sèvres (24963).
This piece, designed by A.-E. Fragonard, is typical of the Restoration period in its use of abundant decoration. Here the motifs are modelled in relief and were executed by Hyacinthe Régnier.

199 *Page from a pattern-book, probably dating from the 1830s on the evidence* ▷ *of the religious group.* Paris, Dagoty and Honoré factory: pattern-book. Cabinet des dessins, MdAd, Paris (CD. 3857, Pl. 22).
Other Paris factories, such as Darte, are known to have made cups in the shape of a swan around 1810. An album of shapes used at different times between 1796 and 1865 at one of the Paris factories, probably Dagoty and Honoré, is preserved in the Musée des Arts décoratifs.

200 *Vase.* Paris, Honoré factory, second quarter of the 19th century. Hard-paste porcelain. H. 22 cm. Mark: 32. Madeleine Castaing Coll., Paris. This extraordinary green vase, its shape reminiscent of vegetable forms, is an example of the wide range of pieces made by Paris porcelain factories.

201 *Pair of vases.* Paris, Denuelle factory, *c.* 1830–1835. Hard-paste porcelain. H. 17.5 cm. Unmarked. MAD, Limoges (ADL 3019, 3020). These unmarked vases were presented to the Adrien Dubouché museum, Limoges, by Madame Denuelle so that their provenance is beyond doubt. Denuelle exhibited 'Etruscan vases' at the 1834 Exhibition.

## Paris

Even during the period when rigid Neo-Classicism was in fashion, the Paris factories were already showing a taste for the unusual. It goes without saying that this tendency was to be even more pronounced in the ensuing period.

### The Discry-Talmours-Hurel Factory

In the first quarter of the nineteenth century the elder of the Darte brothers, Joseph, was the owner of a rather run-of-the-mill porcelain factory situated at 26 rue Popincourt. Discry succeeded him in 1823, improving the wares. He seems to have remained relatively unaffected by the difficulties that caused the failure of many of his competitors. In 1837 he went into partnership with a businessman named Charles de Talmours, but the partnership was dissolved in 1841. Talmours then took Hurel as his partner, while Discry concentrated on the manufacture of ceramic colours.[10]

This factory made several innovations all designed to produce wares that would compete with Chinese porcelains. During the first third of the nineteenth century Chinese influence had not, of course, totally disappeared and there are some pieces, such as the *cache-pots* ('flower-pot cases') probably dating from the 1820s and made at an unidentified factory (now in the Sèvres museum),[11] which are decorated with chinoiseries. However, Discry was not aiming to produce traditional chinoiseries but rather to create porcelain which was close to that made in the East. He experimented with celadon grounds, tried to create a process for obtaining blue grounds by dipping (a technique that gained him a gold medal in 1839), 203 and also devised a decorative process using applied slip. This last was to gain wide popularity at a later date. His applied slips are matt, whereas those produced at Sèvres have a shiny appearance.

202 Discry was also responsible for the creation of new shapes for tea-services. He presented to the Sèvres museum an undecorated service exhibited in 1834. Its scalloped edges are typical of the taste of this period.[12]

202 *Milk jug and cup and saucer from a tea-service exhibited in 1834.* Paris, Discry and Talmours factory, *c.* 1834. Hard-paste porcelain. H. (milk jug) 14 cm; H. (cup) 6 cm. Unmarked. MNC, Sèvres (1692[1] and [5]). English influence is evident in the bulbous shapes and decorative reliefs.

203 *Pair of vases.* Paris, Discry factory, *c.* 1845. Hard-paste porcelain. ▷ H. 46 cm. Unmarked, MNC, Sèvres (4223). These Chinese-influenced vases with their celadon ground and applied slip decoration are exceptional. They must date from before 1851, since they entered the Sèvres museum at that time, proving that Paris factories were quick to react to changing tastes. The applied slip decoration has been left unglazed to emphasize its relief effect.

204 *Covered bowl and tray.* Paris, Jacob Petit factory, mid-19th century. ▷ Hard-paste porcelain. D. (stand) 20 cm. Mark: 36. MNC, Sèvres (23 607). This piece is in the 18th-century style favoured by Jacob Petit. The flowers in relief are reminiscent of Meissen, while the 'partridge-eye' ground repeats a Sèvres motif. The combination of these two sources of inspiration is characteristic of Jacob Petit's work.

## The Jacob Petit Factory

Jacob Mardochée (1796–1868), who married Anne Adélaïde Petit and took the name Jacob Petit, is the most famous French porcelain manufacturer of the period 1830–1860. He had more artistic training than most of his competitors in the porcelain industry, having studied painting under Gros. He was also widely travelled. His first factory at Belleville was soon too small for him, and by 1834 he had established another at Fontainebleau. He enjoyed considerable success, and in 1839 had on the payroll 150 employees at his own workshops and more than 60 people working for him outside the factory.[13] However, he appears to have been better at making porcelain than at dealing with the complexities of finance. In 1848 he was declared bankrupt, but he carried on working and only sold the factory at Fontainebleau in 1862. In 1866 he was still listed in the rue Paradis-Poissonnière. He died in 1868.

The 'Jacob Petit style' is not easy to define since variety is one of its chief characteristics. Petit was particularly fond of creating porcelain that would appeal to people's sense of fun. Much of his inspiration came from eighteenth-century French and German porcelain. His tureens in the shape of animals are based on, and have all the quality of, the zoomorphic tureens in earthenware that had been made at Strasbourg, Höchst and

206   *Teapot.* Paris, Jacob Petit factory, *c.* 1840. Hard-paste porcelain. L. 25.5 cm. Mark: 37. MNC, Sèvres (23 621).
Dark colours became fashionable in the reign of Louis-Philippe (1830–1848), and the black ground of this piece is fairly characteristic of the period. The shape is clearly influenced by English porcelain teapots. The thickly applied gilding is less shiny in appearance than was usual on Paris porcelains.

205   *Veilleuse, or tea warmer.* Paris, Jacob Petit factory, or one of his imitators, mid-19th century. Hard-paste porcelain. H. 32 cm. Unmarked. MNC, Sèvres (23 629).
This piece, extravagantly designed in a manner defying aesthetic judgement, is typical of the 'Jacob Petit style'. It is in four parts: the base; the lady's dress containing a spirit lamp, its ventilation holes formed by the pockets; the bodice forming the teapot itself, its handle in the guise of an arm and its spout formed by the other arm; and the hat or lid of the teapot.

207   *Tobacco jar.* Paris, Jacob Petit factory, second third of the 19th century. Hard-paste porcelain. W. 28 cm. Mark: 39. MAD, Limoges (ADL 3324).
Its function takes second place to its decorative appeal. The subject represents the *amours vendangeurs,* or cupids of the wine harvest. The mark on the base of the jar imitates the Meissen factory mark but cannot be mistaken for it.

208  *Ornament.* Paris, Jacob Petit factory, *c.* 1850. Hard-paste porcelain. H. 32 cm. Mark: 38. MAD, Limoges (ADL 23 592).
This piece seems to have no practical function, despite the presence of the two movable containers on either side of the female figure.

Sceaux in the previous century. His 'snowball' vases are
204 conceived in the Meissen idiom. The 'partridge-eye' grounds he used to decorate some of his pieces were originally developed at Sèvres and were enormously popular in the reign of Louis XVI. Jacob Petit's figures are sometimes copied directly from Meissen models; in the Adrien Dubouché museum at Limoges is a figure of a man with his female companion, both reclining and holding a basket, closely based on Meissen originals. The
289 female figure was also made in England at the Coalport[14] and Minton[15] factories, but the English versions are less faithful to the original. Jacob Petit had in fact visited England in his youth and borrowed some of his shapes from English pieces, especially
206 the shapes of his tea-services.

Jacob Petit's originality is undeniable. At this time the Neo-Rococo style reigned supreme almost everywhere. Only the royal factory clung to the Neo-Classical style, which was barely affected by the element of fantasy introduced by Alexandre-Evariste Fragonard. Jacob Petit was therefore able to assume the mantle of style-setter, which he held on to tenaciously. He drew heavily on the models of earlier periods, mixing elements from one with ideas taken from others, ornamenting his creations endlessly with flowers, jewels, and fruit modelled in relief. He created thousands of different models of *veilleuses,* or coffee or tea warmers, all following the
205 same general principle: the *veilleuse* was formed as a female figure, her dress covering the candle of the warmer and her torso comprising the teapot. One of her arms was the handle while the other formed the spout. The lid of the teapot was her hat. Petit's scent-bottles were made in the shape of cushions or crowns resting on cushions, as pagodas or figures wearing a hat that formed the stopper, and as Gothic or Renaissance buildings. His invention knew no bounds. He has long been the subject of criticism because of his 'bad taste'. In 1906 Chavagnac and Grollier wrote of his work:

> Jacob Petit made a large number of figures, both enamelled and biscuit, which were supposed to imitate Meissen. However, they can always be easily distinguished 207 from their originals because they are in poor taste and clearly Neo-Rococo in style. The same applies to his other pieces, which are often decorated with relief flowers 208 painted in a naturalistic manner. A green ground is most frequently used.
> Clocks, candlesticks, inkwells and so on are common. The pieces are not badly made but unfortunately the models themselves, as we have already said, are in deplorable taste, which is not the maker's own fault, but rather the fault of the age in which he lived.[16]

In 1906 nineteenth-century taste was almost universally condemned, that being an era as yet unaffected by the mania

209 *Vase (showing both sides)*. Paris, unidentified factory, *c.* 1845. Hard-paste porcelain. H. 46.5 cm. Unmarked. MAD, Limoges (ADL 3127-3128). The sombre colours used are typical of the Louis-Philippe era (1830–1848).

210 *Apothecary jar and cover.* Paris, Pochet-Deroche decorating workshop, after 1834. Hard-paste porcelain. H. 46 cm. Mark: 40. MNC, Sèvres (14 588).

Deroche's workshop and its successors, including the one run by Deroche's son-in-law Pochet-Deroche after 1834, specialized in painting porcelain for pharmacists and perfumers. From about 1820 onwards Paris decorators bought 'blanks' from Limoges factories as well as from the steadily decreasing number of Paris factories.

for 'anything old'. Behind the scorn expressed by these authors, one can in fact sense a certain admiration for the exceptional quality of Jacob Petit's work.

Jacob Petit's work has suffered by being associated in most people's minds with the innumerable inferior productions made by various factories imitating Petit. These factories had no hesitation in 'borrowing' Petit's mark if necessary. The pieces which we now call 'Jacob Petit' are only those in his style, rather than those he actually made. There is no criterion except quality that distinguishes genuine Jacob Petit productions from their imitations; the copies themselves give us some idea of the importance of the originals they so poorly reproduce.

### Decorators

During the period 1830–1850 there were no great porcelain-makers in Paris. The activity of the decorators was also reduced in scope, although it did not altogether cease. Many of the decorators whose careers had begun during the First Empire period, like Legros d'Anizy for example, were still active. Other younger decorators were up and coming such as Francisque Rousseau, a porcelain and ceramic-colour merchant, who also decorated porcelain and made a number of technical innovations. He is listed at the rue de Ménilmontant in 1838. At the 1844 Exhibition he was awarded a gold medal for his 'relief decoration in gold, which is both solid and inexpensive, his gilding on ceramic or enamel [i.e. metal] reliefs in white or polychrome, his durable and economical gilding on *garnitures*'.[17] We can see here the beginning of the search for relief gilding that could be cheaply produced. It is difficult not to be aware of the decadence to come: in the second half of the nineteenth century gold decoration was all too often both thick and dull in appearance.

Many anonymous porcelain manufacturers and decorators have left behind a wide range of creations reflecting their clients' changing tastes. The Neo-Gothic style came into fashion in about 1830. Everyday objects were often left almost undecorated, with the exception of a few gilt lines and coloured flowers, though their shapes had more vitality.

## Limoges

At Limoges, the period 1830–1850 was marked by the establishment of several new factories, mostly of minor importance. The effects of economic crises, especially in 1830, threatened the very existence of the biggest factories in both Limoges and Paris. However, the concerns that improved production and lowered manufacturing costs experienced continuous growth. The period was also marked by the appearance of a new style.

◁ 211 *Tea-service*. Paris, unknown factory, c. 1840. Hard-paste porcelain. H. (teapot) 12.5 cm. Unmarked. MNC, Sèvres (18737, 18738).
Neo-Gothic decorative schemes were typical of Romantic taste. These unmarked pieces are difficult to date, except perhaps by referring to other artistic achievements, for example the construction of the Neo-Gothic Church of Sainte-Clotilde in Paris, begun in 1840.

212–214 *Pages from a factory catalogue listing 223 different items of porcelain.* Limoges, engraved catalogue issued by the Bonneval factory, c. 1830. Bibliothèque de l'Ecole des Arts décoratifs, Limoges.
Some pieces are closely related to Dagoty and Honoré wares. Limoges factories supplied 'blanks' for decorating in Paris; they therefore had to make pieces in harmony with Parisian tastes.

215 *Plate from the service made on the occasion of the marriage of Alluaud's daughter, Louise, to Aimé Malevergne in 1834.* Limoges, François Alluaud's factory, 1834. Hard-paste porcelain. D. 28 cm. Unmarked. MAD, Limoges (ADL 6491).
Despite the high-quality painting and the gilt decoration, the service is simply designed.

There was an increase in the number of factories operating in the countryside around Limoges during the reigns of Charles X and Louis-Philippe. In the country labour costs were lower, and wood, and sometimes kaolin, were found locally. The 212–214 Marquis de Bonneval, for instance, owner of the Coussac factory, also owned kaolin deposits, which he tried to exploit directly by using the material in his own factory. Since he was a poor businessman, he was obliged to subcontract the manufacture of porcelain to a succession of skilled men who each tried their luck, one after another, until eventually the factory buildings were turned into a farm in 1858. The Magnac-Bourg factory, situated some 18 miles to the south of Limoges, was plagued by bankruptcies and fires. It regained a measure of stability during the Second Empire period (1852–1870). The crises of 1830 and 1848 seriously affected the Bourganeuf factory, which was forced to close in 1850 for lack of state support.

Two factories were established at Saint-Léonard in 1825: the Récollet factory only ceased production in 1963 and the Pont de Noblat factory is still in existence. The Sauviat factory was studied by Jean d'Albis and Céleste Romanet as a typical example of a small concern prey to numerous difficulties. It was set up in 1836 by timber merchants who hoped to sell their wood to the factory at a good price, and they subcontracted the porcelain-making side of the business. Absolutely no maintenance work was done on the factory buildings, which fell into an incredible state of dilapidation. The factory only recovered under the Third Republic, becoming successful at a time when wood was more and more rarely used as fuel for

firing kilns. At Sauviat, however, it continued to be used, and the quality of the porcelain obtained using these old-fashioned methods ensured the success of the concern at the end of the nineteenth century.

There were in fact serious problems arising from the question of what fuel was to be used in the industry. Alluaud considered the matter during the First Empire period, then Ruaud studied the technology of the kiln and was the first to decide that pit coal should be used. His decision could only take effect in 1857, in the Second Empire, after the construction of the Paris to Limoges railway line, which enabled the fuel to be transported easily to the porcelain factories. Ruaud had in fact perfected the technique of coal-firing long before this time. He occupied the former Monnerie factory, which had premises in the Augustine convent, in the years between 1829 and 1869, and here he introduced mass-production methods.

There were other factories that concentrated exclusively on the production of luxury pieces. The factories we have already mentioned limited their production to everyday items. The Michel and Valin factory, set up by two bronze-founders from Paris, Michel Aaron and Jean-Baptiste Valin, also a sculptor, made pieces in the style normally only associated with Jacob Petit. In 1845 Aaron went to Chantilly, while Valin continued cf. pp. 235– to operate the factory until his death in 1855. After this date his successors made only domestic tableware. The Lesme factory, founded in 1839, confined its activity to decorating 220 wares, though it made porcelain in the Second Empire period.

*Techniques*
To an even greater extent than at Paris, the survival of the Limoges factories was linked to their ability to improve their technical processes. As we have seen, Jean-Baptiste Ruaud was, in the eyes of his contemporaries, most capable of achieving this. There were problems connected with firing methods using wood and coal, the problems with the latter being insoluble until the opening of the railway line to Limoges, even though the technical aspect had been explored by the Belgian engineer, Merkens, and the porcelain-maker, Vital Roux of Noirlac in 1845, with the help of Ruaud. Ruaud introduced a steam-engine fuelled with peat into his factory in 1844, as well as a jigger for plate-making, which operated by lowering a *mu-caliper* vertically on to the plates. These innovations were only adopted by other Limoges concerns twenty-five years later.

Ruaud also carried out research into decorative processes and was the first to fire cobalt-blue at a high temperature.

*Styles*
A large number of pieces made at Limoges at this period are indistinguishable from those produced in the preceding period. Since there is almost no known signed or dated piece made in the period under discussion, we are obliged to rely merely on attributions.

The only piece which can be identified with any certainty is an extraordinary pendulum clock-case in the Adrien Dubouché 216 museum in Limoges. It was shown in the 1839 Exhibition by Michel and Valin and is decorated with the figure of an Arab

216 *Clock-case: Arab Rider Attacked by a Tiger.* Limoges, Michel and Valin ▷ factory, 1839. Hard-paste porcelain. H. 62 cm. Unmarked. MAD, Limoges (ADL 8672).
Pieces of this kind are usually attributed to Jacob Petit. They are more remarkable as pieces of sculpture than for their usefulness. Michel and Valin were awarded a bronze medal at the 1839 Exhibition for this and eleven other pieces.

217 *Vase.* Limoges, unidentified factory, *c.* 1830. Hard-paste porcelain. H. 13 cm. Unmarked. MAD, Limoges (ADL 8804).
The somewhat bulbous oblate shape of this piece was to become characteristic of church vases during the 19th century.

218 *Pierced basket.* Limoges, unidentified factory, *c.* 1830. Hard-paste porcelain. H. 26 cm. Unmarked. MAD, Limoges (ADL 6502).
Exuberantly decorated pieces were being made at Limoges at the same period as Jacob Petit was setting the trend in Paris for porcelain encrusted with reliefs.

220

221

220 *Vase.* Limoges, Lesme brothers' decorating workshop, *c.* 1850. Hard-paste porcelain. H. 34 cm. Unmarked. MAD, Limoges (ADL 2473).
The Lesme brothers specialized in decoration copied from Chinese porcelain but also created original works.

221 *Veilleuse, or tea warmer.* Limoges, unidentified factory, *c.* 1830–1840. Hard-paste porcelain. H. 31.5 cm. Unmarked. MAD, Limoges (ADL 2620).
The Limoges factories sometimes produced pieces as fantastic as those made at Paris. This example is in the Neo-Gothic style.

◁ 219 *Part of a tea-service.* Limoges, unidentified factory, *c.* 1850. Hard-paste porcelain. L. (tray) 30 cm. Unmarked. MAD, Limoges (ADL 2638).
Elaborately decorated pieces discovered in the Limoges region are traditionally attributed to local factories but could equally well have been painted in Paris during the same period.

rider fighting a tiger. Both figures are painted in colours. The clock dial and its movement are incorporated into the base, which is painted sky blue. It stands on four scroll-shaped gilt feet surmounted by small figures in Turkish dress. It is likely that had this pendulum clock not been positively identified as a Limoges product, it would have been attributed to Jacob Petit. The piece is an expression of the Romantic taste of the period. The upper part of this clock has all the violence of a Barye sculpture, while the lower part exhibits the taste for fantasy shared by the best contemporary Paris porcelain. Aaron and Valin had, of course, come from Paris, and a great deal of Limoges porcelain was made for the Paris market. Many Parisians came to work in the Limoges area: the manufacturer-owners of the Récollet factory at Saint-Léonard had done precisely this. For these reasons, the pieces made at Paris and Limoges are often indistinguishable from each other.

217 The collection at the Limoges museum, which is mainly of local origin, does, however, contain pieces that are unlikely to have come from far afield. Church vases in particular are mostly traceable to convents in Limoges itself, as they were loaned to the museum at the behest of the mayor. These vases are in the shape of cornucopiae, growing from a narrow point to a wide mouth, their outline evoking a full-blown, trumpet-shaped flower. At the point they are ornamented with heavy relief motifs or Rococo scrolls, sometimes both, to balance the shape. They are of white porcelain, painted in bright colours, including a characteristic purplish-red. Occasionally they are decorated with a pretty polychrome bouquet or enriched with sumptuous gilding.

219 Although dinner services are difficult to date precisely, tea- and coffee services do not present the same problem. The wide hemispherical cups have gadrooned or shaped rims. Like the Paris models, teapots were based on English shapes and are

218 bulbous. A pierced basket with a twig handle, crudely decorated in colours, shows how the taste for complicated forms had taken hold at Limoges. Other pieces exhibit a charming sense of fantasy. There is a *veilleuse* in the Adrien Dubouché museum, Limoges, still Gothic in taste, which is composed of a crenellated tower, flanked by pinnacles supporting a teapot with a crenellated rim.

The present whereabouts of what is probably the masterpiece of Limoges porcelain remains unknown. This fabulous basket was presented to the Duchesse de Nemours in 1845 and was described by Achille Leymarie, as has been pointed out by Jean d'Albis and Céleste Romanet, who quote him.[18] It included a profusion of sculptural elements as it was 'formed of an intertwined group of animals, fantastic monsters, and flowers'. The art of modelling in porcelain culminated in Pouyat's best works made during the Second Empire.

222 *Vase.* Doccia (Tuscany), Ginori factory, *c.* 1840. Hard-paste porcelain. H. 28 cm. Unmarked. MAD, Limoges (ADL 3279).
Similar pieces with decoration in low relief have often been attributed to Capodimonte. In fact they were a particular speciality of the Doccia factory in the 18th century and were revived in the 19th.

# ITALY

The military upheavals in the early part of the nineteenth century and the ensuing economic crises left only a single porcelain factory still in operation in Italy; this was the Doccia factory. On the death of Carlo Leopoldo Ginori in 1837, his son Lorenzo II (1823–1878) was too young to take over the business. Once again the heir to the firm had to be guided—this time Marchese Pier-Francesco Rinuccini looked after the firm until 1848 when he was succeeded by Marchesa Marianna.

223 *Plate.* Doccia (Tuscany), Ginori factory: Lorenzo Ginori period, 1845. ▷
Hard-paste porcelain. D. 22 cm. Mark: 100. MNC, Sèvres (3522²).
This piece, acquired by the Sèvres museum in 1845, shows the perfection achieved by painters at the Doccia factory at this period. In the centre is a reproduction of a Rubens self-portrait.

224 *Plate.* Madrid, Royal La Moncloa factory, *c.* 1840. Hard-paste ▷
porcelain. D. 24 cm. Unmarked. MAN, Madrid.
Although pictorial scenes on porcelain went out of fashion in the mid-19th century, La Moncloa continued to decorate its wares in this way. The decorator has brought out the picturesque aspect of the scene on this piece.

225 *Pendulum clock-case.* Turin, Dortu, Richard & Cie, *c.* 1840. Hard-paste porcelain. H. 51 cm. Unmarked. Toso Coll., Venaria.
This clock-case, in which the influence of Jacob Petit is evident, is one of the rare more ambitious products of the factory. It can be compared to the clock-case by Michel and Valin at Limoges (Pl. 216).

226 *Plate.* Vista Alegre (Aveiro, Portugal), Ferreira Pinto & Filhos, *c.* 1840. Hard-paste porcelain. D. 25 cm. Unmarked. Museu da Fabrica, Vista Alegre.
Painted by Victor F. Chartier-Rousseau, a Frenchman who was in charge of the decorating workshop at the Vista Alegre factory between 1835 and 1851.

From the technical and stylistic point of view there was no break with the preceding period. The Restoration style had 222 been adopted around 1830 for 'antique' vases such as the amphoras and Medici vases, with their rather heavy interpretation of Classicism. They were overloaded with painted decoration comprising picturesque, military, or landscape subjects. The first egg-shell porcelains with chinoiserie decoration date from this period, as we have already mentioned. Other pieces decorated with delicate garlands enhancing the porcelain body itself are known, but the grossly rounded forms of these coffee-pots, teapots, and water jugs are typical of the nineteenth century rather than the eighteenth. In the later period, elegance rather than comfort was the main consideration. Finally the famous Doccia porcelains with relief 222 decoration of mythological subjects picked out in colours and dating from this period should be mentioned, although they have been discussed *ad nauseam.* About 1830 Marchese Carlo Leopoldo had acquired *'dai beni della Corona di Napoli, di tutti i modelli antichi e le forme per i riproduzioni di essi in porcellana della famosa Fabbrica Reale di Capo di Monte acquistando parimenti il diretto di applicarvi la marca'.* ('property from the King of Naples and all the old patterns and moulds to enable him to reproduce them at the famous Royal Factory of Capodimonte, and at the same time he obbtaie obtained the right to use the [old] mark.') Doccia had in fact already used this type of decoration, called *bassorelievi istoriati* ('figurative low reliefs') in the eighteenth century, and when it was reintroduced in the nineteenth century this decoration was merely the extension of an existing tradition; however, different motifs were used in the later period. Moreover, Capodimonte pieces were never decorated in this way. Confusion has arisen because Doccia often marked its pieces of this type with a crowned 'N', either incised or painted under the glaze. This mark, used by the Royal Naples Factory, was certainly used by the Doccia factory with intent to deceive.[19]

## Turin

Two new factories were set up, or expanded considerably, at this time: one at Turin, the other at Milan. The Turin factory was in a sense an offshoot of the Swiss factory at Nyon, since its founder was the son of Jacques Dortu. Frédéric Dortu went into partnership with Jacques François Richard du Villard and Prelatz in 1823 and occupied the former premises of the Rossetti earthenware factory. Most of their output consisted of printed creamware, which was undoubtedly more profitable than porcelain. However, the manufacture of porcelain commenced in 1827. In 1829, when Prelatz withdrew from the partnership, the firm became known as Dortu Richard & Cie. Jacques François Richard was replaced by his son, Louis, in 1834. Dortu left the concern in 1846, and Louis Richard then went into partnership with Carlo Imoda and later with his sons. After Richard gave up the business, the Eredi-Imodas ran it until the factory closed down in 1864.

The work of this factory is virtually unstudied since few marked pieces are known. Two well-known pieces do, however, show what the factory could produce. One is an ink-well and the other a clock-case surmounted by the figure of a 225 mare protecting her foal from a wolf (?). This piece is in the same vein as the productions of Jacob Petit and Michel and Valin but is certainly not typical of the generally modest pieces made at the Turin factory.

## Milan

The Milan porcelain industry was established during this period. Giuseppe Vanzo had made an unsuccessful attempt in 1828 to found a factory. Luigi Tinelli's efforts were less short-lived. He belonged to an aristocratic faction, which, following a great tradition, believed that it should protect the arts and take part in political life. Tinelli was condemned to exile for having conspired against Austria. He founded the San Cristoforo factory in the suburbs of Milan in 1834 in order to promote an Italian industry that would not be subject to Austria. Following Luigi's exile, his brother, Carlo Tinelli, ran the factory. Production was only on a small scale and in typical Restoration style, using white grounds that emphasized the rather tormented shapes, discreetly decorated with scattered flowers and gilding.[20] In 1841 Carlo Tinelli sold the San Cristoforo factory to Giulio Richard.

## PORTUGAL

### Vista Alegre

Vasco Valente, author of the most important book on the history of the Vista Alegre porcelain factory, has established that the high point of this factory was in the years between 1830 and 1850. Its success was dependent on several factors, including the discovery of extensive deposits of kaolin in 1832.

In 1835 João Ferreira Pinto Basto, brother of the factory's founder, recruited Victor François Chartier-Rousseau, a Frenchman who had sought political asylum in London. He stayed at the Vista Alegre factory until 1851. Chartier-Rousseau, originally a portrait-painter, headed the decorating workshop at the factory. He introduced the revived Rococo style, which dominated the European art scene at that time. Domestic wares assumed more complex shapes as we can see from those illustrated by Régine de Plinval-Salgues.[21] Chartier-Rousseau was influenced by the Romantic movement and is known to have painted portraits of Petrarch and Laura on vases.[22]

Porcelain made at Vista Alegre at this period shares all the stylistic characteristics of European decorative art and the factory can be taken as having been in the mainstream of European porcelain production.

## RUSSIA

### St Petersburg

Tsar Alexander I died in 1825, in the same year as Count Guryev. Under Nicholas I (1825–1855) the imperial manufactories received their own administrator, who was able to attain a certain autonomy, as were the individual managing directors of the factories and also the artists. Important innovations, however, and even major new product lines required the approval of the tsar.

It is probably due purely to a certain structural similarity and to the close links that both factories had with their respective courts that the porcelain produced by the Royal Manufactory in Nymphenburg and the Imperial Manufactory in St Petersburg had much in common during this period. There is no evidence in either place of the concerns mentioned at the

227   *Ornamental plate with landscape.* St Petersburg, 1839. Overglaze decoration, relief gilt ornamentation, etched gilding. D. 25 cm. Mark: 153. MNC, Sèvres (2815²).
The shape and flange ornamentation are suggestive of Neo-Rococo, but the landscape in the centre is resolutely Romantic.

beginning of this chapter, i.e. in the direction of efficient industrial management;[23] modern production methods found no favour here. As before, painting was regarded as making the most important contribution to the artistic whole.

A new generation of painters continued in the style of Swebach, Adam, Moreau, Golov, and Shchedrin.[24] As in western Europe, the paintings in the imperial collections were copied with chromatic precision on to plaques. Paintings in frames also decorate the often enormous vases that probably remained the factory's true speciality. There was plenty of room for them in the many imperial residences, and they were favourites as formal gifts. The achievements of the Empire style were retained, including areas of gilding with ornamental etching and polishing and imitations of precious stones such as lapis lazuli and malachite in ground colours and painting. The chief types of vase were still the crater and the slender Panathanaean amphora, which is like the *vase fuseau* from Sèvres. Very often these were mounted on Neo-Classical bronze socles and given figured ornamental handles. As was the case with the painted plaques, the St Petersburg factory managed to produce bigger vases than any of the factories in western Europe ever achieved—an important fact in an age when technical capabilities had incessantly to be demonstrated.

The state services made for Nicholas I and the tsarina show the same clinging to tradition: the Banquet Service of 1830–1840,[25] for example, which again combined figures and vessels like the Guryev Service and many others before it, used statuettes by S. S. Pimenov. Admittedly these were now gilded to look like bronzes and given pure Neo-Rococo bowls with flower-painted reserves in coloured grounds.

Neo-Rococo also played an important role in the St Petersburg factory in the reign of Nicholas I. Besides enormous

228 *Display vase with flower painting.* Batenin factory, St Petersburg, *c.* 1830. Overglaze painting and gilding. H. 47 cm. Mark: 151. Hermitage, Leningrad (5304).
Crater and amphora were the favourite models for such display vases, which formed an integral part of the interior decoration of state-rooms.

vases in late Neo-Classical crater and amphora shapes, other vases were produced on the basis of eighteenth-century patterns from Sèvres and Meissen. In addition to vases, from the 1830s onwards the factory also produced fire-place surrounds, consoles, clocks, small tables, candlesticks, and mirror frames based on *vieux Saxe* models. Skilfully modelled flower garlands were essential in such compositions. By 1850 decorative painted porcelain plaques were once again inlaid in small pieces of Louis XV style rosewood furniture. In the modelling of the services commissioned by the St Petersburg court, too, Rococo of the Meissen and Sèvres variety again played a part. In 1841 the factory had to complete the blue-ground Sèvres service for Catherine the Great, and in 1843 a new tea-service was created for the tsarina entirely in the *vieux Saxe* style.[26] *Déjeuners* reappeared with delicately coloured grounds with white flower-painted reserves. Blue and green grounds in every shade enjoyed enormous popularity. Statuettes of shepherds and cavaliers joined the repertoire of figures, which was dominated by painted biscuit figures based on characters in contemporary novels and above all costume figures of the different peoples of the Russian empire. As well as Neo-Rococo elements and occasional borrowings from other styles, around 1850 a new taste for naturalism made its appearance. Flower painting gained in *trompe-l'oeil* precision, as did the factory's statuettes. Tankards were produced with plant and figure reliefs, possibly based on English stoneware models.[27] The shell shapes so popular throughout Europe at this time had a distinctive counterpart at the St Petersburg factory in the form of coral motifs. Vases, breakfast salvers, and even jugs and cups are wound round with bright-red, naturalistic imitation coral branches that indicate a new feeling for colour.[28]

### Private Factories

We know very little about the Biedermeier porcelain produced by private firms in Russia. Only very seldom can such wares be dated with any precision; often they have no factory marks, and there are almost no publications on the collections.[29] It appears that private firms, like the Imperial Manufactory, still operated on a purely craft basis and that early industrial production and decoration techniques were not used.

Pieces that are today regarded as typically Russian, such as tobacco jars or mugs in the shape of Cossack heads and pseudo-oriental decoration, were mainly intended for export. For the rest, the Russian factories continued to take their cue entirely from the West. Vases, individual plates and cups, and tea-services in smooth shapes evolved from Neo-Classical ones but with larger, squatter proportions can therefore, like the wares of the factories of western Europe, be attributed without much doubt to the second quarter of the century. Most of them have a wealth of etched gilt decoration and flower designs in

229

234

229 *Writing set.* St Petersburg, 1839. Overglaze decoration and gilding. W. 23.2 cm. Unmarked. MNC, Sèvres (2815).
Bright red branches of coral appear to have grown round a shell in the kind of naturalistic *tour de force* so popular in the mid-century period.

230 *Cache-pot.* St Petersburg, V. Mescheriakov, *c.* 1830. Overglaze ▷ painting, gilding, bronze mount. H. 28.5 cm. Mark: inaccessible. Hermitage, Leningrad (5304).
This low, curved vase with fancy handles exists with many different decorative schemes; our example is decorated with Cupid and the Three Graces.

231 *Two covered cups and saucers decorated with views.* Popov factory, Gorbunovo, near Moscow, *c.* 1840. Royal blue ground, overglaze painting, gilt decoration. H. 12.6 cm. Mark: 148. Kunstgewerbemuseum, SMPK, Berlin (1981, 25).
The borders encircling the large medallions imitate the 'jewelled' glass-bead decoration fashionable in England.

232 *Group with a pug.* Popov factory, Gorbunovo, second or third quarter of the 19th century. Biscuit and glazed, painted porcelain. H. 16.5 cm. Mark: 148. MNC, Sèvres (23 344).
This departure from the usual range of subjects for Russian figure porcelain is a copy of a Meissen Rococo group.

particularly dazzling colours. There is also evidence that the pleasing shapes of the Neo-Rococo style with curved plate rims and vessels with swelling bodies on wave feet painted with gilt flourishes, cartouches, and flowers were in production as early as the 1830s, e.g. at the Filip Batenin factory, which closed in 1839.[30] In addition to the statuettes we have already discussed, depicting representatives of remote Russian tribes in picturesque costumes or peasants and craftsmen at work, many urban types were now modelled: elegant dandies, actors, dancers, and characters from the novels of Walter Scott and Gogol. In the later Biedermeier period these images of urban elegance were often given stands with *rocaille* relief and the peasants provided with earth bases instead of the previously customary square or round plinths. Since this type of figure retained its popularity over several decades, the general opinion in the Russian literature on the subject is that these modified base shapes are helpful for purposes of dating.

### Popov

A particularly versatile factory in the production of painted tableware and show-case porcelain was that of Alexey Gavrilovich Popov at Gorbunovo.[31] Tea-services and cups in straight Neo-Classical or bellied Biedermeier shapes were produced both in the Bohemian manner, with a gold-rimmed white ground and flowers or landscapes, and as a speciality with 231 various blue and green grounds. The gilding and miniature painting are of exceptional quality. Popov appears to have had a particular predilection for the elegant Neo-Rococo style, as witness his tea-services and dessert plates with delicate pastel grounds and gilt cartouches surrounding painted roses. The 233 finest examples are without a doubt the large 'bread and salt salvers', flat plates usually measuring 40 or 50 centimetres in diameter that were used according to Russian custom when receiving guests. Their elaborate flower or *rocaille* decoration in brilliant ground colours is reminiscent of certain Neo-Rococo wares from England, with which Popov may have had close

links even before his marriage to an Englishwoman in 1844.[32] Naturalistic motifs—shells and coral, bark-like surfaces on tankards, branch handles, calyces—were as popular with Popov as with Gardner and the Imperial Manufactory and were probably based on English prototypes.

### Batenin

A number of particularly fine large porcelain vases, cups, and 228 tea-services bear witness to the continued efficiency of the small Batenin factory under its last proprietor, Filip Batenin, before the fire and subsequent closure of the factory in 1839.[33] These wares correspond particularly closely to our idea of the Biedermeier style with their large, bulging shapes and colourful paintings of flowers or views in broad areas of gilding. Batenin appears to have manufactured nothing but tableware. All the other privately owned factories, particularly in the two decades under discussion here, resembled the Imperial Manufactory in energetically marketing a broad range of porcelain figures.

### Gzhel' District

Francis Gardner in Verbilki and Alexey Gavrilovich Popov at Gorbunovo continued to produce the finest figures, in terms 232 both of modelling and of painting.[34] The statuettes of Kuznetsov are not always of such quality as the one illustrated; 235 those of the Afanasiy Leontevich Kiselev factory, on the other hand, which only existed between 1832 and about 1860, are almost invariably of a high standard. Kiselev had one of the largest factories in the Gzhel' district, which like Thuringia, Bohemia, Staffordshire, and the Limousin was an old pottery region that in the nineteenth century became a porcelain centre. The best known of the Gzhel' factories is Popov's, but

233 *Bread and salt salver.* Popov factory, Gorbunovo, mid-19th century. ▷
Overglaze painting and gilt ornamentation. D. 42 cm. Mark: 148, and pattern number. Hermitage, Leningrad (1173).
For his large salvers with their elaborate flower painting on coloured grounds Popov may have been inspired by English ware.

234 *Coffee and tea-service.* Russia, second quarter of the 19th century. Overglaze decoration, rich etched gilding. H. (coffee-pot) 21.5 cm. Unmarked. Kunstgewerbemuseum, SMPK, Berlin (1968,46).
The squat shapes and the comparatively large sugar bowl and milk jug typify the way Neo-Classical vessel shapes developed in the Biedermeier period.

235 *Statuette of a South Russian peasant woman.* Novocharitonovo Kuznetsov factory, second or third quarter of the 19th century. Biscuit porcelain, painted. H. 20.5 cm. Mark: 149 and impressed marks in dots. MNC, Sèvres (10039).
Such figures, prototypes for which date back to the time of Catherine the Great, are the Russian factories' most distinctive creation.

there were countless smaller firms as well, often quite short-lived. It was chiefly large farmers who established these factories, since with the help of their serfs' labour they were able to operate cheaply. They were hardly in touch with the art world, of course, and were largely without ambition in that direction, so that their products tend to be more or less naïve popular reproductions of the porcelain tableware and figures of the more refined factories. Marvin Ross illustrates examples of such products from the Miklashevsky, Guzhev, and Ikonnikov factories as well as other, unknown firms in the Gzhel' district.[35]

# AUSTRIA

## Vienna

### Beginning of the Economic Crisis
The porcelain wares produced by the Imperial Manufactory in Vienna, which thanks to a discriminating clientele had maintained an outstanding level of quality until after the Congress of Vienna of 1815, went slowly downhill during the Biedermeier period. Individual large-scale commissions, as mentioned in chapter II, continued to make great demands on the factory's modellers and painters during the 1820s. Among these creations, which by and large remained loyally Neo-Classical, the Laxenburg Service constitutes an exception. Here the dessert plates with Austrian castle ruins, the centrepieces with their Gothic-style architecture, and the paintings of Habsburg kings by Lorenz Herr are thoroughly historicist and offer an early example of the possibilities latent also in Romanticism as far as porcelain design was concerned. Those possibilities were by no means exploited to the full, however,

for although Austria gained in economic and political importance in the period that followed, neither court nor nobility saw it as their task to support the Imperial Manufactory with major artistic commissions.

As in Meissen in 1820 and in Vienna a little later, it was likewise a question of making economies and concentrating on profitable rather than on artistically outstanding products. When Mathias Niedermayer died in 1827 he was replaced as managing director by a chemist, Benjamin von Scholz, who had established his credentials as early as 1819 with the publication of his study *Concerning Porcelain and Porcelain Clays, Principally in the Austrian States* and who had been deputy managing director since 1825. The appointment of a chemist was thoroughly typical of the time: in terms of surviving the competitive struggle, factory managements from Meissen to Sèvres and from Berlin to Bohemia saw the development of modern technologies as being more urgent than maintaining artistic continuity. But whereas in Meissen and Berlin experiments with new colours and pastes, general modernization of the plant, and the introduction of mass-produced articles really did lead to financial rehabilitation, in Vienna this was not the case. Scholz began his economies by purchasing and using cheaper clays, as Meissen had also done for a time for some of its simpler products but soon stopped doing. Scholz's experiment turned out to be a mistake on two counts, for the new pastes necessitated changing the mode of production just at a time when, with the factory's Bohemian rivals outdoing one another at industrial exhibitions with continuous improvements in their initially unsatisfactory pastes, low-quality porcelain was no longer appreciated anywhere. Even more disastrous was his attempted rationalization by introducing a kind of piece-work; Scholz replaced the earlier system of payment, which was graduated

84

236 *Tray with flower still life*. Vienna, Joseph Nigg, 1834. Overglaze painting, etched gilt rim. H. 30 cm. Marks: 109 and artist's signature. MNC, Sèvres (3314).
Joseph Nigg was the leading flower painter at the Vienna factory for decades.

237 *Cup and saucer with flower painting*. Vienna, *c.* 1830. Overglaze painting and gilding. H. 11 cm. Mark: 109. ÖMaK, Vienna (6362).
Apart from copies of old masters, flower painting played the major role in the Vienna factory's art porcelain.

according to performance, by simple piece-wages. Actual improvements, such as the overdue acquisition of a steam-engine for paste preparation and so on, were thus robbed of their full effect on the firm's accounts. Big savings were made on painting staff: in 1830 only fifty polychrome and five blue painters were employed, whereas in 1805 there had been more than three times that number.

When on Scholz's death in 1833 the physicist Andreas Baumgartner was appointed managing director, the state administration showed that it regarded Scholz's management style as having been the right one. Baumgartner stepped up the industrialization process, concentrated on cheap, mass-produced wares, introduced printed decoration, and did actually manage, as Scholz had done, to make the factory show a small profit instead of needing a subsidy. This was also the most urgent undertaking required of his successor, the chemist Franz Freiherr von Leithner, on his appointment by the government in 1842. For all his austerity, Leithner was able to master the task only until 1848, the year of the Revolution.

Of the products that resulted from such directives, not much has survived, white porcelain wares with or without printed decoration having seldom been carefully preserved. Probably most of the models for cups, services, and plates were taken from the abundant resources of the previous decades.

*Decoration*

The art department with its steadily diminishing staff concentrated on a few specialities: paintings continued to be copied on to plaques, for which experienced painters were 238 available though of course no young ones were being trained any longer. Equal attention at least was paid to flower painting—on plaques as well as on vases and cups. Older models were mainly used for this purpose, together with one or two variants. A squat, facetted cup[36] and a similarly compressed modification of the old crater vase are conspicuous novelties of the Biedermeier period. The most experienced of the flower painters was Joseph Nigg (1782–1863), who was 236 attached to the factory from 1800–1843, although his artistic maturity largely coincided with the Biedermeier period (1820–1840). He received the occasional reprimand from the management for working too slowly, but they could not do without him. His speciality was large plaques and vases with flower still lifes based on Dutch paintings or using his own compositions. His pupil Eduard Pollack, who began making a name for himself in 1825, was from 1834 to 1864 the last head painter of the flower section at the Vienna factory, supervising a number of painters who are known to us by name.[37]

Besides large vases, which were still occasionally commissioned by the court as presents or were produced for industrial exhibitions, it was above all cups that they painted; these sold well, and large numbers of them have survived. The 237

238 *Madonna and Child.* Vienna, Claudius Herr, *c.* 1829. Overglaze painting. H. 67.2 cm. Signed and dated. Mark: 109. ÖMaK, Vienna (Ke 386).
Vienna still had some excellent painters in the second quarter of the century, as this painting after Andrea del Sarto shows.

239 *Family group with the Austrian emperor and empress.* Vienna, after 1855. Biscuit porcelain, base glazed, coat of arms in relief with gilding. H. 23.2 cm. Marks: 109, year stamp, impressed number. ÖMaK, Vienna (Ke 8627).
In contrast to the uniformed emperor, the empress is portrayed in a spirit of bourgeois Realism as a young mother.

delicate, high-quality painting is naturalistic and varied in colour. It is inevitably combined with large areas of gilding—a fashion that was not confined to Vienna. Animals, emblems, allegories, chinoiseries (by Michael Köhler), and portraits of famous contemporaries (by Anton Schwendt) occurred less often as motifs. Following the general trend of the time, very few new figure models were created: a series of biscuit busts of musicians was produced in the 1840s, as was the occasional 239 portrait of a member of the imperial family or—and these are probably the most convincing achievements—a colourful contemporary genre group that might have stepped straight out of a Greuze or Waldmüller.[38]

## GERMANY

### Nymphenburg

While the old factories of Vienna and Meissen were very much caught up in the trend towards industrialization, the more recently established Nymphenburg factory was unaffected by it until 1848, thanks to the special attentions of King Ludwig I. He had already taken a great interest in the factory as crown prince, promoting the painting department in particular, as we have seen, to the status of 'art institute' and showering all kinds of marks of favour upon it. During his reign as Ludwig I (1825–1848), which more or less coincided with Friedrich cf. p. 78 Gärtner's period of office (1822–1848) as overall artistic director, Nymphenburg worked almost entirely on royal commissions. From 1827 onwards the painting staff was busy cf. p. 79 copying pictures from the Royal Pinakothek on to porcelain plaques, as already mentioned; even after 1850 new ones were occasionally added. Contemporary subjects, too, were painted on plaques, plates, and cups, e.g. landscapes and portraits of the royal family. The state services and sets of plates produced at Nymphenburg in the 1830s and 1840s must, artistically speaking, rank as some of the most outstanding porcelain of 112 the period. Production of the Onyx Service, designed by Gärtner and still Neo-Classical in shape and decoration, began in 1835. By the time of Gärtner's retirement in 1848 it is probable that most of the plates and vases painted with figures were finished, though work on many pieces—such as the fruit baskets—had not even been started. Under Eugen Napoleon Neureuther, who took over in 1848, the service was expanded from just under 200 to 700 pieces. In 1842–1845 the Art Institute decorated two complete sets of plates with paintings, one of them apparently realizing a plan that dated from the early years of the century to celebrate the Bavarian landscape on porcelain, the other consisting of a series of portraits of women in national costume. Costume pictures were very fashionable in St Petersburg around this time, and portraits of women were also among the favourite subjects for cups in the Bohemian factories around 1830. Both the Nymphenburg sets probably used drawings by Karl Heinzmann, who had been sent off on his travels in 1823 to draw picturesque views of Bavarian towns and folk costumes. Finally, in the wake of these two sets the Art Institute painted a further series of forty plates 241 in a different, more Romantic style with landscapes and scenes from the Nibelung legend. The designs were supplied by the finest painters of the artistically outward-looking Bavarian capital: Wilhelm von Kaulbach, Julius Schnorr von Carolsfeld, Peter von Cornelius, and Eugen Napoleon Neureuther, who was appointed to succeed Gärtner shortly afterwards.

240 *Display vase decorated with a self-portrait of Albrecht Dürer.* Nymphenburg, c. 1838. Overglaze painting, etched and polished gilding. H. 38 cm. Mark: 137. MNC, Sèvres (1345[1]).
This Gärtner-designed vase was a gift from the Nymphenburg factory to the Musée Nationale de Céramique, Sèvres.

Of the painters who executed the porcelain miniatures, some signed their names and others are known from factory records. The best and oldest of them was Christian Adler (1787–1850), and his finest pupils were said to have been Franz Xaver Nachtmann (1799–1846) and Karl Heinzmann (1795–1846), both of whom also worked in other media as draughtsmen and painters. Heinzmann and Adler also supplied designs for painting large vases, which in Gärtner's day became 240 popular products, being highly suitable as court presents.

With the passing of Neo-Classicism, interest in white biscuit figures in the Classical manner disappeared.[39] A few fresh subjects emerged, but in number and importance they did not begin to rival the creative achievements of the painters. A milkmaid was modelled as early as 1816, shown in her working clothes with a straw hat and milk pails; she was joined between 1830 and 1850 by a buxom young market woman and a wealthy corn merchant. It is not known whether the coincidence of subject-matter with the many Russian folk types, which like the Nymphenburg figures were usually made in painted biscuit, was wholly accidental. A price list of 1831 mentions some presumably older statuettes of members of the Bavarian royal family as well as of Frederick the Great and

241 *Plate with Romantic landscape painting.* Nymphenburg, 1842–1845. Overglaze painting, gilt rims and borders, D. 23.5 cm. Mark: 137. Residenzmuseum, Munich.
Sets of plates on a given theme were a speciality of Nymphenburg's 'Art Institute'; this landscape is from a set dealing with the legend of the Nibelung.

Napoleon, which were available in both biscuit and imitation bronze. Figures added in the following years were made to designs by the Munich sculptor Ludwig Schwanthaler, most of which arose out of his large-scale sculptural works (busts of famous men for Valhalla, the 'hall of fame' near Regensburg, or the 'Bavarian rural districts' for the new Residenz). Certain designs for ethnic figures from rural Bavaria and for animal sculptures are attributed to the painter Sebastian Habenschaden. It was not until around the middle of the century that the factory that had employed Bustelli turned from this 'bourgeois Realism' to Neo-Rococo groups. A memorandum states expressly: 'The introduction of the so-called Rococo taste began in the year 1848.'[40] This is represented by a group in which a man is kissing his female companion's hand and a pastoral group, again in glazed and painted porcelain, which we would no longer wish to judge as harshly as did the factory's chronicler in 1923 (Hofmann).[41]

## Berlin

*Style and Technique*
The Berlin factory occupies an intermediate position between the continuation of the Neo-Classical tradition with conventional methods on the one hand and the switch to modern manufacturing methods on the other.

It had already suffered in the 1820s under new tariff laws that permitted the importation of Saxon, Bohemian, and French porcelain. In the Biedermeier period, further competition came from inside Prussia itself with the products of Moritz Schumann and Son's factory at Moabit, near Berlin (est. 1835),[42] and the Krister factory in Waldenburg (Walbrzych), Silesia (est. 1829).[43] Both factories helped themselves to Berlin's repertoire of shapes but painted and gilded them very much less carefully—and thus more cheaply—and gave their products marks that only the discriminating purchaser could distinguish from the Royal Manufactory's sceptre mark.

On the death of Friedrich Philip Rosenstiel in 1832 the ministry appointed Friedrich Georg Frick as the new managing director of the factory; for years he had occupied the responsible position of technical director. His discoveries in the field of colour technology (green, black) and the development of an exceptionally workable porcelain paste, particularly essential for the successful manufacture of large-scale display vases, had benefited the factory enormously. Frick consistently proved himself to be not only an outstanding technician but also a prudent businessman. Responsible for the manufacture of white porcelain from 1821 onwards, he succeeded during his period as managing director (1832–1848) in making this the economic cornerstone of the factory's entire output. Against all kinds of opposition, he carried out a thorough-going modernization of the factory's technical plant. From 1821 to 1849 Frick's colleague Prössel was in charge of the branch factory that used a porcelain paste resembling stoneware to manufacture what is called 'utility ware'. Between 1810 and 1850 this consistently found a very good market with the middle-class public, but after that it was increasingly superseded by cheaper porcelain from other factories, and in 1865 Berlin stopped producing it but continued to manufacture technical porcelain such as petticoat insulators,

242  *Souvenir cup and saucer.* J.F.F. Schumann factory, Berlin, *c.* 1835–1840. Overglaze painting, gilt ornamentation. H. 15 cm. Mark: 129. Kunstgewerbemuseum, SMPK, Berlin (18,103).
The cup—an Empire shape—is fully gilt inside, and both cup and saucer are decorated with gilt tendril work.

pipes, and weaving equipment.[44] Frick's successor Kolbe wrote of him that during his period of office as managing director he had succeeded in turning the factory into a major concern and increasing output by manufacturing ware that was 'as marketable and as acceptable as possible'[45]—a remark that can be interpreted equally well as praise or as scathing criticism. In fact, Frick did not convert the entire factory to the production of cheap ware but simply sought, by manufacturing utility and technical ware, to give his expensive art porcelain economic support, for the Berlin factory could not, any more than the others, survive on art porcelain alone. In the Biedermeier period the production of luxurious individual pieces was in fact made possible chiefly by commissions received from the court. Following the Wars of Liberation it had been the large services commissioned by Frederick William III for his commanders that had kept the modellers and above all the painters in work for years; between 1830 and 1850 it was primarily display vases that the royal family wished to give as presents to other courts.

*Shapes*

With these wares the emphasis was still on painting; there was clearly no feeling that new shapes were needed. The vase shapes were by artists from the circle of the great Karl Friedrich Schinkel; some of the vases later came to be known as Schinkel vases, though there is no documentary evidence to support the attribution. Their basic lines were laid down before 1830. They are based on the Classical crater and amphora or on a blend of amphora and hydria. Between 1822 and 1832 it seems to have been almost always the crater shape that was used; this was known as the 'Medici vase' and gave rise, through modification of the handles, to other variants with different names (such as the 'Redensche vase'). After 1830 the amphora and its urn-shaped variant gained greater popularity. The latter was known as the 'Munich vase' and stemmed from a type of display vase created by Friedrich Gärtner for Nymphenburg. The Munich vase was commissioned by the court as a gift about 120 times between 1832 and 1847, the French type—a slim amphora with various foliage or griffin handles—about 100 times.[46] It seems almost as if court protocol saw these vases as possessing a kind of standard value, particularly since they were available in graduated sizes. A further variation in their value as gifts arose out of the possibility of composing sets of three or five vases; in 1832–1833, for example, a 79-centimetre-high

243 *Pieces from a simple coffee service.* Berlin, before 1840. White porcelain with gilt rims. H. (coffee-pot) 26.5 cm. Mark: 124. Kunstgewerbemuseum, SMPK, Berlin (1976,25).
Such simple white porcelains—the first step towards modern mass-produced ware—were part of Frick's attempt to restore the fortunes of the Berlin factory.

244 *Pieces from a service in the Neo-Rococo style.* Berlin, 1849–1870. Overglaze painting, gilt decoration. H. (pot) 18 cm. Marks: 125, 128 and incised marks. Berlin-Museum, Berlin.
Not only does the shape of this service go back to the 18th century; even the views are of buildings from that period.

246 *Table top with views of Berlin and Weimar.* Berlin, c. 1835. Overglaze painting, gilt decoration. D. 67 cm. Marks: 123, 128. Kunstgewerbemuseum, East Berlin.
This porcelain table top required the services of the factory's flower and view painters and gilders.

245 *Münchner Vase painted with views.* Berlin, c. 1835–1840. Overglaze painting and rich gilt decoration. H. 61.5 cm. Marks: 123, 128. Kunstgewerbemuseum, East Berlin (1976,269).
This vase shape (here with a view of Berlin's Stadtschloss) was much in demand for court presents in the 1830s and 1840s.

247 *Lalla Rookh vases.* Berlin, 1824. Overglaze painting, gilt decoration. ▷ H. 91, 82 cm. Mark: inaccessible. Hermitage, Leningrad (24 847, 24 846, 24 848).
The 'Persian' shape of these vases commemorating the visit of the Russian crown prince and princess in 1821 was designed by Karl Friedrich Schinkel.

Munich vase went to the court of the tsar accompanied by a pair measuring 61 centimetres in height.[47] Much more important than the shape was the painting, which was always combined with rich gilding and often with stone imitations as well (malachite, porphyry). The choice of motifs was as conservative as the choice of shapes. Framed views of the sights of Berlin were extremely popular, as they had been in the first decade of the century. S. H. Spiker's *Berlin and its Environs in the Nineteenth Century* (1832–1833), illustrated with engravings of drawings by Ahlborn, Eduard von Gärtner, Strack, and many others, often provided the source for these. Besides views we also find battle scenes from the Wars of Liberation, royal portraits, and flowers, used particularly as a decorative accessory. Responsible for the latter until 1849 was Gottfried Wilhelm Völker (b. 1775), who had been head painter since 1803. Trips to Vienna had familiarized him with the naturalistic style of flower still-life painting regarded as exemplary there. The flower motif is usually framed with a wealth of Neo-Classical gilt ornamentation for which the architect Gustav Stier and other successors of Schinkel's supplied the designs.[48]

An attempt in 1824 to break away from Neo-Classicism and strike out in a more imaginative direction had remained without sequel. In 1821, on the occasion of a visit to Berlin by the Russian crown prince and princess, who were received there with much rejoicing, the court had organized a ceremonial procession in oriental costume, based on Thomas Moore's Romantic work *Lalla Rookh* (published 1817), in which the entire court including the Russian visitors took part.

This event was recorded in drawings by the painter Kloeber, and from these the factory had bowls, plates, and vases painted. The only surviving sketch by Karl Friedrich Schinkel for a piece of porcelain stems from this project. His *Lalla Rookh* vase shows an amphora with a somewhat oriental profile, covered with a profusion of decoration that appears to be based on Indian cashmere shawls. Schinkel's Persian vase, executed in 1824, had no artistic sequel in the persistently Neo-Classical programme of the Berlin factory.[49]

There is a somewhat broader spectrum of formal variation in the factory's cups, which remained the favourite gift and collection articles with the less pretentious. These were painted with the same motifs as the vases. Various bell-mug shapes were combined with ornamental handles and often further elaborated with foot rings and little feet. Typical Biedermeier shapes of the 1830s and 1840s are low bell cups with short curved sides, a small strap handle, and a profiled base; a more marginal one is a very shallow bowl with a projecting lip, painted inside with pictorial motifs.[50]

Few complete services appear to have been made. Those that were used earlier shapes, as in the case of the wedding present made for Princess Friederike in 1840, which can today be seen in the Residenz in Munich. This also included a number of confectionery bowls and other centrepieces, for most of which models were reshaped from the 1800 'Mount Olympus' centrepiece.[51] Only a few services had new models, which can probably be attributed to the son of the Neo-Classical master modeller, Friedrich Wilhelm Riese jr., who succeeded his father from 1834 to 1841. He was superseded in 1841 by Julius

cf. p. 70

247

242

244

Wilhelm Mantel (1820–1896). When it came to re-using old service shapes, they clearly did not stop at Neo-Classicism but occasionally, even before 1850, remodelled eighteenth-century shapes and painted them in a blend of Neo-Rococo and contemporary styles with large views framed in *rocaille*—an approach that, however questionable, ultimately stood more chance of replacing Neo-Classicism than Schinkel's *Lalla Rookh* venture.

## Meissen

The support that all the factories mentioned hitherto received from royal commissions and that enabled them to maintain their art departments was something that Augustus the Strong's foundation lacked in the Biedermeier period. In chapter II we gave examples to show that in the first quarter of the century Meissen could very definitely still compete, and in competitive situations such as the making of gifts for the Duke of Wellington came off no worse than Berlin or Vienna. Nevertheless around 1820 voices were again raised, as they had been ten years earlier, in favour of closing the factory down, since for a long time it had been running at a loss. King Augustus III successfully resisted these demands. After 1831, however, when Saxony became the third German state to receive a constitution and the porcelain factory was placed under state ownership with the redefinition of crown property, the king could no longer help. Thus it was of enormous consequence that the financial fortunes of the factory took a turn for the better around this time and that in 1834 income at last began to exceed expenditure once again. This was due not only to Saxony's having joined the German Customs Union but also to a new policy that the management had been pursuing for some time with the primary aim of operating at a profit.

249    *Plate with relief pattern.* Meissen, 1845–1846. Relief decoration, matt and gloss gilding. D. 22 cm. Mark: 136, shape and model numbers. MNC, Sèvres (3603²).
The introduction of plates inexpensively made from pressed-glass moulds and decorated with relief patterns was a major economic breakthrough for Meissen.

248    *Neo-Gothic cup and saucer.* Meissen, *c.* 1835. Relief decoration, 'shiny' or gloss gilding, overglaze painting. H. 11 cm. Marks: 136 and impressed signs. MNC, Sèvres (19694).
Manufactured in large series from pressed-glass moulds, such cups were inexpensively decorated with gloss gilding; additional painting was rare.

### Technical Innovations

The new goal was to beat the competition from cheaper French, Bohemian, and Thuringian wares. This meant that Meissen could no longer base its production on exclusive, laboriously and expensively painted luxury gifts, display vases, and services for which there were no more commissions coming in and which could not be sold on the open market because they cost far too much. Instead it had to look into ways of manufacturing low-cost wares that would sell well and in large quantities. The first efforts were expended in the laboratory: with the development by Heinrich Gottlob Kühn in 1817 of a chrome-green that could be baked in under the glaze, together with the green vine-tendril pattern designed for this colour by Samuel Arnhold, a successful step had already been taken in this direction. Also in 1817 an initial method of applying the ever-popular gilding more cheaply had come into use;[52] but the really significant step was taken in 1827, again by Kühn, with the perfection of the gloss-gilding process. This involves dissolving (sulphur-) gold in sulphur balsam, after which it can easily be worked with a brush, e.g. on relief areas, while simple rims and circles can even be done mechanically with the aid of a 'ring machine'; moreover, with the gold in solution, only a fraction of the quantity is required, as compared with the old method of leaf-gilding. When painted on biscuit body it stays matt after firing, but on glazed surfaces it emerges with a high gloss, thus also eliminating the necessity for polishing with agate, which had always been required before. The new gilding's low resistance to abrasion was somewhat understated at the beginning, and in fact for rims and other places most exposed to wear they preferred to go on using the old method of application. How decisively Kühn's

248–249

250  *Picture plate with Romantic motif: Heimkehr der Königskinder.* Meissen, mid-19th century. Sepia overglaze painting, gilt decoration. D. 21.5 cm. Mark: 136. Exhibition Room, SP, Meissen.
Meissen was concerned right up until the last quarter of the century to maintain a varied programme, which continued to include porcelain painting.

251  *Picture plate with family idyll.* Meissen, Ludwig Richter, *c.* 1830. Overglaze painting, gilt rim. D. 23.8 cm. Mark: 136. Exhibition Room, SP, Meissen.
A drawing tutor at Meissen from 1828 to 1835, Richter contributed a number of designs to the factory's repertoire.

gloss-gilding process benefited the factory can be seen merely by comparing prices: a gilt cup bought around 1814 cost something like three times the price of one made in 1830.[53] Never in the eighteenth century would this invention have made such a difference as it did at this time, when it was common practice to gild the entire sides of vessels. Cups with a gilt vine-leaf design on a white ground were extraordinarily popular and sold very well. By 1830, of course, the days were long gone in which a factory could guard a secret as the 'arcanum' of porcelain itself had been guarded in the eighteenth century. The Bohemian and Thuringian factories in particular were soon imitating Meissen's gloss gilding, although after 1837 Brongniart was still describing it as a 'procédé mystérieux'.[54] In Meissen, logical decorative schemes were worked out in which gloss gilding could be used to particularly good effect. These consisted primarily of relief decoration. Whose idea they were does not appear to have been recorded or handed down; at any rate they proved extraordinarily successful. In 1831 Meissen began using moulds that had been designed and used very recently for the manufacture of pressed glass in France.[55] Clearly these could be used without alteration for porcelain, which manufacturers had meanwhile also begun to pour in rather than press in. The first pressed glass moulds had the Gothic pointed-arch and quatrefoil designs that had just come into fashion in France, usually combined with a false stone effect on the lower part of the cup; a little later on they were using the design borrowed from America of flower tendrils and Neo-Rococo sweeping lines on a 'lacy' spotted ground. With the aid of a few brush strokes the porcelain vessels, which came out of the mould with ready-made relief ornamentation, could be given an extra

touch of luxury by means of gloss gilding, for which skilled painters were not needed.

A further effective method of decoration was developed by Kühn in 1828–1829 in the form of his so-called 'iridescent colours'. A lustrous pink in particular is often found beside slightly worn areas of gilding on Meissen plates, bowls, and cups with pressed glass designs.

*Style*
The introduction from 1833 onwards, of the 'Old-German-Greek taste' mentioned by Kühn,[56] offered further scope both for the factory's relief technique and for sumptuous gilding. It appears to have been mainly decorative plates and vessels that were produced in this style, combining 'Old-German' vine-leaf designs (which today strike us as rather naturalistic) with various ornaments culled from the antique past. Another example of Historicism took a much more specific form as far as Meissen was concerned. Certain of its foreign customers had never really stopped ordering eighteenth-century models; this applied primarily to Russia, but also to Turkey, and from the 1820s onwards also to English buyers.[57] The special interest shown by the English in Kändler models resulted in a whole section of the factory's staff working in the 'English taste'— long before there was any question generally of a new Rococo age. By the late 1830s this kind of resurrection of older shapes from the factory's own model cellars was probably once again worthwhile as far as sales in the home market were concerned as well. It was this aspect of Meissen's production that made a disagreeable impression on the Neo-Classically inclined Berlin jurors at the 1844 Customs Union Exhibition. But after the Bohemian factories, and Elbogen in particular, had also

252 *Monumental vase.* Meissen, before 1849. Overglaze decoration and gilding on relief and sculpted parts. H. *c.* 90 cm. Lost since 1945 except for the cover (H. 18 cm), which has no marks. Porzellansammlung, Dresden (86,92 b / P.E. 6721).
The Meissen management often approached freelance artists for designs—in this case the famous Dresden architect Gottfried Semper.

switched to Neo-Rococo with Meissen copies around this time, the Meissen management could hardly be expected shamefacedly to abandon this style once more.

White porcelain wares with relief stamping in Neo-Gothic, Rococo, 'Old-German-Greek', or naturalistic motifs and broad areas of gilding or iridescent colouring, while they were supremely successful economically, are less satisfactory to the art historian. Faced with the choice of either operating economically or going into liquidation, Germany's first and, in artistic terms, formerly most splendid factory turned into a

mass-producer of technically flawless and advanced wares that were imaginatively conceived but artistically irrelevant.

*Modellers and Painters*
Modellers and painters were, of course, not entirely inactive during these years. Since 1814 the drawing classes for the factory's porcelain painters, previously held at Meissen itself, had been entrusted to the Dresden Academy of Art with the ostensible object of greater effectiveness. The Academy, however, never showed any particular interest but confined

itself to dispatching one of its less illustrious members to Meissen twice a week to correct the painters' work. From 1828 to 1835—when this type of supervision was dropped again—the correcting tutor was Ludwig Richter. Clearly he did not often take a hand in production with designs of his own, any more than did that other famous painter Georg Friedrich Kersting, who as head painter from 1818 to 1847 was in charge of the art department. We have few precise clues as to the nature of their work and their influence on the painters. Occasionally motifs from the paintings of either Richter or Kersting can be found on porcelain dating from the 1830s.[58] Copying from old masters—which in Meissen had been practised in the eighteenth century—was still on the programme during this period, just as it was in the factories of Nymphenburg and St Petersburg. The well-stocked Dresden painting collection acted as a stimulus here. A specialist at this kind of work was the painter Heinrich Gotthelf Schaufuss.

There was no investment in new shapes for show-pieces; again, the factory's Rococo models could be re-used when something was required. Only after this monotonous reliance on its own heritage had been criticized in 1845 did the factory occasionally commission outside artists to produce modern designs. The best-known attempt is that made by Gottfried Semper, who was living in Dresden in these years as the celebrated architect of its opera-house. He designed a very free modification of the Classical crater with a roof-like cover. Painted with a procession of bacchantes, this was presented by Meissen at the first World Exhibition in the middle of its otherwise exclusively Neo-Rococo entries. Like Schinkel's *Lalla Rookh* vases, Semper's vase represents another impracticable attempt to modify traditional shapes. The factory won greater recognition, perhaps not without good reason, with such masterpieces of craftsmanship as its life-sized camelia bush in a pot, which was also on view at the 1851 Exhibition.[59]

## Lithophanes

Berlin and Meissen both enjoyed equal success in the Biedermeier period with lithophanes, a speciality that is today almost forgotten. These are small, thin porcelain plaques that were used as a shade in front of a candle or hung in a window as decorative pictures, the light shining through them to reveal pictorial motifs of the type used in the mezzotints that were so popular at the time. This effect was achieved by converting a copperplate engraving into a wax plate in such a way that the lightest parts of the original formed the deepest impression and the darkest parts the shallowest. From this plate a plaster negative was taken that served as the mould for the final porcelain lithophane. Light penetrates the thinner areas more easily than the thicker areas and gives the desired chiaroscuro effect.

The first lithophanes were produced in France, where Baron Charles P. de Bourgoing received a ten-year patent for them in 1827. Since Brongniart, de Bourgoing has been regarded as the inventor of the process.[60] However, he is known to have served as a diplomat at the Russian and Bavarian courts, for example, and it would seem to be more plausible to see him as an art lover and financier of artistically and economically interesting experiments.[61]

French lithophanes were on offer at the Leipzig Fair as early as 1828.[62] Meissen's managing director, Carl Wilhelm von Oppel, purchased some early samples. Further models were

253 *Woman wearing a domino and carrying a mask.* Meissen, 1830–1840. Lithophane (in a cast-iron frame). H. 20 cm. Unmarked, model number. Berlin-Museum, Berlin.
The singer and actress Wilhelmine Schröder–Devrient, who 'reigned' at Dresden's Hoftheater from 1823 to 1847, was the subject of at least three Meissen lithophanes.

254 *The Princes in the Tower.* Berlin, 1836–1837. Lithophane (in a bronze frame). H. 15.8 cm. Marks: 124 and model number '161'. Private coll., Berlin.
Besides copies of famous old masters, certain subjects by contemporary artists such as this one after J. Northcote by T. Hildebrand also sold well as lithophanes.

255 *Zu Gott.* Plaue, Thuringia, 19th/20th century. Lithophane.
H. 28.7 cm. Marks: impressed PPM and model number '981'. MfKuG,
Hamburg.
As lithophanes retained their popularity, smaller factories too began to
produce them. Kaulbach's guardian angel made a very suitable lampshade.

acquired from a German dealer in the same year and
immediately copied. By 1829 Meissen was already
manufacturing lithophanes to its own designs. The Royal
Berlin Porcelain Manufactory, too, began imitating and
manufacturing them in 1828—probably getting them from
the same sources. Lithophanes immediately became a
tremendous success with the public. In 1829 Meissen even sold
four hundred of them to Berlin, although the factory there was
already producing them itself. They continued to account for
between 6 and 12 per cent of Meissen's output until the 1840s.
Before long Meissen was able to offer some 200 different
motifs, which in terms of subject-matter used the themes most
popular with the painters of the day;[63] between 1828 and 1865
Berlin brought out a total of 650 pictorial motifs. In 1851 the
Meissen management discarded eighty that had gone out of
fashion; these were mainly Romantic, Neo-Gothic motifs.
Others enjoyed unbroken popularity, chiefly copies of
paintings by Raphael *(Sistine Madonna, Madonna della Sedia),*
Correggio *(Holy Night),* and certain more modern painters
such as Mengs *(Assumption of the Virgin, Cupid),* a variety of
atmospheric landscapes, from the view of Vesuvius to the
Russian snowscape with a sleighing party, religious motifs such
as pictures of saints or the Expulsion of Hagar, and finally such
sentimental subjects as guardian angels, the angels' heads from
Raphael's *Sistine Madonna,* or children with bird-cages and
little dogs. In many instances Meissen and Berlin brought out
the same motif. Finished lithophanes from one factory were
probably used by the other to make moulds for its own

production, thus economizing on 'development costs'.
Raphael's *Madonna della Sedia* and James Northcote's *The
Princes in the Tower,* for example, exist in identical examples 254
from both sources. Thanks to J. Kunze's publication of 1981
we have an index of motifs for Meissen lithophanes based on
old price lists,[64] though so far none has been drawn up for
Berlin. Meissen lithophanes are in fact difficult to identify 253
because they have no marks—possibly because they were
regarded as items of little value—whereas their Berlin
counterparts can not only be identified by the sceptre mark
painted in underglaze blue; they are also stamped with model
numbers, with the help of which they can be approximately
dated.[65]

In their time—the Biedermeier period—lithophanes were
not only turned out in their thousands by the two factories
already mentioned as very definitely mass-produced items; they
were also made in smaller quantities by other factories such as
Nymphenburg (where they are mentioned in the 1840s),
Pirkenhammer (as shades for night-lights, late 1830s), the
Imperial Manufactory in St Petersburg, and by the Popov
factory.[66] They were also manufactured at Volkstedt and at
Plaue near Arnstadt in Thuringia, the latter being the only 255
factory that is still (or again) producing them today.[67]

## Thuringia

The factories of Thuringia developed hardly at all during this
period. Neo-Classicism continued in most cases to dictate the 256
shapes employed. Decoration remained similarly conservative, 258
rarely departing from the standard repertoire of views and 257
flowers. Large quantities of utility wares continued to be
decorated with the strawflower pattern in underglaze blue or
with printed patterns of all kinds.

## BOHEMIA

### Private Factories

The Vienna factory had worked since its establishment and
throughout the Sorgenthal and Niedermayer periods for the
upper stratum of society that wanted for its palaces, in addition
to paintings and other works of art, sophisticated table services
and ornaments appropriate to so artistic a setting. The new class
of more or less well-to-do townspeople that had been growing
since the beginning of the industrial revolution was catered for
by the factories that sprang up after 1800 in northern Austria
and Bohemia. They were not, however, concerned with purely
utility ware, since this demand was adequately and
inexpensively covered by stoneware and pewter suppliers. So
they produced fancy painted cups for the glass cabinets of
middle-class homes, fruit and biscuit bowls, vases with gilt
decoration, and painted pipe bowls. It was with such individual
pieces as these that in the 1820s and early 1830s they reached
their artistic peak—while simultaneously their porcelain itself
achieved a satisfactory degree of maturity in terms of paste and
glaze. The Schlaggenwald and Klösterle factories did not have
many painters, but they did include some outstanding ones
who cared about good patterns and colours and produced in
particular cups and *déjeuners* of true artistic quality.

256 *Pipe bowl with view of Jena.* Ilmenau, *c.* 1850. Overglaze painting, gilt rim. L. 13.5 cm. Mark: 133. TM, Eisenach.
Pipe bowls remained a major item in the Thuringian factories' mass-production programme, though few were painted as carefully as this one.

257 *Cup with a painting of St Geneviève and saucer.* Ilmenau, *c.* 1850. Black printed and gilt decoration. H. 10.8 cm. Mark: 133. Kunstgewerbemuseum, Cologne (E 4155).
The picture of St Geneviève and the nursing hind that kept her company was based on an engraving by A. Bosselmann and applied to the cup by the transfer-printing process.

258 *Pieces from a coffee service with views of Weimar.* Ilmenau, *c.* 1851. Overglaze painting, gilt rims. Dimensions and mark: inaccessible. TM, Eisenach.
The Neo-Classical shapes and conventional local views—charmingly though they are painted—typify the stylistic inertia of the Thuringian factories.

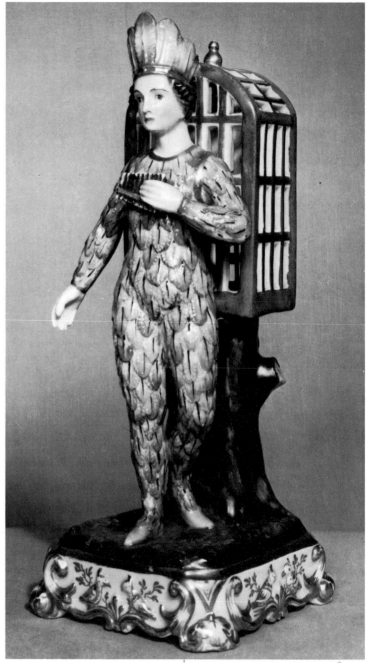

259 *Crater vase with landscape.* Schlaggenwald, 1835. Overglaze painting and gilt decoration. H. 38 cm. Marks: 117 and date. UM, Prague (Z-50). With its traditional 'Medici' shape and view of the Eger (Cheb) valley, this vase is typical of Schlaggenwald's production in the early 1830s.

260 *Statuette of Papageno.* Schlaggenwald, 1838. Painted and gilded. H. 23.8 cm. Mark: inaccessible. UM, Prague (Z-97/127). *Papageno* and *Papagena,* characters from Mozart's *Magic Flute,* are unusual figures among Schlaggenwald's many Neo-Rococo porcelain figures.

With the advent of the 1830s the customers of the Bohemian factories began to demand coffee and dining services, forcing the factories to introduce types of decoration that were cheaper to produce than painted miniatures. Consequently their managements looked at what other factories were doing and began, for example, to imitate Meissen's vine-leaf pattern in underglaze green. Simple blue and gold rims or spots were also used and offered neat solutions, though in the long run they failed to satisfy the customers. As a result, even before 1840 the factories were making extensive use of printing and transfer processes, which for the Bohemian factories represented the beginning of a steady decline to the status of mass producers.[68]

## Schlaggenwald

The most important factory in Bohemia at the beginning of the Biedermeier period was that of Haas and Lippert in Schlaggenwald. Around 1830 something like twenty painters were busy decorating Neo-Classical vases and cups with landscapes and sights of Bohemia, beauty spots, playing-cards, hunting scenes, portraits, and flowers, many delightful examples of which are preserved in the museums of present-day Czechoslovakia.[69] As the painters' confidence grew, so their pictures took up more and more of the available space until in the mid-1830s only the rounded foot of vase or cup was left unpainted to form, as it were, a base for the paintings. There

259

was a particular fashion for miniature portraits of beautiful women, for which the porcelain painters often drew upon Franz Stöber's *Gallery of Female Beauties, a Pattern-Book of Samples for Young and Old,* as well as upon the almanacs. Portraits of royalty also sold well, as did copies of old masters. The white ground that always dominates early Bohemian cups gave way to large areas of gloss gilding, often relieved by borders of polished and etched vine-leaves on the Viennese model. The strict cylindrical and calathus cups gradually disappeared in favour of more engaging shapes. The Vienna factory was no longer adequate as a design source. The young head of the firm, Eusebius August Haas, who had replaced his father Wenzel Haas in 1830, put his faith in a broader, more modern range of wares. A wealth of shapes and particularly of types of decoration characterized Schlaggenwald in the 1830s. These were not variants of one and the same style, as in Vienna from 1800 to 1830, but already manifested a stylistic pluralism that was to be typical of the huge range of wares with which the young porcelain factories of the Biedermeier period competed for the favours of the public at large. For conservative tastes Haas continued to offer 'Etruscan' cups with black-and-white figures.[70] For those who liked modern, naturalistic shapes there were wood-grain imitations or examples in which the cup was modelled as a shell and the saucer as a scallop-shell.[71] The facetted cup shape with applied pseudo-precious stones was borrowed from Vienna, as was the more profusely curved variety of the so-called mother-of-pearl cup, which lent itself to chinoiserie types of decoration. Other echoes of the style of the eighteenth century are replicas of cups in the shape of roses or guelder-rose clusters (examples from 1832),[72] as in use at Meissen around 1740. A comprehensive revival of Rococo porcelain began in 1835. Curvaceous cups and bowls were decorated in relief with voluted rims, raised cartouches, S and C scroll mouldings, and even sculpted flowers on the sides. As at Meissen, this kind of relief decoration gradually replaced the more expensive miniature painting, with the result that the number of painters employed declined steadily after 1835. The relief cartouches and *rocaille* ornaments usually stand on a white ground once again, though occasionally on a cobalt ground, and are trimmed with polished gilding. For more elaborate utensils the factory tended to fall back on more complex modelling. Boxes, vases, inkwells, or mantelshelf clocks were embellished with fanciful handles, voluted bases, cornucopia grips, and *rocaille* and flower decoration. The late 1830s also saw Schlaggenwald's first porcelain figures. An unimportant bagpipe player (1837) was followed in 1838/1839 by the very charming couple representing Papageno and Papagena from Mozart's opera *The Magic Flute,* and before long Rococo figurines were being welcomed by the critics. As in Russia, the better statuettes are painted on biscuit; others have a glaze, which is usually too thick and spoils the contours, and some hastily applied coloured paint. To industrial exhibitions in the 1840s the factory sent relief wares and figures, and instead of painted services it now submitted services with printed decoration. This was done in blue or black under the glaze. In this way the almanac motifs and views, so popular in the 1820s could be

261   *Covered cup and saucer with chinoiserie decoration.* Schlaggenwald, 1836. Overglaze and gilt decoration. H. 10.7 cm. Marks: 117 and date. UM, Prague (21 535).
In the 1830s the Bohemian factories began to vary their products in order to appeal to a wider clientele.

262   *Tea-service in the 'Second Rococo' style.* Schlaggenwald, 1841. Overglaze and gilt decoration. Marks: 116 and date. UM, Prague (B II 171).
'Second Rococo', increasingly popular from 1835 onwards, is characterized by restless shapes, contrasting details, and bright colouring and gilding.

263   *Two mineral-water mugs.* Schlaggenwald and Pirkenhammer, *c.* 1835. ▷
Transfer-printed decoration, gilt rims. H. (left) 11.2 cm, (right) 11 cm. Marks: (left), 114; (right), 117. MNC, Sèvres (14 416, 22 503).
For the many visitors to the nearby spas, the Bohemian factories made tall mugs decorated with printed views for taking the waters.

264 *Teapot with warmer.* Pirkenhammer, *c.* 1835. Overglaze painting, gilt decoration. H. 22.2 cm. Mark: 114. UM, Prague.
The Biedermeier period brought many new types of vessels and appliances. This 'tower' decorated with a view of Karlsbad was devised to keep the teapot warm.

265 *Cup with portrait of a child and saucer.* Elbogen, *c.* 1832. Overglaze painting and gilding. H. 8.2 cm. Mark: 110. UM, Prague.
The cup, with its delightful picture of a little girl sitting in the grass, still shows a strong Viennese influence.

applied cheaply and durably to porcelain. Sometimes they were coloured by the few painters still on the pay-roll. Due to the variety of shapes and decoration that it could supply, and thanks to an ever-increasing production of its cheap wares, the Schlaggenwald factory continued to flourish in the 1830s and 1840s. Wholly owned by Eusebius August Haas from 1847 onwards, following the death of his father's former partner Lippert in 1843, the factory enjoyed excellent sales for its wares through branches in Austrian Italy and Austria-Hungary, in Prague, and last but not least in Vienna. The Imperial Manufactory in Vienna, which from 1848 onwards was continually in need of subsidies, may well have viewed with some bitterness the rise of the Schlaggenwald factory on the basis of increasingly dubious wares.

## Pirkenhammer

Lippert and Haas in Schlaggenwald had a competitor at Pirkenhammer who outdid them in many respects. In 1831 Christian Fischer, the son of one of the founders of the firm, who had trained as a chemist in Prague, became managing director of the Fischer and Reichenbach factory. Fifteen years later he bought out the Reichenbach share, and from 1846 to 1853 he was sole proprietor.[73] Under Christian Fischer the Pirkenhammer porcelain paste was regarded as the finest in Bohemia; with its high degree of transparency it came closest to the French, which was particularly to its advantage on the Italian market, where it adversely affected French sales.[74] Pirkenhammer had installed a copperplate press as early as 1829, which put the factory in an even better position than before to supply inexpensive mass-produced wares, especially cups with views of Bohemian sights. In contrast to such early steps in the direction of industrialization, however, Christian Fischer in other aspects of his output clung to rather more conservative terrain than Schlaggenwald. When in the 1840s Haas had switched completely to relief and above all printed decoration, Fischer was still producing cups and *déjeuners*  264 painted with scenes and landscapes. The best of the Pirkenhammer painters were the Quasts, father and son, Quast senior having emigrated from Ansbach in Bavaria. In order to set the painting off to its best advantage, in the 1840s the Fischer factory even fell back on Neo-Classical cylindrical shapes, which suited miniature painting better than the curved sides of the shapes then in fashion. But of course even here the taste of the time was not ignored, and from the mid-1830s onwards the Pirkenhammer programme included livelier vessel shapes, with scroll handles and applied *rocaille* ornaments as well as naturalistic reliefs.

## Klösterle

In addition to the two big firms in Schlaggenwald and Pirkenhammer it was above all Klösterle and Elbogen that played an important role in the late Biedermeier period. From 1835 Klösterle was under the management of Johann Hillar,

266 *Ice-urn.* Copenhagen: RPF, G. F. Hetsch, 1834. Overglaze painting, ▷ gilt decoration. H. 32 cm. Mark: 146. Christiansborg Palace, Copenhagen. This piece belongs to the magnificent dessert service commissioned for the royal palace of Christiansborg in 1831.

267 *Cup and saucer in the 'Second Rococo' style.* Altrohlau, mid-19th century. Overglaze and gilt decoration. H. 9.2 cm. Mark: inaccessible. UM, Prague. The majority of the smaller Bohemian firms cultivated the sumptuous 'Second Rococo' style from 1835 onwards.

268 *The Rape of Ganymede.* Copenhagen: RPF, after 1839. Biscuit porcelain. H. 18 cm. Marks: 146 and ENERET stamp. RPF, Copenhagen. A porcelain copy of Thorwaldsen's 1817 marble of the boy who became cup-bearer to Zeus, who abducted him in the guise of an eagle.

a university-trained expert like Christian Fischer, who successfully adopted various technological improvements. Before long both paste and glaze were so impeccable that Klösterle could afford to leave its wares white and decorate them in the fashionable manner merely with relief and gilt ornamentation. From 1843 decoration was applied at Klösterle too by means of the advantageous printing process. A special feature of Klösterle are the figures that were modelled there from 1836 onwards: groups of children, flower girls, and the occasional peasant figure or genre statuette, such as the *Dame im Pelz* ('Woman in Furs'), in painted biscuit.[75]

### Elbogen and Smaller Firms

The Elbogen factory continued under the management of the Haidinger brothers, who in the 1830s broke away from the narrow influence of Vienna. Everyday wares were printed in blue on the model of English stoneware. Around 1830 they were producing very up-to-date white porcelain wares with etched gilt vine-leaf borders, but then in many ways they switched to historical models. At the industrial exhibition held in Prague in 1836 they presented on the one hand wares in the Chinese style decorated in underglaze blue and on the other early samples of Neo-Rococo. In the following years they closely imitated eighteenth-century Meissen porcelain, particularly copying the painting of Höroldt, *Neuoziermuster* (the 'new osier pattern'), gold lace, and—with particular predilection and great skill—sculpted flower shapes and decoration. With their guelder-rose cups and their tendrils and little roses painted in colour on bowls, cups, and even mineral-water mugs they went much further in terms of getting close to historical models than the little *rocaille* ornaments and scroll rims commonly used by other factories. As well as this kind of Neo-Rococo, which in Elbogen was adopted earlier and above all more consciously and exclusively from old Meissen patterns

than at Meissen itself, greater tribute was paid here to the current fashion for naturalism than at other factories. Bottles and jugs in the shape of figures or decorated with figures and flowers in relief are reminiscent of contemporary English ceramics.[76]

The smaller Bohemian firms, most of which produced stoneware as well as porcelain, followed the above-mentioned factories in adopting this broad programme that was nevertheless recognizably typical of the time. Dallwitz, near Karlsbad, Giesshübel, Altrohlau (Stará Role), and Chodau went on producing Neo-Classical Viennese cups painted with flowers and views for a long time, as well as similarly decorated mineral-water mugs. For less expensive decoration they chose gold edges and strings of vine-leaves and cornflowers. In the 1840s they used printed decoration; at the same time shapes became more animated and the appearance of relief decoration was linked to Neo-Rococo trends.

## DENMARK

### Copenhagen

*Royal Porcelain Manufactory*
At Copenhagen, still Scandinavia's only factory of any artistic importance, the preservation of the Neo-Classical style in its more refined, courtly form was guaranteed by the continued presence of Gustav Friedrich Hetsch (mentioned in the chapter cf. p. 81 on the earlier period). In the early 1830s state services had to be designed for the royal residences. Hetsch's Neo-Classical shapes were decorated by a group of outstanding painters. King Frederik VI's dessert service for Christiansborg, delivered in 1834, is embellished with a wealth of Classical gilt decoration and flower painting as well as with views of Danish landscapes and towns, which were drawn *in situ* especially for this purpose. Besides flower and view painting, portraits also played a part.

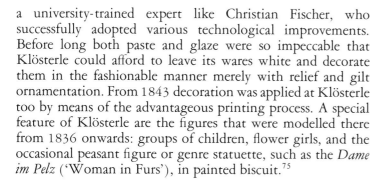

265

267

266

269, 270 *Day and Night*. Copenhagen: RPF, after 1840. Biscuit reliefs. D. 11 cm. Marks: 146 and ENERET stamp. RPF, Copenhagen.
These two round medallions, first modelled in 1840, were the most successful of Copenhagen's Thorwaldsen copies.

Of lesser interest in modelling and painting were Neo-Gothic and Neo-Rococo motifs, although individual examples of the former were mentioned around 1830 and of the latter from 1841 onwards.[77] Sculpture regained an extraordinary importance in the late 1840s—in a very particular direction. It was G. F. Hetsch who initiated the connection with Denmark's great national sculptor, Berthel Thorwaldsen. As early as 1824 small-scale copies were made in biscuit porcelain (9 and 18 cm high respectively) of Thorwaldsen's recent marble busts of Prince Christian Frederik VI. The next attempt did not take place until 1835, but in the late 1840s numerous copies of free-standing sculptures and reliefs by Thorwaldsen appeared in rapid succession. The 1835 statuette of Lord Byron (original 1831) was followed in 1838/1839 by a seated shepherd, *Mercury,* and *Ganymede.* In 1840 the production of biscuit copies of Thorwaldsen's work received a boost from the spontaneous and enormous success enjoyed by the pair of relief tondi, *Day* and *Night* (D. 11 cm): the factory sold over 2,100 of these medallions alone in the first six years.[78] All nineteen statuettes that had so far appeared, as well as twenty-five relief motifs and busts, were on show at the 1851 Great Exhibition and could be assured of a great welcome in London, where of course the comparable Parian statuettes produced by several English factories had been enjoying increasing popularity since around 1840.[79] It remains unclear whether the Danish biscuit statues based on Thorwaldsen are derived from the porcelain figures that the Berlin factory based on Schadow and Rauch.[80] What does seem to us to be certain is that it influenced and was influenced by the Parian statuary of the mid-century. It remains an astonishing fact that in the middle of a period in which painted porcelain favoured refined, fresh, and invariably glowing colours in combination with brilliant gilding, this marble whiteness—the very epitome of colourlessness—

268

269–270

cf. p. 166

should have been so successful where sculpture was concerned.[81] There was nothing like it in Germany, but from 1854 onwards there was a young competitor in Copenhagen itself.

*Bing & Grøndahl Factory*
Two years earlier a skilled modeller named Frederik Wilhelm Grøndahl had left the Royal Porcelain Manufactory and joined the book and art dealers Jacob Hermann and Meyer Hermann Bing to set up a second factory in the city. They managed to obtain the services of the eminent sculptor Hermann Bissen as their artistic adviser, and Bissen established contacts with the Thorwaldsen museum. The new firm of Bing & Grøndahl produced its first biscuit statuettes and reliefs—based on the same models as those of the Royal Manufactory—in 1854; in 1864, at the third World Exhibition in London, they presented a wide range that was in quality in no way inferior to that of its rival.

## ENGLAND

During the reign of William IV (1830–1837) and at the beginning of Queen Victoria's rule (1837–1901), English porcelain became more and more influenced by the revived Rococo style that dominated this period. French influence on English porcelain was superseded by German influence—as indeed had happened in France itself, we have already seen that Jacob Petit was inspired mainly by Meissen. Decorative porcelain had already shown signs of a tendency towards over-ornamentation, and from now on the popularity of pieces encrusted with reliefs, usually flowers, knew no bounds. Gilding, although often of lower quality than during the earlier period, was now used more and more abundantly. In the catalogue of the exhibition 'Staffordshire Porcelain, 1740–1851' Terry Lockett states: 'The overall impression often made in this period is of a lack of control in the design, of a subordination of function to ornament and yet of a ware which

271 *Plate.* Coalport (Shropshire), John Rose &
Co, *c.* 1815. Bone china. D. 23.7 cm. Mark: 167.
V & A, London (C. 1025-1924).
The border decoration is in underglaze blue with
a gilded pattern and polychrome painting in the
centre, evidence that the influence of the 18th
century persisted into the 19th.

272 *Plate.* Caughley or Coalport (Shropshire),
John Rose & Co, decoration attributed to
Thomas Pardoe at Bristol, *c.* 1815. Bone china.
D. 24.9 cm. Unmarked. V & A, London (3143-
1901).
Like their French counterparts, many English
porcelain factories sold 'blanks' to decorators.
The floral painting on this plate is in delicate
shades of green, grey, and mauve.

273 *Oval dish.* Coalport (Shropshire), John ▷
Rose & Co, decoration done in London, *c.* 1820.
Bone china. L. 29.5 cm. Unmarked. V & A,
London (C. 62-1939).
The border of the dish is decorated with
interlaced scrolls and flower sprays in relief under
the glaze in the style originating at Vincennes.
The ground on the border is a beautiful grey
colour, and the colour scheme achieves a
harmonious originality.

274 *Pot-pourri.* Coalport (Shropshire), John
Rose & Co, *c.* 1840. Bone china. H. 29.3 cm.
Unmarked. V & A, London (C. 1250-1917).
Pieces of this type with their encrusted floral
decoration were the pride of the Coalport factory
between 1820 and 1840, about ten years before
similar pieces were made on the Continent.
Examples can be attributed to Coalport on the
basis of factory marks or by comparing unmarked
pieces with the pattern-books preserved at the
factory.

possesses great technical mastery and virtuosity, colourful and
opulent, but somehow foreign to our rather insular tastes (the
British have always preferred Chinese- and Greek-inspired
decoration to Continental!)'.[82] Continental influence may well
be foreign to English taste, but none the less it took hold in
England in a way unsurpassed in France.

The products of two factories above all were the incarnation
of the revived Rococo style: Coalport and Rockingham. Other
firms did, of course, manufacture porcelain in this style but
were more eclectic and used other styles as well.

Another important development was the discovery of Parian
porcelain by Copeland, successors of Spode. It proved well
suited to figure-making and *pâte-sur-pâte* decoration.

## Coalport

The Coalport factory, situated on the banks of the River Severn
in Shropshire, had been run by John Rose since the end of the
eighteenth century and operated under the name of John Rose

& Co. In 1814 John Rose bought the rival factory on the
opposite bank of the river in Coalport itself, and at the same
time he shut down the Caughley factory, which he had been
running since 1799. These three factories, which were in direct
competition with each other in the early nineteenth century,
were in no way exceptional. The body used was a hard, dense
composition covered with a soft glaze. Simple shapes typical of
this period were made, usually decorated with flowers,
landscapes and oriental motifs. After 1814 John Rose
improved the quality of both the body and, especially, the
glaze. In 1820 he bought up the remaining stock from the
Nantgarw and Swansea factories as well as their moulds. In the   273
same year he was awarded the medal of the Royal Society of
Arts for his discovery of a leadless felspathic glaze, which
reduced the health risk to his employees and customers. Other
factories such as Spode soon followed his example and used a
leadless glaze.

Pieces ornamented with flowers in relief, for which the
Coalport factory is renowned, were made from the 1820s
onward.   Applied   flowers,   scrolls,   and   other   relief   274–275

275 *Dish with flowers and fruit in relief.* Coalport (Shropshire), John Rose & Co, *c.* 1830. Bone china. D. 26.4 cm. Unmarked. V & A, London (C. 566-1935).
Coalport is famous for its flower-encrusted vases, soup bowls, pots-pourris, teapots and so on. Here the object is actually made up of relief decoration.

276 *Water jug.* Coalport (Shropshire), John Rose & Co, *c.* 1837. Bone china. H. 16.51 cm. Mark: 168. Coll. of Her Majesty the Queen, Windsor Castle.
This piece with Queen Victoria's monogram is a good example of the style of English porcelain in the 1830s.

277 *Two comports and a plate from the William IV Service.* Swinton ▷ (Yorkshire), Brameld & Co: Rockingham Works, 1830–1837. Bone china. Max. H. 27 cm, D. (plate) 23.8 cm. Mark: 223. Coll. of Her Majesty the Queen, London.
This service is probably the most beautiful example of 19th-century European porcelain. The imaginative design of the comports and the high quality of the painted decoration are quite outstanding. As so often at Rockingham, both relief and painted decoration are used.

278 *Perfume jar and cover.* Swinton (Yorkshire), Brameld & Co: ▷ Rockingham Works, *c.* 1830. Bone china. H. 15.8 cm. Mark: 222. V & A, London (3177 2a-1901).
Like Coalport, Rockingham produced a large number of flower-encrusted pieces.

279 *'Rhinoceros' vase.* Swinton (Yorkshire), Brameld & Co: Rockingham ▷▷ Works, *c.* 1826. Bone china. H. 97.8 cm. Unmarked. V & A, London (C. 47-1869).
This vase, of which there are only two examples, was a special production. Its height, relief and painted decoration, and its abundant gilding, all distinguish it from other Rockingham wares. However, it is not particularly pleasing aesthetically, especially as the gilding is dark and dull in tone. It was painted by Edwin Steele.

ornamentation—often superimposed on each other—virtually obscured, or were sometimes inconsistent with the shape of the vases, teapots, pots-pourris, and baskets produced. Pieces of this type made by Coalport are often known as 'Coalbrookdale' porcelains, since in the 1820s they were marked: 'O D', 'C Dale', 'Coalbrookdale', or 'Coalport'. A pattern-book used by a travelling salesmen working for the factory around 1840 has survived and enables us to attribute to Coalport a number of pieces that are usually unmarked. The pattern-book includes, of course, pieces which were already in production prior to the 1840s. Although Coalport is the best-known factory using relief decoration painted in naturalistic colours, it was by no means the only firm making this type of porcelain.

After John Rose's death in 1841 his nephews carried on the business, making pieces in the revived Rococo style. In addition they began to manufacture copies of Sèvres porcelain. Coalport was stylistically in advance of other European factories, especially those in France, by ten years or so, since it adopted the revived Rococo style in the 1820s and favoured eclecticism in the 1840s.

## Rockingham

The name of the Rockingham factory is indissolubly associated, like that of Coalport, with the manufacture of pieces in the Neo-Rococo style heavily encrusted with reliefs. The factory took its name from its patron, Earl Fitzwilliam, Marquis of Rockingham, rather than from its location. It was situated at Swinton in Yorkshire and taken over by the Brameld

brothers in 1806. It had been making pottery and creamware since the mid-eighteenth century. In 1826 it began to make porcelain. The factory mark was a griffin, the crest of its protector. Although of high quality, the porcelain made there was unprofitable. The Brameld brothers were poor managers, and the factory closed down in 1846.

The Brameld brothers showed a marked preference for specially created pieces, perhaps because they enjoyed noble patronage, unlike any other British factory. Such wares became much more common in the second half of the century as factory owners became increasingly conscious of the international exhibitions. Two examples of a 'rhinoceros' vase are typical of 279

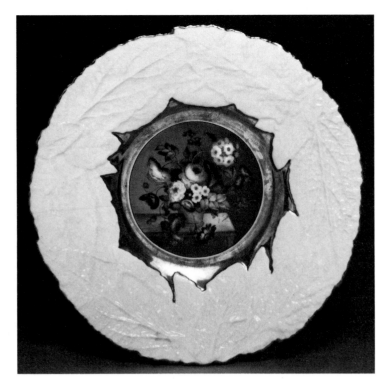

280 *Plate.* Swinton (Yorkshire), Brameld & Co: Rockingham Works, *c.* 1825. Bone china. D. 25 cm. Mark: 224 and incised 'B'. V & A, London (C. 776-1935).
The border has leaf moulding, while the centre is painted with flowers on a gold ground. The decoration is unusual and perfectly executed.

this kind of production. One was made for Earl Fitzwilliam and is now in Rotherham museum, while the other is in the Victoria and Albert Museum, London, and was painted by Edwin Steele in about 1826. He was the son of the Derby porcelain painter Thomas Steele. Although the painting is well executed, the heavily gilded oak leaves, acorns, and twig handles as well as the famous gilt finial in the shape of a rhinoceros are not especially attractive, for the gilding is dull and dark in colour. When W. B. Honey called it 'an excellent illustration of the taste of the period',[83] he seems to have picked on a piece that was in fact rather exceptional.

277   Another specially created work, this time perfectly executed, particularly in regard to its gilding (a sure sign of production quality), is the William IV Service. Although ordered in 1830, it was only used for the first time at Queen Victoria's coronation. The plates bear the Royal Arms in the centre, surrounded by oak boughs on a blue ground, itself decorated with gilding. The numerous dessert dishes and comports are really extraordinary, their stems modelled as coral branches, palm trees, sheaves of corn, or occasionally fruit-bearing branches. Alwyn and Angela Cox have called this service 'A Royal Extravaganza'.[84] There is also abundant painted decoration: the bases of the comports and fruit dishes are decorated with landscape scenes complementing the relief motif. For instance, a shell-shaped cup, its foot shaped as a piece of coral, is decorated with marine subjects. The wine-coolers are painted with scenes from Sir Walter Scott's novels or with reproductions of contemporary English paintings. Thomas Griffin was responsible for modelling the shapes, while George Speight designed and painted the armorial devices. Thomas Brentnall, who had been at the Derby factory, painted the flowers, and William Willis Bailey may have done the landscape scenes. The service was extremely successful and

281 *Vase.* Burslem (Staffordshire), Samuel Alcock & Co: Hill Pottery, after 1844. H. 20.5 cm. Mark: 163. Coll. Godden of Worthing Ltd.
Samuel Alcock produced large numbers of vases of slender form, sometimes with handles. They are decorated either in relief or with hand-painted scenes.

282 *Vase.* Burslem (Staffordshire), Samuel Alcock & Co: Hill Pottery, ▷ *c.* 1856. Bone china. H. 21 cm. Mark: 166. CM & AG, Stoke-on-Trent.
Neo-Classicism once more became fashionable in Europe between 1845 and 1855. Alcock's vases in the Neo-Classical style with their polychrome decoration, have a somewhat strange appearance.

283 *Vase.* Burslem (Staffordshire), Samuel Alcock & Co: Hill Pottery, *c.* 1850. Parian porcelain. H. 28.5 cm. Mark: 164. V & A, London (332-1952).
Parian ware was used above all for figures but occasionally also for more functional pieces.

284 *Figure of Fanny Elssler.* Burslem (Staffordshire), Samuel Alcock & Co: Hill Pottery, *c.* 1851. Biscuit porcelain. H. 36.5 cm. Mark: 165 and 'S.A.' Morris Coll.
This figure, after S. W. Arnold, was exhibited at the 1851 Exhibition. It is biscuit, not Parian, porcelain.

copies of it were ordered by the Duchess of Cumberland, the Duke of Sussex, the Duke of Sutherland, the Duke of Cambridge and the King of Belgium. These orders completed the ruin of the uncommercial Brameld brothers.

Some less extravagantly conceived wares were also made by the Bramelds. They too were of high quality, since the body used was beautifully soft and the painters, many of whom worked on the William IV Service, highly skilled.

Among the painters working at Rockingham were: William Corden, who had been at the Derby factory, George Speight, who sometimes signed his pieces, Thomas Brentnall, Collinson, Llandig (the last three fruit and flower painters), and William Willis Bailey who painted butterflies.[85] Rockingham, although famous for its relief-decorated pieces, should perhaps be more admired for the perfection of its painting. Charming plates decorated around the border with leaves in low relief and with polychrome painting in the central reserve deserve mention in this context.

### Samuel Alcock & Co

The firm owned by Samuel Alcock made porcelain between 1828 and 1853. Most of the pieces, which are of high quality, are typical of the period: some are encrusted with flowers, while services with relief decoration enhanced by painted motifs in the Rococo style were also made. Some of the biscuit figures made by this factory are famous, the statuette of the dancer Fanny Elssler is a much more lively and lifelike figure than many manufactured at this period. For the most part biscuit porcelain was used to represent rather rigid creations based on Classical prototypes. Samuel Alcock was particularly fond of

Classical art, and in the 1850s he manufactured some remarkable vases, the style and iconography of which was based on Greek vases of the fifth century BC. Alcock's pieces, however, were decorated in quite a different manner from the Classical vases: he used pink, yellow, and sea-green, colours quite unknown to Classical potters.

Alcock was not the only potter producing porcelain in the Classical style at the end of the first half of the nineteenth century. The names 'Estruscan', 'Pompeian' and 'Greek' were among those used interchangeably to describe pieces that had an element of fantasy about them absent from the early nineteenth-century productions in the Neo-Classical idiom. A similar style evolved in France at about the same time, as we can see from a porcelain vase symbolizing *Velocitas* made at the Sèvres factory in 1852.[86]

### Minton

Although most relief-decorated English porcelain dating from this period tends to be attributed to Coalport or Rockingham, it was Thomas Minton (1765–1835) who made most of this type of porcelain. He had founded a creamware factory at Stoke-on-Trent in 1793, very near to the Spode factory. Around 1798 he began to make bone china. Although he enjoyed considerable success he gave up making china between 1816 and 1824 for reasons which remain obscure. During the first half of the nineteenth century Thomas Minton and his son Herbert (1793–1858), both gifted with a well-developed commercial and artistic flair, were making pieces in the popular styles of the time. Until 1816 simple shapes were produced mostly painted with the usual Staffordshire subjects, including

285  *Jug and stand.* Liverpool (Lancashire), Case, Mort & Co: Herculaneum Pottery, between 1833–1836. H. 12.1 cm. Mark: 178. V & A, London (C. 659-1935).
The Herculaneum factory was established about 1796; it initially made creamware and then began to make porcelain around 1800. It changed hands several times, closing in 1840. In style it developed along the lines of other English factories. This piece has a dark pink ground and is painted with naturalistic flowers.

286  *Pair of cache-pots (flower-pot cases).* Stoke-on-Trent (Staffordshire), Minton factory, *c.* 1815. Bone china. H. 11.5 cm. Mark: 208. V & A, London (Sch. I. 792).
These pots are decorated with botanical subjects in the simple style popular in early 19th-century Staffordshire.

287  *Plate.* Stoke-on-Trent (Staffordshire), Minton factory, *c.* 1810. Bone china. D. 22.5 cm. Mark: 207. V & A, London (2721-1901).
The underglaze-blue decoration has been embellished with overglaze low-temperature colours and gilt. Unlike conventional chinoiseries, the decoration on this plate is unusually poetic.

288 *Thermometer.* Stoke-on-Trent (Staffordshire), Minton factory, *c.* 1830. Bone china. H. 16.7 cm. Unmarked. V & A, London (C. 770-1935). The most varied objects were created in England in the Rococo style, just as happened at the Paris factories.

290 *Figure of Queen Victoria.* Stoke-on-Trent (Staffordshire), Minton & Boyle factory, *c.* 1837. Biscuit porcelain. H. 29.21 cm. Unmarked. Coll. Godden of Worthing Ltd
Before the invention of Parian ware, the English factories used a special body for figures. This model bears the number '106', which makes it possible to attribute it to the Minton factory.

289 *Figure of a seated lady with a basket.* Stoke-on-Trent (Staffordshire), Minton & Boyle factory, *c.* 1840. Bone china. H. 12.5 cm. Unmarked. Minton Mus.: Royal Doulton Tableware Ltd, Stoke-on-Trent.
The piece is based on a Meissen model that was also copied by the Coalport factory and by Jacob Petit in Paris.

Chinese- and Japanese-inspired motifs (either lustred or printed), flowers, Neo-Classical or rustic scenes. After 1826 287 shapes and decorative motifs alike were affected by the revived Rococo style. Floral decoration was now strongly influenced by 288, 289 Meissen, although French sources of inspiration were also important. In the 1830s Minton copied the eighteenth-century Sèvres *vase à oreilles.*[87] However, even though shapes were copied, the decoration was not. A Minton copy of a *plateau Hébert* dating from around 1840, also created at Vincennes-Sèvres in the eighteenth century, was painted by John Simpson with a Virgin and Child after Raphael.[88] Gothic motifs were used at Minton following French influence.[89] Its dominance, which the French themselves find surprising, was not the only influence affecting Minton; even Chelsea vases with particularly elaborate handles were copied. From the 1830s Minton was characterized as much by its eclecticism as by its taste for richness and Rococo motifs. Most Minton porcelain of this period is unmarked. However, pattern-books surviving at the factory, which is still in production, can be used to identify shapes and decoration in use in this period.

Figures were made in some quantity at this time. Both biscuit and polychrome glazed pieces were produced. Biscuit 290 examples were strongly influenced by pieces made at Vincennes and Sèvres in the mid-eighteenth century. However, Minton occasionally used heavily scrolling bases that are very Rococo in feeling. Glazed figures were based on German models. Some

biscuit-porcelain figures are executed in pure Rococo style such as a seated female figure sniffing a bunch of flowers and symbolizing the sense of smell. It is based on a Meissen original dating from 1772–1774. The figure is wearing a dress trimmed with porcelain lace. The process of making this lace had been invented in Germany in the nineteenth century and was in use at the Derby factory at the same period. This figure dates from around 1842.[90]

## Parian Ware

291–295 Right at the end of the period 1830–1850 Minton began to use Parian porcelain,[91] which had probably been perfected by Copeland & Garrett, successors to Spode.

Josiah Spode III died in 1829. In 1833 William Taylor Copeland, who had been in charge of Spode's London showroom, bought the showroom and the factory in Stoke-on-Trent. He ran both concerns in partnership with Thomas Garrett, Josiah Spode's descendants having preferred the role of gentlemen-farmers to that of factory owners. In 1847 Garrett gave up the business which then became known as 'W.T. Copeland, late Spode'.

During this period, when they were enjoying great success and employed about a thousand workers,[92] Copeland & Garrett made pieces in the popular taste of the time. Perhaps because of the influence of the artistic director, Thomas Battam, there was a slight preference for 'Etruscan' shapes and decoration. Battam played an especially important role in the momentous discovery of Parian ware. Copeland & Garrett's Parian body formula included felspar, china clay, or kaolin, and a frit containing silica, Cornish stone (a felspathic clay) and potash.[93] The composition was known by various names: at Copeland & Garrett it was called 'statuary porcelain', at Minton it was christened 'Parian' and at Wedgwood, where it was occasionally used around 1848, it was marketed as 'Carrara'. These names all alluded to the resemblance between the new material and marble. The name 'Parian' in fact refers to marble quarried at Paros, while the origin of the name 'Carrara' is perhaps more familiar deriving, of course, from the famous marble quarry. To anyone accustomed to the whiteness and the texture of Continental biscuit porcelain, Parian ware has an unfortunate resemblance to soap. Nevertheless it enjoyed great success. It seems to have been discovered by John Mountford, who worked for Copeland & Garrett and had been trained at Derby. He carried out experiments to make biscuit porcelain similar to that made at Derby in the eighteenth century. In 1844, around the same time as Mountford was doing this, Benjamin Cheverton invented a machine that was capable of reproducing figures on a reduced scale from an original. Here at last was the technology necessary for the reproduction of famous pieces of sculpture. The success of the Art Unions was the third, and perhaps the most decisive factor, contributing to the triumph of Parian ware. The Art Unions were societies whose members subscribed to a common fund. Once a year a lottery was held and the winners were awarded a work of art. If this were an engraving or a piece of porcelain then the number of winners could be increased. These associations were officially recognized by a law passed in 1846 that distinguished them from illegal lotteries. Here we can see a conscious attempt, which is peculiarly English, to bring examples of 'good taste' into every home. Even though the formula for Parian porcelain cannot in fact be proven to have been invented

291  *Figure of Narcissus.* Stoke-on-Trent (Staffordshire), Copeland & Garrett factory, c. 1846. Parian porcelain. H. 30.2 cm. Mark: 196. V & A, London (2789-1901).
Modelled after a figure by the sculptor John Gibson, this was the first piece commissioned by the Art Union of London in 1846. On the back is the factory mark and the inscription: 'Narcissus by Gibson R. A. Modelled by E. B. Stephens and executed in STATUARY PORCELAIN by Copeland for the Art Union of London 1846'.

at Copeland & Garrett, it is certainly true that the firm's artistic director, Thomas Battam, was one of the first to realize the importance of the new material. Copeland was awarded the first commission bestowed by the London Art Union; it was for the manufacture of a figure of *Narcissus,* after a work by John Gibson. Other commissions followed. At Minton the success of Parian ware was linked to an enterprise founded by the young Henry Cole under the pseudonym of Felix Summerly. Cole, who later became a member of the curatorial staff at the South Kensington Museum (which was to become the Victoria and Albert Museum) and was ultimately knighted, took it upon himself to 'promote public taste' by setting up the 'Art Manufactures' in 1847, commissioning domestic  292 articles of high quality designed by artists. Cole understood, even better than William Morris in later years, that industrial production could be married to the creation of beautiful things. Minton supplied him with stonewares, earthenware

and bone china jugs, tea-services, vases, and so on. From 1847
Parian ware was used at Minton for figures inspired by Classical
art, including *Ariana,* created in 1816 by the German sculptor
Johann Heinrich von Dannecker.

Henry Cole gave up his business in 1850 as he was taken up
with the preparations for the 1851 Exhibition. Although the
firm was short-lived, its importance was far-reaching, and the
designs it produced for Felix Summerly carried on being made
for a number of years.

Parian ware reached the height of its popularity in the second
half of the nineteenth century and was as much used at Minton
as at Copeland. Among the pieces exhibited by Minton in 1851
was a dessert service purchased by the queen. It combines
polychrome, enamelled and Parian porcelain and has figure

groups of children playing with goats, which are mentioned in
the catalogue: 'The two groups of children sporting with goats
are in Parian,—that exquisite material in which England
remains unrivalled, and which is only second to marble'.[94] The
pieces in the exhibition exploit the possibilities of the new
body much more systematically than the Copeland products.
Copeland made a wider range of pieces, which were still
conceived in a historicist style, called 'Etruscan'. Many were 294
ambitiously conceived on a large scale: plaques designed to be
incorporated in chimneypieces and columns that supported
vases.

The International Exhibition held in London in 1851 had
a strong effect on contemporaries and continued to haunt the
imagination of later generations. It tried to impose an artistic

294 *Figure of Virginia.* Stoke-on-Trent (Staffordshire), W. T. Copeland, late Spode factory, *c.* 1850. Parian porcelain. H. 41 cm. Unmarked. Conservatoire national des Arts et Métiers, Paris (4708).
Since this piece was purchased at the 1851 Exhibition, it was probably the first piece of Parian ware to enter a French public collection.

295 *Figure of Una and the lion.* Stoke-on-Trent (Staffordshire), Colin Minton Campbell factory, 1865. Parian porcelain. H. 36.5 cm. Mark: 185. V & A, London (46-1865).
This piece was modelled by John Bell in 1847 as a pendant to the famous figure of *Ariane Riding a Panther.* It is after a work by the German sculptor Johann Heinrich von Dannecker, created in 1816. Both figures display the arid quality typical of Neo-Classical sculpture.

ideal on industrial production, which was in fact quite out of keeping with the reality of mass-production, each firm having tried to outdo its rivals in making exhibition pieces. The cult of eclecticism received official sanction as we can see from the essay by Ralph Nicholson Wornum that appears at the end of the catalogue of the 1851 Exhibition. It is entitled 'The Exhibition as a Lesson in Taste'. Nine styles that he considered had strongly influenced European civilization were discussed: the three antique styles, comprising Egyptian, Greek, and Roman; the three styles of the Middle Ages, that is the Byzantine, the Islamic, and the Gothic; and the three modern styles, which were 'The Renaissance, the Cinquecento, and the Louis Quatorze'. He declared that these nine styles were the bedrock of contemporary manufacturing activity and that it in turn was dominated by French influence: 'There is nothing new in the Exhibition in ornamental design; not a scheme, not a detail that has not been treated over and over again in ages that are gone, that the taste of the producers generally is uneducated, and that in nearly all cases where this is not so, the influence of France is paramount in the European productions'.[95] Finally, Wornum attacked the dogma of French supremacy in matters of taste, underlining the virtues of English taste: 'First, generally, the English side does not betray that great inferiority of taste which has for so long [been] prognosticated of it'.[96] He takes exception to the prestige of Sèvres: 'Though the Sèvres porcelain takes the lead in point of pretensions, it is not superior in taste, and is certainly inferior in matters of utility, to the specimens of Alderman Copeland, of Stoke-on-Trent'.[97] The desire to prove that when it came to making porcelain the English could outdo the French commercially and aesthetically was not an overriding consideration among English porcelain manufacturers during the second half of the nineteenth century, for they had adopted the technical aspects of French porcelain. In fact, the leading factories, headed by Minton, recruited French workers and achieved greatness through them.

# IV 1850–1880: Historicism

The mid-century really did mark a turning-point for arts and crafts in general due to the world exhibitions, which from 1851 onwards enabled international comparisons to be drawn in the field of the craft industries and made the products of those industries the subject of wider discussion. The exhibitions in London, Paris, and Vienna in 1851, 1862, 1867, 1873, and 1889 also resulted in fresh impulses for porcelain manufacturers. After the 1862 Exhibition in London, for example, the Neo-Renaissance porcelains exhibited by the Worcester Royal Porcelain Company (in imitation of Limoges enamels) together with the same firm's so-called 'Capodimonte' vases were thought fit to be emulated at the Royal Saxon Manufactory at Meissen. Experiments conducted at Meissen as a result led to further interesting developments. Similarly, in the wake of world exhibitions such techniques as *pâte-sur-pâte* from Paris, 'Parian' porcelain from England, and underglaze-blue painting from Copenhagen became common property among European manufacturers. Whatever the jury had bestowed recognition on at a world exhibition became an example to all—until the next great competitive circus. Government commissions attended these international exhibitions in an official capacity and subsequently instructed factory managements at home to turn their attention to the more illustrious achievements of those factories that had won more prizes than they had themselves. Consultative bodies, committees of experts, even 'honorary councils of noted artists' (Berlin, 1851) were attached to managements; programmes and theoretical plans were drawn up for the future. Among the more questionable products of this situation were the 'exhibition pieces' that factories made specially for the occasion and that served no other purpose than to demonstrate just what the firm could do in a particular field. The kind of thing that in earlier decades factories had been required to supply as state presents for foreign royalty they now produced as show-pieces for these international occasions—namely supreme examples of their great technical and artistic skill. Often the firm's own master modeller and head painter were not considered capable of producing a sufficiently competitive design and a well-known freelance artist was called in. For example, in the late 1840s the Meissen factory got the architect of the Dresden opera-house, Gottfried Semper,[1] and the Academy painter Julius Schnorr von Carolsfeld to design a monumental covered vase, which was exhibited in 1851. Today it is difficult to summon up any enthusiasm for this piece by an architectural theorist with a penchant for history; at any rate, it made the return journey from the Great Exhibition to Meissen without a medal. One is more in sympathy with another piece exhibited at the same time, a very lifelike little camelia tree in a pot that for all its conventionality is a charming piece of design and shows off the modellers' virtuoso mastery of their material to perfection. Such demonstrations of purely technical skill were frequently exhibited in the mid-century years. It was largely from the technical standpoint that exhibition juries made their assessments, placing a high value on such qualities as extreme size, variety of colour, or especial hardness and whiteness of body. In their assessments of artistic quality they were as uncertain as present-day jurors. They demanded originality (which very often led to banality), innovation in shape and decoration, and a cosmopolitan approach (that is, for Germanic factories, not always to use Saxon landscapes but also the occasional view of the Rhineland and Switzerland);[2] on one hand they wanted more wit and charm in the spirit of a 'Third Rococo', on the other more dignity and composure in the spirit of a stricter Neo-Classicism, or in general terms a tighter integration of art and industry. Factory managements were always having to comply with such conflicting criteria as best they could, but the steady stream of contradictory demands tended rather to increase the lack of uniformity of porcelain production than to lead to fresh innovations.

## FRANCE

### Sèvres (1848–1870)

The history of the Sèvres factory is so bound up with that of the French state that it can only be divided for the purposes of discussion into periods which correspond with major events in French history. Between 1848 and 1852 the Second Republic challenged the political line that had been pursued by the Restoration monarchy, and between 1852 and 1872, in the Second Empire, measures were taken to ensure prosperity in France. There was a crisis at Sèvres in the first period; during the second period slow growth took place at the factory which was to bear fruit during the Third Republic. In any case the year 1880, our normal cut-off point for other porcelain factories, has no significance either in French history nor for Sèvres.

In 1847 Brongniart died. Two years earlier he had appointed as his joint administrator, Jacques Joseph Ebelmen, a mining engineer, who was to succeed him. Ebelmen, however, unlike Brongniart, could not claim to be a man of taste as well as a scientist. His abilities were confined to the technical sphere so that a new post of artistic director had to be created. It was filled by Jules Dieterle from 1852 to 1855 and by Joseph Nicolle between 1856 and 1871. The chemist Alphonse-Louis Salvetat was technical director between 1846 and 1880. On Ebelmen's death in 1852 he was replaced by the physicist Victor Regnault who resigned in 1871.

During the Second Republic the problems faced by the factory were not connected with labour relations, but rather with politics. Why should a Republic subsidize a factory producing luxury pieces that were of little or no practical use?

At this time Sèvres was placed under the control of the Ministry of Agriculture and Commerce. According to a time-honoured French custom, the Ministry quickly appointed a *Conseil de Perfectionnement des Manufactures nationales* ('Development Board for State Enterprises'). A report was drawn up by Fernand de Lasteyrie. Its conclusion was that state enterprises should be maintained (despite the refusal of the *Parlement* of 1850 to sanction the budget necessary for the survival of the Sèvres factory) so that they could be used to carry out technical research which was too costly for private firms to undertake. Products from the state factories could also be used for furnishing public buildings.

In 1852 luxury articles were once again allowed. Under the Second Empire the Sèvres factory came under the jurisdiction of the Minister of State responsible for the Emperor's establishment. Although part of the factory's output was sold to private clients, most of its production was destined to supply tableware (often extremely plain and decorated only with a simple gilt band) and toilet articles for the imperial residences. It was also expected to produce diplomatic and personal gifts for presentation by Their Imperial Majesties. Finally, the factory had to create pieces that would outdo those made by other concerns participating in the world exhibitions, especially in the 1851 London Exhibition of course.[3]

In 1851 the factory had one hundred and fifty employees. Artists were paid on a piece-work system. Tamara Préaud[4] quotes Victor Regnault's complaint that this system allowed painters to work quickly and then to seek additional employment elsewhere. This situation was only to be remedied under the Third Republic.

### Techniques

*Bodies.* Ebelmen and Regnault were both scientists. They realized that if the ceramic art were to evolve stylistically a new body would have to be developed, which would offer new possibilities to the artists. Therefore, they tried to revive the manufacture of the old soft-paste body, which Brongniart had abandoned in 1804. Ebelmen never had the time to see his research through. Victor Regnault was luckier, at least on the theoretical level, although the production of soft-paste porcelain entailed so many problems that during the Second Empire period it remained in the experimental stage. Examples were shown in Paris in 1855. In 1862 a new product, called *pâte caméléon* was shown, which changes colour according to alteration in lighting conditions.[5]

*Manufacturing Methods.* Casting was more frequently used at this time, especially for monumental pieces and for thin-walled porcelains known as 'egg-shell'. The process of casting in a vacuum was also adopted since it prevented distortion.

Vital-Roux, who was in charge of firings and bodies, perfected coal-firing; coal now began to replace wood as fuel.

### Decoration

When the research into new bodies had been completed, experiments were carried out into colours that would be suitable for use on them. Under the Second Empire this work concerned soft-paste porcelain. The factory chemist, Salvetat, saw the need for careful control of the atmosphere in the kiln during firing, whether it was oxidizing (rich in oxygen) or reducing (deprived of oxygen). That he was working on this from 1848 is shown by seven pieces in the Sèvres museum.[6] These have 'flamed' glazes imitating Chinese porcelain: copper oxide has been fired in a reducing atmosphere at a high temperature. In 1855 the factory was able to show celadon porcelain and uranium-based colours, also as a result of research into firing procedures.

The most important decorative innovation of the beginning of this period was the *pâte-sur-pâte* technique, sometimes known in France as *décor en pâte d'application* or *décor à la* 296, 300 *barbotine*. The procedure consists in decorating the piece by

296  *Vase bijou.* Sèvres, Imperial Porcelain factory, 1862. Hard-paste porcelain. H. 18.5 cm. Mark: 73, signed 'J. Gély'. MNC, Sèvres (5964²). This vase is a porcelain version of a 16th- or 17th-century rock-crystal vase made in Milan and now in the Galerie d'Apollon in the Louvre. Gély has decorated the vase in the *pâte-sur-pâte* technique with medallions containing classically inspired heads in profile. The decoration is well suited to the shape.

means of a brush using a substance composed of liquid clay (barbotine, or slip) coloured with metallic oxides. Retouching can be done before the piece is fired, and a needle is often used to obtain a sharper outline. This type of decoration was enormously popular, initially in France and later in England where French artists, particularly Marc Louis Solon, practised the technique. *Pâte-sur-pâte* pieces were shown in London in 1851. This type of decoration only finally stopped being made at the factory after the appointment of Sandier as artistic director in 1897. Some of the most successful pieces made at Sèvres under the Second Empire were in *pâte-sur-pâte,* as Georges Lechevallier-Chevignard points out.[7]

The Sèvres factory also exhibited biscuit vases with painted decoration in London in 1851. This technique was used only on an irregular basis.

1852 saw the closure of the workshop for painting on glass, which had been established in 1824. The workshop for enamelling on copper was in operation between 1845 and 1872. Like Minton, Sèvres made tin-glazed and lead-glazed wares in the Second Empire period.

*Style*

*Break with the Past.* The most important thing about the Second Empire style at the Sèvres factory was its complete break with the preceding period. Porcelain came into its own again and was no longer trying to imitate oil-painting or any other kind of material. Objects (usually vases) were now conceived as a whole—their decoration integrated with their form. At this period the shape of pieces was rarely entirely obscured by coloured decoration. Most vases had simple shapes, especially in comparison with eighteenth-century pieces, and only their handles were occasionally truly Baroque, as for example those on the 'Rimini vase'.[8] Decoration was in harmony with form.

*Eclecticism.* The eclecticism of the Second Empire has often been stressed and was without doubt part of the stylistic current of the period. It was adopted wholeheartedly at Sèvres in the nineteenth century. Yet between 1850 and 1870 original creations were more important than might at first appear.

*The 'Pompeian' Style.* Between 1845 and 1855 taste in France was again influenced by the Antique. Prince Jérôme's 'Pompeian' house was built during this period and marked the high point of this movement. Sèvres was not unaffected by this fashion as we can see from pieces such as the *vase Adélaïde,* made in 1852.[9] Its decoration is clearly influenced by the 'Pompeian' style. The method of painting in matt colours on biscuit porcelain was designed to imitate decoration on Classical vases and used for Classical subjects.

*Revival of Eighteenth-Century Styles.* The Second Empire saw the return to eighteenth-century styles, notably to the Rococo style dating from the reign of Louis XV.

The Sèvres factory still preserved all the models and moulds that had been used a century earlier, so that it was easy to carry out what is always supposed to have been a wish expressed by the Empress Eugénie. Eighteenth-century shapes were reproduced (for example the *vases balustres Louis XV* the *vases bouteilles à côtes, vases tasses à la Reine*) or only slightly modified (such as the *vases Clodion, vases Boizot*), but most of the decorative schemes were nineteenth-century inventions. In the Musée des Arts décoratifs in Paris is an ewer and basin of the

297  *Vase Adélaïde.* Sèvres, National Porcelain factory, 1852. Hard-paste porcelain. H. 36.5 cm. Mark: 72. MNC, Sèvres (24 964).
This vase, designed by Leloy in 1840, includes Rococo-style handles; the decorative motifs have been arranged all round the extensive surface of the vase. It is in the 'Neo-Pompeian' style and represents one aspect of taste in the years between 1845 and 1855.

shape known as the *feuille d'eau* painted in colours based on those used in the eighteenth century. A *vase Pâris de côté* in the Sèvres museum,[10] like the *vases balustres Louis XV,*[11] has a sky-blue *(bleu céleste)* or a dark blue *(beau bleu)* ground, which could have been painted in the previous century, but the decoration in reserve is clearly 'in the manner of' the eighteenth century. Painting in the style of Watteau and Boucher was frequently used from this time. Pieces made at the Sèvres factory were the forerunners of all the pieces of 'imitation Sèvres' with turquoise grounds, which have been made in such great numbers. Other pieces reproduced eighteenth-century shapes but were painted with scenes in a typically nineteenth-century style, such as a *vase bouteille à côtes* in the Sèvres museum,[12] which has a violet ground, and the numerous *vases Boizot* made of a pink-tinted body with white *pâte-sur-pâte* decoration.

298 *Basin and ewer.* Sèvres, Imperial Porcelain factory, 1865. Hard-paste porcelain. H. (ewer) 18.5 cm, L. (basin) 30.6 cm. Mark: 74. MdAd, Paris (GR 228).
The shape dates from the 18th century when it was known as *feuille d'eau.* The quality of the 19th-century pieces is as high as that of the 18th-century originals.

299 *Covered tazza: Henry II à incrustations.* Sèvres, Imperial Porcelain factory, before 1868. Coloured hard-paste porcelain. H. 28.5 cm. Unmarked. MNC, Sèvres (6564).
White interlaced decoration enclosed between violet lines on a mauve ground has been used on this piece, the shape of which is based on 16th-century Saint-Porchaire earthenware. Although the decorative scheme follows the original in outline, the colours are quite different: the Saint-Porchaire wares are decorated in white and ochre slip. In England the Minton factory copied Saint-Porchaire earthenwares much more faithfully but sometimes produced them in sizes much larger than the originals.

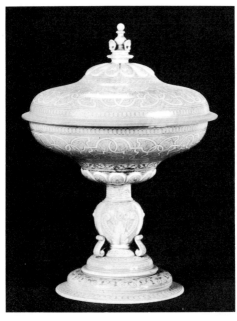

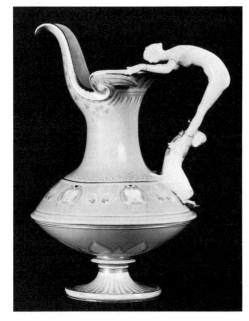

300 *Vase: buire Nicolle.* Sèvres, Imperial Porcelain factory, 1867. Celadon-coloured hard-paste porcelain. H. 31 cm. Mark: 75. MNC, Sèvres (6747).
Joseph Nicolle, who modelled this vase, was artistic director at Sèvres from 1856 to 1871. The use of a female figure to form the handle derives from Classical vases, but the celadon ground and the *pâte-sur-pâte* decoration make this a totally original creation.

*The Neo-Renaissance Style.* It was not only the eighteenth-century styles that were imitated during the golden age of eclecticism. While the Gothic style became less and less popular, the Renaissance style gained ground. It is not always possible to draw a dividing line between it and the 'Pompeian' style, since so many Classical motifs were re-used in the Renaissance period. The *vase bijou* is a case in point; its shape was directly based on a mid-sixteenth-century rock-crystal vase in the Imperial Collections, which is now in the Galerie d'Apollon at the Louvre. Several versions of this piece with differing decoration are known. The example in the Sèvres museum[13] was decorated by J. Gély, who specialized in *pâte-sur-pâte* medallions in the Classical manner.

The model known as the *vase buire Nicolle* (after the name of the designer) shows how far creative imagination could triumph over pure imitation. The handle of this piece is in the form of two nude female figures, one kneeling and supporting on her shoulders the second upright figure. The body and lip of the vase are decorated with floral motifs. Although these motifs are Renaissance in spirit, they have more in common with the Art Deco style of the future.[14]

*Exoticism.* Like other contemporary factories Sèvres too sought inspiration far afield. The names of certain pieces reveal their origin: *buire indienne à incrustations, vases Ly* and *bouteilles persanes,* to take only three examples. Nor did Sèvres stop short at decorating *vases Ly* with Turkish motifs[15] or typically nineteenth-century subjects.[16] As for *zarphs,* these were footed cups with pierced decoration containing a drinking cup and were supposed to serve as coffee cups. They were made in egg-shell porcelain. The *zarph* was foreign to western Europe and demanded all the special skills of the Sèvres workers.[17]

*Originality.* Fantastic creations were also made during this period and must not be forgotten. At least two artists were involved in designing them. We have already mentioned Nicolle and his flagon *(buire),* but he was also responsible for the model called the *vase amphore Nicolle,*[18] which is both sober and bizarre. It has a purplish-pink ground and a pointed base resting on a bronze socle painted green. Marc-Louis Solon was the creator of a strange coffee-pot formed in the shape of an elephant's head.[19] The elephant's trunk forms the coffee-pot's spout.

Domestic wares were produced in quantity and were often quite plain. From this time most imperial residences were provided with an impressive number of table services and toilet articles in white porcelain with a gilt line round the border and, at best, the crowned imperial monogram in gold. In the reserve collections of a château such as Compiègne there are whole cupboards filled with these wares.

Prestige pieces represent the opposite pole to this kind of mass-production. These ambitiously conceived pieces were designed to attract the attention of exhibition juries and to catch the eye of visitors to the exhibition. The Baptistery exhibited in 1855[20] at Paris was the largest piece made in porcelain at this time. The next period would see research into the production of similar gigantic pieces pushed to an extreme point.

*Sculpture*
All the pieces so far mentioned are ornamental and have no function; clearly, sculpture falls into the same category. During the Second Empire there was a rather half-hearted renaissance

of biscuit porcelain figure-making. In 1859 a group entitled *Vénus à la goutte de lait* after Marcellin was produced. Carpeaux's famous *Prince Impérial* was also made in biscuit porcelain, but other pieces after his works such as the busts of Garnier and the figure of a negress were not made until the 1900s.

Attempts were made to revive the tradition of making painted figures. Forgeot and Solon made pieces in celadon or 301 *pâte caméléon,* one for a monumental centrepiece, the other intended as a support for candelabra or footed cups.[21]

## Limoges

Until the end of the Restoration period in France the most active centre of French porcelain manufacture seems to have been Paris. After this time, however, the situation changed and provincial factories took the lead. Practical difficulties such as lack of space for expansion, the high cost and unreliability of labour, and the difficulty of obtaining fuel, all combined to kill off porcelain production in the capital. Only the decorating workshops survived.

In the Limoges area there was a strongly developed spirit of enterprise, which was stimulated by the arrival of various Americans. It played a decisive role in the growth of the industry. Intelligent factory owners realized that good porcelain could not be made in decaying premises, using old-fashioned equipment, and employing an undernourished or even starving work-force. Factories were no longer established in the countryside but in Limoges itself, which was linked to Paris by a railway line in 1857 and to Montluçon by a line opened in 1864. The most successful entrepreneurs making porcelain during this period were Ardant, Pouyat, Gibus, and, of course, in the leading position, Haviland.

*Factories*
Some of the large factories established much earlier were still in operation. The Alluaud factory began to use coal for firing their kilns in 1857 and continued to make profits from selling paste for making porcelain. Pierre Tharaud died in 1843, but his widow took over from him and kept his factory in production until 1865. Ruaud gave up making porcelain in 1869. Under the Second Empire these factories were almost exclusively engaged in the manufacture of domestic articles.

Henri Ardant (1828–1883) was more ambitious. In 1854 he went into partnership with Pierre Poncet who had established a porcelain factory on the premises of the old Royal Factory in 1828. The partnership lasted until 1858. After this Ardant, now working alone, removed to different premises in Limoges and began to make high-quality decorative porcelain using the trade-name 'Henri Ardant et Cie'. Between 1878 and 302 1883 he was in partnership with his son-in-law, Raymond Laporte. The latter, after Ardant's death, set up his own small firm and enjoyed some success making biscuit porcelains and *cabarets,* or small trays with matching tea or coffee cups.

The porcelain made by François Pouyat (1754–1838) at Paris has already been mentioned (see p. 44). Pouyat was originally in the business of selling ready-made porcelain paste, and purchased the Russinger factory in 1799 for his three sons on the profits. In 1825 the sons dissociated themselves from the Russinger factory. The eldest, Jean-Baptiste, returned to Limoges where he inherited the family clay business from his

301 *Female figures from a centrepiece.* Sèvres, Imperial Porcelain factory, 1862–1867. Coloured hard-paste porcelain. H. 72 cm. Unmarked. MB-A, Troyes.
These two figures form part of a centrepiece modelled by Forgeot in 1862. Although centrepieces have traditionally been produced mainly in biscuit porcelain, these two pieces are made of coloured clay. The predominating colour is an unusual celadon-green.

302 *Bust: Autumn.* Limoges, Henri Ardant factory, 1865. H. 32 cm. Mark: 5. MAD, Limoges (ADL 3683).
Modelled by A. Carrier–Belleuse who later worked at the Sèvres factory. He created several female busts for H. Ardant that are often signed, like this example, 'A. Carrier'.

303 *Centrepiece from the Cérès riche Service.* Designed by Comoléra, an animal sculptor. Limoges, Pouyat factory, 1855. Hard-paste porcelain. H. 69 cm. Unmarked. MAD, Limoges (ADL 3545).
This gained the Pouyat factory a first-class medal in the 1855 Exhibition, where it was exhibited with an 'Etruscan' *cabaret*.

father; he also inherited two porcelain factories. Jean-Baptiste kept the firms going until his death in 1849, but nothing is known about his products. His three sons, Emile, Louis and Léonard-Eugène made the family name famous for the well-known *blancs de Pouyat* ('Pouyat's white porcelain'). The beauty of their porcelain body is quite outstanding. For the first time Limoges porcelain surpassed Paris porcelain not in quantity but in quality. A coherent aesthetic emerged at the factory where artists such as Comoléra, Dammouse, and Schoenwerk were employed.

Although less important, the Jouhanneaud and Dubois factory deserves mention. Between 1846 and 1876 it made porcelain for the luxury market. It too employed the sculptor Schoenwerk.

Some exquisite masterpieces in porcelain were made by the firm known as 'Gibus et Cie' from 1853. The concern was run by Gibus, Margaine, and Redon who were in partnership together. Gibus, an excellent practical potter, was the head of the firm; Margaine acted as artistic director, and Redon was in charge of administration. In 1868 the American Charles Haviland wrote: 'I made desperate efforts to manufacture porcelain that would equal the Gibus factory's production'.[22] In fact, from 1865 onwards Gibus sold a significant part of his

304 *Soup tureen and stand from the Cérès riche Service.* Limoges, Pouyat factory, 1855. Hard-paste porcelain. L. (soup tureen) 52 cm, L. (stand) 51 cm. Mark: 14. MAD, Limoges (ADL 3535).
The Pouyats increased the popularity of white porcelain, as the quality of their ware was so high. The body is enhanced by a shiny glaze.

305

306

307

◁ 305 *Monumental ewer.* Limoges, Jouhanneaud and Dubois factory, *c.* 1855.
H. 100 cm. Unmarked. MAD, Limoges (ADL 3800).
This piece is an example of the *tours de force* that porcelain manufacturers were
obliged to produce for exhibitions. L. Dubois used designs by Constant Sévin
and Schoenwerk for his 1855 Exhibition pieces.

306 *Vase.* Limoges, Gibus & Cie, *c.* 1865. Hard-paste porcelain. H. 39 cm.
Unmarked. MAD, Limoges (ADL 3660).
Gibus & Cie exhibited white and coloured biscuit porcelains at the
International Exhibition held in Paris in 1867. The female figures on this
vase are in green-tinted biscuit porcelain. At this time, the factory made
porcelain for Haviland, who then exported it.

307 *Ewer and stand.* Limoges, Gibus & Cie, 1867–1871. Hard-paste
porcelain. H. (ewer) 39 cm, D. (stand) 47 cm. Mark: 9. MAD, Limoges
(ADL 4604).
The black ground, *pâte-sur-pâte* decoration, and silver-plated metal handle
(from the Christofle workshop) evoke 16th-century Limoges enamels.
Gibus's partner Margaine was responsible for this piece.

308 *Plate.* Limoges, Gibus & Cie, 1868. Hard-paste porcelain. D. 35 cm.
Mark: 10. MAD, Limoges (ADL 4590).
Porcelain imitating Limoges enamels became popular all over Europe in the
19th century—the style at least had some *raison d'être* in Limoges itself. The
*pâte-sur-pâte* decoration is signed 'F. Peyrat 1868'.

308

output to Haviland, who then exported it to the United States, the rest being sold to Parisian dealers and decorators.

In 1872 Margaine retired because of ill health. Gibus and Redon built a new factory in the rue des Cazeaux. Here they employed two hundred and fifty workers and henceforth exported their products direct to the United States. However, from this time they specialized in making domestic wares, especially so after Gibus retired. Redon carried on the business alone in the years between 1882 and 1896.

During the Second Empire Americans began to dominate the Limoges porcelain industry. The Havilands were originally New York dealers in and importers of ceramics. They were anxious to offer their customers an alternative to English creamware, and French porcelain was unsuited to Anglo-Saxon needs. For this reason David Haviland, after going to France for the first time in 1840, settled in Limoges in 1842. At first he sent to Haviland Brothers, the parent company, pieces which had been designed for the French market and which were sold all over the American continent. Then David Haviland set up a porcelain-decorating business, which was initially on a small scale but expanded vigorously after 1855. He had two types of dinner service made at Limoges by Alluaud, Pouyat, Gibus and other factories, decorating the porcelain in his own workshop and sending it to America. The Civil War and the ensuing bankruptcy of Haviland Brothers, which occurred in 1865, interrupted these exports. At this time David broke away from the parent company, setting up a new business called 'Haviland & Co' with his sons Charles and Théodore. The elder, Charles, immediately took charge of this new enterprise, providing dynamic leadership.

In 1865 he installed four kilns and began to manufacture porcelain, producing four different types of table service. He continued to deal with other Limoges porcelain manufacturers, buying from them in order to satisfy heavy American demand for tablewares.

Charles Haviland was sufficiently aware to be able to anticipate changes in taste. In 1872 he recruited Félix Bracquemond who had been put in charge of the decorating workshops at Sèvres in the preceding year. Haviland entrusted him with the running of his workshop in Paris, situated in the rue Michel-Ange. At this workshop designs were drawn up for porcelain that was intended to be mass-produced at Limoges. In this way Japonism and Impressionism, a strange marriage of styles, came to influence decoration on Limoges porcelain, which had hitherto been so conventional.

*Techniques*

Between 1850 and 1880 the main development at Limoges did not consist of innovation but rather involved an increasing emphasis on mass-production allied to an improvement in the quality of materials, which now reached their highest level. The Pouyat factory, in particular, made a body of unparalleled whiteness and fineness. However, their *tours de force* only revived processes that were already in use before the middle of the nineteenth century.

*'Blanks' or Undecorated Porcelain.* In the second half of the nineteenth century Pouyat's 'blanks' became immensely successful, from an artistic as well as a commercial point of view. These are often marked with the well-known J.P. (Jean Pouyat, Limoges) mark which had also been used in the preceding period. When pieces were sold as white porcelain not intended to be painted, they could now be marked in the usual way. Even when every Paris factory, as well as Sèvres, was trying to disguise the white porcelain body, covering it with artistic decoration, Limoges porcelain-makers such as Alluaud were making their livelihood mainly from the sale of almost undecorated pieces, often adorned only with a narrow gilt line. The Pouyats realized that the beauty of the body and the quality of the shape were often more important than coloured decoration. This development finds a parallel in the history of tin-glazed earthenware at Faenza during the sixteenth century. After using over-elaborate decoration for a period of fifty years, blue and yellow painting on a white ground, known as *a compendiario* decoration, was devised for relief-ornamented pieces based on metal shapes. Four centuries later, the Pouyats accomplished the same process also using metal shapes: 'Taking bronze and silver objects as a model, the Limoges factories merely catered to an existing market. They had to take account

309 *Vase.* Limoges, Haviland & Co, 1879–1889. Hard-paste porcelain. H. 38 cm. Mark: 12. MAD, Limoges (ADL 3917).
Charles Haviland established a pottery studio at Auteuil in 1879. Bracquemond was put in charge of the enterprise, which was supposed to make innovations to porcelain. The studio never managed to achieve mass-production, but the Haviland factory produced some porcelain in the style originating at Auteuil.

310 *Cup and saucer from the President Hayes Service.* Limoges, Haviland & Co, ▷ 1879. Hard-paste porcelain. H. (cup) 7 cm, D. (saucer) 14 cm. Mark: 12. Limoges, Haviland & Co.
Haviland supplied services for several presidents of the United States. The one made for President Hayes comprised more than 1,000 pieces and was painted under the direction of F. Braquemond. The pieces show a strong oriental influence.

311 *Plate from the service parisien.* Limoges, Haviland & Co, 1876. Hard-paste porcelain. D. 25 cm. Mark: 13. MAD, Limoges (ADL 2818).
Signed on the front 'B. 76' (for Bracquemond 1876), the plate is one of twelve illustrating the Seasons after Japanese prints. They were decorated by means of three different processes: copperplate engraving, chromolithography, and by hand.

312 *Vase.* Limoges, J.-B. Ruaud factory, 1854. Hard-paste porcelain. H. 24 cm. Unmarked. MAD, Limoges (ADL 3950).
Ruaud tried to use high-fired cobalt-blue to imitate Chinese porcelain on an industrial scale. This piece is painted with high-fired underglaze-blue decoration.

of public tastes and needs but soon "art" porcelain became truly ceramic in character, except in the case of certain backward looking factories. This preoccupation can be noticed at an early stage at the Jouhanneaud and Dubois factory'.[23] The strange influence of silversmith's work is clearly visible in Pouyat's products too. Some extraordinary pieces made for the international exhibitions are in the Musée National Adrien Dubouché, Limoges. The firm exhibited a square soup tureen of very plain shape in the Great Exhibition of 1851. However, from 1855 Comoléra was requested to design a centrepiece composed of a bowl on a support of palms and large waterfowl. This piece was more boldly conceived than any yet made in biscuit porcelain. At the same exhibition white porcelain made for Tsar Alexander II of Russia was shown, together with the *Cérès riche* Service. The soup tureen in this service is decorated with ears of corn moulded in relief, recalling the eighteenth-century naturalistic tradition. The 'Etruscan' Service, also exhibited, is in a faintly Neo-Classical idiom, freely interpreted. Over-elaborate decoration was now a thing of the past, and the shapes used were united in the use of white porcelain. The Pouyats proved with their entry for the 1862 Exhibition in London that they could make egg-shell porcelain resembling the Sèvres product; it was used for their so-called *cabaret mousseline*. For the 1878 Paris Exhibition, Pouyat returned to

a monumental production in the same vein as that shown in 1855. This time they showed a huge centrepiece made up of three elements composed of bowls supported by fairies and cupids. The centrepiece was modelled by Dammouse with sculptural work by Schoenwerk.

On dishes and plates in the *Cérès riche* Service the use of a mixture of low-relief motifs (in this case fruits) in biscuit porcelain combined with the glazed porcelain employed for the rest of the piece creates a pleasing effect.

*Biscuit Porcelain.* Other factories used white porcelain in the more traditional unglazed form. Ruaud, at Jouhanneaud and Dubois, employed the sculptors Constant Sévin and Schoenwerk, who created models that were often based on foreign sources. One example of this type is a beer mug with the title *l'orgie allemande* ('German Orgy'), exhibited in 1855. Dubois, another sculptor working for these factories, was inspired by Lepautre's engravings dating from the eighteenth century. Henri Ardant made an attractive series of female busts after Carrier-Belleuse. He also introduced a note of colour into his biscuit porcelain production by tinting the body that was to be used for the parts of the design modelled in relief. Gibus copied this type of decoration.

313 *Part of a centrepiece from the service grains de riz.* Limoges, Pouyat factory, 1878. Hard-paste porcelain. W. 51 cm. Mark: 15. MAD, Limoges (ADL 3606).

A. Dammouse collaborated with the Pouyats as well as producing his own pieces and began by designing this service. The sculptural elements were modelled by Schoenwerk.

## Decoration

Some new processes of decoration were devised during this period. At the Ardant factory differently coloured bodies were used for one piece, a technique which Gibus took up. The Lesme brothers' factory perfected their method of imitating Chinese porcelain with low-temperature decoration, as well as their technique of making porcelain reproductions of Bernard Palissy's lead-glazed wares. They decorated these 'rustic figures' with a lead glaze and low-temperature colours. Jouhanneaud and Dubois also initiated research that was carried out by their factory chemist, Halot, into new porcelain colours that could be fired at a high temperature. Finally Charles Haviland introduced the most far-reaching changes when he began to use transfer-printing, lithography, and chromolithography. Printed outlines were then filled in by hand by his painters, achieving a high standard of decoration.

*'Pâte-sur-Pâte' Decoration.* Pâte-sur-pâte is mid-way between relief and painted decoration. This difficult technique was especially popular at the Gibus factory. Sixteenth-century Limoges enamels were enthusiastically collected by connoisseurs in Limoges and provided a source of inspiration to potters. As the originals were well known, the porcelain copies made by Gibus, Margaine, and Redon had to be of superior workmanship. An ewer bequeathed to the Adrien Dubouché museum, Limoges, by Margaine, and probably made by him between 1867 and 1871, is a masterpiece of its kind. It far outstrips the English copies of Limoges enamels produced at the Worcester factory and painted by Thomas Bott.

*Painted Decoration.* The Haviland factory played a leading role in Limoges as porcelain decorators, buying white porcelain and painting it in their workshops. From 1853 their premises were situated in the avenue du Crucifix. Numerous decorated pieces were shown at exhibitions from 1855 onwards. These included two moulded vases designed by Léon Sazerat and decorated by Baude, which were awarded a silver medal. In 1867 they received another silver medal[24] for a *service gothique* ('Gothic Service')—'Gothic' only in name—made at the Gibus factory and decorated by Saquet at the rue du Crucifix.

Naturally, the orders placed with Haviland by the White House helped to establish the firm's reputation. The Smithsonian Institution in Washington, D.C. has pieces from the presidential services on exhibit, a few examples of which are still preserved by the Haviland factory: a plate from the President Lincoln Service of 1861 and a cup, saucer, and plate from the President Hayes Service, decorated in relief. The

decorating workshop in the avenue du Crucifix continued to produce objects with skilful decoration. The outlines of the motifs were printed and then hand-painted, or decorated with transfer-printed gilding on coloured grounds, in particular the famous *bleu du four,* which imitated the equally renowned Sèvres blue. These techniques were gradually replaced by chromolithography.

It was only after Félix Bracquemond was taken on to supply new decorative schemes at the beginning of the Third Republic that Charles Haviland's pieces began to express a truly original style. Bracquemond realized that by using Japanese decorative principles such as the asymmetrical placing of motifs and the use of stylized outlines he could bring new life to hackneyed European decorative styles. When he supplied decorative designs to the Creil factory, he adopted Japanese principles wholeheartedly. For Charles Haviland, however, he diluted these principles by giving up the use of coloured motifs in low
311 relief. He was more inspired by Impressionist painting than by Japan. Thanks to Bracquemond, Haviland was awarded a gold medal at the exhibition held in 1878.

*Style*
There was no brutal rupture between the Second Empire period and the preceding era. Shapes of both dinner and tea-services remained the same. Decoration mainly consisted of gold bands or thin lines and naturalistic flowers. Certain stylistic tendencies became more marked but were the logical development of earlier styles.

At Limoges, as elsewhere, part of the production was characterized by eclecticism during the Second Empire. The decorators best known for their eclecticism are the Lesme family, who produced fake Chinese porcelains at the same time as copies of Bernard Palissy's pieces. Léon Sazerat wrote admiringly of their Chinese-style porcelain, 'It can hardly be distinguished from the real thing'.[25] In the Sèvres museum there is a Sèvres porcelain vase dated 1852, decorated in Limoges in 1853 by Jules Lesme with 'Chinese enamels in relief', according to a label stuck to the piece.[26] Ruaud made
312 a vase with high-temperature decoration *en camaïeu bleu* ('monochrome blue') right at the beginning of the Second Empire. It too imitated Chinese porcelain. The spirit of imitation and research into technical processes were closely linked together in the work of both Ruaud and the Lesme family, attracting collectors and porcelain specialists. It is likely that Limoges decorators also made imitation Sèvres pieces in the same way as they imitated Chinese porcelains, although in the present state of knowledge this is impossible to substantiate.

## ITALY

In Italy, as in other countries, this period saw the triumph of industrialization, affecting production methods and the products themselves.

## Doccia

315-317 The Ginori family managed to maintain the vitality of their factory at Doccia through a constant process of improvements. In 1848 Lorenzo Ginori II took charge of the firm after having studied porcelain-making techniques all over Europe, and

314 *Plate.* Limoges, unidentified factory, *c.* 1880. Hard-paste porcelain. D. 20 cm. Unmarked. MAD, Limoges (ADL 3317).
The acid-etched gold relief decoration carried out in several colours is typical of the late 19th century. The Japanese influence so popular in the same period is also in evidence here.

especially at Sèvres. He introduced a four-chamber kiln (later to be used at Sèvres), which was extremely economical, and obtained kaolin from the Limoges area. He started making all the fashionable types of ceramics at Doccia such as lithophanes, majolica (in current production at Sèvres and Minton), and egg-shell porcelain. Jafet Torelli, artistic director between 1861 and 1873, Giusto Giusti, the factory chemist, and Paolo Lorenzini, employed between 1854 and 1891, all played their part in assuring the success of Ginori's efforts. The awards received by the firm at the various international exhibitions were a just recompense for all this activity.

From the 1870s Italy was unified and ready to be industrialized. The number of workers employed at Doccia increased from five hundred to one thousand five hundred, but for all that the owners were able to maintain a policy of benevolent paternalism towards their work-force. There was a new emphasis on the production of ceramics for use in the electrical industry and in the developing telecommunications field (the telephone was invented in 1872). Methods of reproducing photographs on porcelain came into use as did chromolithography in 1873.

On Lorenzo II's death, his eldest son Carlo-Benedetto succeeded him and followed in his father's footsteps. Industrial ceramics were manufactured on a large scale and subsidized 'art' porcelain and earthenware. The same policy was pursued at the Società Ceramica Richard: the two firms merged in 1896.

## Milan

In 1841 Giulio Richard bought the Tinelli San Cristoforo factory at Milan. This purchase was in a way symbolic: Richard,

315 *Candelabrum from the servizio per il Kedive d'Egitto ('Khedive of Egypt Service').* Doccia (Tuscany), Ginori factory: Lorenzo Ginori period, 1872–1874. Hard-paste porcelain. H. 85 cm. Mark: 100a. MPD, Sesto Fiorentino.
For once the fashion for eclecticism dominating this period was justified by the nationality of the recipient of the piece.

316 *Peacock vase.* Doccia (Tuscany), Società Ceramica Richard-Ginori, 1902. Hard-paste porcelain. H. 115 cm. Unmarked. MPD, Sesto Fiorentino.
This piece, which was shown at the Turin Exhibition in 1902, was highly acclaimed for its adaptation of the Art Nouveau style, called *stile Liberty* in Italy. It was introduced at the Doccia factory by the painter Buffa under the artistic direction of Luigi Tazzini.

an aristocrat dedicated to the defence of artistic, moral, and political values, turned into a businessman concerned to preserve his country's economy, when it was under occupation, against the colonizing power's own products. Only rapid industrialization enabled the firm to survive. Richard initiated production on a vast scale of domestic earthenwares as well as industrial porcelains for textile, electrical, and chemical use. His aim, which he achieved, was to make Italians 'buy Italian'. The production of luxury porcelain was what prompted him to make these changes, but even such porcelains had to conform to current taste. In the 1877 Exhibition in London a large vase was shown, modelled by Vincenzo Vela and decorated with the emblem of Rome, the she-wolf. A biscuit figure symbolizing Italy, also by Vela, was shown at Milan in 1881, together with plates decorated *en camaïeu rose* ('monochrome pink') after paintings by Del Bona.

Early nineteenth-century Italian porcelain still had its own character, but economic conditions prevailing later in the century necessitated industrialization. When this had been effected, by the second half of the century, the Italian porcelain industry could no longer claim leadership in producing original works of art.

318, 319

# SPAIN

## Pasajez (Viscaya Province)

In 1851 a Frenchman, C. Baignol, arrived in Pasajez and set up a factory in premises belonging to the Society of Jesus, and which had formerly been occupied by ship builders. His most famous product is a service made in 1860 for the inauguration

317 *Plate.* Doccia (Tuscany), Ginori factory: Carlo-Benedetto Ginori period, *c.* 1880. Hard-paste porcelain. D. 24 cm. Unmarked. MPD, Sesto Fiorentino.
Painted decoration with *pâte-sur-pâte* embellishments within a square reserve on a dark green ground. This piece is a good example of the striving for originality.

318 *Plate.* San Cristoforo (Milan), Jules Richard factory, 1855. Hard-paste porcelain. D. 24 cm. Mark: 101. MNC, Sèvres (4823[14]).
In 1855 Jules Richard presented to the Sèvres museum examples of porcelain and creamware that he had shown at the 1855 Universal Exhibition in Paris. This piece was included in the gift.

320 *Cylindrical cup (tasse litron) and saucer.* San Cristoforo (Milan), Jules Richard factory, 1855. Hard-paste porcelain. H. (cup) 5.8 cm, D. (saucer) 11.2 cm. Unmarked. MNC, Sèvres (4823[2]).
In addition to cups of the shape known as *calice* ('flower-cup'), this cup and saucer were exhibited in Paris by the Milan factory in 1855. The pieces are modestly designed and mechanically decorated with landscape scenes printed in black.

319 *Figure of the Marine Venus.* San Cristoforo (Milan), Jules Richard factory, 1855. Hard-paste porcelain. H. 21 cm. Mark: 102. MNC, Sèvres (4823[20]).
Incised on the shell: 'Hen. Keller. Hel,ve 1/Inve. Tscolpit. Romae/Anno 1796', indicating that the original was modelled at Rome in 1796 by the Swiss sculptor Henry Keller. The Richard factory is best known for its domestic or industrial wares, but decorative pieces were also manufactured.

of the Museo Naval in Madrid. The concern was known as Baignol Hnos. Closed down in 1878, it re-opened in 1880 only to cease trading for good in 1905.

## PORTUGAL (1850–1900)

### Vista Alegre

Thanks to the work of Victor François Chartier-Rousseau, the Vista Alegre factory joined the mainstream of European porcelain factories making pieces in the revived Rococo style. Rousseau died in 1852, but another French painter, Gustave Fortier, was taken on at the Portuguese factory in 1851. Under Rousseau's influence, Fortier too plunged into the current of eclecticism. Vista Alegre could remain isolated no longer: it participated in the international exhibitions held at Paris in 1855 and at London in 1862. The products were now extremely diverse, both stylistically and artistically. Fortier introduced the so-called 'pen and ink technique' and lithography. Two lithographic presses were acquired, the first in 1859, the second in 1861. In the same year the factory also purchased a steam-engine. Modernization was taking place in Portugal, as elsewhere.

From the beginning Vista Alegre employed sculptors. The factory exhibited a sculptural work in biscuit porcelain entitled *Nossa Senhora de Penha de França*[27] in 1855. It is worth noting that the factory called its biscuit porcelain *porcelana pariana,*[28] using a term of English origin.

In 1858 Vista Alegre produced a copy of a biscuit group created at Sèvres by Boizot in the eighteenth century and called *Le larcin de la rose* ('pilfering a rose'). Like the rest of Europe

321 *Plate.* Vista Alegre (Aveiro, Portugal), Ferreira Pinto & Filhos, 1855. Hard-paste porcelain. D. 23 cm. Mark: 106. MNC, Sèvres (4886[5]).
The pleasing shape of this plate, with its moulded relief decoration of scrolls, is complemented by gilt friezes. It was shown at the 1855 Universal Exhibition.

322 *Plate with ribbon ornamentation.* Vienna, 1863. Transfer-printed decoration with overglaze colours and gilding. D. 24.3 cm. Marks: 109 and year stamp. ÖMaK, Vienna (Ke 812).
After 1850 Vienna tried to meet the demand for cheaper porcelain by introducing such modern industrial processes as transfer-printing.

at this period Portugal rediscovered the charm of the eighteenth century. Reproductions of Classical vases[29] and Neo-Rococo[30] pieces also formed part of the factory's output.

The decade 1870 to 1880 was a difficult period for the factory and for Fortier's successor, Joaquim José de Oliviera. Vista Alegre suffered from lack of capital, markets, and creativity at this period. However, Oliviera did train some skilful painters. Floral decoration was the most popular type in use, although some pieces were painted with effigies, including representations of the Infante Dom Alfonso Henrique, the Duke of Porto, and Prince Don Carlos.[31] The Portuguese taste, which showed a tendency towards a rather clumsy naivety, is evident in coloured figures of religious subjects.[32]

At the end of the nineteenth century this factory experienced increasing decline. Portugal was isolated from the centres of creative activity, and although Vista Alegre was still capable of producing academic pieces with high quality painted decoration, the factory never became part of the new current of modernism embodied in Art Nouveau.

## AUSTRIA

### Vienna

Two factories that had played a key role hitherto were of little importance in the period 1850–1880: Nymphenburg and Vienna. The decline of Vienna, beleaguered by the state administration's demand for profitability on one hand and by competition from the producers of cheap wares on the other, has already been touched upon. For the 1851 World Exhibition every effort was made once again to obtain a

favourable assessment and make the famous old factory appear in a positive light internationally. The jury did indeed praise its painted vases, dishes, plates, coffee services and statuettes, groups of figures and paper-weights very highly, putting them on a par with the porcelains of Sèvres.[33] In contrast the official catalogue had not a word of praise for the other Austrian factories—Pirkenhammer, Schlaggenwald, Herend, and so on—so that for the English jurors at least Vienna must still have played a very special role.

Day-to-day conditions at the Vienna factory were certainly anything but satisfactory in 1851. Following the revolution of 1848, sales became more sluggish and the then managing director was obliged to ask for subsidies from the state, despite the fact that for a considerable time the production of painted single pieces of art porcelain had quite definitely taken second place to mass-produced utility ware.[34] For the latter the factory's chemist, Franz Kosch, introduced printed decoration in 1853 as well as the gloss-gilding process in use at Meissen since 1829. But neither such steps as these, nor the commitment of the last managing director of the factory, the scientist Alexander Löwe who was appointed in 1856 and who tried once again to promote art porcelain, were able to save the factory. One of Löwe's achievements in its final years was to persuade important modern artists to produce designs that, earlier than at any other European factory, combined simple late Neo-Classical shapes with Neo-Renaissance borders or leaf-work and strap-work in delicate lines and fresh, bright colours. Theophil Hansen, one of the great architects of Vienna's Ringstrasse, designed a particularly beautiful tea-service in 1864 on which the only decoration was gold rays on a white ground.[35] Even costly new decorative techniques were adopted, as on a number of medallions with white *pâte-sur-pâte*

322

323 *Small covered tureen.* Vienna, Johann Wech, after 1866. Overglaze painting and gilt decoration. H. 10.2 cm. Marks: 107, painter's monogram, impressed marks. ÖMaK, Vienna (Ke 600).
This ornate little tureen, reminiscent of Vienna's heyday at the beginning of the century, was in fact decorated by a former factory painter after its closure in 1864.

decoration on a celadon-coloured ground.[36] All this evidence of artistic vitality was to no avail; on 22 August 1864, at the request of the Chamber of Deputies, the emperor decided to close the factory down. An institution that in its heyday had made an extraordinary contribution to spreading Austrian culture was thus written off by the state in the very year in which that same state set up a centre for the promotion of Austrian arts and crafts by founding the Österreichisches Museum für Kunst und Industrie. The winding-up process was not immediate but took two years, and porcelain was still being produced in 1866—for example to complete services already on order.[37] The considerable stock of white porcelain was hastily marked and sold off, in part to the new museum but mostly to private porcelain firms. The subsequent misuse of these wares will probably never be fully sorted out.[38]

# GERMANY

## Nymphenburg

The Royal Bavarian Manufactory at Nymphenburg came close to being dissolved some sixteen years earlier than Vienna. Friedrich Gärtner, artistic director of the factory from 1822, died in 1847. In fact he was only closely associated with it in a supervisory capacity from 1822 to 1829, but as overall artistic director he continued to influence it up until his death. The new artistic director appointed in 1848 was Eugen Napoleon Neureuther (1806–1882). In his day he was an exceptionally well-known painter and illustrator active in many areas of the arts and crafts; for example, he worked with Kaulbach and others on the Nymphenburg factory's Nibelung Service.[39] Neureuther took over a factory whose finances were in a disastrous state, mainly because of the expensive 'Art Institute'.

cf. p. 139

### End of the 'Art Institute'
The object of countless administrative complaints in the past, it continued to function only thanks to the deep commitment

and constant financial assistance of Ludwig I. A few months after Neureuther took over, Ludwig I abdicated in favour of his son Maximilian II, which rather altered the factory's outward situation. The exchequer made strong recommendations that it should be wound up because of its increasing debts and marketing problems. Although the new king had nothing like the same close links with the factory as his father had had, he decreed instead that only the Art Institute should be dissolved and that the Nymphenburg factory itself should continue in existence as an exemplar for private firms. The watchword now, however—as it had been in Vienna and Meissen a generation earlier—was maximum economy. Neureuther endeavoured to make sensible use of the limited means placed at his disposal. The illustrated price list of 1850 shows that he revived the simple, well-proportioned tableware of Johann Peter Melchior, which he was able to sell as white porcelain at favourable prices. A few of Gärtner's Neo-Classical vases remained on the programme too, but soon Neureuther was trying to attract customers with a wealth of new and in some cases undoubtedly very modern articles made to his own designs and ranging from address plates and paper-weights to tooth-brush racks and cigar-holders.[40] Neureuther had promised the state administration to turn the factory from an art institute into an industrial concern in which the principle of beauty would be adhered to for even 'the least little vessel'.[41] The factory's chronicler, Friedrich Hofmann, attributed some four hundred different tableware and vessel designs to Neureuther[42] as well as a certain amount of figure-work such as biscuit busts of famous artists and statuettes of ethnic types.

Work by the Art Institute still played an important part in the image the factory presented of itself at the London International Exhibition, principally in the shape of vases, plates, and plaques decorated with paintings copied from Mieris, Raphael, Albani, and Kaulbach. The illustrations in the exhibition catalogue, however, suggest that the jury preferred the vases and beer mugs based on designs by Neureuther. His 325 'speciality' was sculpted decoration in naturalistic or Neo-Gothic shapes. To modern eyes these seem quite unsuited to porcelain. They are derived from historical stoneware mugs from the Rhineland though with some fashionable modification of the relief decoration: stag's heads sculpted in the round look out from the sides of a tall goblet with foliage decoration, and late Gothic ornaments stand out from the base; fleshy leaves unfold from the side of a vase.[43] Similar work can be found on English stoneware of the same period. In 1852–1853 Neureuther made Maximilian II of Bavaria a Hunting Service that was the most successful expression of his style.[44] In 1853 the state administration asked an advisory committee of Munich artists to report on the factory's products. They were full of praise, but they could not prevent Neureuther from being pensioned off because in his five years in office he had failed to lead the factory out of loss into profit. In the same year a technician and a chemist were appointed to positions of authority, and production increasingly switched to industrial and technical porcelains. But not even petticoat insulators and the like brought in sufficient income, and finally in 1862 the Royal Manufactory was leased to a private entrepreneur and

324 *Pedestal table in the Neo-Rococo style.* Meissen, E. A. Leuteritz, 1853. ▷ Overglaze painting, gilt trimming. Mark: inaccessible. SP, Meissen.
After 1850 Meissen produced not only individual pieces of furniture but occasionally entire rooms in porcelain.

began to decline into insignificance. A later lessee, Alfred Bäuml from Bohemia, was able to revert to the production of art porcelain, initially in the form of remodelled re-issues of Rococo figures, and on that basis to turn the factory decisively in the direction of profitability from 1888 onwards and to build up a good modern production following the historicist path that had already been trodden by Meissen.

## Meissen

### Revival of the Glorious Period

As we have seen, Meissen, as part of its efforts to produce saleable wares, revived some of its eighteenth-century models, notably from the time of Kändler, to meet orders stemming cf. p. 145 particularly from the English market. The mid-century constituted a turning-point for Meissen because of the death in 1847 of its head painter, Georg Friedrich Kersting, the last upholder of the tradition, current since around 1800, that porcelain was primarily a vehicle for lavish miniature painting. In 1849 the head of the modelling department, Carl Gotthelf Habenicht, retired; his successor, until 1886, was the energetic Ernst August Leuteritz (1818–1893). He had already been a modeller at Meissen for some time and had begun producing Neo-Gothic models there. His most significant contribution was to refurbish and remodel countless figures by Kändler and his contemporaries. Thanks to his influence, Neo-Rococo reigned supreme at Meissen in the second half of the century. 'Nearly all the models from Meissen's most splendid period were remodelled or otherwise modified; they included crinolines, harlequins, mythological and allegorical groups, the tailor on the goat, the Bolognese dog, the Paduan cock, and other animals, clocks, girandoles, and centrepieces decorated with figures, and groups of children and putti. Often, however, they lacked the harmonious merging of shapes and the delicate detailing of the eighteenth-century originals. The new perfection allowed neither firing cracks nor glaze bubbles nor the slightest fault. Consequently these remodelled pieces often became stiff in their striving for maximum precision while the flowers became more voluminous and naturalistic and the faces more doll-like. The new decoration makes them appear cooler, the gloss gilding more luxurious.'[45]

Leuteritz's successor, Emmerich Andresen (1843–1902), continued this style after 1886.[46] The execution of the invariably complicated shapes testifies to the enormous skill of Meissen's modellers at that time. Under Leuteritz and Andresen large-scale animals, tables, consoles, mirror frames, 324 and chandeliers were once again, as in the eighteenth century, dispatched to palaces the world over. The royal residence at Ajuda in Portugal contains an entire room decorated throughout with Meissen porcelain, as does King Ludwig II 326 of Bavaria's summer castle, the Linderhof.[47] Designing such ensembles, which consist of countless individually modelled and painted pieces, called for a perfectly trained team of craftsmen. They demonstrated their skill in minor tasks as well, among them the jars, bowls, and vases with applied flowers, birds, and butterflies (for example the 'guelder-rose vases') that became so popular again from 1860 onwards.[48]

One result of the first World Exhibition was probably the appointment of an artistic advisory committee for the factory, which took place at the request of the administrative authorities in 1851. Its members included the painter Julius Schnorr von Carolsfeld (1794–1872) and the sculptor Ernst

325 *Beer mug and pitchers.* Nymphenburg, Royal Porcelain factory, E. N. Neureuther, 1848–1851. Illustration of porcelains at the Great Exhibition of 1851 in London.
Neureuther, artistic director of the Nymphenburg factory from 1848, produced these 'Old German' wares as part of his break with Neo-Classicism.

326 *Phoebus auf dem Sonnenwagen ('Phoebus in the Chariot of the Sun').* Meissen, 1875–1876. Porcelain group with polychrome painting and gilt. H. 31 cm. Mark: inaccessible. VdSSGuS (Ludwig II Museum), Munich.
In the 1870s Meissen received many commissions from Ludwig II of Bavaria for his castles at Linderhof and Herrenchiemsee.

Rietschel (1804–1861). Both did several designs for the factory—not in the Kändler/Leuteritz Rococo style but owing more to Renaissance painting of the Cinquecento. Schnorr von Carolsfeld had already, before 1850, worked with the champion of Neo-Renaissance architecture, Gottfried Semper, on his large covered vase. He helped Meissen with vase decorations for the International Exhibition of 1862 as well, and his round display table with many-figured mythological compositions for the Exhibition of 1867 received the highest praise. Schnorr von Carolsfeld perpetuated the tradition of painted porcelains that, for commissions from a certain clientele, was continued by other painters with copies of paintings on dishes and plates, with fruit and above all flower still lifes, and with landscapes and scenes from Watteau and Boucher.[49]

*Modernization*

In 1849 Heinrich Gottlob Kühn, who had been technical director since 1814 and acting head of the factory since 1833, was finally appointed managing director. His last years in that office were occupied with pushing through—against all kinds of opposition—the construction of a modern factory building with all the latest technical innovations. This work was continued after his death in 1870 by two outstandingly talented chemists, Julius Heintze (from 1873) and Carl Förster. Technological problems were unknown at Meissen, and so, when the artistic advisory committee recommended imitation of the products that other manufacturers had successfully presented at world exhibitions, Meissen had few difficulties. In 1862, for example, the Worcester Royal Porcelain Company enjoyed tremendous success in London with its blue-ground porcelains painted in grisaille on the model of Limousin enamels;[50] by 1865 Meissen was already producing vessels of its own in the Neo-Renaissance style which went one better than Worcester's 'Limoges' porcelains in their complicated effects, e.g. in the use of platinum for painting or with their tortoise-shell-patterned grounds.

Probably also influenced by Worcester, from about 1865 Meissen was manufacturing so-called 'Capodimonte' ware, which was characterized by scenic reliefs dealing with Renaissance themes. Similar porcelains had originally been manufactured in Doccia, near Florence, in the mid-eighteenth century. There they appear to have been revived in the middle of the nineteenth century and given the commercially attractive name of 'Capodimonte', after Italy's most celebrated and historic porcelain factory near Naples. Worcester was the first factory in northern Europe to imitate porcelains with figured reliefs under the label of 'Raphaelesque porcelain'. Meissen's 'Capodimonte' ware too appears to have had its biggest market in England.[51]

The Neo-Renaissance movement bore further rich fruit at Meissen. A series of vase types was created and decorated with ornaments and framed paintings in the style of or dealing with themes from the sixteenth century. One of these designs, Leuteritz's 'snake-handle vase', is still in production today.[52]

327 *Ornamental vase decorated with a procession of bacchantes.* Meissen, E. A. Leuteritz, 1863. Overglaze painting in *grisaille* on a platinum ground. H. 29 cm. Mark: 136. SP, Meissen.
Worcester and Sèvres copies of Limoges enamels of the Renaissance period were earlier, but Meissen's were more refined.

328 *Large amphora-shaped vase in the Neo-Renaissance style.* Meissen, 1878. Overglaze painting and rich gilding. H. 57 cm. Mark: 136. UM, Prague (Z-136-2018).
Conventional Neo-Renaissance vases were decorated with 16th- and 17th-century paintings—here the *Rape of Europa* after a ceiling from the Palazzo Farnese in Rome.

Versatility was the watchword from the late 1860s onwards, so that once again there were vases and plates with coloured grounds as in the early Marcolini days. At the 1862 International Exhibition in London a *déjeuner* employing Neo-Baroque shapes was exhibited with borders, featuring polychrome painted foliage on a dark ground, that were inspired by Renaissance or Islamic ornamentation.[53] It is particularly charming and has a counterpart using similar shapes with lily-of-the-valley decoration. Thanks to the experiments of the factory's chemist, Julius Heintze, the *pâte-sur-pâte* technique could be applied to Meissen's hard-paste porcelain from 1878. It was much used for figure decoration on small jars, bottles, and vases until the turn of the century, though because of the high production costs involved large-

329 *Coffee service with oriental-style borders.* Meissen, E. A. Leuteritz, *c.* 1862. Overglaze and gilt decoration. H. (coffee-pot) 16 cm. Mark: 136. SP, Meissen.
The surprising thing about this *déjeuner* is the economy of decoration, although the shapes are Neo-Rococo.

330 *Pieces from a coffee service with lily-of-the-valley decoration.* Meissen, E. A. Leuteritz, W. Gruner, 1861. Overglaze painting, gilt decoration. H. (coffee-pot) 20 cm. Mark: 136. SP, Meissen.
As one of Prince Albert's favourite craftsmen, Gruner may have been taken on by Meissen with a view to the second World Exhibition in London in 1862.

331 *Amphora-shaped vase decorated with scenes from mythology.* Meissen, E. A. ▷ Leuteritz, shortly before 1893. Overglaze painting, gilt decoration. H. 100 cm. Mark: 136. SP, Meissen.
The shape was designed by Leuteritz in 1865; the impressive paintings of Diana the Huntress were done for the 1893 World Exhibition in Chicago.

332  *Small covered pot with head of Minerva.* Meissen, before 1897. Underglaze painting, engraving, and *pâte-sur-pâte* decoration. H. 4.5 cm; D. 7 cm. Mark: 136. MfKuG, Hamburg (1897.489).
This pot with its Mantegna-like head and almost Art Nouveau scratched ornamentation typifies the German use of the *pâte-sur-pâte* technique.

333  *Déjeuner decorated with a painting after Watteau.* Meissen, 1896. Overglaze painting, gilt decoration. W. (salver) 38.7 cm. Mark: 136. Exhibition Room, SP, Meissen.
A good example of the work of Emmerich Andresen, who continued to cultivate and even develop the *vieux Saxe* style after 1880.

scale works remained rare exceptions. Now and again, however, for publicity occasions such as national or world exhibitions, monumental *pâte-sur-pâte* porcelain was produced—a table-top, for example, or even door panels.[54]

In numerical terms all these experiments with various historical styles or new techniques remained a tiny minority in comparison with the vases, plates, fruit baskets, centrepieces, groups of figures, clocks, and dessert and table services based on eighteenth-century prototypes taken from the factory's own store-rooms. Whatever new ideas or stimuli the technicians, artists, or advisory committee came up with remained ephemeral, for public and management were basically of one mind: they wanted to see *vieux Saxe.* Consequently Meissen was probably the first German factory to pursue the regrettable policy—and one that remains that of Berlin and Nymphenburg today—which consists in making no more concessions to modernity than are absolutely necessary but concentrating resources on the reproduction of eighteenth-century models.

For use in middle-class households the old 'onion pattern' in underglaze blue achieved quite unprecedented popularity in the late nineteenth century (from about 1880 onwards). The original plates and bowls with their curvaceous Baroque shapes were now complemented by every conceivable service item and sold in vast quantities. What the 'strawflower' or 'shell pattern' (also originally from Meissen) came to mean to the Danes, the 'onion pattern' was to the Germans. Easily the most popular crockery pattern during the late nineteenth century, it was already being produced by the rival private factory of Carl & Ernst Teichert in Meissen by the end of the 1880s.[55]

### Berlin

The successes recorded by Meissen with the revival of eighteenth-century models did not go unnoticed by its closest rival, the Royal Prussian Manufactory in Berlin, though for a long time Berlin was unable to make up its mind whether to

follow suit. Friedrich Georg Frick, managing director for the previous two decades, had died in 1848. This great ceramic technologist, whom Köllmann compares with Alexandre Brongniart,[56] was replaced in 1850 by Heinrich Gustav Kolbe (1809–1867), a civil servant from the finance ministry who, though he had no technical training, was interested in the factory and committed to making a success of it.[57] In the 1840s Frick had had to step up production of sanitary ware and white porcelain for economic reasons, because Berlin did not have Meissen's readily saleable semi-luxury porcelains such as lustre-coloured wares[58] and those made in pressed glass moulds. The Kolbe period was characterized by efforts to promote more ambitious trends in porcelain manufacture. Frederick William IV personally wanted the factory to flourish as an 'art institute'—a desire in which Ludwig I of Bavaria had recently been frustrated (see p. 184). In Berlin—and again there were precedents in Sèvres, Meissen, and Nymphenburg—the managing director of the factory was now given an 'Honorary Council of Noted Artists' to stand by him with help and advice. The intention was good but the help remained minimal since the artists represented were still wholly rooted in Romanticism or Neo-Classicism. A galvanizing spirit of innovation was hardly to be expected of them, if only on grounds of age. The sculptor Christian Daniel Rauch was seventy-three, the painter and director of the Academy, Peter von Cornelius, was sixty-seven, and Friedrich August Stüler, though only fifty years of age, was totally absorbed in the Neo-Classicism of his fellow-architect Schinkel, which the factory had been cultivating for decades in its display porcelains. However, Kolbe did not just wait to be helped. He and his top artists went on study trips, and other painters were sent to Sèvres for further training. In line with the prevailing historicist approach to art, Kolbe purchased old wares in order to build up a specimen collection of ceramics—again on the pattern of the Musée céramique et vitrique at Sèvres. His head painter from 1849 to 1874 was the academic painter Hermann Looschen, who was succeeded on his death in 1874 by his son of the same name. The man responsible for all vessel and figure

cf. pp. 140–

modelling from 1841 to 1884 was Julius Wilhelm Mantel (1820–1896).

### Exceptional Pieces

At the Great Exhibition of 1851 in London the Berlin factory won a medal for its extremely heterogeneous entry, which ranged from the crater vase and the 'Persian' vase designed by Schinkel to experiments in the 'Old German' style (a vase with the figures of the twelve apostles after Peter Vischer) and included large numbers of vessels and plaques with copies of paintings, lithophanes, biscuit figures, service items with flower and landscape decoration and paintings after Watteau, even imitation majolica, thus offering a complete panorama of the stylistic pluralism of the mid-century period.[59] Subsequent world exhibitions were little different. Each time the factory concentrated on presenting the jurors with an entry that would elicit prizes by the sheer variety, size, and complexity of the pieces shown—and would usually be awarded, of course, on grounds of technological excellence alone. The reports of the exhibitions contain bewildering descriptions of these incoherent entries, now criticizing the lack of a consistent stylistic direction, now complaining of persistent reliance on too few types and on the 'architectural art trend currently prevailing in Berlin'.[60] Little has survived from this period (which quickly fell into disrepute), particularly since Berlin, unlike Meissen, Vienna, and Sèvres, did not have a factory or local museum in which important works were preserved. However, we can assess the enormous variety of ware produced simply by looking at the display vases that went from the World Exhibitions of 1855 to 1867 into what was then the finest of all collections, that at London's South Kensington Museum.[61] In addition to traditionally shaped amphora vases

334  *'Calendar cup and saucer'*. Berlin, 1849. Overglaze and gilt decoration. H. 8.5 cm. Mark: 125. Kunstgewerbemuseum, East Berlin (Hz. 682).
An example of the striving for originality that preoccupied all porcelain manufacturers around the middle of the century.

335  *Corinthian capital*. Berlin, 1855. Biscuit porcelain. H. 42.2 cm. Unmarked. Kunstgewerbemuseum, SMPK, Berlin (1980,190).
Only Berlin, the stronghold of late Neo-Classicism, could have produced a full-size Corinthian capital in porcelain, as it did for the 1855 World Exhibition in Paris.

and craters going back to the Schinkel circle, with figure and scene painting as well as imitation stone and gilt painting, there was also a modified gadrooned crater (1855) in celadon-green with entwined handles and a procession of horsemen represented in Classical style painted in white to imitate cut cameos round its wide neck, a large wine jug on a trefoil-shaped saucer (1867) with polychrome grotesque painting, a supremely successful example of the freshest kind of majolica imitation, and an urn-shaped vase (1867) with Irish guilloche ornamentation and paintings based on the Germanic folk tales.

Kolbe and his team were anxious to get away from using porcelain purely as a vehicle for painting—the 'dead end' that had dominated the entire first half of the century. Sculpted decoration had characterized much of the pottery and porcelain at the first World Exhibition, from English relief stoneware with mainly naturalistic decoration (there was something similar from south Germany in the 'Old German' idiom) to the Neo-Rococo porcelains of Meissen and Bohemia. Kolbe tried likewise to give a new look to Berlin porcelain with sculpted elements, relief ornamentation, 'spectacular' handle formation, 'the use of sculpted groups as bearers of vessels or accompaniments thereto', and the 'incorporation of sculpted flowers, masks, and human and animal heads'.[62] Consequently in 1862 the factory exhibited several centrepieces with figure supports as well as biscuit figures and busts representing an obvious attempt to compete with the 'Parian' figures that had been popular in England for years.[63] Kolbe based his 'new direction', which principally occupied his master modeller Mantel, more or less convincingly on the creations of the Italian Renaissance.

The universal Neo-Renaissance movement that had begun around 1860 and with which Berlin now fell in, provided further stimuli.[64] The vessels modelled in the new spirit were painted with the grotesque ornamentation of the Cinquecento, with the painters trying for reasons of stylistic purity to reproduce the exact colour of tin-glazed earthenware. German Renaissance pottery was also imitated with castings of Raeren or Westerwald stoneware pitchers, which became successful export items.[65]

It was also in these years that Berlin began imitating Chinese porcelain,[66] though the twenty simple flower vases illustrated in the 1875 price list did not become important for Hermann Seger's coloured glazes until after 1880.

### Crisis in the 1870s

In 1867 the factory received a new managing director—another civil servant, Gustav Müller (1826–1881), who clearly allowed things to go on as he found them; there were no changes either in the artistic staff or in the production programme. For reasons that are not entirely clear, sales of porcelain fell off in the years around 1870.[67] When in 1877 the factory required a subsidy for the first time, steps were taken from outside. The 'Honorary Council of Noted Artists' appointed in 1851 had not met for years. Now another committee of 'experts' was called together by the ministry responsible to decide the factory's fate. The result of their deliberations, the so-called 'Berlin Protocol',[68] contained some ideas that bore thinking about and others that were absurd. The factory's not always brilliant reviews at past world exhibitions

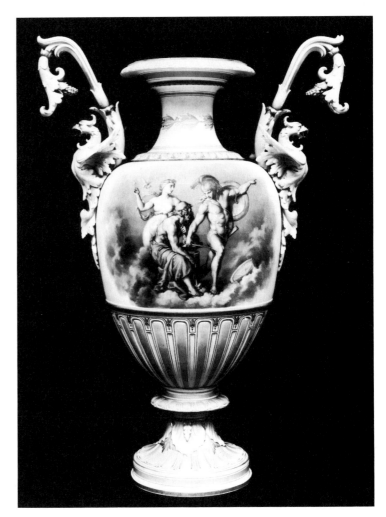

337 *Ornamental vase.* Berlin, 1867. Biscuit porcelain, painting in matching shades of violet, gilt ornamentation. H. 80 cm. Marks: 125, 128. V & A (Bethnal Green Mus.), London (942-1869).
This great display vase with its griffin handles and careful *grisaille* painting represents a quite different kind of Neo-Renaissance porcelain.

◁ 336 *'Majolica' jug.* Berlin, 1867. Overglaze decoration. H. 40.5 cm. Marks: 125, 128. V & A (Bethnal Green Mus.), London.
One product of Berlin's borrowings from Renaissance art were majolica-type wares such as this jug with imitation 16th-century grotesque painting.

were taken in a positively masochistic way as a prophecy of doom as far as the current standard of production was concerned. They overlooked the fact that the verdicts of which they took particular note, for example those of the 1855 World Exhibition in Paris, did not have a good word to say for anybody except the national factory at Sèvres, and that comparisons between Sèvres and the commercial porcelain manufacturers were basically unfair in that Sèvres was able to experiment without having to worry about economic considerations. The authors of the protocol analysed and criticized—objectively, as they thought, but with hindsight we can see that they were very much 'of their time' in condemning the Neo-Renaissance works based on majolica and stoneware that were just then going out of fashion. They made suggestions that, again with hindsight, we can see to have been of questionable value. But the inquest did undoubtedly have one important result: the managing director was henceforth assisted by an artistic director and a technical director. With the first technical director, who headed the technochemical research institute set up shortly before the meeting, they struck gold straight away in the person of Hermann Seger, whose radical innovations are discussed in chapter I. The first artistic director was Louis Sussmann-Hellborn (1828–1908), a sculptor with only a local reputation but with wide-ranging

338 *Beer pitcher*. Berlin, after 1870. Relief stamping and overglaze decoration. H. 35 cm. Marks: 125, 128 and impressed marks. Sotheby's, London (23.10.1980).
Various 'Old German' beer pitchers based on stoneware models formed part of Berlin's Neo-Renaissance production programme. They sold very well abroad.

interests in the field of the arts and crafts. Two surviving statuettes of his depicting 'ladies of fashion' indicate that he helped to prepare the ground for a style that, under his successor Alexander Kips (1858–1910), became definitive from 1888 onwards—the so-called 'Third Rococo'. Long out of favour, though since 1851 it had been repeatedly cropping up in certain shapes and motifs, Rococo now gained ascendancy as the style to be followed. A generation later than Meissen, Berlin now adopted the course of unreservedly reasserting its own heritage. Kips enthusiastically embraced the possibilities that porcelain offered to the artist with a gift for decoration and designed vases, clocks, boxes, candlesticks, and even such monumental items as fire-place surrounds that were full of pathos and delighted in exaggerated shapes.[69] At the same time old models were reworked and decorative motifs sought on the eighteenth-century pattern; display vases were even painted with portraits of the imperial family. Everything Kips designed was on a grand scale; it was his idea, for example, to clad whole walls with porcelain pictures made up of

339

individual tiles, an idea that in conjunction with his ornamental vocabulary dominated Berlin's entry at subsequent exhibitions.[70] At the time the critics were full of praise, but in the perspective of art history Kips's efforts, which he continued until 1902, soon fell into second place behind those of Hermann Seger.

## Thuringia

In the second half of the century Meissen's lead was followed by the porcelain factories of the dukedoms of Saxe-Coburg-Gotha, Saxe-Meiningen, Saxe-Weimar-Eisenach, Schwarzenburg-Rudolstadt, and Schwarzburg-Sondershausen, in other words the firms we know generically as the porcelain factories of Thuringia; the same programme was also pursued by firms in Saxony (C. Teichert in Meissen and Thieme in Potschappel) and in the province of Silesia (Tielsch & Co in Altwasser and Carl Krister in Waldenburg, among others). The older Thuringian factories at places like Gotha, Gera, Ilmenau, and Rauenstein continued to produce porcelain but now concentrated to a greater or lesser extent on utility ware, younger foundations having taken over the 'luxury' market. In the first half of the century some twenty new factories had been established in Thuringia; the decade between 1850 and 1860 alone brought a further fifteen.[71] Factories in Blankenhain, Elgersburg, Gotha, Grossbreitenbach, Ilmenau, Kahla, Lichte, Limbach, Neuhaus am Rennweg, Ohrdruf, Rauenstein, Rudolstadt, Schaala, Sitzendorf, Tambach, Volkstedt, Wallendorf and Zwickau enjoyed a certain reputation. Some firms confined themselves entirely to producing utility porcelain such as hotel and catering ware, toilet sets, door and curtain knobs, haberdashery, children's services and dolls' heads, which had recently been ousting faience and metal articles. Others were already concentrating on chemical and technical wares such as pipes and insulators. Many of them operated in both areas, also covering the more elegant end of the production spectrum with 'luxury and fantasy articles', holy images (crucifixes, Madonnas, figures of saints), holy-water basins, clock cases, cigar and match accessories, pipe bowls, writing utensils, vases—often with applied sculpted flowers—*jardinières*, bowls and dishes with painted decoration, toilet sets, or simply cream pots. In this third quarter of the century the variety was almost infinite, from dining, tea-, and coffee services, open-work dessert services and centrepieces to figures, groups, and 'knick-knacks',[72] both in glazed and in biscuit porcelain. Most firms had their own painting department. A surprising number of them clearly worked predominantly or exclusively for the export market, with the English-speaking countries as well as Central and South America as the chief customers. Special export articles listed in the 1883 Directory of the Ceramic Industry[73] were significantly 'mugs', 'candlesticks', 'flowerholders' (Heubach in Lichte), 'penny toys' (Unterweissbach, Coburg), Turkish coffee cups, and 'Portugal cups' (Lochotin in Pilsen [Plzeň]).

The biggest sales success abroad were figures in the 'Meissen genre': ornamental vessels (bowls, small baskets), candlesticks, 340

339 *Neo-Rococo vase with portrait of Wilhelm II*. Berlin, c. 1903. Overglaze painting, gilt trimming. H. 67 cm. Marks: 125, 128 and impressed marks. WL, Stuttgart (1969-18).
The appointment of Alexander Kips as Berlin's artistic director in 1888 ushered in fifteen years of the sumptuous style known as 'Third Rococo'.

and clock cases, modelled in pseudo-Rococo shapes, decorated with sculpted flowers, colourfully painted, and ornamented with gilding. Themes for figures and groups included saints for certain Catholic countries (including even India and South America), putti, cavaliers and Rococo ladies, shepherds and gardeners in an *ancien-régime* manner far removed from reality, so-called 'Mozart groups', and from 1880 at the latest 'crinoline groups'. These were figures of fashionable ladies that, before being fired in the porcelain kiln, were given elaborately flounced skirts made of real lace dipped in porcelain paste. The lace burned away in the kiln, leaving a delicate filigree of porcelain that still delights innumerable purchasers today.[74] Candlesticks and centrepieces, richly modelled and always combined with figures, were supplied in large quantities and sometimes excellent quality by the Carl Thieme firm at Potschappel-Freital near Dresden (est. 1872).[75]

Simpler vessel shapes, primarily vases, were often in the last third of the century painted with delicate Watteauesque and Chinese scenes, battles and so on after eighteenth-century Meissen patterns. There must have been quite a number of firms that simply concentrated on porcelain painting, of which that of Helena Wolfsohn in Dresden is particularly appreciated today.[76]

Inexpensive imitations of Meissen's blue-and-white patterns (onion, strawflower) were supplied mainly by C. Teichert in Meissen (est. 1863).[77] Römer & Födisch at Fraureuth (est. 1866) made utility services whose thin walls won approval at international exhibitions, but it was not until after 1900 that Fraureuth, along with Friedrich Kästner at Oberhohndorf (est. 1883), gained a reputation for ornamental porcelains.

### Bavaria and Silesia

In the Bavarian Forest, which was similarly rich in kaolin deposits to neighbouring Thuringia, subsidiaries of the Thuringian factories were established from 1815 onwards. Bauscher at Weiden (est. 1881) produced utility wares and was noted for cobalt-blue ornamental articles in the 'Third Rococo' style with gilt decoration; J. N. Müller at Schönwald (est. 1879) supplied painted and unpainted utility ware; and two large firms founded by members of the old Thuringian porcelain family of Hutschenreuther at Selb (est. 1857) and Hohenberg (est. 1815) produced in the 1880s all the usual porcelain wares from utility tableware to picture dishes and painted service items in the older styles, 'exquisitely decorated'. Most of these firms had a staff of anything from a few dozen to several hundred. Very much larger were the two Silesian firms of C. Tielsch at Altwasser (est. 1845) and Carl Krister at Waldenburg (1831), which in 1883 employed 1,500 and 1,250 people respectively and supplied—at low prices—everything from technical to luxury porcelain.[78]

### Fürstenberg

The Duke of Brunswick's porcelain factory at Fürstenberg was hard hit by increased competition in the second third of the century and visibly declined. In 1859 it was leased out to private entrepreneurs.[79] The new management was successful in its efforts to bring the factory into line with the new market situation. Only cups were still produced in the firm's old Empire style, while as early as 1861 a radical attempt at renewal was embarked upon with ten coffee and tea-services in the contemporary eclectic manner. Spouts in the shape of animal heads, flower knops, branch-shaped handles, and strap-work ornamentation were some of the many historical motifs quoted.[80] The painting department, abandoned in 1828, was now reorganized and found plenty of work decorating the newly designed services that began to appear in regular succession. In 1880 Fürstenburg began remodelling some of its

polished gilding, already popular before 1850, retained its popularity for a long time. These porcelain factories were joined by one or two new ones, for example the rapidly successful factory established by Karl Knoll at Fischern, near Karlsbad, in 1849.

## Pirkenhammer

The porcelains of the Pirkenhammer, Klösterle, and Prague factories are of vastly superior artistic quality to those of the firms mentioned above. The largest of these was Pirkenhammer, which in the second half of the century was managed by Rudolf Fischer and Ludwig von Mieg. Although here too there was greater emphasis on mass-production, following the departure of Christian Fischer in 1853, the factory continued to produce carefully modelled single pieces with high-quality painting.

Under the influence of Vienna, in the 1860s and 1870s Pirkenhammer complemented its popular gilt-trimmed Neo-Rococo lines with simply shaped plates and other items of tableware decorated with a Neo-Renaissance ornamentation that has a charm all its own.[81] Figure sculpture, too, was produced here, though it appears to have been of inferior quality to that of the Prague factory.

## Prague

In Prague an old faience factory had begun to specialize in the manufacture of porcelain figures, for which there was an excellent market in the growing city. In addition to the pseudo-Rococo types also well known from Thuringia, Prague is noted for busts and statuettes of contemporary politicians, actors, dancers, poets, musicians, numerous costume figures from the heterogeneous Austrian empire, rural and city characters such as the Russian factories also made, suitably costumed historical characters, caricatures, and such unusual motifs as the anthropomorphic flowers based on Grandville illustrations. The quality of the modelling was determined by Ernst Popp, a pupil of the celebrated Munich sculptor Ludwig Schwanthaler.[82]

342 *Bottle vases decorated with paintings after Watteau.* Dresden, Richard Klemm's porcelain painting shop, after 1871. Overglaze painting, gilt decoration. H. 48.5 cm. Mark: inaccessible. Sotheby's, London (15.9.1980). In the late 19th century several firms in the Dresden area were producing wares based on 18th-century Meissen models—sometimes forging Meissen's marks.

own eighteenth-century designs, thus joining the then prevalent Neo-Rococo trend in German porcelain.

There was now a constant demand for porcelain tableware and appliances from all sections of the population. For the middle classes it still had the status of 'white gold', lending itself to display. And the lower the social bracket, the stronger the demand for shapes and types of decoration that at least had the appearance of costliness. Elaborately shaped, heavily decorated, and sumptuously gilded porcelain thus retained its popularity up until the turn of the century and beyond, particularly with those factories that could produce it cheaply. This applied to most of the privately owned factories in the German provinces as well as to those in nearby Bohemia.

## BOHEMIA

By the middle of the century the Bohemian factories had long had a solid clientele that on the one hand required sturdy but at the same time pleasing utility ware and on the other hand wanted attractive but sensibly priced display pieces. The large Haas & Cžižek factory at Schlaggenwald was, together with Fischer & Mieg at Pirkenhammer, the biggest supplier of utility tableware combining sturdy, rarely experimental shapes stylistically between late Biedermeier and Neo-Rococo with printed—and therefore inexpensive—decoration. Dallwitz, Elbogen, and Altrohlau appear to have followed the Neo-Rococo style even more single-mindedly; here relief decoration on simplified *rocaille* shapes with polychrome painting and

343 *Tea-service.* Schlaggenwald, before 1873. Overglaze decoration. H. (teapot) 20.3 cm. Mark: 120. UM, Prague (74.973-979)
For their utility tableware the Bohemian factories of the period used simplified Biedermeier shapes with painted or printed borders.

344 *Washing set.* Elbogen, 1853. Overglaze painting and gilding. H. 24.8 cm. Marks: 111 and year. UM, Prague.
This small basin and ewer typify the sumptuous, richly gilded, brightly painted 'Second Rococo' style favoured by the Bohemian factories.

345 *Display vase.* Pirkenhammer, K. Mannl, 1885. Overglaze painting, gilt decoration. H. 75 cm. Mark: 115. UM, Prague.
A typical exhibition piece—in contrast to the two examples (Pls. 343–344) of the Bohemian factories' everyday production in the second half of the century.

346 *Empress Elizabeth on horseback.* Prague, fashioned by Ernst Popp, 1854. ▷
Biscuit porcelain, painted. H. 27.5 cm. Mark: inaccessible. UM, Prague.
The finest porcelain statuettes from Bohemia in the second half of the century were produced by a former stoneware factory in Prague itself.

347 *Pieces from a dining service.* Klösterle, 1851. Gilt decoration. H. (tureen) 38 cm. Mark: 113. UM, Prague.
Variants of the 'Ferdinand shape' in white and gold are regarded as the finest Bohemian porcelains of the second half of the century.

348 *Cup with a view of Schloss Sagan and saucer.* Tiefenfurt, Silesia, after 1883. Overglaze painting, gilding. H. 8.2 cm. Mark: 143a. MNC, Sèvres (14 559).
A good example of the way the 'Second Rococo' style persisted in provincial Germany throughout the second half of the century.

## Klösterle

The most remarkable factory in this period both for figures and for tableware was Count Thun's porcelain factory at Klösterle. In 1848 this had received a new managing director in the person of Karl Venier, who had trained at the Prague Polytechnic and was an experienced craftsman. He brought the factory right up-to-date technologically and paved the way for a broad and varied production that in terms of both shape and decoration was more interesting than that of all the factory's Bohemian competitors. A number of large and more than usually ambitious services were produced at the time of the first

347  World Exhibition. They were based on the 'Ferdinand' shape, named in honour of the emperor who had abdicated in 1848, a curvaceous Neo-Rococo design with foliage and scroll reliefs on surfaces and rims and with elaborate handles, spouts, and knops. There were variants with vertical and slanted fluting, the so-called Emperor Service (1851) and the *Thunsche Service,* made in 1854–1856 for the proprietor of the factory, Count Josef Maria Thun. Both are unpainted, their decoration being limited to gilded relief elements and coats of arms. Single pieces of tableware in the same shape with dense floral painting preserved in the Prague museum are very much less satisfactory than the white-and-gold services.[83] A welcome tendency towards austerity characterizes other, almost Neo-Classically simple services from Klösterle.

For the world exhibitons, to which Klösterle usually submitted an entry, less harmonious display pieces were made in an attempt to meet the requirements of contemporary fashion for a broad reworking of historical themes. In 1855 the factory exhibited in Paris a wine-jug 80 centimetres high inspired by the decorative tankards of the Renaissance and covered with figures representing the Victory of Wine; in 1876

349 *Covered cup with chinoiserie decoration.* Herend, 1885–1891. Overglaze painting. H. 8 cm. Mark: 157. Kunstgewerbemuseum, Cologne (E 4439).
Moritz Fischer of Herend specialized in copies of 18th-century porcelains to complete existing services.

it showed in Philadelphia a monumental vase in an almost grotesque mixture of styles with snake-handles, masks, dolphins, imitation stone trimmings, and so on—probably also seen as paying homage to Renaissance art.[84]

# HUNGARY

## Herend

An exhibition report written around 1870 mentions as the only porcelain factory of any note in central Europe, apart from Meissen, the one established at Herend (near Vesprem in Hungary) by Moritz Fischer in 1839.[85] Fischer specialized exclusively in what he called 'facsimiles'.[86] At first rather overshadowed by the small factories of central Germany and Austria, he found his true vocation when Prince Esterhazy's family brought him an old Meissen service and asked him to make up the missing parts. Soon the Fischer factory at Herend was doing nothing but reproducing patterns from Meissen, Vienna, Capodimonte, and Sèvres. In 1851 he had his first international success at the Great Exhibition in London with imitation Chinese porcelains. Some old Chinese porcelains belonging to the Turin court had been brought to him for completion shortly before. Imitations of all the popular Chinese porcelains with *famille rose, famille verte,* and Imari decoration together with such variants as double-walled and pierced vessels became a further speciality of Herend in the years that followed. The heyday of the factory, which employed no independent designers but some outstanding craftsmen, was brief. It went bankrupt for the first time as early as 1874, following the departure of its founder, but continued in production. In the Directory of the Ceramic Industry of 1883 Herend announced utility and ornamental porcelain with, as a speciality, 'antique genres' for which, in addition to the Herend factory mark, the beehive stamp—the old mark of the Imperial Porcelain Manufactory in Vienna—was offered 'to order' in underglaze blue.[87] In this respect Herend came closest to Samson of Paris.[88]

349

# DENMARK

## Copenhagen

*Royal Porcelain Manufactory*
The mid-century period had brought the Copenhagen factory welcome popularity through the sale of Thorwaldsen biscuit replicas. The 1850s and 1860s saw new motifs added to this branch of the factory's production. These figures could be produced in series and therefore relatively inexpensively, and they sold to a wide public. At the same time extravagant display vases with views and portraits were individually made to commissions from private and royal customers.

268

Christian Hetsch (1830–1903), the son of the factory's long-serving artistic adviser, continued his father's Neo-Classical style but enhanced it with historicist elements. Admittedly, in principle his vases still reflected the basic Classical shapes, but now the highly coloured decoration was very much to the fore. The *horror vacui* so characteristic of the time finds expression in intricate and elaborate relief, gilt, and painted decoration covering everything.

350

Here and there an historicist shape or piece of decoration marred the overall late Neo-Classical/Biedermeier picture; in 1863 the *Flora Danica* Service—with far fewer pieces and some different motifs—was reissued for the first time for the trousseau of a Danish princess.

Financial problems had already supervened before 1850, despite the excellent sales of the factory's biscuit statuettes. The

350 *Display vase with portraits of the reigning king and queen.* Copenhagen: RPF, Christian Hetsch, before 1867. Overglaze painting, rich gilt decoration. H. 52 cm. Mark: 146. Christiansborg Palace, Copenhagen.
The Royal Porcelain factory continued the Neo-Classical tradition after 1850, though in a more elaborate version in which the display aspect was often paramount.

351 *Service in the Neo-Renaissance style.* Copenhagen, Bing & Grøndahl, Heinrich Hansen, before 1862. Overglaze painting, sculptural and gilt decoration. H. (coffee-pot) 17 cm. Mark: 144. Factory collection, Bing & Grøndahl, Copenhagen.

Typical of Bing & Grøndahl's experimental approach to historical styles in the 1860s, the only conventional feature of this *déjeuner* are the views of Copenhagen.

352 *Plate from the Service with the Oldenburg Kings.* Copenhagen, Bing & Grøndahl, Christian Hansen, 1861. Overglaze and gilt decoration. D. 21.5 cm. Mark: 144. Factory collection, Bing & Grøndahl, Copenhagen. One of the factory's many successful decorative experiments, with coats of arms and cameo portraits neatly inserted in an ornamental border.

353 *'Vienna Plates'.* Copenhagen, Bing & Grøndahl, Heinrich Hansen, 1870. Overglaze and relief gilt decoration. D. 24.5 cm. Mark: 145. Factory collection, Bing & Grøndahl, Copenhagen. These plates took up again a type of decoration that had had its heyday in Vienna in the Neo-Classical period.

354 *Tureen from the Rosenborg Service.* Copenhagen, Bing & Grøndahl, Heinrich Hansen, *c.* 1870. Overglaze and gilt decoration. H. *c.* 40 cm. Mark: 145. Factory collection, Bing & Grøndahl, Copenhagen.
Bing & Grøndahl's state service for the Rosenborg Palace was based loosely on 18th-century Meissen designs.

story was the same as elsewhere in this age of industrialization: the small factory could not go on in the old way, producing high-quality and at the same time profitable work by hand; first it required subsidization, and eventually it was put up for sale by a state that did not see itself as a patron of the arts. From 1 January 1868 the old Royal Manufactory was royal in name alone, being in fact in private hands. Not until 1882 did it regain its place among the artistically important factories when it was taken over by the flourishing Aluminia faience factory.

*Bing & Grøndahl*

Meanwhile the second Copenhagen porcelain factory of Bing & Grøndahl, established in 1852, was faring somewhat better. It not only enjoyed great success with its biscuit statuettes through an unusual outlet—the book trade—but it also created a sound basis for itself with utility porcelains and from 1857 with technical porcelains (insulators). Grøndahl's early death in 1856 changed nothing. He was succeeded by the modeller C. Schjeltved, and the landscape painter Andreas Thomas Juuel (1817–1868), who had come to Bing from the Royal Manufactory in 1853, set a high standard in the field of decoration. Bing & Grøndahl did not aspire to a pioneering role. With biscuit figures, painted display vases, cups, and plates they followed the already available types and with them captured their market step by step. When on Juuel's death in 1868 the architectural painter Heinrich Hansen (1821–1890) was appointed to succeed him, the Neo-Renaissance made a timely appearance in the factory's programme, a style that was

355 *Decorative vase with a portrait of John Locke.* St Petersburg, before 1862. Overglaze painting, rich gilt decoration, gilt bronze mount. H. 70 cm. Mark: 154. V & A (Bethnal Green Mus.), London (9093-1862).
Tsar Alexander's gift to the London museum after the 1862 Exhibition appropriately bore a portrait of the great English philosopher.

never reflected in the output of the Royal Manufactory. Hansen had already supplied attractive designs in a modern historicist style for the International Exhibition of 1862, and of these a Neo-Renaissance service with views of Copenhagen has survived. Its complicated overall shape with the emphasis on individual parts and with its animal-head spouts and figured handles can be compared with similar services from Meissen (contemporary), Berlin, and Sèvres (later). The finest pieces have views of Danish royal castles painted by Hansen himself. Other examples of this imaginative artist's work are ornamental plates with cameo painting (1861) or in the Viennese Empire style (1870) and the display vase with a view of St Peter's, Rome, made for the Universal Exhibition of 1873 in Vienna.[89]

## RUSSIA

### St Petersburg

When Tsar Alexander II came to the throne in 1855, the Imperial Porcelain Manufactory at St Petersburg received a new managing director, and a new general managing director, Count Stenbock, was appointed to oversee all the imperial manufactories (porcelain, glass, crystal, tapestry, wallpaper). But the technical and artistic staff actually responsible for the day-to-day running of the factory changed but little. The administration had had to make greater efforts than simply promoting the usual contacts with western European factories in order to bring a fresh impetus to the antiquated concern. From 1855 to 1859 and again from 1862 the porcelain painter Lippold came from Dresden, but he appears to have been more of a copyist than an innovator, rather like the master modeller August Spiess, who preferred to work in the Meissen or Sèvres

356 *Plate with Russian 'national' decoration.* Kornilov factory, after 1891. Overglaze and gilt decoration. D. *c.* 26 cm. Marks: 155 and 'Made in Russia by Kornilov Bros'. M. M. Post Collection, Hillwood.
Patterns based on Russian peasant embroidery emerged with the nationalist movement around 1870 and were promoted mainly by art schools.

style. The painting department continued to employ qualified figure, flower, historical, landscape, and ornamental painters, and there were two further posts for *amours et études de femmes* and *genre japonais*.[90] As a result the St Petersburg factory returned from the World Exhibitions of 1862, 1867, and 1873 with honourable mentions and prizes for the technical perfection of its painting. The lack of originality, however, became positively obtrusive. There was little encouragement from the imperial court itself during this period. From 1870 the staff had to be cut, but porcelain production was not—like the work of most of the other imperial manufactories—discontinued in that year. In 1871 the tsarina ordered a reorientation towards new western and above all English patterns. Consequently the last traditional *bravura* pieces—the copies of paintings and the plaques with pictorial compositions in muffle-colour painting—were abandoned without anyone being in a position to put anything truly new in their place. Suggestions that the old folk art should be taken as the basis for a modern and specifically Russian porcelain do not appear to have produced any conspicuous results at the Imperial Manufactory.[91]

### Private Factories

The number of privately owned factories in Russia dropped during these years and the gap was filled by a few large concerns.[92] They appear to have cultivated a Historicism oriented mainly towards Rococo, but at the same time the discovery of the 'national style' constituted a genuine enrichment for them. A decisive contribution to the formulation of this was made by the work of the Moscow School of Arts and Crafts, whose pupils and teachers copied old Russian manuscripts in all the libraries to which they could gain access and published a collection of a hundred prints in 1870.[93] The declared aim of the book was to offer Russian artistic craftsmen a compendium of shapes in the national style. The designers at the porcelain factories did indeed make enthusiastic use of these patterns, which formed the basis of colourful, highly original decorative schemes on ornamental plates and vessels, of which we have quite delightful examples from the Popov, Kornilov, and Kuznetsov factories.

### ENGLAND

The Great Exhibition held in London in 1851 brought out more strongly than ever the keen spirit of competition affecting French and English porcelain manufacturers in the mid-nineteenth century. In a somewhat curious way each suffered from feelings of inferiority in regard to the other. The English were afraid of being accused of 'bad taste', while the French also feared the same accusation as well as that of producing wares which were impractical. It was against this background that some firms, notably Coalport and Minton, vigorously launched the production of 'imitation Sèvres' pieces.

### Coalport

The Coalport factory had a head start over its competitors in making this type of porcelain. In 1820 John Rose had purchased from Billingsley and Samuel Walker both their

357  *Pair of vases.* Coalport (Shropshire), John Rose & Co, *c.* 1850. Bone china. H. 33 cm. Mark: 169 (only one marked). V & A, London (C. 561-1935).
Known as *vase flacon à cordes* at Sèvres in the 18th century, the pink ground on these pieces is successful. On one side of the vases are scenes in the style of Boucher attributed to James Roux and somewhat heavily painted, but the flower painting on the reverse has been skilfully executed.

358  *Vase.* Coalport (Shropshire), John Rose & Co, *c.* 1850–1860. Bone china. H. 39.3 cm. Mark: 169. V & A, London (C. 1258ᴬ-1917).
This vase has been decorated with a green ground and partridge-eye gilding. When Coalport pieces of this type are of high quality, they almost reach the perfection of Sèvres porcelain.

359 *Plate from the Tsar Nicolas I Service.* Coalport (Shropshire), John Rose & Co, second quarter of the 19th century. Bone china. D. 26 cm. Mark: 'A.B.' and 'R. P. Daniell' printed in gold. V & A, London (C. 3386-1901). This service was commissioned by Queen Victoria and exhibited at the Great Exhibition in London in 1851. It includes all the characteristics of services with armorials made in numerous English 19th-century factories: lobed fluted border, strong ground colour and thick gilding. The piece is evidently designed to impress by means of its rich decoration rather than to arouse admiration for its quality of production.

360 *Covered cup and saucer.* Coalport (Shropshire), John Rose & Co, *c.* 1850. Bone china. D. (saucer) 12 cm, H. (cup) 10 cm. Mark: inaccessible. Conservatoire national des Arts et Métiers, Paris (4669).
The shape and decoration of this piece derive from oriental models. It is made of thin-walled 'egg-shell' porcelain. The pink ground is decorated with a gilt 'vermiculated' pattern, often found as an element of a decorative scheme but rarely used alone as on this object, which was shown at the 1851 Exhibition.

361 *Cups and saucers.* Coalport (Shropshire), John Rose & Co, third quarter ▷ of the 19th century. Bone china. H. (covered cup) 9.5 cm, D. (saucer) 12.7 cm, H. (remaining cups) 6.1 cm, D. (remaining saucers) 13.2 cm. Mark: interlaced LLs imitating the Sèvres factory mark on the saucer of the covered cup. V & A, London (3370[A]-1901, 3368[B]-1901, C. 228-1935).
Coalport is imitating mid-18th-century Vincennes porcelains here. On either side are cups based on the *tasses Hébert;* the centre cup, cover, and saucer is based on the *gobelet litron.* Like the best Vincennes pieces these have blue grounds, but the polychrome decoration of the Coalport examples is slightly more abundant than it would have been on Vincennes porcelains.

secret formulas and the moulds they had used at Swansea and Nantgarw to make copies of Vincennes porcelain. (The factory that later moved to Sèvres, in 1756, was originally set up at Vincennes in 1738.) After John Rose's death in 1841, his brother, Thomas Rose, together with his son, William Frederick Rose, and William Pugh took over the firm keeping the name 'John Rose & Co' until 1889. William Pugh was the sole owner of the factory between 1862 and his death in 1875.

After John Rose's death the factory abandoned the Rococo style and discontinued the manufacture of pieces with floral decoration in relief. German influence gave way to French, but now the famous Sèvres vases, which were the pride of the Royal factory in the second half of the eighteenth century, were copied rather than Vincennes pieces. The Coalport factory even made use of fake marks, which copied those of Sèvres. Both the shapes and the coloured grounds used for Sèvres vases were imitated. Coalport and Daniel, the latter a London businessman who acted as the factory's agent, showed porcelain decorated with *rose du Barry*[94] and *bleu-céleste* grounds at the 1851 Exhibition, as well as baskets with glazed decoration. These were supported by Parian figures similar to ones exhibited by Minton, which had been made for Queen Victoria. A certain number of painters at Coalport specialized in Sèvres-type decoration, among them John Randall, a bird painter; William Cook, a flower and fruit painter; and James Roux who painted figures and decorative motifs. Such were the talents of these painters and the quality of English porcelain that these Sèvres copies are dazzling. They are very far from the numerous outright fakes of Sèvres porcelain, mostly of French manufacture. These 'fake' pieces—doubtless made in the second half of the nineteenth-century—have tarnished the reputation of the Royal Factory in the eyes of the French.

Coalport also copied eighteenth-century Chelsea vases especially pieces with coloured grounds and Rococo handles, in other words those that most resembled Sèvres vases.

## Minton

In the second half of the nineteenth century most of the pieces made at Minton, Stoke-on-Trent, were a reflection—sometimes faithful and sometimes fanciful—of eighteenth-and nineteenth-century Sèvres and of various French ceramics and enamels. Under the management of Herbert Minton in the years between 1836 and 1858 and then under Colin Minton Campbell many foreigners, especially Frenchmen, were taken on at the factory. The foremost of these was Léon Arnoux (1816–1902). Arnoux began his career at the Valentine factory in Toulouse. As business became more and more difficult, he accepted a post at Minton in 1849 as artistic director and factory chemist. The high quality of Minton's output in the second half of the nineteenth century is linked to the vital

361

362 *Pair of pots-pourris and covers.* Coalport (Shropshire), John Rose & Co, *c.* 1850–1860. Bone china. H. 25.7 cm. Unmarked. V & A, London (C. 563ᴬ-1935).
Although based on Sèvres pieces, the deep pink ground would never have been used on French 18th-century porcelain. The scenes in reserve are painted in brownish-black, restoring an element of sobriety to the palette. The Sèvres model on which these pieces are based has no cover and is known as a *cuvette courteille* (Brunet and Préaud, 1978, p. 161, figs. 111, 111a).

363 *Vase.* Coalport (Shropshire), John Rose & Co, *c.* 1850–1860. Bone china. H. 27.8 cm. Mark: 170. V & A, London (3365-1901).
After 1850 Coalport copied a large number of Sèvres vases. The factory also produced imitations of Chelsea vases and used the Chelsea factory mark.

fusion between the porcelain body (either bone china or Parian ware) and the colours used to decorate it. These in turn were closely related to the actual styles of decoration adopted by the factory. Léon Arnoux was responsible for combining these various elements into a harmonious whole. In 1851 the Minton factory exhibited pieces of so-called majolica (known as *faïence fine* in France), which imitated Bernard Palissy's work in the sixteenth century or else imitated Saint Porchaire ware (Minton called their pieces 'Henri II Ware'). These objects were in no sense accurate copies and were often of monumental size. So successful were these wares that the Sèvres factory set up an earthenware studio in 1852. This, however, never achieved the same prominence as its counterpart at Minton.

As the leading exponent of the French influence at Stoke-on-Trent, Léon Arnoux, who was mainly concerned with decorative porcelains, encouraged the production of vases that were exact copies of eighteenth-century Sèvres. In principle most of these Sèvres copies are clearly marked with the Minton mark. The factory in fact obtained from Sèvres between 1837 and 1842 details of their shapes and models,[95] and also had at

its disposal public collections of eighteenth-century Sèvres pieces such as that belonging to the china-dealer W.J. Goode. Léon Arnoux was remarkably successful in reproducing the Sèvres shapes in bone china (not, of course, in the same soft-paste porcelain material as had originally been used) and in capturing the ground colours. These are perhaps almost too perfect when compared to the originals. Turquoise-blue, high-temperature blue, yellow, the so-called *rose Pompadour* and various greens were all used as grounds enclosing reserves painted with extremely high quality decoration. The painters responsible for carrying out the scenes and motifs on these vases included Thomas Allen, Christian Henk, and Désiré Leroy, a Frenchman who was to end up at the Derby factory.

In his *Victorian Porcelain,*[96] one of the few English publications giving a comprehensive account of the subject, Geoffrey Godden includes copious details about the painters employed during the eras of Herbert Minton and Colin Minton Campbell. The painters who decorated these luxurious productions were not allowed to sign their work around the middle of the century but later were given permission to do so.

364 *Tazza and cover.* Stoke-on-Trent (Staffordshire), Minton factory, *c.* 1858. Bone china. H. 25.5 cm. Inscribed: 'Minton & Co. Stoke Upon Trent' and signed 'SL'. V & A, London (4773-1859).
The shape and decoration of this piece are faithful imitations by Pierre Reymond of 16th-century Limoges enamels. Stephen Lawton was responsible for the painting. This piece is much closer to the French Renaissance originals than the Worcester examples decorated by Thomas Bott.

365 *Vase.* Stoke-on-Trent (Staffordshire), Colin Minton Campbell factory, *c.* 1865. Bone china. H. 49 cm. Mark: 186. Minton Mus., Royal Doulton Tableware Ltd, Stoke-on Trent.
The shape of this vase was created at Sèvres, where it was known as the *vase fil et ruban.* The Watteauesque theatrical scene on this piece was painted by Louis Jahn. Sèvres rarely used Watteau paintings on its own productions as they were out of fashion in 18th-century France; however, copies of Watteau's paintings are often found on 19th-century copies of Sèvres porcelains.

Thomas Allen (1831-1915) is a notable example of an artist whose life was dedicated to the decoration of ceramics. Joining Minton while still very young, he painted pieces exhibited in 1851. He left the factory temporarily to perfect his technique first at the Art School at Stoke-on-Trent, then at the National Art Training School, South Kensington. He painted figures and flower subjects, signing very few examples of his work. The last years of his working life, between 1875 and 1904, were spent at Wedgwood. Thomas Kirkby (1824–1891) was also a figure and flower painter and decorated both pseudo-Sèvres vases and earthenware pieces. The Frenchman Emile Lessore (1805–1876), employed as a figure painter at Sèvres between 1853–1855, was only at Minton for a short time. He is known above all for his painting on Wedgwood earthenwares between 1859 and 1876.

Christian Henk, who was at Minton from about 1842 and died in 1905, was of German origin. His background may account for his liking for Watteauesque decorative schemes. These are so rarely found on porcelain made at Vincennes or Sèvres and so frequent on nineteenth-century pieces that their very presence is an almost sure sign that the piece was not in fact made at the Sèvres factory but manufactured 'in the Sèvres style'. Louis H. Jahn was also of German origin. In 1862 he came from Vienna to Minton where he stayed for ten years. He then left the factory only to return in 1895 when he succeeded

366 *Centrepiece.* Stoke-on-Trent (Staffordshire), Herbert Minton & Co, ▷ *c.* 1850. Bone china and Parian porcelain. H. 61.7 cm. No mark visible. Coll. of Her Majesty the Queen.
Exhibited in London in 1851 and mentioned in the official catalogue, this piece was part of a dessert service purchased by Queen Victoria. Glazed bone china, partly enamelled in sky-blue, and Parian porcelain have been used, the latter for the sculptural elements of the piece.

367 *Vase.* Stoke-on-Trent (Staffordshire), W.T. Copeland, late Spode ▷▷ factory, 1851. Bone china. H. 39.2 cm. Mark: 203. V & A, London (2775-1901).
This piece was shown at the 1851 Exhibition and was painted by Daniel Lucas junior. It is somewhat Classical in style, and richly decorated.

368 *Garniture.* Worcester, Worcester Royal Porcelain Company, 1864. ▷ Bone china. H. 55.9 cm, 44.4 cm. Mark: 234. DPM, Worcester.
The figures of Sibyls were skilfully painted by Thomas Bott. These vases were shown at the 1867 Universal Exhibition in Paris.

369

370

369 *Plate.* Stoke-on-Trent (Staffordshire), Colin Minton Campbell factory, *c.* 1860. Bone china. D. 23.5 cm. Unmarked. V & A, London (7344-1862).
The pierced border of this plate and its refined decoration of flowers, fruit, and butterflies, painted by John Latham, is a perfect illustration of the elegance of Victorian taste in the 1860s.

370 *Plate from the service made for Lord Milton.* Stoke-on-Trent (Staffordshire), Colin Minton Campbell factory, *c.* 1870. Bone china. D. 23.5 cm. Mark: 187. Stoke-on-Trent, Minton Mus., Royal Doulton Tableware Ltd, Stoke-on-Trent.
The border decoration is in acid-etched gold (a mechanical process), while the centre of each plate is hand-painted with a scene depicting Lord Milton's adventures in Canada. This scene is entitled *The Forest Fire.*

371 *Candelabrum.* Stoke-on-Trent (Staffordshire), Colin Minton Campbell factory, *c.* 1870. Bone china. H. 67 cm. Mark: 188 and Phillips' mark (retailer). V & A, London (C. 1236-1917).
This object is in the characteristically eclectic style of the 1870s. The tritons are based on Classical models that were extremely popular in the Renaissance period. The scrolls and serpent tails that form the upper part of the piece supporting the candleholders and drip-pans, and above all the use of turquoise, are typical of French 18th-century porcelain.

372 *Comport.* Stoke-on-Trent (Staffordshire), Colin Minton Campbell ▷ factory, *c.* 1877. Tinted and glazed Parian porcelain. H. 60 cm. Mark: 191. Minton Mus., Royal Doulton Tableware Ltd, Stoke-on-Trent.
Parian ware is ideally suited to sculptural works and had been used for making figures since its discovery. It is also responsive to the *pâte-sur-pâte* technique of decoration.

Léon Arnoux as artistic director until 1900. He painted many pieces submitted to the various international exhibitions.

In the middle of the nineteenth century there was a group of flower painters at Minton led by Jesse Smith. In the 1850s the factory used a very soft glaze that absorbed the enamel colours used to decorate pieces assigned to the most skilled painters. G.A. Godden notes[97] that such pieces bear a special mark, the so-called ermine mark. A new generation of painters came to the fore in the following decade. They had been trained in the state-aided art schools and included Richard Pilsbury (1830–1897), a former pupil of Burslem School of Design, who was employed as a flower painter at Minton between 1866

373 *Plate.* Stoke-on-Trent (Staffordshire), Colin Minton Campbell factory, 1878. Bone china. D. 24.2 cm. Mark: 189. MAD, Limoges (ADL 3318).
The style of this plate is typical of pieces made at London in the South Kensington studio. It was set up in 1871 under the direction of W. S. Coleman and closed in 1875 (see Ex. Cat. Aslin and Atterbury, 'Minton 1798–1910', 1976, Cat. H 64).

374 *Pair of pilgrim flasks.* Stoke-on-Trent (Staffordshire), Colin Minton Campbell factory, *c.* 1878. Tinted and glazed Parian porcelain. H. 25 cm. Mark: 190. Minton Mus., Royal Doulton Tableware Ltd, Stoke-on-Trent. These pilgrim flasks were exhibited at the Exposition Universelle held in Paris in 1878. They demonstrate Marc-Louis Solon's taste for depicting young female figures playing with cupids.

and 1892. Charles Toft, who had attended the Stoke-on-Trent Art School, was another leading painter who tended to specialize in the decoration of earthenwares.

In the 1870s new artists were taken on. Some came from France at the time of the Franco-Prussian War, others were young Englishmen. One of the latter was William Stephen Coleman (1829–1904), who joined Minton in 1869. He had

been trained as a painter in oils and a water-colourist and was able to create and carry out extremely refined decorative schemes either on glazed or unglazed porcelain. In the latter technique the glaze was applied with a brush after the coloured decoration had been painted on the biscuit piece. In 1871 the firm established the Minton Art Pottery Studio at South Kensington for the decoration of earthenwares. The pieces 373  were made at Stoke-on-Trent and taken to London where they were painted either by Minton artists under the direction of Coleman, or by pupils of the National Art Training School. This was one of the nineteenth-century experiments, carried out in England as well as in Europe, to stimulate artistic activity and train talented artists to produce art that could be applied to industry. The Minton venture somewhat resembles the enterprise set up by Charles Haviland at Auteuil in 1872 and in which, under Bracquemond's direction, new models were to be created that could be mass-produced in porcelain at the Limoges factory. Minton's Art Pottery Studio, like Felix Summerly's Art Manufactures in the preceding period, was active only for a short time. In 1873 Coleman resigned and in 1875 the studios burnt down. Strictly speaking, the South Kensington studio was concerned with decorating earthenwares, but its research into new methods necessarily also affected techniques of porcelain decoration.

Minton porcelain in the 1870s was, in addition, deeply affected by the arrival of several French painters. The most famous of these, Marc-Louis Solon, will be discussed later as his work in *pâte-sur-pâte* decoration puts him into a category separate from the enamel painters. Antonin Boullemier (1840–1900) worked at Sèvres between 1859 and 1862; he started working at Minton in 1872. A skilful painter, capable of endowing the smallest cupid with a grace evocative of the eighteenth century, he was inevitably called upon to paint vases imitating Sèvres models.

Désiré Leroy, also French, arrived at the factory at the same period but left to go to Derby in 1890. Most of his work consisted of painting that achieved effects similar to the *pâte-sur-pâte* technique. Mussill, another decorator, does not seem to have been at Sèvres, despite what has been written about him.[98] At Minton he was particularly concerned with earthenware decoration. He occupied a leading place in the expatriate colony of French painters working under the direction of Léon Arnoux.

During the second half of the nineteenth century the Minton factory was not totally under French influence, but as happened in France, there was a growing interest in Far Eastern and Middle Eastern art. This was evident in the pieces shown at the International Exhibitions of 1867 and 1871. In fact there was intense interest in oriental ceramics in nineteenth-century Europe before 1867. In the Victoria and Albert Museum, London, is a vase which could easily be thought to be Chinese were it not signed by Léon Arnoux.[99] It dates from around 1862. In France a *vase Ly* (its name alone signifies a Far Eastern origin) is in the Sèvres museum.[100] This shape was created in 1849, and the vase in question bears a label inscribed: '*pièce d'essai de décoration en relief. Modelée au pinceau sur engobe céladon à la manière des Chinois par Mr Ambroise Choiselat Sèvres 1850*' ('trial piece with relief decoration, the relief effect achieved by

375 *Vase.* Stoke-on-Trent (Staffordshire), Colin Minton Campbell factory, ▷ *c.* 1880. Tinted and glazed Parian porcelain. H. 52 cm. Mark: 192. Minton Mus., Royal Doulton Tableware Ltd, Stoke-on-Trent.
The *pâte-sur-pâte* decoration by Solon of cupids playing by a stream exhibits the high quality of execution and the gaiety of mood typical of his work.

Mr Ambroise Choiselat of Sèvres in 1850 using the Chinese method of applying layers of celadon slip'). It should also be emphasized that *pâte-sur-pâte* decoration was originally conceived in imitation of Chinese techniques. At Minton and other English and Continental factories oriental influence was stimulating and took many diverse forms. Minton's production, always of high quality, includes pieces based on Chinese and Japanese porcelains, lacquer-work, enamels, and bronzes. Both bone china and earthenware were subject to oriental influence. Occasionally *pâte-sur-pâte* decoration was used to create pieces with Eastern-inspired decoration.

*Marc-Louis Solon*
Apart from Mussill, the most important painter working at the Minton factory during the last thirty years of the nineteenth century was Marc-Louis Solon (1835–1913).[101] Solon was born at Montauban and worked at Sèvres between 1857 and 1871. At this period the French Royal Factory was creating its best works in the *pâte-sur-pâte* technique which involved mixing metallic oxides with the porcelain body and building up layers of decoration in relief using liquid clay (slip). After glazing the colours were translucent in appearance. During the Second Empire period and at the beginning of the Third Republic some of the most outstanding works of Sèvres were created in this medium. The ground colours used set off the relief decoration to advantage and large pieces could be delicately decorated. Minton could not fail to be aware of the novelty and high quality of this technique, especially after purchasing pieces by Solon from 1867. In fact Parian porcelain, when tinted, proved to be a better vehicle than hard-paste porcelain for decoration by this technique. Solon was then working at the Sèvres factory and decorating porcelain in his spare time for E. Rousseau, a Paris dealer.[102] In France he signed his pieces not decorated at Sèvres 'Miles'. A piece in the Sèvres museum[103] bears the usual factory marks used during the Second Empire and is also signed 'L.M.S. 68', for Marc-Louis Solon, 1868, on the vase itself. This piece, along with plaques decorated by Solon on a freelance basis, a group of which are in the Adrien Dubouché museum at Limoges, is proof that Solon had developed a style of his own, which guaranteed his success even before his arrival in England in 1870. In France a large number of decorators were technically capable of producing competent *pâte-sur-pâte* decoration, but Solon alone endowed his work with an unvarying and highly characteristic brand of humour. He used few themes; indeed he can almost be said to have had only one motif: a discreetly erotic female figure semi-clothed in transparent drapery and playing with putti. Naturally the drapery only serves to emphasize the semi-voluptuous/semi-academic outline of the female who recalls both the flowering of antique art as well as the styles inspired by Classical models: the French Renaissance, the Directoire period (around 1800), and the style of the years between 1845 and 1850 are all evoked. Solon composed endless variations on this one theme. Nearly all his compositions are unique, however, and exist in one version only. Despite the length of time needed to execute this type of decoration, Solon made a quantity of pieces between the time of his arrival in Stoke-on-Trent and his retirement in 1904. Between 1904 and 1913 he continued to work on a freelance basis. At the factory he used apprentice painters to carry out friezes or other decorative motifs. Some of these apprentices such as Alboine Birks (1861–1941), Lawrence Birks, H. Hollins, Frederick Rhead, H. Sanders, T. Mellor, A. Morgan, and T.H. Rice continued to practise this technique, either at Minton or elsewhere, until the very end of the nineteenth century.

Other English factories tried to imitate the *pâte-sur-pâte* technique so successfully mastered at Minton. G.A. Godden[104] lists the following firms who worked in this technique: W. Brownfield & Sons, Moore Brothers, the Worcester Royal Porcelain Company and Grainger's, Worcester, and George Jones's Trent Pottery. *Pâte-sur-pâte* decoration went out of favour at the end of the nineteenth century in England as in France but perhaps for different reasons. Alexandre Sandier of Sèvres rejected it in order to create pieces in a totally new decorative style—Art Nouveau—which demanded different processes. In Great Britain, however, there was no such sudden and brutal stylistic change. Even though factories like Minton did make pieces in the avant-garde Secessionist style in the early years of the twentieth century, most English porcelain factories remained resolutely traditional in outlook. The crux of the problem was that the *pâte-sur-pâte* process was clearly not susceptible to mass-production methods. G.A. Godden quotes Solon's dictum apropos of his competitors: 'They discovered to their cost it did not bear mediocrity of execution'.[105]

376 *Pot-pourri*. Stoke-on-Trent (Staffordshire), W. T. Copeland factory, third quarter of the 19th century. Bone china. H. 30 cm. Mark: 295. Spode Mus., Stoke-on-Trent.
The shape was called the 'Derby pierced shape'. In fact it was created in 1752 at the Vincennes factory under the name *pot-pourri à jours*. The painter C. B. Brough has decorated the vase with two panels of exotic birds and two panels of fruit very much in the French spirit.

377 *Two-handled vase*. Stoke-on-Trent (Staffordshire), W.T. Copeland, late Spode factory, c. 1861. Bone china. H. 70.6 cm. Mark: 202. Spode Mus., Stoke-on-Trent.
The painting on this piece is signed by Hürten. Besides actual copies of Sèvres vases, vases were also made that were more loosely based on 18th-century French porcelain. Pale green is a rather rare ground colour.

378 *Figure of Beatrice*. Stoke-on-Trent (Staffordshire), W. T. Copeland, late Spode factory, c. 1860. Parian porcelain. H. 56.6 cm. Mark: 200, inscribed: 'Beatrice'. Spode Mus., Stoke-on-Trent.
Between 1850 and about 1880 huge numbers of Parian figures were made but few are marked. This piece is a reproduction of a work by Edgar Papworth junior.

379 *Figurine*. Stoke-on-Trent (Staffordshire), W. T. Copeland, late Spode factory, c. 1860. Parian porcelain. H. (incl. base) 66.5 cm. Mark: 201. MAD, Limoges (ADL 3733).
In general Parian ware was little appreciated in France, but the Adrien Dubouché museum at Limoges, which is a ceramic museum, has a fine collection of 19th-century English porcelain, including two Copeland figures.

380 *Pierced vase and cover*. Stoke-on-Trent (Staffordshire), W. T. Copeland & Sons, c. 1870. Bone china. H. 17.2 cm. Mark: 297, signed by the gilder W. Ball. Private coll.
The shape of this vase, conceived as an egg carried by a serpent, was certainly inspired by the Near East and is a rather fanciful creation. The decoration includes small drops of enamel applied in relief. This so-called 'jewelling' was popular in Britain at this period.

381 *Vase and cover*. Stoke-on-Trent (Staffordshire), Colin Minton Campbell factory, 1873. Tinted and glazed Parian porcelain. H. 33.5 cm. Mark: 193, signed 'H.H.'. Thomas Goode & Co Ltd, London.
The Japanese-inspired decoration on this vase was executed by a pupil of Solon's, H. Hollins.

376

377

378

379

380

381

382 *Lobed dish.* Stoke-on-Trent (Staffordshire), W.T. Copeland, late Spode factory, 1865. Porcelain. L. 25.8 cm. Mark: 202. Private coll.
The delicately painted flowers, the work of C.F. Hürten, are in a naturalistic style that is somewhat unusual for this period.

## Copeland

The other large-scale porcelain factory also situated, like Minton, at Stoke-on-Trent, expanded too, but perhaps in a slightly less creative fashion. 'W.T. Copeland, late Spode', called 'W.T. Copeland & Sons' after 1867 continued to produce Parian figures and groups in large quantities under the name of 'statuary porcelain'. G.A. Godden states that hundreds of thousands of these pieces were manufactured.[106] They included reproductions on a small scale of sculptural works, some of them well known, and figures as supports for comports or baskets intended as centrepieces. Some remarkable copies of Sèvres vases are on display at the Spode factory museum, but these pieces were never as important a part of Spode's output as at Coalport or Minton. All the pieces mentioned correspond to those made contemporaneously by the Minton factory.

More characteristic of Copeland's production between 1860 and about 1890 are pieces decorated with drops of enamel in relief imitating pearls and called jewelled decoration. At the end of the eighteenth century similar pieces had been created at Sèvres by the painter Cotteau. In both cases the porcelain was meant to imitate jewellery. Other English factories also produced wares with this type of decoration at the same period.

In the second half of the nineteenth century Copeland's porcelain was strongly influenced by the talents of the painters working at the factory. David Evans, who painted floral decoration until the middle of the century, was succeeded by the German painter Charles Ferdinand Hürten who worked at the factory from 1859 until 1897. His flower paintings have the vitality and impact of real flowers. Daniel Lucas junior, as was often the case with Hürten, had to paint his scenes in reserve on vases with strongly coloured grounds enhanced by elaborate gold friezes. Lucas's figures in landscapes were inspired by the pictures of painters as unlikely as Turner, but the quality of the copy and of the porcelain itself remained constant. The gilded decoration is always of an extremely high standard. In 1870 Daniel Lucas junior left Copeland to set up his own firm. Lucien Besche, a figure painter, was taken on at

this time and executed Watteauesque decoration on pieces shown at the Universal Exhibition held at Vienna in 1873. In 1885 he gave up painting on porcelain. The most important Copeland painter, Samuel Alcock, worked there at the end of the nineteenth century.

## Worcester

Minton and Copeland are seen by Continental Europeans as the best factories operating in the second half of the nineteenth century both technically (the gilding on pieces made at these factories is a sure indication of the quality achieved there) and aesthetically (though clearly judgements on this aspect are purely subjective). Chamberlain's Worcester factory, whose products were very popular in Great Britain, is in a different category. This concern was much less open to Continental influence and represents in a sense the quintessence of the English aesthetic during this period.

*The Kerr and Binns Factory*
The period did not begin well for Chamberlain's Worcester factory at the time of the Great Exhibition of 1851. The company, formed in 1840 as a result of the merger of Flight, Barr, and Barr and the Chamberlain factory, never really took off. Walter Chamberlain eventually retired and the partnership was reorganized in 1852 under the name of Kerr and Binns and lasted until 1862. R.W. Binns, acting as artistic director, began his long and fruitful career with the production of the distinguished Shakespeare Service exhibited at the Dublin Exhibition in 1853. Scenes from Shakespeare can be found on porcelain made in the preceding period, but the novelty of this service lay in its presentation of these subjects in the form of Parian figures from his plays supporting bone china comports. The figures were modelled by William Boyton Kirk and are quite lifelike; otherwise the pieces were conceived in the Neo-Renaissance style. Josiah Davis was responsible for the gilding on this service, while Thomas Bott (1829–1870), who was later to become famous, painted the figures of Tragedy and Comedy in the small medallions.

Thomas Bott had been trained as a painter on glass before joining Kerr and Binns in 1853. His work is faithful to the contemporary taste for the Renaissance, which, as we have seen, was popular at Minton. From 1854 he perfected the technique of painting in white enamel on a high-temperature blue ground, in imitation of sixteenth-century Limoges enamels. His work achieved considerable success and was especially favoured by the factory's prestigious clientèle, notably Queen Victoria. However, it is not comparable with several contemporary French pieces of the same type: an ewer decorated in white *pâte-sur-pâte* on a black ground by Gibus of Limoges is a much finer example of the genre (the French Renaissance enamels have black grounds). In 1857 the *Art Journal* noted that Bott's figures were inspired by Raphael and Flaxman, which may explain their rather stiff appearance. Nevertheless, Bott's success lasted until his death at the early age of forty-one in 1870, by which time he had begun to produce polychrome pieces. His most important work was his last. It consists of a pair of vases with an ewer and dish painted with scenes of the Norman Conquest commemorating the anniversary of the Conquest of England by the Normans in 1066 (although they were executed in the years 1868 to 1870), after drawings by Daniel Maclise. The pieces were shown at the

383 *Comport, tureen and cover from the Dublin, or Shakespeare, Service.*
Worcester, Kerr & Binns, 1853. Bone china and Parian porcelain. H. (comport) 38.1 cm. Mark: 233. DPM, Worcester.
This service is either known by the name of the town where it was first exhibited in 1853 at the 'Art festival' or by the name of the author whose works inspired its decoration. The figures represent characters from *A Midsummer Night's Dream* and were modelled by William Boyton Kirk. The medallions were painted by Thomas Bott, and the gilding was the work of Josiah Davis.

384 *Plate*. Worcester, Kerr & Binns, *c.* 1855. Bone china. D. 24.1 cm.
Mark: 233. DPM, Worcester.
The elegant richness of this piece with its pierced border and turquoise ground, its coloured floral decoration and gilt embellishments is characteristic of one aspect of Victorian taste.

1871 and 1873 Exhibitions. Their inspiration was drawn from Classical rather than Renaissance sources.

Besides Thomas Bott, Kerr, and Binns managed to secure the talents of other gifted artists whose names are listed by G. A. Godden.[107] They included Josiah Rushton and the figure painters, the brothers James and Thomas Callowhill; Joseph Williams, a figure and landscape painter; Robert Perling, an animal painter; James Bradley, John Hopwell, and James Weaver, who all specialized in painting birds; and Baker, David

Bates, and James Sheriff, all flower painters. Special mention should be made of the figure painters who were all excellent artists capable of reproducing on porcelain the Classical style of Italian or Italian-influenced painters. The gilders Josiah Davis and Samuel Ranford were as gifted as their painter colleagues.

Kerr and Binns excelled themselves at the 1862 Exhibition held in London. The factory exhibited a dessert service with a sky-blue (bleu-céleste) ground made for Queen Victoria. The various elements composing the centrepiece were ornamented with Classical figures in Parian porcelain, and the whole was embellished with luxurious gilding. The service is a direct descendant of the one made at Minton for Queen Victoria at the time of the Crystal Palace Exhibition of 1851. The first pieces of Worcester 'ivory porcelain' were also shown at the 1862 Exhibition. Henry Sandon describes this material as having 'a soft creamy tone'.[108] 'Ivory porcelain' is glazed porcelain of the Parian type and is not pure white in colour. From the outset 'ivory porcelain' was used for pieces created in the 'Raphaelesque' style. These are decorated with pseudo-Renaissance motifs in relief, imitating Doccia porcelains, which were attributed at that time to the Capodimonte factory. The 'ivory porcelains' in the so-called Raphaelesque idiom were particularly successful in the succeeding period, especially when they were used to manufacture models designed by James Hadley.

Binns was undeniably responsible for the inclusion of the Worcester factory among the group of leading English porcelain manufacturers during the period under consideration. Kerr left the company in 1862, and Binns then formed the Worcester Royal Porcelain Company, which is still in production and is best known simply as Royal Worcester.

### The Worcester Royal Porcelain Company

In an important book devoted to Worcester's main factory at the end of the nineteenth century, Henry Sandon, formerly Curator of the factory museum, the Dyson Perrins Museum, traces a complete outline of the factory's history.[109]

386 *Comport in the form of a siren holding a shell.* Worcester, Worcester Royal Porcelain Company, 1877. 'Ivory porcelain' (glazed Parian porcelain). H. 20.3 cm. Mark: 236. DPM, Worcester.
This type of decoration in low relief imitating Doccia porcelain (see Pl. 222) was known at Worcester as 'Raphaelesque'. The piece was modelled by James Hadley who was inspired by Italian Renaissance models; Thomas Callowhill was responsible for the painting on the shell.

385 *Tea-service.* Worcester, Worcester Royal Porcelain Company, 1875–1877. Bone china. H. (teapot) 13.9 cm. Mark: 236. DPM, Worcester.
Replica of a service made for the Countess of Dudley in 1865. The rich decoration is almost grotesque. T. S. Callowhill was responsible for painting the portraits; Samuel Ranford for the gilding.

As R. W. Binns continued to direct the concern there was little drastic change in the factory's production when it changed its name. Its success was underlined by important commissions at a time when specially created pieces were normally destined for international exhibitions. Among its greatest achievements was a tea-service made for the wedding of the Prince of Wales and Princess Alexandra of Denmark in 1863. In 1865 another special tea-service was created for the marriage of the Countess of Dudley. A copy of this service was made at the factory in 1877 and has been kept there. The entire surface of these pieces is covered with a network of tiny enamelled dots in turquoise and white, imitating pearls, on a gilt ground executed by Samuel Ranford. The decoration also includes small medallions in reserve painted with profile heads by Thomas Scott Callowhill. In 1875 another dessert service was made, this time for the Prince of Wales.

387 *Vase commemorating the Norman Conquest.*
Worcester, Worcester Royal Porcelain
Company, 1868–1870. Bone china. H. 50.8 cm.
Mark: 235. DPM, Worcester.
The vase is part of a group of pieces including a
companion vase and an ewer, specially designed
to commemorate the 800th anniversary of the
Conquest. The decoration is painted in white
using Thomas Bott's technique, which imitates
painted Limoges enamels of the Renaissance.
Daniel Maclise was responsible for the decorative
scheme; Josiah Davis carried out the gilding.
Bott's technique consisted in painting in white
enamel on an underglaze-blue ground, which did
not give as accurate an imitation of Limoges
enamels as the use of the *pâte-sur-pâte* technique.

388 *'Potters' vases'*. Worcester, Worcester
Royal Porcelain Company, 1878. 'Ivory
porcelain' (glazed Parian porcelain). H. 72.5 cm.
Mark: inaccessible. DPM, Worcester.
These two pieces modelled by James Hadley show
potters at work. On one side is the *Furnace*
(Firing) and on the reverse the *Modeller*. These
scenes are based on the illustrations in the potter
Piccolpasso's 16th-century treatise *Li tre libri dell'
Arte dell' Vasaio*. Here the desire to produce a
technical *tour de force* has resulted in a creation
whose overall conception lacks harmony.

389 *Pair of figures.* Worcester, Worcester Royal Porcelain Company, 1870. Glazed Parian porcelain. H. 39.4 cm. Mark: 235. DPM, Worcester.
Modelled by James Hadley, who created a large number of diverse pieces designed to appeal to a wide clientele. His eclecticism was remarkable even for the period.

390 *Vase.* Worcester, George Grainger & Company, *c.* 1870. Parian porcelain. H. 27.9 cm. Unmarked. DPM, Worcester.
The contrast between the green ground of this vase and the relief decoration in white is extremely successful.

The Worcester factory experienced a moment of triumph at the 1873 Exhibition where it was awarded first prize, shared with Minton. The variety of pieces shown was a testimony to Binns's determination to command respect for his successes ('ivory porcelain' was used for a huge variety of objects) and also demonstrated the eclecticism of current styles. Some important pieces were still designed in the Neo-Renaissance idiom, although the influence of the East was now beginning to be felt. Thomas Bott's last pieces on the theme of the 387 Norman Conquest were shown for the first time at this exhibition. During the preceding decade Binns, foreseeing the birth of a new fashion, had begun to collect an important group of Far Eastern porcelain. This collection, dispersed after Binns's death, included no less than ten thousand pieces,[110] and these were used as models at the factory.

With the arrival of the so-called 'Aesthetic Movement'[111] Japanese influence came to the fore. The leaders of the movement advocated the creation of works in a naturalistic style that was married to their function. These demands were allied to a strong admiration for Japanese art, especially from

the time of the 1862 and 1868 Exhibitions held in London and Paris respectively. Worcester adopted the Japanese style not just as a result of the pervading eclecticism but also as an expression of the high regard felt by artists and critics at the time for this particular source of artistic inspiration.

We have chosen two 'ivory porcelain' figures by James 389 Hadley dating from 1870 as an illustration of the Japanese taste. Renaissance influence is well represented by Hadley's so-called 'Potters' vases' also made of 'ivory porcelain'. These 388 curious vases of flattened gourd shape are supported by figures in high relief within a panel sunk into the body of the vase. The figures are shown in poses as drawn by Piccolpasso in his sixteenth-century treatise on the art of ceramics.[112] The vases were shown at the Paris Exhibition of 1878.

Worcester was very successful at the 1878 Exhibition. In the report of the French national commission highly favourable comments were made on the factory's wares.[113]

*The Grainger Factory*
There was another porcelain factory in the town of Worcester.

391 *Covered basket.* Belleek (Co. Fermanagh, Ireland), D. McBirney & Co, late 19th century. Glazed Parian porcelain. L. 23.1 cm. Mark: 160. MAD, Limoges (ADL 4509).
Belleek specialized in making pieces of this type. The porcelain imitates basketwork with floral relief decoration.

390 It was established in 1800 by Thomas Grainger. Most of its pieces are direct copies of those made at the town's main factory, though there were some new products such as 'semi-porcelain' created in 1851 for utiliarian purposes. In the 1880s *pâte-sur-pâte* techniques were used for decoration. It is worth noting that this factory was one of the few (but not the only English factory) to make lithophanes.

## Derby

Like the Worcester Royal Porcelain Company, Derby in the mid-nineteenth century virtually ignored the fashion for pieces in the French taste. The Derby concern then in operation was not the same firm as the one in existence at the beginning of the century which had closed down in 1848. Fearing unemployment, factory workers from the original firm formed their own company under the leadership of one of their

number, William Locker. They established their own works at King Street and carried on making pieces in the traditional Derby style using the trading name 'Locker & Co Late Bloor'. After Locker's death in 1859, the partners changed and the name of the firm altered several times: it was known as 'Stevenson Sharp & Co', then in 1863 changed to 'Stevenson & Hancock'. Stevenson died in 1866 and Sampson Hancock took over the firm, running it until his death in 1898.

In the main this factory concentrated on decorating 'blanks' of eighteenth-century Derby models bought from larger firms. 'Japan' patterns called 'Witches', 'Roses', 'Garden', and 'Old Japan Patterns' were the main decorative patterns produced. Floral decoration of a good standard was carried out by Sampson Hancock and James Hill, while Richard Ablott and Edward Prince painted landscape scenes. James Rouse, employed for a long time at Coalport to produce copies of Sèvres porcelains, joined the King Street factory in 1875, working there until 1882. Flower-encrusted pieces, especially mirror frames, in a now long-outmoded style, were kept in production at this factory. Painted porcelain figures also continued to be made. All these pieces prove that there were still buyers whose taste remained traditional.

Renewed impetus was given to porcelain making at Derby with the creation of a new factory at Osmaston Road under the

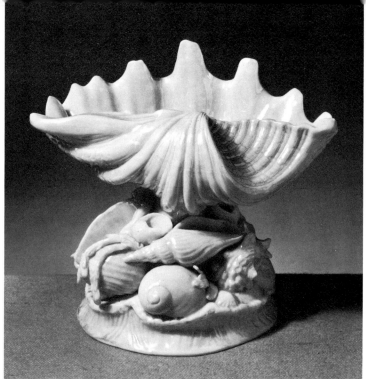

392 *Tea-service.* Belleek (Co. Fermanagh, Ireland), D. McBirney & Co, *c.* 1885. Porcelain. L. (tray) 37.5 cm. Mark: inaccessible. Coll. Godden of Worthing Ltd.
Belleek is most famous for its original creations, which are indeed technically remarkable, but the factory also made practical wares.

393 *Shell comport.* Belleek (Co. Fermanagh, Ireland), D. McBirney & Co, 1868. Parian porcelain. H. 13.6 cm. Mark: 161. V & A, London (848-1878). R.W. Armstrong and his wife modelled a large number of pieces imitating shells for the Belleek factory. The pearlized glaze was ideally suited to these shapes.

394 *Bust of Clytie.* Belleek (Co. Fermanagh, Ireland), D. McBirney & Co, *c.* 1860–1870. Partly glazed Parian porcelain. H. 27.9 cm. Mark: 162. V & A, London (140-1914).
The bust shows a clever use of the contrast between the matt unglazed surface of Parian ware and the shiny, partly glazed areas of the piece.

name 'Derby Crown Porcelain Company'. It began production in 1877, and its history belongs to our next chapter.

## IRELAND

### Belleek

Either in 1857 or perhaps in 1863, a new factory was set up in County Fermanagh, in Ireland.[114] A Dublin architect, Robert Armstrong, had submitted felspar discovered in the north of Ireland to the Worcester factory where it was mixed with Cornish kaolin and tested. When the experiments proved successful David McBirney provided the capital to set up a factory at Belleek, which was initially known as 'D. McBirney & Co' and then as 'Belleek Pottery & Co'. In addition the factory purchased a patent from the Frenchman, Jules-Joseph-Henri Brianchon, for the production of a bismuth-based lustre, or iridescent pearl-like glaze.

Belleek wares, although a varied range was produced, all share the same unified style that is both characteristic of the factory and typical of the Victorian era. Technical *tours de force* were favoured by this enterprise, which produced thin-walled egg-shell porcelain and moulded pieces imitating basketwork.  391
Decorative objects inspired by marine life, such as shell-shaped  393
or oyster-shaped pieces, were manufactured to justify the use of the iridescent glaze. Figures in Parian ware showed the  394
contrast between the matt unglazed body and the pearlized glaze.

The success of these pieces prompted imitators in the United States, at Trenton, New Jersey, to begin production at the end of the nineteenth century and the beginning of the twentieth. The pieces made there were sometimes of excellent quality.

The Belleek factory, which is still in existence, maintains its old traditions, producing numerous pieces from nineteenth-century models.

# V Eclecticism and Art Nouveau

## FRANCE

### Sèvres

The short-lived Second Republic (1848–1852) and Second Empire (1852–1870) were succeeded by the Third Republic (1870–1940), a much more lasting phenomenon, making conditions much more difficult at the Sèvres National Porcelain Factory. The crisis of 1848 seemed at first to be repeating itself. There were an increasing number of attacks on the factory especially by other porcelain manufacturers who wanted to see its budget, regularly allocated by the government, turned into a series of grants or subsidies. The Minister of Public Instruction and Fine Arts, under whose control the factory came, once again set up a commission of enquiry, this time under the chairmanship of the architect Eugène Viollet-le-Duc. The latter submitted his final report in 1875. He strongly criticized previous directors of the factory who had tried to turn it into a technical research centre: 'The factory makes a superior type of porcelain; skills have been developed to a high degree of perfection and are capable of fulfilling every need relating to the potter's art in the matter of raw materials, glazes, and colours, but standards must be maintained in the future. For the most part the artists display unparalleled virtuosity. They have nearly all the necessary qualities, including taste, grace, and the delicacy associated with our national temperament. Only education and instruction are lacking to complete the picture, and there is a great deal to be accomplished in this direction.' Summing up, Viollet-le-Duc thought that the artists' virtuosity was wasted since it was not informed. Great efforts were to be made to ensure that the pieces made were more harmoniously conceived. It must be admitted that these efforts met with little success before the arrival of Alexandre Sandier in 1896.

Victor Regnault had submitted his resignation in 1871 and was replaced by Louis Robert, formerly head of the painters' workshop. Robert held the post of Administrator until 1879. At this time the factory removed to the present-day premises at the edge of the Park of Saint-Cloud on the banks of the Seine, leaving the buildings it had occupied since 1756. In 1879 Charles Lauth took over the running of the factory from Robert. He succeeded in obtaining monthly salaries for the painters who up until this time had been paid by the piece. Loud protests were made by the artists as the 1889 Exhibition drew near, since they could no longer do private work. A vigorous press campaign, in which pieces made at Sèvres were attacked, added force to the artists' complaints, and Lauth was obliged to resign in 1887. He was succeeded by the potter Théodore Deck who died soon afterwards in 1891. Emile Baumgart, an administrator pure and simple, replaced him.

Viollet-le-Duc's report of 1875 had emphasized the factory's need to impose a coherent style. In 1876 the sculptor A. Carrier-Belleuse was created artistic director. We shall see that he had a profound impact on the factory. Between Carrier-Belleuse's death in 1886 and the date of Alexandre Sandier's appointment in 1896, the post of artistic director was filled by artists who carried out little work at the factory.

The factory did so badly at the 1889 Exhibition that in 1891 the Parliamentary Commission in charge of voting the factory's budget refused to grant any funds. For the first time French industrial potters rallied to the defence of the factory, claiming they had benefited from its renown; however, they wished to be able to draw more freely on its technical know-how. Finally the budget was passed but only on the condition that the factory be completely reorganized. This took place in 1896 when Sandier was appointed.

#### Techniques

The technical staff at the factory, discouraged by their inability to develop soft-paste porcelain suitable for mass-production, continued to pursue their research into ceramic bodies. The so-called *pâte Brongniart* fired at 1410 °C did not allow a wide enough range of colours, since most of them cannot withstand this high temperature. Repeated firings are costly, and the French ceramic industry was anxious that Sèvres should develop a material that could be fired at a lower temperature.

Alphonse Salvetat arrived at a formula for a paste known as *pâte Salvetat* or *pâte japonaise* but never perfected a system of firing or glazing it. As a follow-up to Salvetat's efforts, Charles Lauth and Georges Vogt discovered the formula for their *pâte Lauth–Vogt* or 'new porcelain' *(pâte nouvelle)* in 1880. Viollet-le-Duc had recommended in his report of 1875 that the firing temperature should be 1280 °C so that the so-called *demi-grand-feu* colours ('medium-intense-firing colours') could be used. There is a wider range of colours available that can be fired at 1280 °C, and these merge more successfully with the glaze than the high-temperature colours.

In 1889 Théodore Deck perfected and exhibited two new ceramic bodies: the *pâte tendre siliceuse* ('siliceous soft-paste'), which was quite successful as it had the effect of brightening

the colours used to decorate it, and the paste known as *grosse porcelaine*. It was designed to be used by sculptors for freely modelled figures since it was very malleable. After Deck's death in 1891 these bodies were abandoned and the old ones came back into production.

The 'new porcelain' body was devised in order to obtain a new range of colours. It also led to the development of new types of decoration including 'flamed' or 'flambé' glazes *(les flammés)*. These are obtained by firing copper oxide in a reducing atmosphere and were extremely popular in the nineteenth century. Crystalline effects in glazes, resulting from the presence of zinc oxide, were initially firing accidents.

*Style*

Until Carrier-Belleuse was appointed as artistic director, Sèvres porcelains did not change much in style. Viollet-le-Duc's first report of 1872 includes the following criticism: 'Decoration in colours ... is at present totally lacking in overall arrangement. Large white surfaces are mostly covered with foliate motifs without any attempt to organize the ornamentation. The result is an indeterminate effect, which affords the eye no pleasure, but tires it with morbid and useless effort!' The factory was still capable, when it remained faithful to the Second Empire style, of producing harmonious pieces, such as the *vases feuilles d'eau*.[1] Little by little the harmony of traditional shapes was eroded by the introduction of dissonant elements. A *vase Bertin* in the Sèvres museum,[2] a shape dating from 1850, has a black ground decorated before 1878 with a coloured *pâte-sur-pâte* bouquet of flowers that emphasizes the ground colour. The vase measures no less than 111 centimetres in height. The same shape was used again in 1875 and given two small elephant heads in relief in place of handles. The best that can be said of these ornaments is that they detract from the nobility of the piece, although the coloured *pâte-sur-pâte* decoration of a peacock retains its sumptuousness. This slight tendency towards the ridiculous seems to have disappeared by 1877. On a vase made in that year called the *vase de la Manufacture*[3] workers and artists at the factory depicted themselves in the guise of charming putti!

Carrier-Belleuse in effect endowed Sèvres production with its own style. Its unity was apparent at the exhibition held in 1884 at the Palais de l'Industrie in Paris. He designed a large number of vases himself. Some have a simple outline, as for example the *vase Pompéï* and the *vase Saïgon*, allowing the use of continuous decoration. Others, like the *vase Houdon* and the *vase bouteille toro* are firmly divided into different registers: foot, base, body, shoulder, and neck were joined one to another but lacked any organic link. At best they could be unified by the decorative scheme; at worst this could accentuate the disparate nature of the composite parts of the piece. In the cases we have examined it is of little practical importance whether the piece is made of porcelain or not, it could just as easily have been created in another medium and its effect would have remained the same. At times Carrier-Belleuse seems to have remembered that he had been trained as a sculptor and recollected his taste for Renaissance works of art. His *déjeuner à la chimère* and *buire de Blois* with their handles and lip ornamented with sphinxes in relief are markedly Neo-Renaissance in style. Before Carrier-Belleuse's arrival, some of these same decorative elements in sculptural form were achieved by using bronze mounts.[4]

*Decoration*

Many different decorative techniques were in use at Sèvres during this period. Painted decoration was, of course, still extensively employed. Some painters' personal style is fairly easily recognizable; E. Froment worked in the Neo-Renaissance idiom whose Classical overtones are typical of the era of the Third Republic; Madame Apoil, whose career lasted from 1865 to 1892, employed a palette of mellow tones, mixing together figures with branches or garlands of flower to create an effect resembling tapestry. Carrier-Belleuse himself sometimes decorated pieces. A *vase Pompéï* in the Sèvres museum is one of the most accomplished and remarkable works of the period, with its dancing figures seen in outline it evokes Carpeaux's group for the façade of the Paris Opéra. Most of the other painters took their style from the piece they were told to copy. For example Abel Schilt copied Watteau's *Embarkation for Cythera*[5] in 1872 and in 1876 decorated a *vase potiche silène* with delicately painted figures in Chinese costume; between 1877 and 1878 he painted a *service à thé ovoïde*[6] with nude female figures and cupids in a highly academic style.

The fashion for *pâte-sur-pâte* decoration continued, and some extremely important pieces were created in this period which were very much in the Second Empire style. Although certain well-known craftsmen specializing in this technique left the factory, including Marc-Louis Solon, who emigrated in 1871, others like Gély and Gobert carried on working there for years. Taxile Doat on the other hand only joined the factory in 1879, remaining there until 1905. He worked in an academic, somewhat humorous, style.

Under the direction of Carrier-Belleuse, who was his teacher at that time, Auguste Rodin worked at the Sèvres factory between 1879 and 1882, and again in 1888. Mastering the *pâte-sur-pâte* technique, he attempted to introduce a variation of the process by creating grooves engraved into the paste. Rodin's decorated porcelains are only rather pale reflections of his sculptural works, perhaps because of the decorative technique he used.

Finally, it was during Carrier-Belleuse's period of employment as artistic director at Sèvres that reduction firing

395 *Vase commemorating the opening of the new factory premises.* Sèvres, National Porcelain factory, 1876–1877. Coloured hard-paste porcelain. H. 97 cm. Mark: inaccessible, inscribed: 'Manufacture Nationale de Sèvres/ Inauguration de la nouvelle Manufacture/par le maréchal de Mac Mahon, duc de Magenta. Président de la République française/Le 17 novembre de l'année 1876', (painting) 'J. Larue invenit 1877'. MNC, Sèvres (9265).
Details of the decoration on the body of the vase are shown in Pls. 1–8. Putti have been rather delightfully chosen to represent the factory operatives. The vase is made in three pieces and can be dismantled.

396 *One of a pair of 'Rhodes' vases.* Sèvres, National Porcelain factory, 1874. Hard-paste porcelain. H. 95 cm. Mark: inaccessible. MNC, Sèvres (18 246²). Charles Barriat painted this piece, which is an outstanding example of eclecticsm, with strange figurative motifs in the Egyptian style.

397 *'Bertin' vase.* Sèvres, National Porcelain factory, before 1878. Coloured hard-paste porcelain. H. 111 cm. Unmarked. MNC, Sèvres (7702).
Although it only went on the market in 1878, this vase shows extremely well what porcelain manufacturers were striving for during Napoleon III's reign. The shape, devised in 1850, is as simple as possible; the dimensions of the piece are monumental; its black ground is technically perfect, and the *pâte-sur-pâte* decoration by Gély relieves the sombre appearance given by the ground colour. The vase shows absolutely no trace of eclecticism.

398 *Vase: potiche 'Silène'.* Sèvres, National Porcelain factory, 1876. Lauth-Vogt porcelain. H. 35 cm. Mark: 79, signed 'AS [for Schilt] 1876'. MNC, Sèvres (7217²).
This vase *(potiche)* is in oriental style. Three members of the Schilt family were employed as painters at the Sèvres factory: Louis-Pierre and Léonard Schilt were flower painters; Abel Schilt painted figures. The latter worked in a poetic style rather unusual at this period.

395

396

397

398

399 *Elephant-head 'Bertin' vase.* Sèvres, National Porcelain factory, 1874. Coloured Lauth-Vogt porcelain. H. 111 cm. Mark: 79. MNC, Sèvres (7529²).
The shape of the 'Bertin' vase dates from 1850. Doubtless to Third Republic taste it appeared somewhat in need of ornamentation and so it was given elephant-head masks.

400 *'Houdon' vase with ornaments.* Sèvres, National Porcelain factory, 1882. Hard-paste porcelain. H. 55 cm. Mark: 78. MNC, Sèvres (8979).
Albert Carrier-Belleuse created this shape in 1880. Its white ground is decorated in relief and gilt. The almost architectural form of the piece, with its various well-structured elements, including its tubular body and neck, represents the culmination of Carrier-Belleuse's experiments. The scrolls and female forms are in the Neo-Renaissance style.

401 *'Pompeian' vase.* Sèvres, National Porcelain factory, 1884. Hard-paste porcelain. H. 31 cm. Mark: 81, decoration signed 'A. Carrier-Belleuse. 1884, invenit et execudit' *[sic]* and inscribed 'Bacco' and 'B' in blue. MNC, Sèvres (8916).
Carrier-Belleuse was artistic director at Sèvres between 1871 and 1887. He created numerous shapes, including the 'Pompeian' vase in 1880. The nymphs and satyrs painted on one side of the piece show an unexpected liveliness and naturalism, while on the other side of the vase Carrier-Belleuse painted a somewhat academic figure of Bacchus.

402 *'Pompeian' vase.* Sèvres, National Porcelain factory, 1884. Hard-paste porcelain. H. 32 cm. Mark: 80, signed 'Rodin 1882'. MNC, Sèvres (8522).
Carrier-Belleuse designed the shape of this vase, which was decorated by Auguste Rodin. Rodin tried to refine the *pâte-sur-pâte* technique by cutting away the raised areas to a greater depth than usual. In this way he attempted to render perspective depth using only a thin layer of porcelain paste as his medium; however, the sublety of his techniques has little decorative merit and is not well suited to porcelain.

403 *'Hong-Kong' vase.* Sèvres, National Porcelain factory, 1883. Lauth-Vogt porcelain. H. 18 cm. Mark: 79. MNC, Sèvres (9243).
At Sèvres flambé glazes enjoyed their greatest period of popularity between 1883 and 1893. They were used on pieces in a vaguely oriental style, as here, and also on purely European shapes.

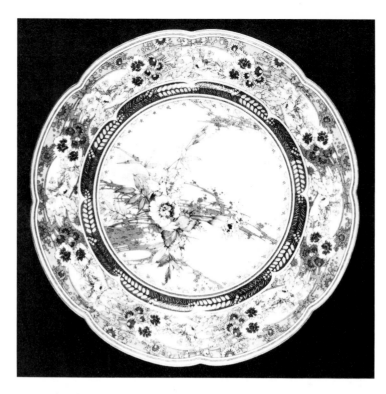

404 *Plate from the service lobé ('Lobed Service').* Sèvres, National Porcelain factory, 1888. Hard-paste porcelain. D. 25.5 cm. Mark: 84. MNC, Sèvres (9148).
The decoration was designed by Haber-Dys and painted by Bonnuit. Its use of elaborate vegetal forms is characteristic of the late 19th century and appears in 'official' art as well as in Art Nouveau.

403, 405 of copper-glazed pieces in the Lauth-Vogt paste or in the 'new porcelain' took place. Flambé glazes were enormously successful at the exhibition held in 1884 at the Union centrale des Arts décoratifs in Paris. This type of decoration, which is essentially non-figurative, prepared the way for the coming stylistic evolution that renounced the use of the human figure as a decorative element.

### The Crisis and Reorganization of 1891
The end of the nineteenth century was a difficult period for the State Porcelain Factory. The painters, who were furious at being obliged to present themselves regularly at the factory when they had been used to being paid by the piece, organized a vigorous press campaign attacking the institution they should have been protecting. The factory's showing at the 1889 Exhibition was disastrous, since no great innovations had been made at that time. In 1891 the Parliamentary Commission in charge of proposing the factory's budget recommended that the state enterprise should be closed. Finally it was decided to reorganize it, and Emile Baumgart was appointed as Administrator. He occupied this post between 1891 and 1909. New principles were set out relating both to the technical and the aesthetic side of the factory's activities, and this time they were adhered to. The new artistic director, Alexandre Sandier, the first worthy successor to Carrier-Belleuse, was employed in the years 1896 to 1916. He initiated innovations in both shapes and decoration. Regulations drawn up in 1891 allowed the factory to employ artists on an annual basis and to dismiss them if their work proved unsatisfactory, thus allowing Sandier to surround himself with new artists. Like Lechevallier-Chevignard we shall quote Baumgart's list of

objectives laid down by those responsible for the direction of the factory. The list was drawn up in 1900. It called for:

1 Perfecting of Sèvres hard-paste porcelain body.
2 Decoration of hard-paste porcelain in the high-temperature kiln.
3 Replacement of old models with shapes not requiring mounts.
4 Search for decorative motifs complementing the shapes on which they were to be used and composed of naturalistic elements.
5 Extension of the range of high-temperature coloured glazes.
6 Modification of decorative processes for the new hard-paste porcelain body.
7 Rediscovery of soft-paste porcelain to be used with modern shapes and harmonious decorative schemes.
8 Development of applications of stoneware in architectural and interior design contexts.[7]

### Technical Innovations
Among the objectives suggested to the factory in 1891 when it was reformed were some of a technical nature. One of the aims was the perfecting, at state expense, of new processes to help privately owned potteries make technical progress without having to bear the expense of carrying out their own research. In 1900 the public could see that the factory had made a number of improvements. Pieces in four different materials were exhibited. These included the old hard-paste body *(pâte Brongniart),* which had been in continual production, the new hard-paste *(pâte Lauth-Vogt),* soft-paste used for small pieces (Vogt had rediscovered the eighteenth-century methods of producing this body), and especially stonewares (which had already been in fashion for some time).

The factory perfected new methods of decoration suited to each of its new bodies. On hard-paste porcelain decoration in high-temperature colours was applied either under or over the 407 glaze. High-temperature decoration requires no special firing technique and is therefore cheaper than other methods. The development of these colours, which could withstand intense heat, should have appealed to other ceramic manufacturers, but as the colours obtained were pale in tone they were hardly used except at Sèvres. The new hard-paste body was especially well suited to flambé glazes and crystalline effects, as well as *pâte-sur-* 403, 405 *pâte* ornamentation, low-temperature colours, and high- 408, 410 temperature grounds. For special effects certain pieces were composed of stoneware and porcelain elements.

### The Art Nouveau Style
Although the factory's 'style'—and it cannot be denied that it does have one—can be said to have been characterized by its diversity, Alexandre Sandier, taking advantage of technical improvements and assisted by certain artists, succeeded in imposing on the factory a special type of production which is readily identifiable. Each porcelain body was used in the most appropriate way, either for small decorative or utilitarian pieces or for the monumental objects designed to show off the factory's technical prowess. Certain vases made at this period in the old hard-paste body measure more than a metre in height. Even larger objects had been made at the factory, but the ones dating from around 1900 were designed and executed in one piece.

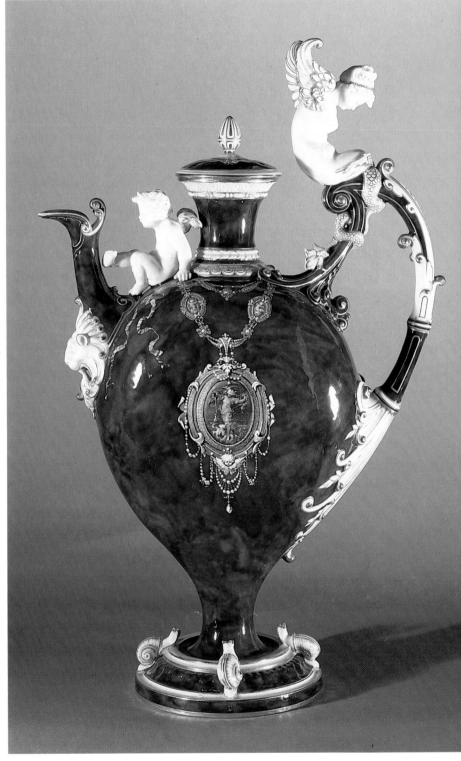

405 *Vase: Kin-te-chin garni.* Sèvres, National Porcelain factory, 1886. 'New porcelain'. H. 33 cm. Mark: 83. MdAd, Paris (D. 886).
Only rarely did Sèvres flambé glazes reach the point of perfection represented by this greyish-blue example.

406 *Vase: buire de Blois.* Sèvres, National Porcelain factory, 1884. Hard-paste porcelain. H. 42 cm. Mark: 82. MdAd, Paris (D. 420).
The vase bears the number '589', its catalogue number in the eighth exhibition held by the Union centrale des Arts décoratifs. Its tortoise-shell ground is unusual for the period and contrasts with the ivory-coloured relief motifs.

**407** *Plate*. Sèvres, National Porcelain factory, 1897. Hard-paste porcelain. D. 24 cm. Mark: 85. MNC, Sèvres (12 689).
The Art Nouveau style prevailing at this time was characterized by fluid forms, but Sèvres persisted in producing a large number of plates with circular borders. Any movement had therefore to be confined to the decoration of the piece. This plate is painted with a flower garland in shades of brown, pink, and green.

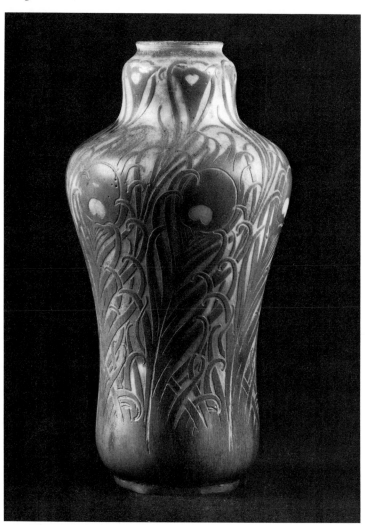

These pieces in fact fulfilled one of the objectives laid down at the time of the reforms made in 1891. Pieces with mounts fixed to them by means of nuts, screws, and other expedients were no longer in favour, the major inconvenience of these mounts being that they necessitated the drilling of holes in the base of the piece, which was thus no longer watertight. Vases made during Sandier's era are decorative enough to stand on their own merits, especially when they are of monumental size. They can also be used as flower vases if they are of suitable size.

Pieces made at this period are conceived as a whole, their shapes designed by A. Sandier, L. Kann, or H. Brécy are sinuous, and their decoration follows the contours of the object. The human figure was no longer used at all as a decorative motif. Louis Trager, Henri Lasserre, Louis Mimard and others painted vegetable or floral motifs that sometimes included insects. Winding tendrils are found swirling around the body of vases or disappearing over the edge of the rim of plates faithfully following the Art Nouveau style that the state factory had adopted. However, there were limits to the factory's application of the style and, at least in porcelain, it never exhibited the exuberance characterizing the best turn-of-the-century European porcelain production. The pieces that display the most marked sense of fantasy, and which are today thought most successful, are the stonewares. The *vase aubergine*[8] created by L. Kann in 1900 epitomizes the rejection of the spirit of prudence and academic values. To design pieces in stoneware the factory called upon Hector Guimard who had designed the Parisian Métro stations. He was responsible for three models created for Sèvres, including the monumental *jardinière colonne* of 1902.

*Sculpture*

Sculpture regained its position of importance around 1900. Models that had been produced some years earlier were reissued in biscuit porcelain, and busts were made after Carpeaux such as the portrait bust of *Charles Garnier* or the figure of a *Negress,* dating from 1900 and 1903 respectively.

In this aspect of the factory's output, curiously enough, academicism was not rejected. This can be seen from a *surtout mythologique* after Emmanuel Frémiet, which consisted of the

◁ **408** *'Bagneux' vase*. Sèvres, National Porcelain factory, 1898. 'New porcelain'. H. 24 cm. Mark: 86. MNC, Sèvres (10 878).
'New porcelain', like the Lauth-Vogt paste that it closely resembled, is ideally suited to flambé glazes. This vase was thrown by Poncelain and the incised decoration executed by Gebleux.

**409** *Three figures from the Surtout de l'écharpe ('scarf-dance centrepiece')*. Sèvres, ▷ National Porcelain factory, 1900. 'New porcelain'. H. (each figure without base, left to right) 42 cm, 42 cm, 32 cm. Marks: 90–92. MNC, Sèvres (17 260², 17 266², 17 263²).
The centrepiece, designed by Agathon Léonard, comprises 15 figures in all. It was produced in three different sizes at Sèvres as it was so popular. The famous dancer Loïe Fuller provided the inspiration for the figures.

**410** *'Bagatelle' vase*. Sèvres, National Porcelain factory, 1900. 'New ▷ porcelain'. H. 18 cm. Mark: 87. MNC, Sèvres (15 773).
Crystalline glazes give a fugitive effect. This glaze is particularly fine.

**411** *'Saigon' vase with cover*. Sèvres, National Porcelain factory: decorated by ▷▷ Thesmar, 1895. Soft-paste porcelain. H. 24 cm. Mark: 97. MNC, Sèvres (15 576).
At the request of the Director of the School of Fine Arts, Thesmar decorated Sèvres porcelain from 1893. In 1895 he was given his own workshop where he could work on his own creations. His speciality was the use of cloisonné enamels on *paillons* ('gold foil') applied on to porcelain.

412

413

414

415

232   ECLECTICISM AND ART NOUVEAU · FRANCE

Chariots of Diana and Minerva, the Triumph of Hercules, and The Deliverance of Andromeda (1900).[9] However, the most successful centrepiece, which is still selling, is known as the *surtout du jeu de l'écharpe* ('scarf-dance centrepiece'), designed by Agathon Léonard in 1900 for the International Exhibition. It consists of fifteen female figures inspired, so the story goes, by the dancer Loïe Fuller. Like the best pieces of contemporary sculpture produced by artists in this period, from Bourdelle to Despiau, the centrepiece has something of the spirit of ancient Greek sculpture, especially in its use of flowing drapery. The centrepiece was made in three sizes and has been copied, not especially skilfully, by various German factories.

The new hard-paste porcelain body was used for sculptural pieces made at this period because its surface is softer to the touch than that of the old hard-paste porcelain body and it is easier to fire.

Finally mention should be made of the enameller Fernand Thesmar, who had his own personal studio within the factory's premises. There he decorated soft-paste porcelains with translucent enamels deposited on jeweller's foil. The resulting works were of extraordinary brilliance.

## Limoges

Two completely different types of ware were made from 1880 to 1905. The first depended on technical virtuosity and was a continuation of the style popular in the 1870s. The second was avant-garde and has more in common with Art Nouveau.

Charles Haviland remained the leading firm for the production of pieces in the traditional style. In 1881 Félix Bracquemond left the studio set up at Auteuil by Haviland and was replaced by Ernest Chaplet between 1881 and 1885. In 1885 Chaplet purchased the workshop, which had moved to Vaugirard in 1881. Théodore Haviland broke away from his brother in 1891, but in the same year Charles Haviland went into partnership with his son Georges, although his firm still operated under the same name until 1937 when it was taken over by G. D. A. (Gérard, Dufraisseix, and Abbot). Between 1892 and 1919 Théodore Haviland ran his own enterprise, which was remarkably modern in outlook. Working in co-operation with various leading artists, he obtained the Grand

Prix at the Exhibition held in 1900. Technical specialists such as Edouard Peyrusson, working outside the major factories, tried to make an impact on the market. Men like Charles Ahrenfeld junior and William Guérin were above all industrial porcelain manufacturers specializing in mass-production of high quality domestic articles.

In practice the G. D. A. factory was the only Limoges concern that adopted the Art Nouveau style. The factory itself was of long standing, having been established by the Alluauds in the Casseaux district of Limoges. In 1876 it had been taken over by one of Charles Haviland's relatives, a certain Charles Field Haviland. Since 1859 the latter had been competing with Haviland and Company for a share of the American market. Despite considerable efforts, Charles Field Haviland was relatively unsuccessful and in 1881 sold out to Gérard, Dufraisseix, and Morel who modernized the factory. They retained Charles Field Haviland's initials as their factory mark in order to break into the American market. In 1890 Morel resigned. In 1900 the new partner, named Edgar Abbot, took over the American export business and the firm became known as 'G. D. A.'.

Gérard, Dufraisseix and Company began to make Art Nouveau ceramics at the request of the Paris dealer, Samuel [or Siegfried] Bing. Bing had commissioned models from Georges de Feure and Eugène Colonna, for his shop 'Art Nouveau'. These pieces were manufactured in Limoges. The *service Canton* ('Canton Service') was hugely successful at the 1900

412 *'Igny' vase.* Sèvres, National Porcelain factory, 1900. 'New porcelain'. H. 14.5 cm. Mark: 88. MNC, Sèvres (15 778²).
Most Sèvres vases made at this period were small, like this example. They could be mounted in bronze and were sometimes even provided with bronze covers.

413 *'Bourget B' vase.* Sèvres, National Porcelain factory, 1901. Soft-paste porcelain. H. 18 cm. Mark: 93. MNC, Sèvres (16 072).
On this piece, which was modelled by Sandier, Uhlrich painted clover-shaped flowers with long stems in the Art Nouveau style. The upper part of the vase is related to the lower by means of the fluid plant forms. Strong colours and gold embellishments make the vase much more striking than many pieces produced at this time.

414 *'Gourd' vase.* Sèvres, National Porcelain factory, 1900. 'New porcelain'. H. 21 cm. Mark: 89. MAD, Limoges (ADL 7704).
About 1900 Louis Kann modelled several shapes based on naturalistic forms. This gourd-shaped vase is one example of his work; it has a flambé glaze.

415 *'Apremont' vase.* Sèvres, National Porcelain factory, 1902. 'New porcelain'. H. 35 cm. Mark: 94. MNC, Sèvres (15 913).
Designed in 1898 by Sandoz, this vase was modelled by Henry in 1902. The 'new porcelain' body could be easily used for freely modelled pieces, which were fashionable around 1900.

416 *Vase.* Limoges. G. D. M. (Gérard, Dufraisseix, and Morel) factory, 1881–1890. Hard-paste porcelain. H. 20.6 cm. Mark: 8. MAD, Limoges (ADL 4372).
This 'aesthetic' piece inspired by Japanese art is based on a rather geometric shape, despite the wave-like form enveloping the body of the vase.

417 *Dish from the service Canton.* Limoges, G. D. A. (Gérard, Dufraisseix, and Abbot) factory, 1900. Hard-paste porcelain. D. 29 cm. Mark: 6. MAD, Limoges (ADL 4437).
Eugène Colonna designed the 'Canton Service' for Samuel Bing's shop, 'Art Nouveau', in 1900. It is simply conceived and the incised porcelain is ivory-coloured, with a sea-green line around the border.

418 *Lamp base.* Limoges, decorated by Edouard Peyrusson, *c.* 1879. Hard- ▷
paste porcelain. Max. H. 33.3 cm. Unmarked. MAD, Limoges (ADL 4569).
Edouard Peyrusson began to perfect a wide range of high-temperature colours from 1865. This piece is decorated in high-temperature blue with gold flecks imitating lapis lazuli.

419 *Vase.* Limoges, G. D. A. (Gérard, Dufraisseix, and Abbot) factory, *c.* 1900. Hard-paste porcelain. H. 10.5 cm. Marks: 6, 7. MdAd, Paris (AD 15 266).
In common with many Art Nouveau porcelains, this piece has a square base and a circular mouth.

Exhibition, but Bing's death in 1905 put an end to this aspect of the factory's production.

*Techniques*
Industrialization of production methods was introduced during the period under discussion. It included the use of coal and even electricity for firing the kilns, the introduction of continuous-firing kilns, down-draught kilns, and so on. Not every factory experienced instant modernization, and some remained strongly traditional in their production methods. Edouard Peyrusson[10] perfected his own range of high-temperature colours, which were bright in tone and were used by the leading factories.

418

*Style*
Traditional styles depended on the maintenance of existing processes. Only Charles Haviland and Chaplet carried out research allowing them to develop new styles. But moves to put a type of artistic activity that was as personal as Chaplet's on an industrial basis were doomed to failure. Théodore Haviland was commercially successful because he employed artists such as Lindeneher, Bracquemond, and Dammouse, but his porcelain was not stylistically innovatory.

De Feure and Colonna, however, created a style that was quite new. Certain pieces had somewhat strange shapes which were in line with contemporary taste. These include standing cups with a circular base and square section, but on the whole their production was characterized by restraint. Decorative

420 *Vase.* Limoges, G.D.A. (Gérard, Dufraisseix, and Abbot) factory, *c.* 1900. H. 31.4 cm. Mark: 6. MAD, Limoges (ADL 4392).
The shape of the piece is not typical of the Art Nouveau style, despite the supple elegance of the plant forms used to decorate it.

421 *Vase.* Limoges, G.D.A. (Gérard, Dufraisseix, and Abbot) factory, *c.* 1900. Hard-paste porcelain. H. 32.5 cm. Mark: 7. MAD, Limoges (ADL 4393).
Both shape and decoration of this piece are unusual.

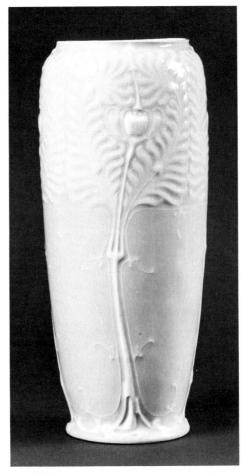

422 *Part of a coffee service.* Chantilly (Oise), Michel Aaron factory, *c.* 1850. Hard-paste porcelain. H. (coffee-pot) 22 cm. Unmarked. MAD, Limoges (ADL 2927–2930).
In the 18th century Chantilly had been one of the leading soft-paste factories. It continued manufacturing porcelain in the 19th century. Michel Aaron left Limoges in 1845 to establish a factory at Chantilly in partnership with Charles Alphonse Chalot; it closed in 1870.

motifs were, in the main, rather soberly designed and were sometimes very unobtrusive in character. The *service Canton* is one example of this tendency: it is delicately decorated in pale green on an ivory-coloured ground. The charm of pieces such as this lies in the perfect marriage of form and decoration.

## Other Factories

In a sense the history of many porcelain factories during the second half of the nineteenth century is less well known than that of the early years of the century. Although Limoges factories have been examined in detail, the same is not true for the Parisian concerns. Despite the decline of the industry in Paris there were still some painters working there who were mentioned by Chavagnac and Grollier whose writings are almost contemporary. Lesur and Tardy[11] also give some decorators' names, but their information has to be treated with caution as no sources are given. We are therefore obliged to turn to the only existing documentary evidence for this period, the reports made by the juries at the various international exhibitions. Once again we shall rely heavily on the collections

of the Sèvres museum and the Adrien Dubouché museum to supplement the reports.

Provincial factories continued to become more and more widespread. In the first half of the century this had occurred because of shortage of space in Paris for the modernization of existing plants and because of the need for cheap labour. In the second half of the century the overriding concern was the need to be close to a source of fuel, that is coal, or to be near a railway line. Although factories moved away from the Paris region, they were not isolated from it, since by this time there was a network of railway connections all over France. Paris attracted both men and products for the Great Exhibitions—and they travelled by rail.

In some ways characteristics we examined in chapter IV were prolonged and even amplified after 1870, but the very end of the century saw the birth of a totally new generation of 'artist-potters'. They worked outside the large traditional factories where production methods were rigidly controlled and instead experimented on their own. Under the influence of Théodore Deck they frequently made or decorated earthenwares, but stoneware was also produced, popularized by Jean Carriès who was inspired by Ziegler. Occasionally some of these potters worked in porcelain.

Close links between different provincial factories, Paris, and Limoges existed at this period. Michel Aaron, for instance, left Valin, with whom he had worked at Limoges, to set up a factory at Chantilly. In 1845 he revived the Bougon-Chalot factory, which had been manufacturing pieces in the Paris style since 1817. Aaron concentrated on the production of domestic wares in porcelain.

The factories that systematically turned their talents to the production of copies of Chinese, Sèvres, and Meissen porcelain should not be forgotten. The Samson factory is the best known of these; however, many worked at producing copies in greater secrecy.

### Mehun-sur-Yèvre

In 1851 the Swiss Charles Pillivuyt established a factory in Mehun-sur-Yèvre in the Berry region, where he made use of local coal. In 1899 he was succeeded by his son Louis. In 1855 the factory managed to secure the services of the chemist Halot, who left Limoges where he had been employed by Jouhanneaud and Dubois. Halot carried on his experiments into high-temperature enamel colours at Mehun. Throughout the second half of the nineteenth century the factory produced domestic tablewares and objects specially designed for the international exhibitions such as the dish exhibited in 1889[12] which is in typical Third Republic style. Its shape is very traditional, yet its decoration must have seemed modern to contemporaries: large areas of white space on which flowering branches are asymmetrically placed.

### Vierzon

Adolphe Hache and Pépin-Lehalleur were working at Vierzon from 1845 onwards. They were well known in the nineteenth century, particularly for their finely formed 'egg-shell' porcelains. This extremely thin porcelain was often used for delicately fluted cups and saucers. The dull colours used such as celadon and grey were very much to the taste of the Third Republic. Even the pinks and blues employed were not as bright as usual. Flowering branches and birds, the most frequently used motifs, were stereotyped but extremely well executed.

423　*Wine cooler.* Mehun-sur-Yèvre (Cher), Charles Pillivuyt & Co, *c.* 1870. Hard-paste porcelain. H. 17.5 cm. Mark: 16. MAD, Limoges (ADL 3844). Factories in the Cher region produced mainly domestic wares, although occasionally they attempted more ambitious pieces. This wine cooler is decorated with a rustic scene in the *pâte-sur-pâte* technique on a celadon ground.

424　*Teapot.* Vierzon (Cher), Hache and Pépin-Lehalleur factory, late 19th century. Hard-paste porcelain. H. 26.3 cm. Unmarked. MAD, Limoges (ADL 2742).
At the end of the 19th century the Hache and Pépin-Lehalleur factory specialized in making coffee and tea-services of egg-shell porcelain. The pieces have fluted sides and are decorated in sombre colours.

Bordeaux is particularly famous for its eighteenth-century tin-glazed earthenwares and its nineteenth-century creamware. But Jules Vieillard (1813–1868), who took over the management of David Johnston's creamware factory in 1845, began experimenting using coal as fuel to fire porcelain between 1849–1850. In 1851 he was able to present a group of pieces to the Sèvres museum. In the same year he participated in the Great Exhibition in London. The catalogue mentions a patent he took out for his method of 'firing simultaneously in the same kiln, during the same firing, hard- and soft-paste porcelain, ironstone china, stoneware, pipe-clay and all kinds of earthenware.'[13] Vieillard was obsessed with fighting against English competition, as his writings show. One is entitled: *Reflexions sur le Traité de Commerce à intervenir entre la France et l'Angleterre* ('Reflections on a Commercial Treaty between England and France').[14] The English industry was characterized by the making of earthenware and porcelain under the umbrella of one factory and in the same kind of kiln, and Vieillard achieved this too.

Driven by this desire to compete with English factories, so close to Bordeaux in their outlook and production, Vieillard began to make Parian ware. The report of the tenth Exposition Philomantique held at Bordeaux states, 'he organized his factory so as to make only hard-paste porcelain, ideal for domestic use and not produced in England'.[15] He enjoyed remarkable success, employing 1,050 workers in 1866 (Charles Haviland employed only 500 people in 1865).

On Jules Vieillard's death in 1868 he was succeeded by his sons Albert and Charles. The factory continued to flourish, receiving a gold medal in 1878 and employing, 1,400 people. It seems, however, that creamware became the favourite vehicle for 'art wares'. These were decorated with exotic scenes or motifs, often in the Japanese manner or based on an imaginary vision of the past. Between 1875 and 1885 Amédée de Caranza was artistic director at the factory.

After this period of brilliance, however, decline was rapid and the factory closed down in 1895.

*Decorating Workshops in Paris*

It is not possible to mention by name all the porcelain factories active in the second half of the nineteenth century. However it is necessary to give some idea of Paris production and decoration at this period, even if the picture remains incomplete. Rousseau worked in an eclectic style typical of the Second Empire period, while Faugeron, in the era of the Third Republic, decorated some brightly coloured pieces of porcelain in a brilliant and imaginative fashion.

Other Paris artists carried on working in much the same style as their predeccessors, characterized by curiosity and creativity. Rivart was one of these; he had become particularly skilled in encrustation techniques using porcelain. The Sèvres museum recently acquired a table decorated with a flower garland of stunning technical ability. The table bears a copper plaque with the engraved arms of Charles-André Comte de Manneville and of his wife, Marie Félicité Benoist, whom he married in 1861, and it is likely that the table was made at that time.

### Albert Dammouse

The work of Albert Dammouse (1846–1926)[16] is much more closely allied to the general development of the arts.

425   *Figure of the Virgin and Child.* Bordeaux (Gironde), J. Vieillard & Cie, 1851. Hard-paste porcelain. H. 36 cm. Mark: 2. MNC, Sèvres (4216[1]). In order to compete with England, Vieillard introduced industrial methods into his factory, which manufactured creamware and porcelain. In 1851, well in advance of other French factories, he was using coal to fire the kilns.

426 *Tea-service.* Paris, Clauss factory, *c.* 1860. Hard-paste porcelain.
L. (square tray) 26 cm, (teapot) 26 cm. Mark: 18. Michel Bloit Coll., Paris.
The Clauss factory, established in 1805, was one of the few Paris porcelain
factories to remain in production after the 1850s. It was sold to the Bloch
family in 1880 and is still in operation under the name 'Porcelaine de Paris',
although it is now merely a decorating studio for porcelain made at Limoges.
In the first half of the 19th century it provided Paris decorators' workshops
with blanks.

427 *Plate.* Paris, V. Rousseau workshop, *c.* 1860. Hard-paste porcelain.
D. 33 cm. Mark: 44. MAD, Limoges (ADL 3896).
The *pâte-sur-pâte* technique used here, although technically inept, shows that
Paris factories were trying to keep abreast of new decorative processes. The
identity of V. Rousseau, whose mark appears on this piece, is uncertain,
although there was an important Paris decorating workshop run by the
Rousseau family. Solon sold pieces decorated in the *pâte-sur-pâte* technique
through the retailer Emile Rousseau.

428 *Plaque.* Paris, decorated by Marc-Louis Solon under the name 'Miles', *c.* 1860–1870. Hard-paste porcelain. H. 31 cm, W. 18.2 cm. Unmarked, signed: 'Miles'. MAD, Limoges (ADL 4333).
Like most of the painters at the Sèvres factory, Solon also worked on a freelance basis, signing himself 'Miles'. The pieces he decorated in the *pâte-sur-pâte* technique were almost certainly blanks made at Limoges.

429 *Table with porcelain marquetry.* Paris, Rivart factory, 1861. Brazilian rosewood, copper, bronze, and hard-paste porcelain. H. 77 cm. L. 1.44 m. Signature engraved on the lock: 'Rivart Bté / Bart Beaumarchais 26'. MNC, Sèvres (24 600).
Rivart established his firm in 1849 in premises on the rue de Normandie, moving to the boulevard Beaumarchais in 1860. He obtained a patent for 'porcelain marquetry forming bouquets of flowers, groups of fruit, ornaments, subjects, etc. inlaid into wood'. His pieces were awarded numerous prizes at the Universal Exhibitions of 1851, 1855, and 1862. This table can be dated by the armorial device combining the arms of Charles-André Comte de Manneville and his wife, Marie Félicité Benoist, whom he married in 1861.

430 *Footed bowl.* Paris, Faugeron decorating workshop, *c.* 1880. Hard-paste porcelain. W. 25 cm. Mark: 30. MAD, Limoges (ADL 3276).
The elaborate and highly coloured floral decoration of this piece is typical of late 19th-century taste, forerunner of the 'modern style'.

Dammouse was trained during the Second Empire period and died well after the First World War. His output reflects the various styles current during his working life. He never worked at the Sèvres factory but passed his youth in its shadow, as his father, Pierre-Adolphe Dammouse, was a sculptor-decorator there. In addition he was taught the *pâte-sur-pâte* technique by Marc-Louis Solon. He could hardly have had a better teacher. In fact, Albert Dammouse was the equal of his master from the technical point of view in his control of this type of decoration.

Dammouse established himself in the town of Sèvres but had to send his porcelain to be fired at Limoges as he had no kiln of his own. He marked his pieces with his initials 'AD' above the word 'Sèvres', which of course he was quite entitled to do as he was working at Sèvres; however, the mark has tended to confuse collectors. Pieces in an elegant but mannered and somewhat cold 'Renaissance' style probably date from the early years of Dammouse's career. They bear some stylistic affinity with Solon's work but lack his humorous touch. His entry for the 1874 Exposition de l'Union Centrale des Arts décoratifs was very successful and gained the attention of the Limoges manufacturers preparing for the Universal Exhibition of 1878.

313 Dammouse designed the rather Rococo shapes of the *grains de riz* ('grains of rice') Service for Pouyat. Between 1882 and 1885 he worked at Vaugirard in a workshop situated in the rue Blomet under Chaplet's direction with funds provided by Charles Haviland. He also worked in collaboration with Théodore Haviland and Gérard, Dufraisseix et Cie. All his designs for Limoges were marked by a well developed taste for shapes in the revived Rococo style. Some of his creations included sculptural pieces emphasizing this tendancy towards the Rococo.[17]

432 From 1892 Dammouse ran what amounted to a workshop at Sèvres. Here numerous pieces of hard-paste porcelain were made, decorated either with painted motifs or in the *pâte-sur-pâte* technique. Stoneware and *pâtes de verre* (types of glass paste) were produced, and pieces designed by artists such as Charlotte Bernard, who had no knowledge of ceramics, were fired on his premises.

433 By virtue of his training in the fine arts and his Sèvres factory background, Dammouse was firmly situated in contemporary avant-garde circles. He was acquainted with Bracquemond and familiar with Japonism. His shapes tended naturally towards the curved line characteristic of the Rococo style. His customers, drawn from the middle classes, liked abundant decoration, muted colours, novelty without excess, and good quality worksmanship. Dammouse satisfied their needs. In most cases he had to content himself with decorating Limoges porcelains according to a tradition that already went back a century. Borrowing without compunction certain motifs from the most varied of styles and countries (Persian, Classical, oriental, and *rocaille* decoration all inspired him), he married brown, grey, celadon, and blue grounds. He set off the appearance of the white porcelain body by his clever placing of scrolls, a flowering branch, birds, a landscape scene, or floral ornament in a sufficiently asymmetrical position to conform with the new taste for Japonism. He used delicate touches of slip and gilding to enhance his decorative schemes. Few artists have been so adept at expressing the style of an era. The number of pieces signed by Dammouse that are still in existence a century later is an eloquent testimony to his popularity. All this did not prevent Dammouse, whose artistic facility and talent are undeniable, from creating stoneware and *pâte de verre* pieces that were far more modern in style.

431 *Dish.* Sèvres (Hauts-de-Seine), Albert Dammouse studio, *c.* 1875. Hard-paste porcelain. D. 32 cm. Mark: 49. MAD, Limoges (ADL 4619). Albert Dammouse employed the *pâte-sur-pâte* process with as much skill as the Sèvres decorators, including Solon—but although Dammouse was a superb craftsman he lacked Solon's wit.

432 *Pin tray.* Sèvres (Hauts-de-Seine), Albert Dammouse studio, 1893. Hard-paste porcelain. L. 15.6 cm. Mark: 51. MNC, Sèvres (9544).
The swirling form and thickly applied floral motifs of this experimental piece (its decoration has clearly suffered in the firing) show that Dammouse was coming under the influence of modernism in the last years of the century.

433 *Vase.* Sèvres (Hauts-de-Seine), Albert Dammouse studio, 1877. ▷ Hard-paste porcelain. H. 23.4 cm. Mark: 50. MNC, Sèvres (7203[1]).
Dammouse worked in Sèvres itself and not at the National Porcelain factory. He bought undecorated white porcelain, mainly from the Limoges factories, and embellished it with scenes loosely based on Japanese motifs interpreted in a somewhat eclectic style, which appealed to contemporary middle-class taste.

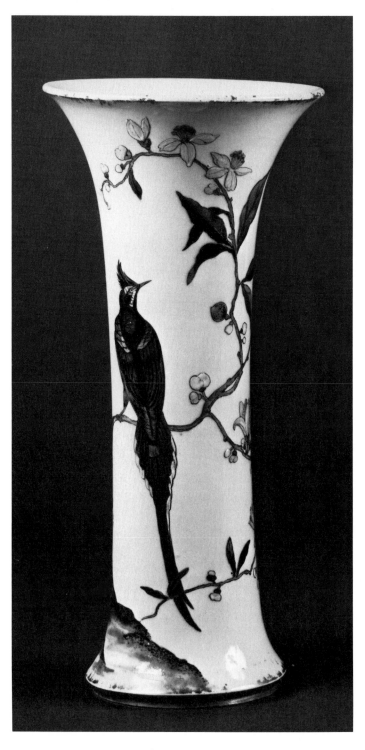

434 *Vase cornet* ('trumpet-shaped vase'). Sèvres (Hauts-de-Seine), Optat Milet studio, 1877. Hard-paste porcelain. H. 25 cm. Mark: 96. MAD, Limoges (ADL 4517).
At the end of the 19th century Optat Milet began to produce porcelain in Sèvres itself (Albert Dammouse seems to have been content to work merely as a decorator.) His pieces are heavily influenced by oriental art.

435 *Bottle*. Bourg-la-Reine (Hauts-de-Seine), Chaplet studio, 1896. Hard-paste porcelain. H. 27.5 cm. Mark: 3. MNC, Sèvres (10105).
At the end of the 19th century Chaplet strove to produce flambé glazes. His pieces were highly acclaimed at the Universal Exhibition in 1900.

Dammouse's work is a good guide to the stylistic development that took place in the years between the Second Empire and the dawn of the twentieth century.

### Artist-Potters around 1900

In the 1880s Jean Carriès who, like Bracquemond, was influenced by Japanese pottery, set a fashion for stoneware pottery that seems to have lasted ever since. Artists who wanted to 'express themselves' without bothering about enlarging their clientele, unlike Dammouse, adopted stoneware, which was heavy, opaque, and could be coloured. Only the most able of these artists, such as Chaplet and Delaherche, periodically returned to using porcelain.

Auguste Delaherche (1857–1940) only used porcelain much later, in the years between 1925 and 1930, although he worked in a style that had much in common with the late

nineteenth-century idiom. Ernest Chaplet (1835–1909), like Dammouse, originally came from Sèvres and like him was a specialist in slip decoration, except that Chaplet used an earthenware body. Taken on by Charles Haviland as Bracquemond's successor at Vaugirard in 1881, Chaplet discovered the possibilities of stoneware there and then moved on to porcelain in 1884. As was the practice at Sèvres during the same period, he used a porcelain body for the production of flambé glazes, many of which are remarkably successful. The shapes he used, inspired by Chinese porcelains, are well suited to these glazes. In fact Chaplet's shapes are rather better chosen than the ones used at the Sèvres factory, where pieces of totally western conception were given copper-red oriental glazes. Chaplet's success with flambé glazes at the International Exhibition of 1900 was quite remarkable, but it proved to be his swan-song. In 1904 Chaplet went blind and was unable to carry on working.

## DENMARK

### The Royal Copenhagen Porcelain Manufactory

'The technicians and artists of the Copenhagen factory are the masters of modern European porcelain manufacture. What Meissen was to European porcelain in the eighteenth century, Copenhagen was in the late nineteenth century.'[18]

Otto Pelka's statement, delivered in 1924, still stands today. The Royal Copenhagen Porcelain Manufactory, which in previous decades had followed unobtrusively in the wake of the major European factories, had been sold to a private entrepreneur in 1864 and in 1882 passed into the ownership of the ten-year-old Aluminia faience factory. In charge at Aluminia was the engineer Philipp Schou (1838–1922), a brilliant businessman and sometime Member of Parliament who in the same year as he took over the porcelain factory became chairman of the 'Society of Industry' set up to promote Danish national art. Under Schou's management the Royal Manufactory (it was allowed to retain the name) changed very rapidly. First the factory buildings and the technical plant were modernized, then some younger staff were recruited. In 1885 Schou took on a young architect, Arnold Krog (1856–1931), who soon exceeded all expectations and became artistic director. Hitherto works of his in Neo-Renaissance or Moorish style had shown him to be wrapped up in the historicist preoccupations of his time. At the porcelain factory, too, he initially kept to traditional porcelain design, experimenting with Neo-Rococo and Islamic ornamentation. His subsequent preoccupation with seventeenth- and eighteenth-century Delftware, with Chinese porcelains, and with the hundred-year-old Copenhagen *musselmønstret* ('strawflower pattern') put him on the right path. To start with he raised the standard of strawflower ornamentation, which had degenerated into sketchy line drawing, and designed new tableware shapes. But beyond that he played a truly pioneering role with his fundamental discovery of the harmony that existed between porcelain white and underglaze blue, which was probably something that only a newcomer to the industry could have seen behind the over-familiar combination. He was fascinated by the 'slightly greyish-green whiteness and its dreamy indigo-blue that lay within'.[19] Travelling with Philipp Schou in 1885, Krog saw in Antwerp, probably at the World Exhibition, some of the porcelains produced by other factories. He described later

436 *Clover leaf serving dish.* Copenhagen: RPF, Arnold Krog, 1887. Underglaze decoration. 25 × 20 cm. Mark: 146. RPF, Copenhagen. Krog's revival of underglaze-blue decoration based on the strawflower pattern began a boom period for Copenhagen.

how two vases from Sèvres with blue-and-red painting enhanced with gilding had impressed him and confirmed him in his decision to take a fresh look at blue underglaze painting. In 1886 he made his first trip to Paris at the invitation of the wealthy collector Wilhelm Salomonsen. Visiting the Far Eastern collector and well-known dealer Siegfried Bing, Krog became an enthusiastic admirer of Far Eastern art and himself purchased several Japanese pieces; Dyveke Helsted mentions some woodcuts.[20] It seems to us conceivable that either in Antwerp in 1885 or on his visit to Bing in 1886 Krog saw other modern porcelains that influenced him: plates such as Albert Dammouse, for example, had been painting since 1880, with Japanese ornaments and motifs applied in delicate shades of blue and grey beneath the glaze,[21] and works by the Japanese Miyagawa Kozan, known as Makudso, which were shown, probably not for the first time, at the Paris World Exhibition of 1889. These were painted in blue, green, and brown underglaze colours; in their concentration on a few pictorial, animal and plant motifs and in the looseness of their composition they are very similar to Krog's designs of the late 1880s.[22]

### The Triumph of Underglaze Painting

Soon after 1886 the Copenhagen factory produced its first ornamental vessels in simple shapes with Japanese-style underglaze painting. In that year Krog entered various vases with butterflies and plants in the model book, himself noting that they were 'based on Japanese motifs'. A covered vase in what was generally known as the 'ginger-jar' shape, a plate with a fan and bird motif, and another with flounders hanging from a branch, preserved from this early period, constitute unambiguous evidence of this influence. The hanging fish have in fact been traced to a Japanese drawing-manual.[23]

437 *Small bottle vase.* Copenhagen: RPF, Arnold Krog, August Hallin, 1889. Underglaze-blue decoration. H. 18 cm. Marks: 146, painter's monogram, and other impressed marks. MdAd, Paris (5704).
The decisive impetus towards a new porcelain style came from the Far East, witness the sparse 'Japanese' decoration on this simple vase.

438 *Picture plate with landscape motif.* Copenhagen: RPF, Arnold Krog, August Hallin, 1886–1888. Underglaze decoration. D. 39 cm. Marks: 146, painter's monogram, and other signs. Factory collection, RPF, Copenhagen.
A new treatment of a traditional device for decorating porcelain, the town view—here in underglaze blue with a Japanese-style foreground.

This new type of porcelain decoration, for which underglaze blue was soon being used in the most delicate shades and nuances and was joined by chrome-green and a red derived from gold, was made possible for Krog by the technological advances of the factory's French-born chemist Adolphe Clément (1860–1933). Philipp Schou engaged him in 1885, and he remained with the firm until 1891. The team of Krog and Clément very soon progressed beyond the linear shell pattern in a single shade of blue. Krog's predominantly non-linear motifs were no longer applied with the brush but with the aid of a compressed-air atomizer known as an aerograph. The use of protective stencils and several applications of paint made it possible to achieve differentiated effects of texture and colour.

The first time the new porcelains were shown to the public in large quantities was at the Nordic Exhibition held in Copenhagen in 1888. The exhibition was organized to celebrate the fiftieth anniversary of Denmark's Society of Industry, one of the declared aims of which was to promote national arts and crafts, and it attracted visitors from all nations. It was vitally important that the Royal Porcelain Manufactory should make a good showing on this occasion. Philipp Schou, who was himself an important man in the Society of Industry, presented a cross-section of the factory's

production: besides a selection of Krog's newer works, this included his new versions of the strawflower pattern as well as apparently Neo-Rococo porcelains and biscuit statuettes. The exhibition offered an opportunity to test the reaction of the critical public to Copenhagen's new porcelains before they were sent to the World Exhibition due to be held in Paris in 1889. Ever since the advent of porcelain in Europe, decoration in underglaze blue and (from 1817) green had been used only on the cheapest utility ware.[24] Artistic designs centred entirely on extending the overglaze palette, and technologists at all factories had scored their highest achievements in this direction with the development of a range of colours that made it possible to produce exact copies of paintings. So it was well within the bounds of possibility that Copenhagen's attempts to revive underglaze painting would be criticized as a dead-end and a mistake or would simply be ignored. The official representative that the German ceramic-industry magazine *Sprechsaal* sent to Copenhagen for the exhibition did in fact completely fail to see the novelty of the Krog-Clément porcelains. He simply reported the reappearance of biscuit figures and *vieux Saxe* (strawflower pattern) tableware.[25] But the thoroughly positive reaction of other art critics encouraged Philipp Schou to pursue what he had begun and put his fire-proof decoration at the centre of the Copenhagen entry for the

439 *Ornamental vase with ducks.* Copenhagen: RPF, Arnold Krog, August Hallin, 1887. Underglaze painting. H. 17 cm. Marks: 146, painter's monogram, and other signs. Kunstindustrimuseet, Copenhagen (B73/1910).
An example of 'negative' underglaze decoration with the design in lighter shades of blue or reserved in white.

World Exhibition of 1889 in Paris. There they won him the *grand prix* and were the sensation of the whole arts and crafts section. Edouard Garnier from Sèvres, the author of one of the official exhibition reports, mentions the Copenhagen entry as the only non-French one and calls it 'une révélation inattendue'.[26] There was universal praise for the variety that the factory managed to wring from the few colours suited to the high temperatures of the high firing and for the softness of the overall colour atmosphere. As well as using numerous Japanese-inspired motifs, Krog had meanwhile also tried to comply with Schou's request that the Royal Manufactory develop a 'national' style. For Far Eastern plants and animals he substituted indigenous ones, putting them in their familiar setting. The pattern of a stork standing on a stone in the shallows by the bank of a stream before an overcast sky from which rain is falling in slanting parallels is one of the loveliest examples dating from 1889.[27] Often details of landscapes are included, viewed slightly from above with, in many cases, abrupt gradation from foreground to background so that exaggeratedly large foreground motifs with a markedly decorative character seem to push the remaining elements of the landscape into a remote background. The frequently rather melancholy landscapes with fields, meadows, and lakes are no longer imprisoned in cartouches and medallions, as was usual for porcelain decoration hitherto, but spread over the whole vessel. In order to give them their full effect, from 1887 onwards Krog used a series of very simple vessel types: the bowl-like plate without a flange, cylindrical and bottle-shaped vases, and the so-called 'ginger jar'. These were usually based on Far Eastern prototypes, although some of them were already popular with European ceramists working in the historicist style. They all offered a maximum of surface to be painted and were thus primarily pictorial vehicles. In terms of colour, Krog's compositions were always based on the interplay of blue and white, with the dazzling white of the glazed porcelain body often playing an important role, not merely as a ground but also as a colour, for example to depict snow, sky, clouds, flower petals, or animal fur, for which purposes it was left blank within a darker field. Even the blue could be delicately shaded by means of multiple applications. The blue and white of underglaze painting always produces a cool atmosphere, which was regarded as peculiarly Nordic.

Krog's designs reached their high point as early as 1889, but they were retained and varied in the years that followed; not until after 1905 did Copenhagen occasionally return to polychrome overglaze painting. Soon after 1889 a number of artists who are known by name were working alongside Arnold Krog. One consequence of the enormous demand for Copenhagen porcelain that followed closely upon the success of the World Exhibition was that from 1893 onwards artists' hand-painted pieces were reproduced in series of varying sizes. These mass-produced pieces bore only the factory mark, whereas the pieces modelled and painted by artists were signed by them from the start (1885).[28]

### Sculpture

As soon as he arrived at the factory Krog began to look into the possibilities of reviving porcelain sculpture. This was certainly long overdue, the factory having for decades cultivated exclusively the tradition of biscuit statuettes based on sculptures by Thorwaldsen and his school. It is hard to imagine a more radical change than that which actually took place. The first sculpture, a kangaroo with underglaze painting, appeared in 1885 but remained without sequel. The beginning of a continuous development was marked by a fish that Carl Frederik Liisberg modelled for Arnold Krog in 1888. The fish was followed immediately by other animals, most of which were drawn from the fauna of the Nordic countries. Several kinds of fish and shell-fish were modelled, together with seals, polar bears, sea-gulls and many other birds, and also domestic animals, culminating in the cat modelled by Liisberg in 1896. The fact that the Copenhagen animals are distinguished by having no base of any kind led Annelore Leistikow-Duchardt to the conclusion, for which there is a good deal of evidence, that Japanese animal bronzes, netsukes, and prints provided the inspiration for this entire genre.[29] The very adoption of animal sculpture as a genre is also clearly due to Japanese influence, for in Europe animals had hardly been used as subjects for small sculpture since the Renaissance.[30] Nevertheless Copenhagen quickly developed a style of its own, which was less interested in realistic portrayal of the animal's form than in a particular kind of stylization which arose from a style of modelling in softly contoured, slightly concave or convex surfaces and the use of paint to accentuate this in shades of blue, grey, and brown, and sometimes from a renunciation of colour altogether.[31] From the outset the critics approvingly stressed the way in which the Copenhagen modellers got to grips with

440 *Fish*. Copenhagen: RPF, *c.* 1900. Underglaze painting. L. 30 cm. Mark: 146, painter's monogram and other signs. Kunstindustrimuseet, Copenhagen (1227). Copenhagen initiated its lively programme of animal sculptures in 1888, concentrating on fish and other sea creatures, which soon became fashionable in all the German and Scandinavian factories.

the 'animal soul', which is a distinguishing feature of this sculpture. Also popular were vessels with animals modelled on them, for example the bowl with a fish forming part of its rim, a vase with lateral handles in the shape of snails, or bowls in the shape of leaves or ponds in which a frog is swimming or on the 'surface' of which stands a polar bear. Here again the stimuli may have come from the Far East or even from France.[32] Not until after 1900 was the factory's sculpture programme extended to include human figures to any appreciable extent. The sculptor Christian Thomsen, following the tradition of the animal sculptures, found his models in the everyday world about him—among villagers, farmworkers, and fishermen. Only occasionally, however, are these statuettes as convincing as the animal sculptures.

## Bing & Grøndahl

The second Copenhagen porcelain factory, Bing & Grøndahl, took up the style initiated by Schou and Krog immediately after the Royal Manufactory's first successes. In 1883 the factory passed to the second generation, and from 1885 the managing director was Harald Jacob Bing (1848–1924). In the very next year, 1886, he appointed the painter, ceramist, and writer Pietro Krohn (1840–1905) as his artistic director. Krohn, who breathed new life into the factory's traditional programme, was an enthusiastic admirer of Japanese art. His first and greatest design for the factory was the *Hejrestellet* ('Heron Service') that combined freely modelled animal sculpture with vessels in a quite new way. In terms of subject it has often been compared with Kändler's Meissen Swan Service for Count Brühl: there the swan was the chosen *leitmotiv* that reappeared on every piece; here it was the long-legged, long-beaked heron. Three of these birds—modelled by the sculptor Ludwig Brandstrup—form the base of the centrepiece, the bodies of two crouching birds form the large, oval, bulbous covered tureen, and heron motifs decorate the bottoms of the plates—each time combined with stylized water plants. In its fusion of animal body with vessel shape and its highly decorative use of plants and bird, the Heron Service comes close to the new style of the Royal Manufactory. Its overall appearance, however, is much more reminiscent of Neo-Baroque tableware. We must not forget, of course, that Krohn's work up until then had been confined to purely ornamental porcelains and that the creation of a service poses very different problems from that of a vase.[33] The chief item in Bing & Grøndahl's entry at the 1888 Society of Industry exhibition in Copenhagen, the Heron Service was less positively received than the products of the Royal Manufactory. Apart from the pseudo-Baroque heaviness and the iconography, the critics complained of its dark colouring. Krohn had in fact already given up polychrome muffle-colour painting—undoubtedly under the influence of Krog's experiments—but he used an excessively dark cobalt-blue with the result that, when combined with gilding, it gave a rather sombre impression. In later editions the high-temperature blue became lighter and more delicate—very much to the benefit of the design. For Krohn porcelain was not necessarily a pictorial vehicle, as it was for Arnold Krog. His flower-shaped cups are reminiscent of eighteenth-century Meissen porcelain or Biedermeier cups, and he also designed vases with applied insects and flowers based on Far Eastern prototypes. With the Heron Service he had begun to bring the sides of his pieces out in relief. This became very much a feature of Bing & Grøndahl porcelains in the following period. F. August Hallin took up the idea for plates and vases with floral decoration, as did Jens Ferdinand Willumsen (1863–1956), who was Bing's artistic director from 1897 to 1900, Pietro Krohn having been appointed director of the newly founded Copenhagen Craft Industries Museum (Det Danske Kunstindustrimuseum) in 1893. Willumsen was an unusually controversial yet original and imaginative painter. A stay in Paris and some contact with Paul Gauguin were early influences, but he was also fascinated by the Nordic tradition; he leaned towards Symbolism and worked in some unusual media. In the 1890s he exhibited paintings that were combined with copper and wood reliefs, and on occasion he had also worked in stoneware.

441 *Pieces from the Reiherservice ('Heron Service')*. Copenhagen, Bing & ▷ Grøndahl, Pietro Krohn, 1886–1888. Underglaze and gilt decoration. H. (tureen) 17 cm, L. 28 cm. Mark: 145. Factory collection, Bing & Grøndahl, Copenhagen.
Copenhagen's 'other' factory also began looking for new shapes in the 1880s, and the Heron Service was the first major step in this direction.

442 *Urn*. Copenhagen, Bing & Grøndahl, J. F. Willumsen, 1897–1900. ▷ Relief and underglaze decoration. H. 28 cm. Mark: 145. Bing & Grøndahl's Mus., Copenhagen.
Willumsen was the artistic director who introduced such severe shapes around 1900; Ingeborg Plockross-Irminger modelled the stylized frieze.

443 *Pot-pourri*. Copenhagen, Bing & Grøndahl, Jo Hahn Locher, ▷▷ *c.* 1898. Relief and underglaze decoration. H. 28 cm. Marks: 145 and artist's monogram. MNC, Sèvres (16935).
Grey fern is modelled in relief with greenish-yellow lady's slipper and white orchids on a grey-green and blue ground.

jade carvings. In terms of colour, too, he broke new ground with the help of the firm's chemists, finding new colours that suited his style and that for some years caused a sensation, particularly a metallic black and bronze-brown obtained from iron oxide. Willumsen trained a great many artistic assistants. They included Ingeborg Plockross-Irminger (1872–1962), who was responsible for one of the most famous Symbolist funerary urns with the monumentally treated faces of a man and a woman between crouching babies, and Effie Hegermann-Lindencrone (1860–1945), who produced friendlier versions of Willumsen's motifs. Their vessels, with a heaviness of structure that stems from their master, have relief and open-work carving in flower and animal motifs in stylized rows; they always used the dark colours with restraint, combining them with large areas of white. The Swedish porcelain painter F. A. Hallin, who had worked with Carl Liisberg at the Royal Copenhagen Manufactory since 1885, came to Bing & Grøndahl in 1895, in other words before Willumsen. He used his experience from the rival factory to improve Bing's underglaze painting both technically and artistically. In his first year at the factory, responding to an idea of Harald Bing's, he produced the first Copenhagen Christmas plate. After the stormy but brief Willumsen interlude, Hallin became deputy artistic director, a post he held until 1924.

*Sculpture*

Many Bing & Grøndahl porcelains are more closely related to those of the Royal Manufactory than the ones in which Willumsen had a hand, especially those with delicately coloured plant motifs. The animal sculpture of the two factories is almost indistinguishable, many sculptors having done designs for both firms. Soon after 1900 Bing & Grøndahl were also producing figure sculpture. Ingeborg Plockross-Irminger, who under Willumsen had modelled objects of deep symbolic significance, now found the sphere of activity that really suited her in child figures and groups of mothers with children playing.[34]

**SWEDEN**

**Rörstrand**

The Copenhagen style reached the Swedish factory of Rörstrand at Lidköping when the painter and sculptor Alf Wallander (1862–1914) became its artistic director in 1895. By about 1900 Rörstrand's porcelains were presenting the two Copenhagen factories with serious competition. Wallander basically took over Krog's simple vessel shapes and underglaze painting, although he extended the palette and used primarily delicate greens, pinks, and violets, which he combined with a great deal of greyish off-white in compositions of the utmost delicacy. Like Bing & Grøndahl, Rörstrand developed a predilection for relief work—though of a very different kind from that of Krohn and Willumsen. Flower stems, petals, and fruits, painted on the sides of vases, stand out from the ground

444 *Snowy owl.* Copenhagen, Bing & Grøndahl, Dahl Jensen, 1899. Unpainted (underglaze grey on eyes, beak, and talons). H. 44.2 cm. Marks: 145 and scratch signs. MfKuG, Hamburg (1900.207).
Not merely a show-case knick-knack, this large snowy owl represents a major contribution to the sculpture of the turn of the century.

*Shapes and Techniques*

Under his influence Bing & Grøndahl's porcelains began to assume heavier shapes. Willumsen's characteristic design is the shape—alien to porcelain—of a funerary urn. The thick body and the closed shapes look as if they were designed for stoneware, yet they were undoubtedly capable of giving porcelain an unprecedented monumentality and magnificence when combined with suitable decoration. Willumsen divided the sides into horizontal strips, chose subjects for his figured friezes from the symbolic Nordic sagas, and derived his ornamentation from early Scandinavian guilloche patterns. Plant decoration is severely stylized and rectilinear boundaries subordinated. For them in particular Willumsen retained the reliefs and carved open-work decoration that Pietro Krohn had introduced so successfully, and he extended its repertory of shapes on the basis of ideas borrowed from Chinese lacquer and

445 *Two vases with flower decoration.* Rörstrand, Lidköping, Waldemar ▷ Lindström, Alf Wallander, 1897. Relief and underglaze decoration. H. 28.7 cm, 23.5 cm. Marks: 158 and artist's monogram. Kunstgewerbemuseum, SMPK, Berlin (98,14/98,391).
Alf Wallander developed his own version of the 'Copenhagen style' with flower decoration emerging in sharp-edged relief.

at their extreme edges in thin, brittle reliefs. This may occur in the middle of the side or at the rim, which is then modelled entirely in leaf shapes—the organic form merging completely with that of the vessel. Besides poppies, daffodils, tulips, cyclamens, and orchids, seaweed or even sea-spray were similarly treated in relief; sometimes sea creatures—a lobster, a fish, a crab—take the place of plants. They speak most plainly of Copenhagen influence, as do the shallow bowls with applied mermaids and animals and the free animal sculptures with fire-proof painting. On the other hand an effective original feature were Wallander's pale flower decorations on a dark ground. The vessel was covered with a velvet-black glaze out of which the flower decoration was reserved and painted in delicate pastel colours. The outlines are blurred in these decorations because the black glaze spread slightly beyond the precisely drawn edges during firing (it is said to 'exhale'). This slightly hazy effect lends the restrained flower decoration a particularly unreal, magical quality.

Alf Wallander's attempts to transfer the new style to tableware are not without importance. Here again he went beyond his Copenhagen prototypes. Some of his tableware wholly embraces the mannerisms of Art Nouveau, for example the tureen with handles in the form of sea-horses, but most of it uses restful shapes, and the lilies or cyclamens raised in delicate relief and painted in the subtlest shades of high-temperature colour give it unusual charm.[35]

'The Danish porcelain style, despite its brief period of existence, spread far beyond the frontiers of the Scandinavian North, with even the stoutest pillars of historical tradition, the factories of Meissen and Sèvres, submitting to its influence', wrote Richard Borrmann in 1902.[36] The managements of the German factories certainly could not close their eyes to the fact that in the last years of the century the new style from Denmark was enjoying brilliant reviews everywhere and selling in vast quantities.

# GERMANY

## Meissen

The first German factory to take up underglaze painting was Meissen. Here decoration in blue and green high-temperature colours (onion, strawflower, and vine-leaf patterns) had long been traditional for utility tableware just as they had in Copenhagen (strawflower pattern). In the wake of the historicist experimentalism of the 1870s, the head chemist, Julius Heintze, had begun in 1878 to extend the limited palette of high-temperature colours, such colours being needed for the then fashionable *pâte-sur-pâte* painting on hard-paste porcelain. But it was a long time before they were used for underglaze painting of the Copenhagen type. Not until 1897 did the factory include porcelains 'in the Copenhagen manner' in exhibitions of modern Meissen ware in Leipzig and Dresden.[37] It was particularly in preparation for participation in the 1900 World Exhibition in Paris that high-temperature decoration played a part—quite rightly so since Meissen had a richer palette at its disposal than any of its German competitors. Plates with impressionistic flower painting by Ludwig Sturm and Otto Eduard Voigt bear witness to this,[38] as do the monumental vases by Andresen and Hentschel that were sent to the World Exhibition.[39] The unusually full, rich colours earned critical approval, but the highest praise was reserved for Konrad Hentschel's *Krokusservice* (1897), which was based on organic shapes but was slightly insipid and self-conscious in terms of formal organization.[40] Hentschel was responsible both for the shape and for the crocus decoration in delicate browns, greens, and pinks, thus creating Meissen's first homogeneous work of art that was wholly in the Art Nouveau manner. The success of the Crocus Service, which sold twenty-five times over at the exhibition itself, caused the administration very late

446 *Three vases*. Rörstrand, Lidköping, K. Lindström and Nils Lindström, *c.* 1898. Decoration in fire-proof colours. H. 13.6 cm, 31 cm, 22 cm. Marks: 158 and artists' monograms. Bröhan Coll., Berlin.
Rörstrand developed a highly effective type of decoration with pastel-coloured flower motifs on a black ground.

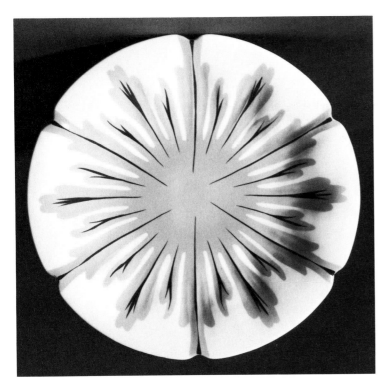

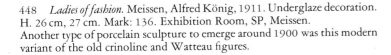

447 *Plate from the Krokusservice.* Meissen, Konrad Hentschel, 1897–1902. Underglaze decoration. D. 19.9 cm. Mark: 136. Bröhan Coll., Berlin (II, 2, 446).
Note how the brown and green underglaze decoration blends perfectly with the flower shape on this piece from Meissen's first successful Art Nouveau service.

448 *Ladies of fashion.* Meissen, Alfred König, 1911. Underglaze decoration. H. 26 cm, 27 cm. Mark: 136. Exhibition Room, SP, Meissen.
Another type of porcelain sculpture to emerge around 1900 was this modern variant of the old crinoline and Watteau figures.

on—in 1906—to welcome with open arms a female decorator who had formerly worked with Arnold Krog. From 1906 to 1909 Marianne Höst adapted the well-known Copenhagen painting motifs—plants, decorative insects, birds—to Meissen porcelain. In the field of animal sculpture, too, Meissen was the first of the German factories to follow Copenhagen's lead. Having confined itself entirely to remodelling its eighteenth-century Kändler designs for the 1900 Exhibition, in 1903 the factory engaged the Swedish-born Otto Jarl to model animals in the modern spirit. But there is undoubtedly a greater degree of independence about such small figure sculptures as the children modelled by Konrad Hentschel (from 1904), and the 'ladies of fashion' by Konrad and his brother Rudolf Hentschel, Theodor Eichler, Philipp Lange, and Alfred König.[41]

While ornamental pieces with landscape, flower, and animal motifs, bowls with sculpted mermaids, large vases, and small statuettes were ultimately no more than variations on Copenhagen inventions, in the field of fine utility porcelain in the Art Nouveau manner Meissen played a pioneering role. Konrad Hentschel's Crocus Service (1897) was followed by others in the early years of the new century. During an interregnum following the death of the artistic director Emmerich Andresen and the premature retirement of the head painter Ludwig Sturm in 1902, when the factory was without a clear artistic lead, a sense of insecurity frequently prompted it to employ freelance designers from outside. Through the good offices of the 'German Workshops' in Dresden-Hellerau, not only did Henry van de Velde—then in Berlin—design a service in 1903/1904 but also Richard Riemerschmied, a co-founder of the 'United Arts and Crafts Workshops' (a Munich association for promoting modern handicrafts) who at that time was teaching at Nuremberg Art School, in 1897. Riemerschmied's service, in 'folksy', bulbous shapes decorated with an unpretentious dot pattern, came on the market in 1905, but with its radical departure from Meissen's invariably elegant style it stood little chance of success. More modern and certainly more in character with the factory was Van de Velde's service with its streamlined shapes and sparse decoration based on segments of the circle and executed in deep underglaze blue and later also in gold. His wave-decoration service influenced another service made in 1904 by a member of the factory staff, Otto Eduard Voigt, down to the very details of the modelling.[42] An entirely independent effort and possibly the most confident of all the factory's services was the so-called *T Glatt* Service on which the Hentschel brothers collaborated in 1901, with the non-representational 'wing pattern' in celadon-green and blue.

449 *Pieces from the 'T glatt' Service with 'wing-pattern' decoration.* Meissen, Konrad and Rudolf Hentschel, 1901. Underglaze decoration. W. (tureen) 25 cm, D. (plate) 21 cm. Marks: 136 and scratch marks. Kunstgewerbemuseum, SMPK, Berlin (1977,80/106).
Another very successful Art Nouveau service by the Hentschel brothers was this wing-pattern design of blue lines and areas of celadon-green.

450 *Plate with 'whip-lash' pattern.* Meissen, Henry van de Velde, 1903–1904. Underglaze decoration. D. 27 cm. Mark: 136. Bröhan Coll., Berlin (II, 2, 449).
When Meissen commissioned a service from the architect Henry van de Velde, his entirely new conception of ornamentation produced a very striking plate flange.

## Thuringia

Following the example of Meissen, some of the more ambitious Thuringian factories took up Copenhagen's ideas. In the first decade of the twentieth century the firm of Heubach Brothers at Lichte, which since about 1870 had been producing ornamental porcelains as well as tableware, made a name for itself with vases and animal sculptures.[43] Its simply shaped vessels, most of them based on Krog patterns, have flower and landscape decorations in bluish green, and grey fire-proof colours that stand out with great delicacy against large areas of dazzling white. Greater value was placed on the creation of animal sculptures, for which Richard Heubach engaged the services of a series of well-known sculptors and modellers including Sigismund von Werneking, Eduard von Otto, and Paul Zeiller. From 1898 the firm of Swaine & Co at Hüttensteinach also produced simple vases with painting running right round the wall or placed freely and at random as at Lichte, as well as vessels with applied flower reliefs on the Rörstrand model. In this field Theo Schmuz-Baudiss (1859–1942) began experimenting in that year on behalf of the United Arts and Crafts Workshops.[44] Like Willumsen and Wallander he was a painter by training; he had been familiarizing himself with ceramics since 1896, but the job with Swaine & Co represented his first encounter with porcelain. Taking Danish decoration as its starting-point, Schmuz-Baudiss's style developed in the direction of increased ornamentation. It was characterized by an emphasis on linear contours and experiments with geometrical figures and with symmetry. His porcelain brought Swaine & Co success at the Paris World Exhibition. As a result, in 1902 he was summoned to the Royal Porcelain Manufactory in Berlin, where he was artistic director from 1908 to 1926.

451 *Badger eating a turnip.* Heubach Brothers, Lichte, Paul Zeiller, shortly after 1900. Underglaze painting. L. 25 cm. Marks: 132a and artist's signature. Kunstgewerbemuseum, SMPK, Berlin (WA 90).
Liisberg's Copenhagen animals prompted various German factories to develop their own animal sculpture, using a magnificent range of fire-proof colours.

452 *Ornamental vase.* Meissen, *c.* 1899. *Pâte-sur-pâte* and fire-proof ▷ decoration. H. 17.5 cm. Marks: 136 and incised marks. Rijksmuseum, Amsterdam.
Meissen was the first to use *pâte-sur-pâte* on hard-paste porcelain, at the same time developing fire-proof colours to go with it.

## Berlin

As at Swaine & Co, his first task here was to build up a department for underglaze painting, for which the chemist Alfred König, engaged in 1899, had created excellent technological conditions. Berlin, like Meissen, had not only the Copenhagen range of blues at its disposal but also brown, red, and yellow shades. Schmuz-Baudiss designed a large number of ornamental vessels—some with bases and some with handles and other applied elements that resembled wood-carving—small bowls, and single cups; he did not produce his first services until 1903. His decoration, which made use of large areas of colour and was sometimes entirely non-representational, is often extremely bizarre. His attempts at an approximation to floral patterns are more convincing. Schmuz-Baudiss's painting talent did in fact find its true fulfilment in expressions of nature, particularly in the landscapes that he painted on flat plates and large vases from 1903 onwards. His subjects were broad, flat landscapes with groups of trees, fields, and meadows in spring, summer, autumn, and under their winter covering of snow. The mountains of Bavaria and the pine-clad slopes of the Brandenburg March, always seen in detail and depicted in a highly atmospheric manner, are his answer to the Nordic nature studies of the Copenhagen factory. Schmuz-Baudiss cultivated his predilection for two-dimensional stylization in these landscapes, flower decorations, and so on through the use of a technique of his own that he evolved out of his work with popular Bavarian pottery before 1897. He applied the *sgraffito* technique, in which designs are scratched on to slip-coated earthenware, to porcelain. Using a burin, he engraved the outlines and internal contours of his compositions in the fired porcelain body. This enabled him to achieve a precision that is almost unattainable with underglaze colours, which tend to 'exhale' when fired—in other words they fuse so completely with the white body that they become blurred at the edges—and in this way Schmuz-Baudiss was able to emancipate himself from his Copenhagen prototypes.

*Sculpture*

Berlin's animal sculpture, on the other hand, evolved in close imitation of its Danish counterpart under his direction. The first models appeared in 1909, and about fifty more followed in the period up until 1914. Berlin was the last of the major factories to turn to this branch of modern porcelain production. Its figure and genre sculpture, for which there are earlier examples, culminated in the eighteen figures of the centrepiece designed by Adolf Amberg for the wedding of Crown Prince Wilhelm.[45] The central figures of the bride and groom are accompanied by allegorical figures of the nations paying homage, who form a procession. Each individual figure is imaginatively conceived, from the horn-playing Negro to the tambourine-playing Persian girl, and the vigorous modelling and delicate colouring make this exquisite ensemble one of the Art Nouveau masterpieces of the Berlin factory.

Around the same time the 'Schwarzburg Workshops' established and operated by Max Adolf Pfeiffer at Unterweissbach in Thuringia began producing excellent figure and animal sculpture.[46]

453 *Cup and saucer with cornflower decoration.* Berlin, Theo Schmuz-Baudiss, 1903. Underglaze decoration. H. (cup) 4.8 cm. Marks: 127 and artist's seal. Kunstgewerbemuseum, SMPK, Berlin (66,21).
The Art Nouveau designs that Schmuz-Baudiss introduced at Berlin invariably tended towards schematic linear ornamentation.

454 *Picture plate.* Berlin, Theo Schmuz-Baudiss, *c.* 1902. Fire-proof decoration, underglaze painting. D. 22.8 cm. Marks: 127, 128 and artist's seal. Kunstgewerbemuseum, SMPK, Berlin (66,18).
Schmuz-Baudiss invented a technique of engraving the fired porcelain body in such a way as to permit accurate drawing with fire-proof colours.

## Nymphenburg

The most extensive contribution in the field of animal sculpture was made by the Nymphenburg porcelain factory, where between 1905 and 1920 well over a hundred models were designed and produced. From 1887 onwards the Nymphenburg factory was in the hands of a private lessee, Albert Bäuml, who at last managed to put it back on the map as far as the wider development of porcelain was concerned. Following the success of an initial non-historicist service at the World Exhibition of 1900 in Paris, Bäuml tried further

455 *Bowl and vase.* Berlin, 1900. Seger porcelain with flow glazes. D. (bowl) 17.6 cm, H. (vase) 18.5 cm. Marks: 127, 128 and scratch signs. Kunstgewerbemuseum, SMPK, Berlin (64,4/61,12).
The soft-paste porcelain developed by Seger around 1880 was an excellent vehicle for coloured glazes inspired by the Far East.

456 *Figures from the Hochzeitszug ('Wedding Procession').* Berlin, Adolf Amberg, 1909–1910. Underglaze painting, bases with gilding. H. 29.5 cm, 28.3 cm, 26.5 cm. Marks: 127, 128 and impressed signs. Kunstgewerbemuseum, SMPK, Berlin (WA 39/37/27).
Designed (but not used) for the wedding of the crown prince, this lively ensemble was one of the few major Art Nouveau table decorations.

experiments in the new style. During the World Exhibition he made certain contacts with the 'Ecole de Céramique' at Sèvres and managed to recruit some staff from there. A graduate of the school, Louis Levallois (b. 1881), worked at Nymphenburg from 1901 to 1912, and from 1902 the factory employed the services of the chemist Albert Keller, also from Sèvres. Together they developed an Art Nouveau programme for Nymphenburg based on underglaze painting. In 1904 the young sculptor Joseph Wackerle, possibly inspired by Meissen, designed a fashionable figure for Nymphenburg. *Die Dame mit Muff* ('Lady with a Muff') proved an enormous success, and other figure sculptures followed. But it was a year later, with the appointment of the sculptor Theodor Kärner (1885–1966), that the most successful branch of Nymphenburg's Art Nouveau production began, namely animal sculpture.[47] In

459

parallel with his job, Kärner took a course at the Munich Academy under the outstanding animal painter of the day, Heinrich von Zügel. He stayed at Nymphenburg as a modeller until 1918 and spent the rest of his life modelling porcelain animals for a variety of factories. He may have been the most important but he was far from being the only animal modeller at Nymphenburg; Willy Zügel, the son of the animal painter, is another who deserves mention. The inspiration for the Nymphenburg animals came from the animals and birds of Bavaria but also in very many cases from those of the Munich zoo, so that in fact different fauna were at the centre of interest here than at the Copenhagen factory, which constituted only a remote influence. Animal painting (with muffle colours) adorned the factory's first modern tableware, as we have already seen. Hermann Gradl, a young Munich painter, had combined

457 *Plate from a 'Fish Service'.* Nymphenburg, Hermann Gradl, before 1900. Overglaze painting, gilt ornamentation. D. 23.5 cm. Marks: 138 and other signs. Bröhan Coll., Berlin (II, 2, 538).
Nymphenburg's first Art Nouveau venture was a service using the animated organic curves of the 'Modern' shape.

458 *Vase with a mermaid.* Nymphenburg, Ludwig Tischler, *c.* 1899. Unpainted glazed porcelain. H. 24.5 cm. Mark: 138. HL, Darmstadt (Kg. 56:2).
Rarely was French Art Nouveau influence as clear as in this vase dating from the period shortly before Nymphenburg had found its own style.

459 *Pair of peacocks.* Nymphenburg, Theodor Kärner, 1905. Underglaze decoration. H. 38.2 cm. Marks: 138 and other signs. Bröhan Coll., Berlin (II, 2, 551).
Animal sculpture was one of the glories of Nymphenburg's Art Nouveau production, and Kärner was its leading animal sculptor.

460　*Pieces from a coffee service.* Weiden, Bauscher factory, Peter Behrens, 1901. Green underglaze decoration. D. (plate) 19.5 cm. Unmarked. Private coll., Saarbrücken.
The members of the Darmstadt Artists' Colony designed all their own tableware, which was made for them by relatively unknown factories in the Bavarian Forest.

461　*Cup and saucer with 'Upright Hearts' pattern.* Selb, Rosenthal, United Darmstadt Artisans, 1904. Underglaze decoration in blue and green. H. (cup) 7 cm. Marks: 142 and additional stamp. Kunstgewerbemuseum, SMPK, Berlin (66,8).
This coffee and tea-service shows the Darmstadt group's leaning towards a Viennese rather than a French interpretation of the new style.

462　*Coffee service.* Burgau, Selle, Henry van de Velde, 1907. Polished gilt decoration. Unmarked, but Van de Velde's impressed mark. MB, Zurich (1958,88).
For the small Selle factory at Burgau, near Jena, Van de Velde supplied a quieter version of a design he had produced for Meissen in 1903.

457 sea creatures and water plants depicted in outline for his Fish Service. Soon after that he was also designing Art Nouveau services for the Fürstenberg factory; at Nymphenburg, on the other hand, porcelain was produced from drawings by Adelbert Niemeyer as early as 1905; in its use of the simplest cylindrical shapes accentuated only by gilt rims or box friezes it already belonged wholly to the *neue Sachlichkeit* ('New Objectivity') style.[48] Niemeyer's Nymphenburg services even outdo in radical simplicity those created from 1901 onwards by the members of the 'Artists' Colony', that was set up by Grand Duke Ernst Ludwig on the Mathildenhöhe in Darmstadt. Hans Christiansen designed a number of plates and services with decoration reminiscent of the Scottish Art Nouveau movement; Peter Behrens produced porcelains with purely linear decoration, Albin Müller severely stylized blossom 460 patterns, and the 'United Darmstadt Artisans' heart-shaped leaves on swirling stalks.[49] This tableware renounces any attempt to charm, having invariably smooth rims, sometimes facetted walls, and always angular handles. The young designers intended their new porcelains for everyday use so that most of them also have a thicker, more robust body than had been usual in artist-designed services hitherto (the *Stehende Herzen* ['Upright Hearts'] Service is an exception). The decoration is invariably printed and was executed in underglaze colours. The mass-produced porcelain of our own day is unmistakably heralded by the Darmstadt Artists' Colony designs, and it is no accident that even at that time they were produced not by the old factories but—with the exception of Nymphenburg—by younger, up-and-coming factories in the

460
462 Bavarian Forest (Bauscher at Weiden, Rosenthal at Selb) and Thuringia (Ferdinand Selle at Burgau).[50]

Around 1905 a reaction set in and criticism of underglaze painting on porcelain began to make itself heard, particularly with reference to its pale, insipid colours. In 1906 Ernst Zimmermann, the influential curator of the historic Dresden porcelain collection, wrote on the occasion of an exhibition of arts and crafts that as far as porcelain was concerned the 'bad example' of the Copenhagen style had at last disappeared.[51] In fact this was by no means true, yet by 1910 Neo-Biedermeier figure and flower decoration in brightly coloured overglaze painting was beginning to oust the Copenhagen style.

## New Glazing Techniques

Far Eastern prototypes provided the inspiration not only for blue-and-white wares but also for monochrome glazed porcelains. Even the eighteenth-century porcelains with coloured grounds go back to Chinese vases in which the entire side is covered with glaze stained with metallic oxides. On European porcelains of the eighteenth century the coloured grounds are in pastel shades and are combined with polychrome miniature painting in white reserved panels. In the late nineteenth century European craftsmen once again turned their attention to Far Eastern porcelains with coloured glazes as exquisite examples of old Chinese porcelains appeared at the world exhibitions and reached the first private collections of Far Eastern art. Experiments with monochrome glazes on faience were begun by Théodore Deck in France in the late 1870s. From 1880 onwards the development of monochrome coloured glazes in the laboratories of Europe's porcelain factories was a favourite preoccupation of chemists. Their interest centred not, as in the eighteenth century, on pastel colours but on the full, dark, rich, so-called 'ox-blood red' that was based on cuprous oxide and came about through reduction during firing. Controversy about who first invented this and who was the first to use it successfully began as early as 1883. The chemist A. Bünzli, who operated a small factory at Krummnussbaum, near Vienna,[52] claimed the honour for himself as well as for Théodore Deck of Sèvres and attacked Hermann Seger of Berlin, who had published his process in 1881 and made out that it was his own achievement.[53] The Sèvres factory collection contains proof that experiments conducted at Sèvres by A. L. Salvetat to manufacture a *sang-de-bœuf* glaze produced positive results as early as 1848, but at the time only a few trial pieces were made. Thus in 1883 Seger was able to say that only he succeeded in that year in firing vessels
465 with an ox-blood glaze without any waste, whereas Bünzli's and Deck's ox-blood glazes were often still imperfect.[54]

In 1878 a 'Techno-Chemical Research Institute' had been attached to the Royal Porcelain Manufactory in Berlin and the chemist Hermann Seger placed in charge of it. His experiments invariably aimed at systematic exploration of the field. The 'Seger cones' that he invented in 1880 and put on the market in 1886 (they are made of clay containing silicate and melt at exactly predetermined temperatures) offered the first possibility of controlling firing temperatures precisely and are still in use today. His thoroughgoing efforts to revive the Royal Porcelain Manufactory began with the development of new porcelain pastes such as had been demanded by the 'committee of experts' appointed in 1878.[55] As at Sèvres, experiments were aimed at finding softer pastes more like the Far Eastern ones and

463 *Ingwertopf (ginger jar).* Copenhagen: RPF, Valdemar Engelhardt, 1893. Soft-paste porcelain with flowing crystalline glaze. H. 13 cm. Marks: 147 and artist's monogram. MdAd, Paris (7780).
The Far Eastern shape is less happily matched with a conventional European rosebud knop than with the blue, pink, and grey 'flow' glaze with bright blue crystalline stars.

culminated in what came to be known as 'Seger porcelain', first made public in 1880. Thanks to a larger proportion of quartz and a correspondingly smaller amount of clay body (45% quartz instead of the 21% usual in Berlin's hard-paste porcelain), it can be fired at very much lower temperatures. This makes it a suitable vehicle for a great many glazes stained with metallic oxides and also for the most difficult of them all, the ox-blood glaze. Once they had managed to fire faultless red glazes without waste, they went on experimenting on this basis. The fact that air admitted at the reduction stage of firing made the copper-red turn into shades of green, blue, and violet was exploited artistically in so-called 'flamed glazes', which 465 very soon became as popular as their monochrome counterparts. 'Flow' glazes were also developed, in which two or three coloured glazes were made to run into one another. This was achieved by coating several coloured glazes with a fondant containing boric acid and having a low melting-point; as it melted, this took some of the coloured glaze with it. The same kind of experimentation produced 'crackle glazes', which resulted from two coloured glazes with different coefficients of expansion being laid one on top of the other in such a way that one of them crazed during firing.

464   *Vase with tiger's-eye glaze.* Copenhagen: RPF, Valdemar Engelhardt, before 1900. 'Flow' glaze. H. 17 cm. Marks: 147, VE monogram, and model number. Kunstgewerbemuseum, SMPK, Berlin (00,683).
One of the very few completely successful examples of Copenhagen's amber-coloured, semi-transparent 'tiger's-eye' glaze.

465   *Three ox-blood vases.* Berlin, Hermann Seger, after 1882. Seger porcelain with 'flow' glazes. H. 15.5 cm, 16 cm, 17 cm. Marks: 127 and scratch signs. Kunstgewerbemuseum, SMPK, Berlin (64,76/64,53/64,3).
Monochrome glazes on simple vessel shapes usually based on Far Eastern models became one of Art Nouveau's prime means of artistic expression.

466 *Dragon vase.* Berlin, before 1888. Seger porcelain: 'flow' glaze and gilt drawing. Mark: 127. ÖMaK, Vienna (Ke 3550).
This vase, with its Chinese 'ox-blood' glaze, was given additional decoration to underline its Far Eastern character.

467 *Gourd-shaped vase.* Copenhagen: RPF, Valdemar Engelhardt, *c.* 1900. Soft-paste porcelain with crystalline glaze. H. 18.7 cm. Marks: 147, artist's monogram, and numerals. MNC, Sèvres (96 637).
Crystalline glazes were among the most interesting results of the experiments Copenhagen's chemists began in 1880 with low-temperature pastes and glazes.

The chemists Lauth and Dutailly reported successful crackle glazes from Sèvres in 1887. A year later they were in possession of the key to another ornamental glaze with far greater potential but failed to exploit it. They issued a warning at that time to the effect that contamination of coloured-glaze pastes with zinc silicate or titanic acid and titanic-acid salts could lead to deposits of crystals. The technical manager of the Royal Copenhagen Porcelain Manufactory, Adolphe Clément, took their warning as a challenge. In 1889 he showed the first porcelain vessels on which fields of crystals formed an additional decorative element on coloured glazes. These 'crystalline glazes' immediately met with an enthusiastic reception. In the very next year Copenhagen's Paris representative, Siegfried Bing, sold 120 crystalline-glazed

463

vases to museums and collectors. The Sèvres factory did not begin to use crystalline glazes until 1897. In Copenhagen, following the departure of Adolphe Clément, they were perfected by his successor, Valdemar Engelhardt.[56] In Berlin Hermann Seger's successor, Albert Heinecke, head of the Techno-Chemical Research Institute from 1888–1914, concentrated on the manufacture of crystalline glazes from 1898.

469

Coloured glazes, particularly ox-blood red, were used in Copenhagen, Berlin, and Sèvres on soft-paste porcelain. In Meissen, however, Julius Heintze managed as early as 1883 to produce an ox-blood red glaze on hard-paste porcelain.[57] Not until 1895 were different soft-paste porcelains developed at Meissen too in order to meet the growing demand for 'flow'

468

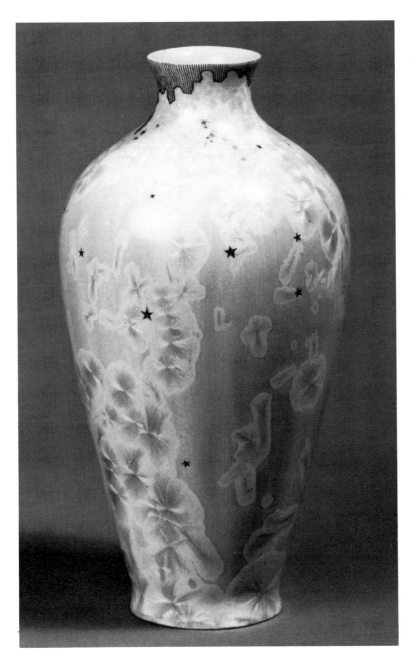

468 *High-shouldered vase.* Meissen, *c.* 1900. Soft-paste porcelain with crystalline glaze; gilt decoration (stars). H. 17.5 cm. Marks: 136 and incised marks. Hetjens-Museum, Düsseldorf (1963,51).
Having developed both coloured glazes and underglaze colours for hard-paste porcelain, Meissen still had to produce a soft-paste porcelain to meet the demand for crystalline glazes.

469 *Bottle vase.* Berlin, Albert Heinecke, *c.* 1900. Soft-paste porcelain with flowing crystalline glaze. H. 35 cm. Marks: 126 and scratch signs. SSuG, Berlin.
Glazed porcelains, always rather scorned by the artistic staff, called for intensive experimentation if they were to be aesthetically successful.

and crystalline glazes. Meissen presented its first crystalline-glazed vases for design patents in 1898. The factory had been experimenting with crackle glazes since 1882 and was able to produce them by 1887 at the latest.

The development of monochrome glazes together with the variants derived from them went hand in hand with the emergence of new, invariably simple shapes. Like underglaze painting, red, blue, flamed, and crystalline glazes were effective only on plain vessels. Cylinder, baluster, bottle, gourd, and egg shapes are the most usual ones, as with the Chinese Song porcelains that provided the inspiration for European glazed porcelain. Many of these vase types had been developed at the factories earlier on, though they had little in common with those that followed the European historicist taste. Albert

Heinecke in Berlin used a lot of high-shouldered vases and stacked them one on top of the other in the kiln in such a way that some of the crystalline glaze dripped from the upper one on to the shoulders of the one below. Delicately coloured crystalline glazes were used not only for ornamental vessels but also, in the Scandinavian factories and in Berlin at least, for animal sculptures. 469

Coloured glazes were of enormous importance for the process of artistic renewal in porcelain design. With them manufacturers presented at exhibitions for the first time ornamental vessels that were successful without any figure or even decorative painting and without either relief or gilding. They represent an essential step on the way to *neue Sachlichkeit,* the Functional-Realist arts and crafts style of

'form without decoration'. As early as 1883 the Berlin Kunstgewerbemuseum arranged an exhibition of new porcelains from the Royal Porcelain Manufactory for the specific purpose of showing a large group of flower tubs, *jardinières,* vases, and bowls with coloured glazes.[58]

Because these glazed porcelains were always produced singly and therefore at relatively high cost, production of them was gradually cut back at all factories during the first decade of the twentieth century; after 1910 in Germany only Meissen and the Schwarzburg workshops continued to produce 'flow' and crystalline glazes.[59] Managements and art departments everywhere had reservations about them.[60] With occasional exceptions, when perhaps a gilt design provided additional ornamentation on the densely coloured ground, they went straight from the laboratory into the kiln and were regarded as the province of the chemists—not to be taken entirely seriously in artistic terms.

## Other Factories

If no other firms have been mentioned in this section apart from the Scandinavian and German manufacturers it is for want of a distinctive character or outstanding achievements. The Vienna factory, with its long tradition, had ceased to exist in 1864, and Austria did not again begin to produce really interesting work until after the period covered by the present volume. The factories of Bohemia by and large went on working in the traditional style, with the occasional exceptions only proving the rule. Most Thuringian and Bavarian factories, too, did not follow the modernist movement in the arts and crafts to any significant extent except in a few cases and then only after 1900.

## RUSSIA

470 In Russia at this time, most of the small, privately owned factories, once so numerous, had been bought up by a few large concerns, with the two giants Kornilov and Kuznetsov dominating the market. 'National' designs retained their popularity and were exported by Kornilov as far afield as America.[61] In 1891 the second oldest Russian factory, that of Francis Gardner, which had always maintained a high standard of quality, was itself swallowed up by the Kuznetsov concern, which from then on marked some of its products with the famous Gardner 'G'.[62]

## St Petersburg

The Imperial Manufactory in St Petersburg must have been in a sorry enough state at the beginning of Alexander III's reign in 1881, but even the personal interest of the tsar brought little change for the better. Count D. A. Guryev, who had already served under Alexander II, attempted various reforms—probably not all of them aimed in the right direction. Nevertheless overdue technical and constructional improvements were initiated after several of the technicians responsible had made a study trip to Saxony, Bohemia, and France in 1884, a practice that they repeated at regular intervals. Three new kilns were built, modelled on those of Berlin, Meissen, and Sèvres respectively; paste and white

470 *Mocha cup and saucer with lily relief.* Dulyevo, Kuznetsov factory, *c.* 1900. Relief, underglaze, and gilt decoration. H. 6.5 cm. Mark: 149a. Hermitage, Leningrad (4615/4516).
Continuing to draw their inspiration from the West, the few remaining large Russian factories adopted the techniques and motifs of Art Nouveau.

porcelain were imported from Limoges. Guryev's attempt to place the factory under the Academy of Arts met with failure. The fifty-three painters and twelve modellers employed in 1881 were not very much to boast of, training was in a bad way, and the wages were too low to attract good new recruits. Guryev's decision to close the factory's obviously not very effective art school and rely on graduates of the private Stieglitz Art School also turned out to be a mistake. The factory turned in on itself more and more, and from the early 1880s onwards all outside sales were discontinued and the staff worked exclusively for the tsar and the needs of the court administration. Alexander III continued at first to commission the traditional copies of vases and paintings, but he subsequently became increasingly interested in new patterns and techniques from abroad. *Pâte-sur-pâte* paintings were produced at his request, and the usual miniature paintings in muffle colours were joined from 1892 onwards by underglaze decoration on the Copenhagen model—a field in which the factory's tried and tested painters K. Krasovsky and S. Romanov successfully tried their hands. With the help of the painter Liisberg, recruited from Denmark, they also learned how to produce coloured glazes, and from 1889 these were being manufactured in large quantities. But the Imperial Manufactory did not really find a new life of its own before it was nationalized in 1917; its last managing director, Baron Wolf, whom we have to thank for at least the basic history of the factory, said of Alexander III's reign something that applies to the whole of this late period: 'On croyait toujours encore qu'on pouvait se borner à copier des modèles étrangers.' ('Innovation was still limited to copying shapes and patterns from abroad.')[63]

471 *Pieces from a tea-service.* The Hague, Rozenburg, J. Kok, S. Schellink, *c.* 1900. Egg-shell porcelain with overglaze painting. H. (cup) 5.2 cm. Marks: 159, artist's monogram, and other signs. Kunstgewerbemuseum, SMPK, Berlin (1972,33).
At his short-lived Rozenburg factory Juriaan Kok produced wafer-thin frit porcelain in various unusual shapes with Indonesian-inspired decoration.

## NETHERLANDS

### Rozenburg

Far greater interest attaches to the products of a short-lived small Dutch factory. Since the closure of the porcelain factory at The Hague in 1790, the Netherlands had made no further contribution to European art porcelain. Not until the last years of the nineteenth century were fresh efforts made in this direction at Rozenburg, near The Hague. Here the architect Juriaan Kok (1861–1919) took over, in 1894, a small faience factory that in the preceding five years, under the direction of the highly talented Dutch craftsman Theodorus Colenbrander, had already been producing densely coloured faiences that had no parallel elsewhere. Kok was lucky enough to find a congenial colleague in the person of the chemist M. N. Engelen, who created for him exactly the material he wanted. This was not a hard-paste porcelain as such but a paste containing a great deal of frit that was extremely workable and transparent and could be fired to a wafer-thin body. Kok designed vessels which, in their greater complexity and brittleness, differed from the organic as well as from the simple Chinese shapes of Art Nouveau. They are often facetted, frequently switch from angular to rounded sections, and feature tall arches on spindly columns. They could not be turned or modelled but were—in common with most porcelain at that time, in fact—cast in plaster moulds. To decorate his sharp-edged, wafer-thin fantasy shapes Kok too looked for his inspiration outside the European tradition. He found it, however, not in China but in the art of the Dutch East Indies, now Indonesia. Much of his decoration is reminiscent of Javanese batik patterns. Non-representational ornamentation merges into flowers, birds, and insects, all joined together by a curious wan colouring with harsh oranges, yellows, and browns, always with a large area of white ground in between and areas of delicate dots or a dust-like finish. Kok

created these unreal, extremely fragile covered jars, pots, vases, and tea-services with the aid of a large staff from 1899 to 1913, when this highly artificial style went out of fashion.[64]

## ENGLAND

It is a well-established fact that at the end of the nineteenth century English art was relatively uninfluenced by the modernist movement and Art Nouveau. This general consideration naturally also applies equally to ceramic art. Despite the international exhibitions, porcelain production remained intimately bound up with market forces. Intense industrialization only emphasized this phenomenon, even if a book of this nature tends to concentrate upon works that are creative, even exceptional, rather than upon mass-produced articles and domestic wares. The 'modern style' originating in Continental Europe was only adopted in France on a superficial basis. In Great Britain it was virtually ignored. Manufacturers there sought to win customers by producing a variety of traditional wares in eclectic styles. The clientèle included not only the home market but also territories within the British Empire, which provided a great deal of business. The search for markets was intense around the turn of the century, and no fundamental stylistic change in English porcelain is noticeable at the end of the nineteenth century and the beginning of the twentieth.

### Derby

One of the factories which was most concerned to maintain its adherence to eclecticism, in accordance with the demands of its clientele, was the Derby Crown Porcelain Company. It became The Royal Crown Derby Company in 1900 and is still in production at the same premises at Osmaston Road in Derby.

472 *Vase.* Derby, Derby Crown Porcelain Company, 1886. Bone china. H. 60 cm. Mark: inaccessible. Royal Crown Derby Mus., Derby. This pseudo-Persian piece is painted in blue, pink, and red. Relief gold has been abundantly used to ornament it and was often employed to excess; it succeeded the flat-looking gilding used at Derby in the early years of the century.

473 *Vase.* Derby, Derby Crown Porcelain Company, 1898. Bone china. H. 21 cm. Mark: 174. Coll. Godden of Worthing Ltd.
The white painted decoration on a blue ground imitating the *pâte-sur-pâte* pieces made in the 1870s is typical of Désiré Leroy's work. The piece is heavily gilded and shows how little British taste evolved in the last thirty years of the 19th century. Gilding was now far too heavily applied.

John Twitchett and Betty Bailey have written about this firm in their book;[65] and the non-chronological layout of the illustrations emphasizes the homogeneity of this factory's production over a century. For example a plate of 1892 decorated with musical trophies (p. 60) can be compared with another decorated in 1955 with a portrait of King Faisal of Saudi Arabia (p. 160). In both cases ground colours are particularly important, and this holds true for most of Derby's output. However, even more attention was paid to gilding. 'Raised gold' decoration (relief decoration that has been gilded) was Derby's downfall. In order to produce an impression of luxuriousness without increasing the cost of production to any great extent, many factories, both British and European, used relief gold at the end of the nineteenth century and the beginning of the twentieth. Twitchett and Bailey give the recipe for 'raised gold', which is never especially bright in tone. Leaving aside this aspect of Derby's output, the remainder is decorated with printed scenes, very few pieces being hand-painted. The best painter working at Derby at the end of the nineteenth century was Désiré Leroy (b. 1840). His apprenticeship is not recorded in the Sèvres factory archives, despite reports to the contrary.[66] He could have been trained by Sèvres painters, however, as his technique is similar to theirs. He joined Minton in 1878, which gives an indication of his talent, and in 1890 he was taken on by the Derby Crown Porcelain Company and carried on working there until his death in 1908. One type of decoration he favoured was the use of white enamel (for flowers and birds) on an underglaze-blue, turquoise blue, or pink ground. He also painted on white porcelain grounds, his motifs sometimes, but not invariably, being enclosed in reserves. His style is typically late nineteenth-century, but he managed to preserve the grace and finesse associated with the eighteenth century. Some Derby porcelain collectors consider him the best painter to have worked at the factory at any time.[67]

474 *Plate and vase.* Derby, Derby Crown Porcelain Company, 1891. Bone china. H. (vase) 31.6 cm, D. (plate) 21.6 cm. Unmarked. Royal Crown Derby Mus., Derby.
Decorated by Désiré Leroy. This piece represents one of the rare experiments at Derby to express the prevailing current of taste at the end of the 19th century. The painted decoration on this piece is designed to merge with the coloured ground.

475 *Vase.* Worcester, James Hadley's factory, *c.* 1900. Bone china. H. 35 cm. Mark: 232. V & A, London (C. 253-1976).
Between 1896 and 1905, James Hadley, who had designed pieces in many differing styles for the Worcester Royal Porcelain Company, made porcelain at his own factory. He produced pieces with floral decoration in a well-defined style that appealed to late 19th-century taste. The painting on this vase is signed 'Chair'.

476 *Vase.* Stoke-on-Trent (Staffordshire), W. T. Copeland & Sons, *c.* 1895. Bone china. H. 78.7 cm. Mark: 198. Spode Mus., Stoke-on-Trent.
The Copeland factory was saved from disaster at the end of the 19th century by the talent of the painter Samuel Alcock. He painted contemporary figure subjects, as well as Biblical or Classical ones. The figures on this vase represent Naomi and Ruth.

477 *Vase.* Burslem (Staffordshire), Doulton & Co Ltd, *c.* 1900. Bone china. H. 32.5 cm. Unmarked. Minton Mus., Royal Doulton Tableware Ltd, Stoke-on-Trent.
At the beginning of the 20th century the Doulton factory was already one of the most vigorous firms in Britain. It was therefore able to create original works that married 19th-century eclectic taste with a decorating technique similar to that practised on the Continent around 1900. Enamel colours that fused with the glaze were used. This piece of 'Lucian Ware' was painted by Walter Nunn.

478, 479 *The Aesthetic Teapot.* Worcester, Worcester Royal Porcelain Company, 1882. Bone china. H. 15.2 cm. Mark: 237. DPM, Worcester. Inscribed on the base 'Fearful consequences through the laws of Natural Selection and Evolution of living up to one's teapot'. The joke refers to Oscar Wilde and his circle of 'Aesthetes'. The Aesthetic Movement in fact strongly affected Worcester's output; however most of their humorous pieces were less elegant than this one.

480 *Pierced vase and cover.* Worcester, Worcester Royal Porcelain Company, 1892. 'Ivory porcelain' (enamelled Parian porcelain). H. 43.2 cm. Mark: 238, signed by G. Owen. DPM, Worcester.
George Owen specialized in creating these amazing *tours de force* in a vaguely, Persian style.

## Worcester

### *The Worcester Royal Porcelain Company*

The Worcester Royal Porcelain Company was in the same situation as the Derby factory in that it carried on into the twentieth century producing pieces in the late nineteenth-century style without being able to adapt to changing times. Under the direction of R. W. Binns who only retired in 1897 (d. 1900), James Hadley carried on until 1896 creating the majority of models used by the factory. He effortlessly adapted all the various oriental and western styles. Among his more ambitious creations are large figures such as the Japanese couple; his more modest pieces are represented by children in the Kate Greenaway style. Painted and gilt decoration is invariably Persian, Indian, or Japanese in style.

All through this period, as in the preceding era, Hadley and his followers produced numerous diminutive pieces such as figures of contemporary politicians and other personalities

drawn from the various *milieux.* These were modelled in the form of menu-holders or candle-snuffers, the latter incorporating grotesque figures of different famous characters. Decorative porcelain slippers based on Indian footwear were made in 'ivory porcelain'; other items made included small vases held by cupped hands, candlesticks, pin-trays, and so on, all of which were aesthetically well below the level of competence of Hadley and his fellow artists. Some pieces, however, retain a charming element of fantasy, including the famous teapot formed as a female head on one side and as a male head on the other. It is known as the Aesthetic Teapot. The 478, 479 inscription underneath is an ironical reference to Oscar Wilde and his circle and the Aesthetic Movement. The teapot was modelled in 1882.

Among the innovations made in this period—although faithful to past styles, the factory still carried out research—was

the pierced work practised by George Owen, who died in 1917. His reticulated vases are extraordinary *tours de force*. As 'ivory porcelain' declined in popularity at the end of the nineteenth century, the factory also initiated research into glaze effects including the 'coral' glaze of 1893, 'shot enamels', produced in 1894, that were iridescent, 'prismatic colours' imitating the effect of a kaleidoscope, the reproduction of Tiffany glass in porcelain, 'shaded pink' and 'Sabrina ware'. This last is the name of a glaze effect on a Parian-ware body and was in use from 1897 until about 1930. It has a slightly iridescent appearance and was highly successful. The glaze is difficult to control in the kiln and was made around the same time as the crystalline glazes produced at the Sèvres and Copenhagen factories; thus the Worcester factory was clearly conscious of the Art Nouveau style. The same adaptation to changing taste can be seen in certain pieces made slightly after 1900. These vases or ewers, their shapes sharing many characteristics of nineteenth-century pieces, are decorated with long-stemmed flowers characteristic of Art Nouveau. Even so these pieces represent only a small part of the factory's output, most of which completely ignored the transition from the nineteenth to the twentieth century.

### Other Factories

Besides the main factory at Worcester—the Worcester Royal Porcelain Company—there were other factories in production in the town. The Grainger factory merged with the Worcester Royal Porcelain Company in 1889 and was closed down in 1902. Edward Locke's firm was founded in 1895 and ceased production in 1904. James Hadley's concern was by far the most important of the smaller companies. Hadley, the modeller who was largely responsible for creating the Worcester Royal Porcelain Company's style, set up his own business in 1875, although he continued to work for his original employers for whom he had already done so much. In 1896 he began to manufacture porcelain, making his so-called 'Hadley wares'. These were decorative vases painted in subtle luscious colours with floral motifs on an off-white ground. Highlights in the form of coloured slip add a note of liveliness to some of these pieces. On Hadley's death in 1903 his sons carried on the business. It was absorbed by the parent company in 1905 but kept in operation by Louis Hadley. 'Hadley wares' were hardly avant-garde in style, but they appealed to the generally prevalent taste for flower-decorated pieces.

### Stoke-on-Trent

Even large factories such as Minton and Copeland, which had concentrated all their efforts on creating new pieces, marked time at this period. The high standard of their output was maintained, but there was no adaptation to avant-garde taste, at least in so far as the bulk of their production is concerned.

### Copeland

Artistic directors at Copeland were Thomas Battam, who died in 1864, George Eyre (1818–1887), and Robert Frederick Abraham who held the post until his death in 1895. Abraham's son, Robert John Abraham, was a flower painter at Copeland.

A highly talented painter named Samuel Alcock employed at the Copeland factory enabled it to progress easily from the nineteenth to the twentieth century. Alcock was a figure painter in an era marked by a preference for floral decoration. His figures, sometimes depicted in Classical dress but often shown in modern costume, are simply rendered in a rather poetic fashion on the white porcelain ground. His decorative schemes owe some of their charm to the exquisite quality of the porcelain body used (which never exhibits any firing defects), ornamented with perfectly executed motifs such as enamel 'pearls' or with gilt decoration. Spode-Copeland has remained in production for two hundred years largely because of the quality of its wares and is still on the same premises that it occupied during the nineteenth century. The firm is now known as 'Spode Ltd'.

### Minton

Like Copeland, Minton carried on making pieces of a high standard at the end of the nineteenth century and into the ensuing period without turning to modernism, which would have upset its customers. However, this was only true for its porcelain production; between 1902 and about 1912 Léon V. Solon and John W. Wadsworth designed earthenwares in the Vienna Secessionist style. Porcelain was made in the style popular in the previous period and remained eclectic. Pseudo-Sèvres pieces, imitation Chelsea porcelains, and copies of Chinese vases all formed part of Minton's output. The oriental style remained most subject to free interpretation, since the original Far Eastern pieces had nothing in common with western aesthetic conceptions, and as a result, often gave rise to real creativity. As for Solon he carried on working at Minton itself until 1904, thereafter working as a freelance until 1913. *Pâte-sur-pâte* pieces continued to be produced in the twentieth century by one of Solon's pupils, Birk, and even by one of Birk's followers, Richard Bradbury.

### Doulton

There was one factory, which was destined for a great future, that started making ornamental pieces at this time without

481 *Dessert plate*. Stoke-on-Trent (Staffordshire), W. T. Copeland & Sons, *c*. 1895. Bone china. D. 22.5 cm. Mark: 199. Spode Mus., Stoke-on-Trent. The delicate Rococo shape of this plate, which is signed by Samuel Alcock, is characteristic of late 19th-century taste.

renouncing the prevailing current of eclecticism. This concern is known as Doulton–Burslem. It takes its name from its founder, John Doulton, and from his son, Henry Doulton. John Doulton was a far-sighted businessman who had a large and prosperous pottery in Lambeth, South London, making industrial, architectural, and sanitary wares. It enabled him to set up a 'studio pottery' at Lambeth and to set up factories for the production of industrial ceramics in other parts of Britain and even in Paris. In 1877 he bought shares in the Pinder, Bourne & Co factory, operating in premises at Nile Street, Burslem, Stoke-on-Trent. Within a few years Henry Doulton had become sole proprietor of this concern, which had originally made only industrial ceramics and earthenware. In December 1884 he agreed to begin manufacturing porcelain as suggested by his associates, who included J. C. Bailey and J. Slater. At the 1893 Exhibition held in Chicago the firm had considerable success with its showing of about 1,500 pieces. This is understandable, given the attitude of the factory's owner: 'Of course public taste cannot altogether be disregarded; and if a master is to provide for the dependent army of workers the demand must to some extent regulate the supply. Although the intelligent and enterprising manufacturer will always endeavour to lead the public taste, certainly if he leaves it at too great a distance it is at great cost'.[68] An extraordinarily varied range of pieces in bone china and earthenware were made with the assistance of Charles Noke, the factory chemist who also designed shapes; Slater, who devised new ceramic bodies, glazes, and colours; and a whole team of painters. They were either former employees of other factories or ex-pupils of the local art schools. A wide diversity of styles were employed from floral decoration of large blooms that seem to melt into the glaze and are typically Victorian in flavour, to Neo-Renaissance motifs. Flambé glazes and crystalline glaze effects were also in production. Certain pieces that seem typical of the nineteenth century or of the beginning of the twentieth are often of much later date. In contrast, some pieces made in our period are original, and these include the 'Holbein wares'. These are made in hard-paste porcelain with slip decoration under a characteristic ivory-coloured transparent glaze. They are painted with portraits in a Holbeinesque style by artists such as W. G. Hodgkinson, H. Tittensor, and W. Nunn. Despite its name the technique, which came into use in 1895, was also employed for other types of decoration including Art Nouveau floral motifs and rustic

483

482 *Vaisseau à mât, or ship-vase.* Stoke-on-Trent (Staffordshire), Minton factory, 1880. Bone china. H. 44.6 cm. Marks: 209 encircled by Mortlock's mark (retailer), incised 'John Mortlock & Co/Oxford St/London 1880', monogram 'UR' and crown in gold. Coll. of Her Majesty the Queen.
Like Coalport, Minton copied 18th-century Sèvres porcelain, with perhaps even greater daring. In the 19th century bone china lent itself best to the imitation of French soft-paste porcelain. Minton obtained old moulds, and the painters who decorated these pieces were remarkably talented.

483 *Centrepiece.* Burslem (Staffordshire), Pinder, Bourne, & Co (Doulton-Burslem), c. 1893. Bone china. H. 35 cm. Unmarked. Minton Mus., Royal Doulton Tableware Ltd, Stoke-on-Trent.
Henry Doulton's factory at Lambeth, London, which made domestic and industrial stoneware, was extremely successful. In order to gain a foothold in the Potteries, Doulton bought the Pinder, Bourne, & Co factory, which continued to trade under its original name until Doulton's death in 1899. It provided the basis for his expansion in Staffordshire, where the Doulton group of factories is now one of the largest producers of ceramics in Britain. Under pressure from his partners he began to make porcelain and was immensely successful at the Chicago Exhibition in 1893, where this centrepiece modelled by C. J. Noke was shown.

484 *Vase.* Stoke-on-Trent (Staffordshire), Colin Minton Campbell, *c.* 1880. Bone china. H. 57.5 cm. Mark: 194. Coll. Thomas Goode & Co Ltd, London.
Oriental influence was strongly felt at Minton, as at every other European porcelain factory operating in the last quarter of the 19th century. However, the quality of Minton's productions was much more uniformly high than that of pieces made at other English factories.

485 *Vase.* Stoke-on-Trent (Staffordshire), Minton factory, 1895. Coloured and glazed Parian porcelain. H. 22 cm. Mark: 210, signed by L. Solon and dated '10.1.95'. Minton Mus., Royal Doulton Tableware Ltd, Stoke-on-Trent.
This piece, which is signed by (Marc-) Louis Solon, is decorated with *pâte-sur-pâte* cupids playing in the water in Solon's usual charming manner.

scenes. 'Rembrandt wares', made from around 1898, are very similar but are earthenware rather than porcelain. The bone china 'Hyperion wares' are entirely hand-painted, frequently with floral motifs. 'Lucian wares' are painted over the glaze with enamel colours that melt during firing to fuse with the glaze. *Pâte-sur-pâte* decoration was done at Doulton on a special type of felspathic Parian ware; around 1900 this technique was used for the extremely rare 'Lactalian wares'. At about the same time lustred porcelains in the Hispano-Moresque style were manufactured. Soon afterwards the first 'flambé' wares were produced and were exhibited for the first time at the St Louis Exhibition of 1904. Although relatively common in France, where they were mainly the work of artist-potters such as Chaplet or Dalpeyrat rather than mass-produced factory pieces, porcelain and stoneware with flambé decoration has never been made in great quantity in Great Britain, despite the work of artist-potters such as Bernard Moore who set up their own studios for the production of these glazes. Doulton's flambé pieces, although they belong to the twentieth century (the French taste for flambé was typical of the 1880s), are therefore especially important. Crystalline glazes were also made at

Doulton at the beginning of the twentieth century, in other words later than at Copenhagen.

Research encompassing both the aesthetic and technical aspects of porcelain production, which looked to some extent to ceramics made in other periods and other places, was to be carried out at Doulton well into the twentieth century. The prolongation of this practice shows once again that in England there was no great change of outlook around 1900. Naturally some artist-potters as well as factory designers did create pieces quite foreign to the prevailing eclectic taste, as also happened in France, but stoneware or pottery (tin- or lead-glazed earthenware ) were more common vehicles for these creations than porcelain.

The most notable factor affecting English porcelain manufacture during the period under discussion is economic growth. It enabled the factories mentioned, as well as Wedgwood where porcelain was made once again at the end of the nineteenth century, to face international competition under favourable economic conditions, so that they could supply the demand for ceramics of every sort in the British, colonial, and English-speaking markets.

# Conclusion

All aspects of the arts and crafts of the nineteenth century have had to wait until our own day for a scholarly approach to be applied to them, and as far as the porcelain of the period is concerned the research is still very far from complete. This is the first book to be devoted to nineteenth-century porcelain in the whole of Europe, rather than concentrating on individual factories.

In England, where the whole Victorian era was very much an object of appreciation and study at a time when the corresponding period on the Continent was still being passed over in shamefaced silence, the production of the country's porcelain factories has been thoroughly examined both in comparative studies and in individual monographs. There are company histories for most of the major Continental factories too, with jubilees often providing the occasion for their publication, but in the case of the older firms their nineteenth-century output is usually, in comparison with that of earlier periods, represented most unkindly as decadent or of only peripheral importance. The achievements of Vincennes-Sèvres in terms of eighteenth-century soft-paste porcelain have often been extolled in print, but the first exhibition devoted specifically to nineteenth-century Sèvres porcelains, accompanied by a poorly illustrated catalogue, was not held until 1975. The first book satisfying modern requirements on the subject of Paris porcelain appeared in 1972. The fact that Hans Meyer was able to write a comprehensive and still standard work on Bohemian porcelain as early as 1927 was probably due to the absence, in that particular case, of any earlier national achievements. The comparable productions of the Thuringian manufacturers in the nineteenth century had to wait for a thorough study until Helmut Scherf's 1980 publication, and even then the chief emphasis was clearly on the porcelain produced during the eighteenth century. For details of the production of the Vienna factory after its heyday in the Sorgenthal period (pre 1805), we had to wait until Waltraud Neuwirth began publishing her research around 1974. Erich Köllmann's two-volume work on the Berlin factory, published in 1966, devotes only some 30 of its more than 300 plates to the period between the end of the Wars of Liberation and Art Nouveau.

The picture is even bleaker when we look at general books on the subject. They begin basically enough with the circumstances leading up to the rediscovery of porcelain at Meissen, but as a rule the general histories end soon after 1800. Here too, the few exceptions only confirm the rule.

As with the literature, so it is with the contents of public and private porcelain collections—apart from works museums, which by no means all factories possess. They are not all as fortunate as Sèvres, where as early as 1812 Alexandre Brongniart began systematically collecting samples of contemporary ceramic ware. Generally speaking, nineteenth-century porcelain has everywhere been collected only fragmentarily and without enthusiasm. Usually in museums of arts and crafts there is a more or less comprehensive but always carefully composed and proudly presented survey of eighteenth-century porcelains from the principal manufacturers. Generally there are also a few Neo-Classical pieces and in addition—probably taken on as a bequest from a private collector—one or two Biedermeier items and some inevitably recent acquisitions of Art Nouveau porcelain.

So as far as preparing this book was concerned, the inventories of works museums were of enormous importance. The collection that Brongniart started (now the Musée National de Céramique in Sèvres) is in the doubly fortunate position of possessing not only large numbers of its own pieces but also an unusually broad spectrum of material for comparison, including, for example, the previously unpublished cups from Berlin and Meissen dating from the early years of the nineteenth century, which entered the collection before 1810. It was possible to illustrate the part of this book dealing with French porcelain very largely with examples from the Musée National de Céramique, with some additions from the museum in another porcelain centre, Limoges. This had the further advantage that with the help of inventories many unmarked pieces could be attributed with certainty to particular factories.

The illustrations in the section dealing with the English factories are with few exceptions drawn from the relevant works museums or from the Victoria and Albert Museum in London. In the German section we were able to fall back on a well-stocked works museum only in the case of Meissen. Even the Viennese collections are not over-endowed with Biedermeier, and especially not with historicist, porcelain. German porcelains of the period between Louis XVI and Art Nouveau appear to be particularly poorly represented in Germany itself, both as regards the large factories such as Berlin—whose display pieces, as sent to the world exhibitions, are easier to come by in England than in their country of origin—and as regards the smaller firms. To our knowledge there are no systematic surveys at all. The porcelain stocks of

the many state, municipal, and local museums fail to provide a clear picture because the items are almost never dated and their attribution is based purely on the assumption that the geographically nearest factory is the one most likely to be their place of origin. The only sizable collection of Bohemian porcelain is to be seen in Klösterle, a branch of the Prague Arts and Crafts Museum. The Prague museum itself, with its quite exceptional collection, has been closed for forty years! The situation is almost worse as regards Thuringian porcelain: hundreds of thousands of pieces must have been produced in the nineteenth century, yet even in the museums of the immediate vicinity (Weimar, Gotha, Erfurt, Eisenach) there is hardly anything to be seen. Had it not been for the few publications we have mentioned, we could have got hold of no illustrative material on the subject for this book. Things are no different as far as Russia is concerned: the museums of Leningrad and Moscow have made only a fraction of their collections available for viewing. Since the great works of Baron Wolf (1906) and G. Lukomski (1924), all that has appeared has been a few slim picture books with brief commentaries. An attempt to obtain illustrations of some of the many display vases and state services that adorn palaces around Leningrad today ran into insurmountable difficulties.

Nevertheless the material we have managed to assemble in this book to illustrate the history of porcelain in the nineteenth century is sufficient to give the reader an impression going far beyond anything that has been available hitherto—not least because of the possibility of drawing comparisons between the different factories. The wealth and variety of the porcelain produced during the nineteenth century emerges quite clearly, as does its eventful development. We leave it to the reader to decide as to which was the highest of the many high points in that development—the Neo-Classical porcelains with the vivid contrast between their simple shapes and exquisite painting, the technologically extraordinary display pieces produced for the world exhibitions, such artistic discoveries as the transfer of the effects of Limoges enamel painting onto porcelain, those cameo-like *pâte-sur-pâte* reliefs, or the underglaze painting and coloured glazes of the Art Nouveau period. What strikes one in every case is an intense preoccupation with the material itself, porcelain, from which ever-new effects were obtained, whether through varying the paste to produce a brilliant white body or give it a marble-like quality, even various pastel shades, delicate vessels with egg-shell-thin walls or alternatively robust laboratory equipment, or whether through a thousand different types of ornamentation from the finest miniature painting to the cheapest moulded or transfer-printed decoration.

Historical events are preserved in the succession of gem-like royal tableware and the pseudo-gold of early bourgeois pomp. When comparisons are made, the outputs of the various factories backed by royalty throughout Europe, from Sèvres to St Petersburg, unexpectedly start to show a resemblance to one another, while on the other hand so do those of the private or sometimes state-owned enterprises that had to operate economically, producing ware for a quite different clientele and consequently adopting a different style. The striking similarity between porcelains that, of the examples illustrated, can definitely be attributed in the one instance to Paris-Limoges and in the other to Bohemia also shows how far we are from being in a position to classify a great deal of porcelain, that is to say almost all of the ware on which we do not have marks to give us at least a geographical location.

What we should like to demonstrate—to colleagues, to collectors, and not least to today's manufacturers—is that the period as a whole does not deserve the neglect with which it has been treated hitherto. The nineteenth century was already having to struggle with the very modern problems of competition and the need for rationalization, with high wages, low purchasing power, and uninformed taste on the part of the customer. Nevertheless, out of the mass of products in which these exigencies are only too apparent, there clearly emerges a stratum of creations in which a tireless striving for perfection and variety, a successful coming to terms with a material and its inherent possibilities, and a productive collaboration between technician and artist find full and glorious expression.

# Notes

The full titles of the books cited in abbreviated form below can be found in the Bibliography on page 290.

## Chapter I

1 Albis and Romanet, 1980, p. 138.
2 This 'bible' of ceramics in three volumes and an atlas is immensely important; see the Bibliography for successive editions.
3 Published originally without date and place of publication being given; republished recently, 3rd ed., Paris: Léonce Laget, 1977.
4 Plinval de Guillebon, 1972, pp. 112–120.
5 Albis and Romanet, 1980, pp. 181–199.
6 Brongniart, 3rd. ed., 1877, vol. II, p. 255.
7 Three different terms have been used without distinction to designate this glassy covering. The word enamel is used by the potters themselves, while the term glaze is more often used by ceramic historians. Another word, *couverte,* for which there is no English equivalent, is used for a glaze that is fired on to the pot at its first, or 'biscuit' firing. Theoretically, the glaze (*glaçure*) is applied to a pot that has already undergone the biscuit firing, as it cannot withstand the high temperature necessary to vitrify the body. *See Cahiers de la Céramique et des Arts du Feu,* no. 6 (1957): 97 f.
8 Brongniart, 3rd. ed., 1877, vol. II, p. 264.
9 *See* Lauth and Vogt, 1885.
10 Plinval de Guillebon, 1972, pp. 112–114; Brongniart, 3rd. ed., 1877, vol. I, p. 107.
11 Brongniart, 3rd. ed., 1877, vol. II, p. 281 and atlas, pl. 55, fig. 11a.
12 Magnier, 3rd ed., 1977, pp. 200–222.
13 Albis and Romanet, 1980, p. 183.
14 Plinval de Guillebon, 1972, p. 114.
15 Magnier, 3rd ed., 1977, p. 349.
16 Albis and Romanet, 1980, p. 191.
17 *Ibid,*
18 Brongniart, 3rd. ed., 1877, vol. II, p. 621.
19 *Ibid.,* p. 640.
20 *Ibid.,* pp. 640 f.
21 Plinval de Guillebon, 1972, p. 119.
22 *Ibid.,* p. 120; Brongniart, 3rd ed., 1877, vol. II, p. 645.
23 Magnier, 3rd ed., 1977, p. 260.
24 Albis and Romanet, 1980, p. 192; Magnier, 3rd ed., 1977, p. 287; Brongniart, 3rd ed., 1877, vol. II, pp. 600–604, 644 f.
25 Albis and Romanet, 1980, p. 192.
26 Brongniart, 3rd ed., 1877, vol. II, p. 600.
27 Magnier, 3rd ed., 1977, p. 294.
28 Plinval de Guillebon, 1972, p. 117.
29 Sèvres, inv. MNC (4223) for both vases.
30 Quoted in Godden, 1961, pp. 171–173.
31 Cf. the figure by Forgeot, in the Sèvres museum (5460); it is made of the so-called *pâte changeante* and is inscribed: *essai de draperie en pâte rapportée, no. 1 F* ('trial for drapery in slip-decoration technique').
32 Sèvres, inv. MNC (7100) for all seven items.
33 Lauth and Vogt, 1885, p. 33.
34 Brongniart, 3rd ed., 1877, vol. II, p. 418.
35 *Ibid.,* pp. 418 ff.
36 *Ibid.,* vol. I, pp. 193 f. and atlas, pl. XII, fig. 1.
37 *Ibid.,* vol. II, pp. 421 ff.
38 Brongniart, 2nd ed., 1854; on German and Bohemian factories, *see* pp. 368 ff.
39 'Systematik der Tonwaren', in Kerl, 3rd ed., 1907, pp. 484–487. More recent and more readily accessible literature on the subject (*see* Bibliography) includes Liebscher and Willert, 1955; Rada, 1960; Weiss, 3rd ed., 1970; relevant chapters in Köllmann, 1963; Berling, reprint, 1972; Hofmann, 1921–1923, and Wolf, 1906.
40 Brongniart, 2nd ed., 1854, p. 378.
41 The Prague Polytechnic, for example, played a major role in training technicians for the Bohemian factories from *c.* 1830 onwards.
42 *Sprechsaal,* 1876 ff., *Thonindustrie-Zeitung,* 1877 ff.
43 Kerl, 1907, pp. 1374 ff., 1371.
44 *Ibid.,* pp. 1538 f.
45 *Ibid.,* pp. 468 f.
46 At Mägdesprung in the Harz; *ibid.,* p. 396.
47 *Ibid.,* p. 1408; *see also* literature on Meissen and Vienna.

48 *See* drawings in *ibid.,* pp. 1411, 1413.
49 *Ibid.,* pp. 297 ff.
50 *Ibid.,* p. 1419.
51 Jaennicke, 1879, p. 832.
52 Kerl, 1907, p. 1488.
53 *Ibid.,* pp. 1448 ff., and Neuwirth, 1979, pp. 517 ff. (original formulae of the Vienna factory around 1815).
54 *Ibid.,* pp. 1443 ff.
55 *Ibid.,* p. 1461.
56 *Ibid.,* pp. 1463 f.
57 Berling, reprint, 1972, p. 132.
58 *Ibid.,* pp. 135 f.
59 *See* Treskow, 1971, ills. pp. 150–160.
60 *See* chapter V, pp. 258–260.
61 *Ibid.*
62 Kerl, 1907, pp. 1479 ff.
63 *See* Whiter, 2nd ed., 1978, pp. 174 f.
64 Brongniart, 3rd ed., 1877, vol. II, p. 466.
65 *Ibid.,* p. 452.
66 Whiter, 2nd ed., 1978, p. 174.
67 Magnier, 3rd ed., 1977, p. 505.
68 *Ibid.,* pp. 506 f.
69 *Ibid.,* p. 509.
70 *See* Godden, 1961, pp. 152–162.
71 *Ibid.,* p. 162; Magnier, 3rd ed., 1977, p. 509.
72 These technical details have been taken from Whiter, 2nd ed., 1978, pp. 141 f., 182–184 and from Brongniart, 3rd ed., 1877, vol. II, pp. 648–658.
73 Whiter, 2nd ed., 1978, p. 181.
74 Twitchett and Bailey, 2nd ed., 1980, pp. 51 f.
75 Whiter, 2nd ed., 1978, p. 185.
76 *Ibid.,* pp. 186 f.
77 Godden, 1961, p. 94.
78 Sandon, 1973, pp. XXIV–XXV.

## Chapter II

1 Louis de Launay, *Une grande Famille de savants: les Brongniart...* Paris, 1940. This interesting book describes the social and artistic framework in which Alexandre Brongniart lived.
2 *See* Brongniart and Riocreux, 1845, 2 vols.
3 For more details, *see* Lechevallier-Chevignard, 1908, part I, pp. 129–150; Verlet, Grandjean and Brunet, 1953, pp. 54–57; Brunet and Préaud, 1978, pp. 241–244.
4 Brongniart, 3rd ed., 1877, vol. II, p. 459.
5 *Ibid.,* p. 462.
6 *Ibid.,* p. 464.
7 *Ibid.,* p. 465.
8 Lechevallier-Chevignard, 1908, part I, p. 133.
9 Brunet and Préaud, 1978, p. 252.
10 Brongniart, 3rd ed., 1877, vol. II, pp. 298–308 and atlas, pls. L, LI.
11 *Ibid.,* pp. 644–648.
12 *Ibid.,* pp. 648–658.
13 Sèvres, inv. MNC (1320).
14 Brongniart, 3rd ed., 1877, vol. II, p. 653.
15 Ex. cat., Grandjean and Brunet, 'Les Grands Services de Sèvres', 1951, no. 34.
16 Lechevallier-Chevignard, 1908, part I, p. 136.
17 Verlet, Grandjean and Brunet, 1953, p. 42.
18 Sèvres, inv. MNC (1823).
19 Portraits of Josephine: Sèvres, inv. MNC (1801, 2008); portraits of Marie-Louise: Sèvres, inv. MNC (4995, 1803).
20 There is an example in the Sèvres museum, inv. MNC (13 022).
21 Sèvres, inv. MNC (6160).
22 Sèvres, inv. MNC (23 582).
23 Sèvres, inv. MNC (8157); illustrated in Lechevallier-Chevignard, 1908, part I, p. 145.

24 Illustrated in Verlet, Grandjean and Brunet, 1953, pl. 109.
25 Illustrated in Brunet and Préaud, 1978, p. 291, ills. 355.
26 Sèvres, inv. MNC (23 408); illustrated in Brunet and Préaud, 1978, p. 256, pl. LXIV.
27 Sèvres, inv. MNC (2626, 2627).
28 Sèvres, inv. MNC (7252).
29 Sèvres, inv. MNC (7645, 7641, 7644).
30 Sèvres, inv. MNC (7259); illustrated in Brunet and Préaud, 1978, p. 254, pl. LXIII.
31 Sèvres, inv. MNC (7662).
32 Quoted in ex. cat., Grandjean and Brunet, 'Les Grands Services de Sèvres', 1951, p. 47.
33 Sèvres, inv. MNC (1793).
34 Sèvres, inv. MNC (1808).
35 Sèvres, inv. MNC (1804).
36 Sèvres, inv. MNC (3566).
37 Plinval de Guillebon, 1972, p. 86.
38 Ibid., p. 92.
39 It is probably Sèvres porcelain; see Chavagnac and Grollier, 1906, p. 562; Sèvres, inv. MNC (2931).
40 Sèvres, inv. MNC (2976).
41 Plinval de Guillebon, 1972, p. 206 and ills. 103–105.
42 Ibid., pp. 231–235.
43 Ibid., pp. 186 f.; ills. 139–140.
44 Ibid., pp. 222–227.
45 Other pattern-books exist, for example in the Bibliothèque Nationale, Paris, and in the Musée des Arts décoratifs, Paris, but these come from unidentified factories.
46 Paris, MdAd, inv. (C.D. 3857).
47 Plinval de Guillebon, 1972, p. 86.
48 Ibid., p. 92.
49 Sèvres, inv. MNC (710) for the series.
50 Brongniart, 3rd ed., 1877, vol. II, p. 657.
51 Plinval de Guillebon, 1972, pp. 248–250.
52 In the Sèvres museum, inv. MNC (14 718, 20 068). There is a sample plaque from the Nast factory in the Adrien Dubouché museum, Limoges, illustrated in Plinval de Guillebon, 1972, pp. 282, 290; ills. 210, 217.
53 Sèvres, inv. MNC (1892), museum archives (A.n.02² 927-13-21).
54 See Albis and Romanet, 1980.
55 Quoted in Albis and Romanet, 1980, p. 78.
56 Leymarie, Bulletin... du Limousin, 1890, 1891, 1893, 1894, 1901.
57 Quoted in Giacomotti and Verlet, 1965, p. 58.
58 Albis and Romanet, 1980, pp. 73 f.
59 See Banès and Desteney, 1939, pp. 308–318.
60 Archives of the Sèvres museum.
61 Brongniart, 3rd ed., 1877, vol. II, pp. 354 f.
62 Chavagnac and Grollier, 1906, p. 421.
63 Cat., Deroubaix, 1958, p. 47.
64 See Demeuldré-Coché, 1980.
65 Merveilleuse porcelaine de Nyon, Lausanne, 1973.
66 See Caròla Perrotti, 1978.
67 Quoted in Morazzoni, 1960, vol. I., p. 130.
68 Ibid., pp. 52 f. and pls. 145–146.
69 See Brongniart and Riocreux, 1845, vol. I, pp. 301 f.
70 Morazzoni, 1960, vol. I, p. 84.
71 See Liverani, 1967.
72 Valente, 1949, pp. 47 f., figs. 26–27; Plinval-Salgues, Museu, 1961, pp. 7 f.
73 Valente, 1949, p. 50, figs. 29–30; Plinval-Salgues, Museu, 1961, pp. 6–11, figs. 1, 6.
74 Plinval-Salgues, Museu, 1961, p. 8, fig. 2.
75 Valente, 1949, p. 54, figs. 37–38; Plinval-Salgues, Museu, 1961, p. 10, fig. 4.
76 Claudius Innocentius Du Paquier had begun manufacturing porcelain in Vienna in 1719, using formulae from Meissen. This makes Vienna the second oldest porcelain factory in Europe. In 1744 it had come into the possession of the Austrian emperor. For the Sorgenthal period (1784–1805), see especially Falke, 1887; Ernst, 1925; Neuwirth, 1979, pp. 367 ff.
77 On Kothgasser as a glass painter, see Gustav Pazaurek in Cicerone XIV (1922) and Neuwirth in Keramos LXXXIV (1979): 69 ff.; bibliography, p. 89.
78 In 'Weisse Ware Wien', Antiquitäten-Zeitung XV (1980).
79 E.g. P. F. H. d'Hancarville, Antiquités Etrusques, Grecques et Romaines, 4 vols., Naples 1766–1767, including the Gavin Hamilton vase collection.
80 Meissen can be shown to have used cylinder shapes at a very much earlier date—probably, in fact, for the first time in the Swan Service (c. 1740) as vermouth cups; ill. in Walcha, 1973, p. 472/62.

81 See Neuwirth, 'Weisse Ware Wien', Antiquitäten-Zeitung XV (1980) and idem, 1979, pp. 353 ff. with ills.
82 The finest illustrations are in Ernst, 1925.
83 See Bibliography.
84 Cf. an example from Berlin, pl. 92.
85 Even picture galleries collected such porcelain copies, apparently because of their particularly brilliant colouring. Viennese copies of paintings were supplied to picture galleries in Paris, Dresden, Turin, and Vienna itself (see Ernst, 1925, p. 11).
86 Maué in Keramos XC (1980). Later on, paintings by Angelika Kauffmann were particular favourites for transfer application to porcelain (cf. Neuwirth, 1979, pp. 383 f.).
87 See p. 138 (Nigg).
88 See Cat., Baer and Lack, 1979, on the subject of 'Plants on Porcelain'.
89 In an essay by the future managing director, B. von Scholz, 'Über Porzellane und Porzellanerden, vorzüglich in den österreichischen Staaten' (1819); reprinted in Cat., Mrazek and Neuwirth, 1970, pp. 13 ff. but particularly p. 16.
90 Meyer, 1927, p. 6.
91 Frick, who accompanied Brongniart, kept a diary of this trip, though it has not survived. Brongniart gave an account of it in his Traité.
92 Quoted in Meyer, 1927, p. 19.
93 Meyer, 1927, pp. 28 ff.
94 Ibid., pp. 110 f.
95 Ibid., pp. 184 ff. (Giesshübel), 264 ff. (Dallwitz), and 219 ff. (Elbogen).
96 Ibid., p. 196 (Pirkenhammer, pp. 193 ff.).
97 A porcelain factory had been established in the Prussian capital in 1751 by a businessman called Wilhelm Caspar Wegely and operated with the assistance of staff from the older Höchst factory, but it closed in 1757. Johann Ernst Gotzowski tried again in 1761, and from him Frederick the Great purchased an already flourishing business with 146 employees in 1763.
98 See Baer, in Cat. Arenhövel, ed., 'Berlin und die Antike', 1979, no. 486. On the general subject of Berlin porcelain and its classical prototypes, see idem., pp. 251 ff.
99 The best source for illustrations is Köllmann, 1963, vol. II, pp. 186 ff.
100 See Hofmann, 2nd ed., 1980, ill. 256.
101 The order probably came from P. A. B. Count Daru, Napoleon's general manager (see H. W. Lack and W. Baer, 'Ein "botanisches" Porzellanservice aus Berlin für Kaiserin Joséphine', Willdenowia VIII [1978]: 235–259).
102 The last documentary evidence of the Berlin Service is in the Malmaison inventory drawn up after the empress's death; subsequently it was regarded as lost, but since 1965 single plates have several times appeared in the trade (see the Lack and Baer article referred to in note 101).
103 Cat., Arenhövel, ed., 'Berlin und die Antike', 1979, nos. 519, 199. Classical statues and reliefs were similarly adapted (see Catalogue, nos. 511–514).
104 Arthur Wellesley, Duke of Wellington (1769–1852). The service can be seen today in Apsley House, the duke's London residence, as can those from Sèvres, Meissen, and Vienna. On the subject of these gifts, see Köllmann, Keramos X (1960): 86 ff., and Mrazek, Alte und moderne Kunst, series 11, LXXXI (1965).
105 Preserved in the Hermitage, Leningrad (see Köllmann, 1963, vol. II, ill. 217).
106 Pieces preserved in Berlin (Staatliche Schlösser und Gärten, Belvedere).
107 König, Keramos XLVIII (1970). The first mention in the records is for Easter 1820.
108 For pieces by Riese, see Köllmann, 1963, vol. I, ills. pp. 137, 140.
109 On Posch, see G. Lenz, 'Die Arbeiten des Leonhard Posch für die Berliner Kgl. Porzellanmanufaktur', Kunst und Kunsthandwerk, XXI (1918): 1–19.
110 Commissioned to do so by King Augustus the Strong of Saxony, Johann Friedrich Böttger began experimenting in Dresden in 1707 with the object of inventing, or rather reinventing, porcelain, which until then had been known only from the Far East. By 1709 he had in principle succeeded, and the first European hard-paste porcelain was in continuous production at Meissen from 1710.
111 Walcha, 1973, p. 171, ills. 182 ff.
112 R. Rückert and J. Willsberger, Meissen: Porzellan des 18. Jahrhunderts, Vienna, etc., 1977, pl. 147.
113 Walcha, 1973, pp. 174 f.
114 See note 85 above.
115 Cf. note 104.
116 Walcha, 1973, p. 185, and idem, Keramos XV (1962).
117 See Scherf, 1980, pp. 21, 201.

118 Scherf, 1980. There is a shortage above all of illustrations of products from the late nineteenth century, and it is hard to form one's own picture for lack of accessible pieces. Nineteenth-century Thuringian porcelains are exhibited in minute numbers in a few East German museums (Eisenach, Gotha, Erfurt); their repositories are not accessible.
119 Scherf, 1980, pp. 85 ff.
120 Also known from St Petersburg, Fürstenberg, and other factories.
121 *See* Scherf, 1980, ill. 108.
122 *Ibid.,* pp. 197 ff.
123 *Ibid.,* pp. 241 ff. (for Grossbreitenbach), 309 ff. (Rauenstein), 277 ff. (Ilmenau).
124 *Ibid.,* ills. 257 ff.
125 Ill. in Krause, *Keramos* LXXXVI (1979).
126 Hofmann, 1921–1923, vol. III, p. 615.
127 *Ibid.,* p. 628.
128 In 1923 Hofmann counted almost a hundred pieces; *see* Hofmann, 1921–1923, vol. II, p. 631.
129 Hofmann, 1921–1923, vol. III, p. 632.
130 Over 700 pieces are preserved in the Residenzmuseum, Munich.
131 On Gerverot, *see* Ducret, *Keramos* XXVIII (1965).
132 On the *Flora Danica* Service, *see* Cat., Baer and Lack, 1979, pp. 19 ff., 41 ff. The largest collection of pieces can be seen today in the Rosenburg Palace, Copenhagen. Remodels from 1862.
133 There were other Scandinavian factories, for example at Rörstrand in Sweden, where in 1797 an old faience factory also began producing porcelain, entirely on the basis of English prototypes. Another former faience factory at Gustavsberg in Sweden began producing porcelain in 1822.
134 J. G. Georgi, *Beschreibung aller Nationen des Russischen Reichs, ihrer Lebensart, Religion, Gebräuche, Wohnungen, Kleidungen und übrigen Merkwürdigkeiten,* 4 vols., St Petersburg, 1776–1780; others came from J. G. G. Geissler, *Malerische Darstellungen der Sitten, Gebräuche und Lustbarkeiten bey den Russischen, Tartarischen, Mongolischen und anderen Völkern im Russischen Reich,* Leipzig, 1804, with 40 coloured engravings.
135 Names and dates taken from Wolf, 1906, pp. 346 ff.
136 *Vase étrusque à rouleaux* with painting by Swebach and decoration by Moreau, 1816–1820, (*see* Lansere, 1968, pls. 100 f.); spindle vase with Cupid and Psyche by Adam and Moreau, 1816–1818 (*ibid.,* pl. 106).
137 It was enlarged and completed in 1857. A representative portion of the Guryev Service is on show in Pavlovsk Palace, near Leningrad. Ills. in Lansere, 1968, pls. 83 ff.
138 *Ibid.,* ills. 117, 119.
139 *Ibid.,* ills. 134 f., 146 f.
140 Not enough has been published about Russian porcelain. The most informative work on the Imperial Factory is still Wolf, 1906. Unfortunately both it and the extensive source material are in Russian; only the (very full) summary in French is more accessible to western European readers. The few more recent publications are almost exclusively picture books, and even the number of illustrations they contain is tiny in comparison with the vast stocks of Russian porcelain held by Soviet state museums. There are no recent Russian publications dealing with the products of the privately owned factories. The best source here is Ross, 1968.
141 Ross relates that the papers of the Gardner factory were burned in 1925 after the manor-house had been converted into a kindergarten. On the subject of Gardner, *see* Ross, 1968, pp. 3-156.
142 Ross, 1968, pp. 157 ff.; Cat., Baer and Lack, 1979, p. 87.
143 Ross, 1968, pp. 161 ff. The factory burned down in 1839 and was subsequently sold to the porcelain manufacturer Kornilov.
144 *Ibid.,* pp. 203–250.
145 *See* Barrett and Thorpe, 1971, p. 81.
146 *The Old Derby China Factory: The Workmen and Their Productions.*
147 Sandon, 1978, pp. 199–209.
148 *Ibid.,* p. 106.
149 *Spode: A History of the Family, Factory and Wares from 1733 to 1833.* .
150 Whiter, 2nd ed., 1978, p. 27.
151 *Ibid.,* p. 30.
152 One is in the archives of the factory; the other is in the United States, in the Downer Manuscript Collection of the Henry Francis du Pont Winterthur Museum, Winterthur, Delaware; *see* Whiter, 2nd ed., 1978, pp. 90 ff.
153 *Ibid.,* p. 125.
154 *Ibid.,* p. 183.
155 That is, gold which is rubbed with a metal point to give varying tones and modelled effects rather than being burnished with a hardstone.
156 Whiter, 2nd ed., 1978, pp. 181 f.
157 *See* ex. cat., Mountford *et al.,* 'Staffordshire Porcelain, 1740–1851', 1979, pp. 30 f.
158 *Ibid.,* p. 72.

## Chapter III

1 Sèvres, inv. MNC (7547).
2 Sèvres, inv. MNC (7557).
3 Ex cat., Grandjean and Brunet, 'Les Grands Services de Sèvres', 1951, no. 32.
4 *Ibid.,* no. 33.
5 The nature of the process means that many fakes have been made; few Sèvres services have been forged as often as this one. I visited a Paris factory, closed in 1945 but left intact, where the reproduction of this service had been the main output.
6 Ex. cat., Grandjean and Brunet, 'Les Grands Services de Sèvres', 1951, no. 34.
7 Sèvres, inv. MNC (7535).
8 Brunet and Préaud, 1978, pp. 258 f.
9 Sèvres, inv. MNC (24 963).
10 Plinval de Guillebon, 1972, p. 232.
11 Sèvres, inv. MNC (23 352), gift of the Marquise de Paris.
12 Sèvres, inv. MNC ($1692^{1-5}$); *see* Plinval de Guillebon, 1972, p. 217, ill. 157.
13 *Ibid.,* p. 252.
14 An example is preserved in the Victoria and Albert Museum, London.
15 An example is in the Minton museum, Stoke-on-Trent.
16 Chavagnac and Grollier, 1906, p. 636.
17 Quoted in Plinval de Guillebon, 1972, p. 294.
18 Albis and Romanet, 1980, p. 102.
19 Lane, 1954, pp. 38–40 and Morazzoni, 1960, vol. I, pp. 86–89.
20 *See* Morazzoni, 1960, vol. II, pls. 385–393.
21 Plinval-Salgues, *Museu* (1961): 5–14, figs. 3, 6, 9.
22 *Ibid.,* fig. 49.
23 Financial problems were solved with unvarying liberality (*see* Wolf, 1906, p. 352).
24 Many painters for whom there is documentary or signatory evidence during this period are listed on the basis of the factory's archives in Wolf, 1906, p. 357.
25 *See* Lansere, 1968, ills. 140 f.
26 *See* Wolf, 1906, p. 355; he also illustrates a 'guelder-rose' vase in the Meissen style, dating from 1840 (ill. 283).
27 *See ibid.,* ill. 313; a similar example from the Gardner factory (a jug with a hunting scene) is illustrated in Ross, 1968 (ill. 33; cf. English stoneware).
28 Wolf, 1906, ills. 303 ff.; Cat., Nikiforowa, 1973, colour pls. 107 f.
29 The largest collections are in the Hermitage in Leningrad (*c.* 10,000 pieces), the Historical Museum in Moscow, and the Porcelain Collection at Kuskovo, near Moscow, and for which, as far as I known, there are no catalogues. This makes Ross, 1968 (a catalogue designed as a reference book), all the more invaluable.
30 Ross, 1968, ill. 66.
31 *Ibid.,* ills. 75–97, colour pls. LVIII ff., and Cat., Nikiforowa, 1973, ills. 72 ff. Following the death of the founder Alexey Gavrilovich Popov in the 1850s, the factory passed through the hands of various heirs before closing finally in 1875. The models, however, were sold to other firms— some of them probably before 1875. The Sèvres museum has some statuettes with the Popov stamp and an additional sticker: 'Moscou, Fabr. de Mr. A. Roudakoff 1866'.
32 Ross, 1968, pp. 204 f.
33 *Ibid.,* p. 161, ills. 61 ff.
34 Examples illustrated in *ibid.,* and Cat., Nikiforowa, 1973.
35 Ross, 1968, ills. 123 ff., 135.
36 Model no. 338; illustrated in Neuwirth, *Antiquitäten-Zeitung* XV (1980): ills. 123 f.
37 Names given in Neuwirth, 1979, p. 555, and *idem.,* 1976.
38 Cat., Mrazek and Neuwirth, [1970], pl. 98
39 The sources show that in 1829 the only biscuit figure still selling well was a crucifix; all the rest had had no market for years. See Hofmann, 1921–1923, vol. III, p. 555.
40 *Ibid.,* p. 554.
41 *Ibid.,* p. 521.
42 By 1844 the Schumann factory was the largest in Germany, with 443 employees producing utility and luxury articles, but in 1880 it no longer existed. Its marks were SPM or sometimes SCHUMANN A MOABIT, with a vertical line instead of a sceptre or eagle (probably also a line without additions, like Krister's).
43 The factory established by Carl Franz Krister went on producing porcelain in Waldenburg until 1945. Subsequently moved to Landstuhl, near Kaiserslautern, it is today part of the Rosenthal concern. The Krister mark is KPM with a sceptre-like vertical line and exists in many variants (*see* Danckert, 4th ed., 1978, p. 504).

44 'Health porcelain', which was manufactured in simple shapes with a relatively thick body, took its name from the fact that it dispensed with the lead glaze used on ordinary earthenware and already recognized as damaging to health (*see* Köllmann, 1963, vol. I, pp. 60 ff.). The branch factory's mark was a variant of that of the Royal Porcelain Factory, being applied, for example, in underglaze green.

45 Kolbe, 1863, p. 244.

46 *Ibid.*, p. 257.

47 These vases returned to Berlin after 1918 by way of an auction of works of art from the tsar's collection. Today the property of the 'Staatliche Schlösser', they are on show in Schloss Charlottenburg, Belvedere (*see* Scheffler, 1963, ills. 14 f.).

48 Copies of paintings on vases, common in St Petersburg and Nymphenburg, seem not to have been popular in Berlin.

49 Some *Lalla Rookh* vases and service pieces are preserved in the Hermitage, Leningrad. A set of vases remodelled at a later date was sold at Sotheby's in 1965 (*see* Köllmann, 1963, vol. I., ill. 79; ill. 78 shows a study).

50 *See* Scheffler, 1963, pp. 62–67, 68 ff. (vases).

51 *See* Köllmann, 1963, vol. II, p. 70.

52 The gold was applied in solution in mercury oxide.

53 Kunze, *Keramos* LXXXVI (1979): 62. A further economy applied only to the period 1817–1824, namely the use of cheaper pastes for everyday ware (*see* Just, *Keramos* LI and LIV [1971] and cf. Vienna, p. 62).

54 Brongniart wrote that the 'light gilding' process was not yet known in 1836 but that it was purchased against licence fees before 1843 (*see* 2nd ed., 1854, vol. II, p. 376).

55 In the first catalogue of the large French glassworks of Baccarat and St Louis, published by their Paris agents Hautin, Launay & Cie in 1837, we find the prototypes for porcelains of this kind. Presumably the first pressed glass wares, together with the presses, were shown at the Leipzig trade fair as soon as they were invented, and were there acquired for Meissen, much as we are told happened with lithophanes (*see* Kunze, *Keramos* XCII [1981]: 4).

56 Berling, reprint, 1972, p. 87.

57 Jedding, 1981, p. 8.

58 A cup with *Kinder am Fenster* ('children at the window') after Kersting's oil-painting of 1834 is illustrated in Jedding, 1981, p. 56.

59 On the Semper vase, see K. P. Arnold, 'Gottfried Semper—zum 100. Todestag', ex. cat., Dresden, 1979, pp. 316 ff.; camelia bush illustrated in Hofmann, 2nd ed., 1980, ill. 280.

60 Brongniart, 3rd ed., 1877, p. 741.

61 During his term in Russia, for example, he sent Brongniart samples of Russian porcelain to the Sèvres museum (*see* Brongniart and Riocreux, 1845, nos. 193 f.). A modified process, the exploitation of which Bourgoing leased to the firm of Alexis du Tremblay at Rubelles, is that of *émaux ombrants* in which engraving in the stoneware body is filled with coloured transparent glaze. There are examples in all major decorative arts collections.

62 All information about Meissen lithophanes taken from Kunze, *Keramos* XCII (1981).

63 The same motifs were at the same time sales successes as copperplate engravings and later as oleographs.

64 *See* note 59.

65 Index of model numbers in Leichter, *Der Bär von Berlin*, 1974, vol. 23, offprint, p. 9.

66 Other countries tended to regard them as a German speciality, though they were also produced—in very much smaller quantities—in France and also in England, where they were in fact known as 'Berlin transparencies'.

67 Plaue manufactured primarily 'health ware' from 1816–1817 and later the typical Thuringian range of ornamental porcelains. When the factory began producing lithophanes is not revealed in any source published hitherto, but they still form part of the production programme of the VEB porcelain factory, Plaue, today (*see* Scherf, 1980, pp. 432, 466; note 367 refers to a typescript dissertation by W. Leber, *150 Jahre v. Schierholzsche Porzellanmanufaktur Plaue*).

68 Under Kühn printing was used at Meissen for rims and borders as early as about 1814. We read of many major factories that they dabbled in this type of decoration, which was aimed at stoneware manufacturers, during the Wars of Liberation but in most cases dropped it again quite quickly. Not until the second half of the century did it become general practice to use printing processes on mass-produced wares.

69 The largest collection is that of the Arts and Crafts Museum (Uměleckoprůmyslové Muzeum) in Prague. However, this has been closed since 1945 and has been able to show only a fraction of its collection in branch museums in the provinces. Some of its Biedermeier porcelains are on show to the public in Klösterle Castle (Klàšterec nad Ohří) near Karlsbad (Karlovy Vary) (summer months only).

70 Porcelains painted in the manner of classical vases existed very much earlier at Sèvres, Vienna, and elsewhere.

71 Shell cup illustrated in Meyer, 1927, pl. XXVIII, 3.

72 Rose cup illustrated in Meyer, 1927, pl. XXVIII, 1.

73 In 1853 he brought his son-in-law Ludwig von Mieg into the firm and himself effectively left it to found a new factory in Zwickau. After 1853 Pirkenhammer traded as Fischer & Mieg.

74 *See* Meyer, 1927, p. 199.

75 *Ibid.*, pl. XXXV.

76 *Ibid.*, pl. XVIII, 5 and 6.

77 Grandjean, 1962, p. 182.

78 Grandjean, 1978; *Day* medallion no. 86.

79 *See* Shinn, 1971. Unlike the Copenhagen factory's statuettes, each of which was carefully copied by a modeller, many of the English figures were reduced mechanically with the aid of a highly advanced three-dimensional pantograph.

80 Suggestion put forward by Erik Lassen in Lassen, 1978, p. 11.

81 Cf. the poor sales of biscuitware mentioned in connection with Nymphenburg around 1830 (*see* pp. 139–140 and note 39, ch. III).

82 Ex cat., Mountford *et al.*, 'Staffordshire Porcelain, 1740–1851', 1979, p. 75.

83 Honey, 3rd rev. ed., 1977, p. 374.

84 Cox, *The Connoisseur*, no. 756 (1975): 90–97.

85 Quoted in Honey, 3rd rev. ed., 1977, p. 374.

86 Sèvres, inv. MNC (24 964).

87 *See* ex. cat., Aslin and Atterbury, 'Minton 1798–1910', 1976, no. C 9.

88 *Ibid.*, no. C 12.

89 *Ibid.*, no. C 3.

90 *Ibid.*, no. B 21; for a Derby example, *see* Twitchett, 1980, p. 286, pl. 384.

91 *See* Shinn, 1971; Godden, 1961, pp. 147–169.

92 Godden, 1961, p. 47.

93 Shinn, 1971, pp. 20 f.

94 Ex cat., *The Crystal Palace Exhibition; Illustrated Catalogue*, 1851 (reissued: New York, 1970), p. 115.

95 *Ibid.*, p. V***.

96 *Ibid.*, p. VII***.

97 *Ibid.*, p. XVIII***.

## Chapter IV

1 Camelia bush illustrated in Hofmann, 2nd ed., 1980, ill. 280.

2 Berling, reprint, 1972, p. 90.

3 At least as far as its repercussions are concerned. See ex cat. *The Crystal Palace Exhibition: Illustrated Catalogue*, 1851 (reissued: New York, 1970).

4 Brunet and Préaud, 1978, pp. 268–270.

5 A small undated statue by Forgeot, in *pâte caméléon*, is preserved in the Sèvres museum. The effect achieved is quite amazing; the colour of the body changes from pink to grey depending on the light. Sèvres, inv. MNC (5460).

6 Sèvres, inv. MNC (7100).

7 Lechevallier-Chevignard, 1908, part I, p. 137.

8 Brunet and Préaud, 1978, p. 296, fig. 388.

9 Sèvres, inv. MNC (24 964).

10 Sèvres, inv. MNC (6872).

11 Sèvres, inv. MNC (7694).

12 Sèvres, inv. MNC (6701).

13 Sèvres, inv. MNC (5964²).

14 Sèvres, inv. MNC (6747).

15 The *vase Ly* in the Sèvres museum, inv. MNC (6540), is decorated with a pattern based on Turkish ceramics from Iznik.

16 The vase with a black ground in the Sèvres museum, inv. MNC (5458), is painted with a poppy.

17 Sèvres, inv. MNC (7592, 7593).

18 An example is preserved in the Adrien Dubouché museum, Limoges, inv. ADL (7737); illustrated in Brunet and Préaud, 1978, p. 298, fig. 397.

19 An example in the Victoria and Albert Museum, London, inv. (C. 8055-1862), is illustrated in Brunet and Préaud, 1978, p. 297, fig. 392.

20 *See* Brunet and Préaud, 1978, p. 296, fig. 386.

21 A model by Solon in *pâte caméléon*, entitled *femme et enfant pour candélabres* ('woman and child for candelabra'), is preserved in the palace at Compiègne, inv. (C. 768 C), and illustrated in Brunet and Préaud, 1978, p. 307, fig. 445.

22 Quoted in Albis and Romanet, 1980, p. 128.

23 Leymarie, *Réunion des Sociétés...*, (1904): 368.

24 Ex. cat., 'L'Art en France sous le Second Empire', Paris: Grand Palais, 1979, no. 108.

25 *Ibid.*, p. 116.

26 Sèvres, inv. MNC (4602¹).

27 Valente, 1949, fig. 64.

28 Plinval-Slagues, *Museu* (1961): 9.

29 Valente, 1949, fig. 55.

30 *Ibid.*, fig. 52.

31 *Ibid.*, figs. 83, 84.

32 *Ibid.*, fig. 76, entitled *The Child Jesus,* and fig. 77, entitled *St Sebastian.*

33 Cat., 'Official Descriptive and Illustrated Catalogue', 1851, p. 1038: 'Imperial factory, that equals Sèvres'.

34 In 1841, out of 195,192 pieces of porcelain only 799 were fine quality work (*see* Cat., Mrazek and Neuwirth, [1970], p. 29).

35 Tea-service with gilt decoration illustrated in Hofmann, 2nd ed., 1980, ill. 296 b.

36 Falke, 1887, cat. nos. 288, 290.

37 *See* Neuwirth, *Antiquitäten-Zeitung* XV (1980): IV.

38 Neuwirth is informative in several places on the subject of forgeries and misappropriations of Viennese porcelains during this period, most exhaustively in *Wiener Porzellan: Original, Kopie, Verfälschung, Fälschung,* 1979; further reading is suggested there on p. 15.

39 Neureuther: *see* Thieme and Becker, 1907–1947.

40 Price list of the Bavarian Royal Porcelain Factory, Nymphenburg, Munich, 1850.

41 Hofmann, 1921–1923, vol. III, p. 643.

42 *Ibid.*, p. 644.

43 *The Crystal Palace Exhibition: Illustrated Catalogue,* London, 1851, pp. 34 f.

44 The Hunting Service was intended for Schloss Hohenschwangau, which Maximilian had had rebuilt in the historicist style (Hofmann, 1921–1923, vol. III, ill. p. 437).

45 Jedding, 1981, p. 19; illustrations in Berling, reprint, 1972, pl. 26 and figs. 221 ff.

46 Illustrations of Andresen models in Berling, reprint, 1972, figs. 257 ff.

47 Illustrated in M. Petzet *et al.*, 'König Ludwig II. und die Kunst', ex. cat., Munich, 1968, p. 134.

48 Jedding, 1981, ills. 54 f.

49 Copies of paintings have appeared in large numbers in England since the reappraisal of the nineteenth century, but they are almost non-existent in German collections and occur only rarely in the trade in Germany. It looks as if Meissen's porcelain miniatures—like Berlin's—were made specifically for the English market and exported direct.

50 Similar porcelains were manufactured at Sèvres at an earlier date and possibly with even greater elegance, yet they never achieved the international reputation of Worcester's products. One reason for this may have been that France did not exhibit at all the London world exhibitions.

51 For examples of 'Raphaelesque porcelain' from Worcester, *see* Sandon, 1973; for examples from Meissen, *see* Walcha, 1973, pl. 201, and Jedding, 1981, ill. 86. They crop up fairly frequently at London auctions (*see* Sotheby's catalogues from 1971).

52 Jedding, 1981, ill. 85.

53 The salver from this service (Jedding, 1981, ill. 81) has scenes after Watteau on a blue ground.

54 Berling, reprint, 1972, p. 136; small pieces illustrated in Jedding, 1981, pp. 90 f.

55 On the 'onion pattern', *see* Jedding, 1981, pp. 20 f. Imitations of the onion pattern by the 'Meissen Kiln and Porcelain Works, formerly C. Teichert' prompted Meissen from around 1890 onwards to put its swords mark on the front of the ware as well (*see* Jedding, 1981, p. 77). The 1873 price list of the Royal Porcelain Factory, Berlin, includes several services with onion-pattern decoration and flowers in underglaze blue.

56 Köllmann, 1963, vol. I, p. 86; in fact he was closer to Kühn in Meissen.

57 Kolbe wrote the first history of the Berlin factory, *Geschichte der königlichen Porzellanmanufaktur zu Berlin…,* 1863.

58 Experiments with lustre colours were undertaken in the 1850s.

59 *See* the Cat., 'Official Descriptive and Illustrated Catalogue', 1851, p. 1060.

60 Cat., 'Amtlicher Bericht', 1867–1869, p. 212.

61 Now in the Bethnal Green Museum, the annexe of the V & A housing non-British articles from the nineteenth century.

62 Kolbe, 1863, p. 274.

63 For a survey of the Berlin Royal Porcelain Factory's stand at the 1862 International Exhibition, *see* Köllmann, 1963, vol. I, p. 89.

64 There were at least one or two earlier Neo-Renaissance forerunners: a jug based on Florentine semi-precious stone vessels from the sixteenth century in the possession of Ulrich Gronert of Berlin is dated 1847.

65 The variants of stoneware pitchers from the Rhineland constitute one of the central points of criticism in the 'Berlin Protocol' of 1878 (*see* note 68 below). Nevertheless production of them continued because they obviously exported well. The archives of the state-owned Sèvres factory

contain a model of a similar jug, and Count Thun's porcelain factory in Klösterle also produced 'stoneware imitations'.

66 In the 1875 no. 3 price list, flower vessels nos 1–18 on pp. 8 f. and further unnumbered ('Chinese') ones on p. 10 reveal unambiguously Chinese vase shapes. So do the Renaissance beer pitchers, variants nos 1–12.

67 The 1860s were a difficult time for porcelain manufacturers everywhere, with the closure of the Vienna factory in 1864 and the leasing of Fürstenberg in 1859, of Nymphenburg in 1862, and of Copenhagen in 1868.

68 The 'Berlin Protocol' is in fact the minutes of the conference of 3–8 June 1878. Reprinted in Treskow, 1971, pp. 269–277.

69 *See* note 62.

70 Kips drawings in the archives of the Royal Porcelain Factory, Berlin; tile picture illustrated in Köllmann, 1963, vol. II, ill. 240.

71 At the beginning of the twentieth century there were 395 porcelain firms operating in Thuringia (*see* Scherf, 1980, p. 395).

72 'Statuettes in the French style, particularly nudes' (Jaennicke, 1879, p. 903).

73 *Adressbuch der Keramischen Industrie…,* 1883.

74 Lace figures with such 'genuine' skirts were manufactured *en masse* at Meissen around the mid-century; 66 figures 'with lace trimming' were exhibited at the 1862 International Exhibition as against 54 without (*see* Jedding, 1981, p. 10). In Berlin, too, they were regarded as a speciality—even before 1836 (*see* Brongniart, 2nd ed., 1854, p. 401).

75 On the luxury porcelains of the firm of Thieme at Potschappel, in the Meissen style but also in some cases with (forged) Viennese marks, *see* Neuwirth, 1979, pp. 239 ff., 333 ff.

76 Helena Wolfsohn established a porcelain-painting business in Dresden in 1843. In 1888 she was represented at the German National Exhibition in Munich with 'a collection of porcelain objects with hand-painted decoration after the manner of the old Meissen, Berlin, and Sèvres factories as well as new shapes in modern patterns of original design'. In 1879 the firm began putting Meissen's 'Augustus-Rex' (AR) marks on its plates, whereupon Meissen took it to court (*see* Danckert, 4th ed., 1978).

77 At the beginning of the twentieth century (?) Meissen granted the firm of Teichert a licence to use the onion pattern. When Teichert closed in 1930, Hutschenreuther of Selb took over the licence. According to Danckert, 4th ed., 1978, it is also held by Metzel Brothers of Könitz in Thuringia.

78 *See* note 73.

79 The first lessee was a man who had been technical manager for many years, J. C. Proessel, together with a businessman partner, but they were replaced after only two years by new lessees, Heinrich Witte and Wilhelm Freitag, who were responsible for the factory's return to prosperity.

80 Some post-1861 Fürstenberg products are illustrated in Wolff Metternich, 1976, but the main source is Cat., Spies, 'Fürstenberger Porzellan. Empire–Gegenwart', 1972.

81 There is a Pirkenhammer service with Neo-Renaissance decoration in the Arts and Crafts Museum in Prague (*see* Cat., Brozŏvá, 'Historismus umelecké remeslo 1860–1900', 1975–1976, nos 136 f.).

82 On Popp, *see* Poche, 1956, pp. 53, 55; ills. 126 ff.

83 The *Thunsche Service* (Poche, 1956, ills. 38–40) is preserved in the collections of the Klösterle Castle Museum, an annexe of the Prague museum; the *Kaiser* Service is in Vienna, in the former Court Tableware and Silver Pantry (*see* Parenzin, 1980, ill. 24).

84 Wine-jug (1855) in Poche, 1956, ill. 55; state vase (1874) *ibid.*, ill. 54.

85 Falke, in Cat., 'Amtlicher Bericht…' 1867–1869, p. 112.

86 *Adressbuch der Keramischen Industrie,* 1883, p. 24.

87 *See* note above.

88 In addition to the literature referred to under Austria-Hungary (Herend), *see* Neuwirth, 1979, pp. 298 ff., 370.

89 Cf. Lassen, 1978, p. 16.

90 Wolf, 1906, p. 360.

91 *Ibid.*, pp. 373 ff.

92 V. de Boutovski, *Histoire de l'ornement russe du Xe au XVIe siècle d'après les manuscrits,* Musée d'art et d'industrie de Moscou, Paris and Moscow, 1970.

93 *See* Ross, 1968, pls. LXXXII, LXXVII, fig. 130.

94 There is no historical reason for this term. In 1757, when the Sèvres factory discovered the pink ground, Madame du Berry was not yet the mistress of Louis XV; furthermore, the same colour is often termed *rose Pompadour,* a name as unjustified as the first.

95 Sèvres, factory archives, portfolio T 5, L 1 to D 1.

96 Godden, 2nd ed., 1970, pp. 90–104.

97 *Ibid.*, p. 94.

98 *Ibid.*, p. 100. Mussill's name is not on the list of decorators at Sèvres compiled by Brunet, 1953.

99 London, V & A, inv. (281-1864).

100 Sèvres, inv. MNC (4178).

101  *See* Godden, 2nd ed., 1970, pp. 170–185.

102  The decorators working at Sèvres at the time were paid by the piece; therefore, those that worked quickly could do a second day's work for private factories or for themselves.

103  Sèvres, inv. MNC (7692), illustrated in Brunet and Préaud, 1978, p. 300, fig. 406.

104  Godden, 2nd ed., 1970, p. 176 and pp. 187 f.

105  *Ibid.*, p. 188.

106  *Ibid.*, p. 51.

107  *Ibid.*, p. 123.

108  Sandon, 1973, p. 5.

109  *See* Sandon, 1973.

110  *Ibid.*, p. 8.

111  *See* E. Aslin, *The Aesthetic Movement: Prelude to Art Nouveau,* New York, 1969.

112  *See* C. Piccolpasso, *Li tre libri dell' Art del Vasajo,* n.p., [published in the mid-16th century]. Translated and edited by B. Rackham and A. Van de Put, London: Victoria & Albert Museum, 1934.

113  Report quoted in Sandon, 1973, pp. 14 f.

114  Smith, 1979, p. 6 gives the date as 1857; Godden, 1974, p. 41 gives proof for a date of 1863.

## Chapter V

1  Sèvres, inv. MNC (7711).

2  Sèvres, inv. MNC (7702).

3  Sèvres, inv. MNC (9265).

4  Brunet and Préaud, 1978, p. 300, fig. 408.

5  Sèvres, inv. MNC (7662).

6  Sèvres, inv. MNC (7717).

7  Quoted in Lechevallier-Chevignard, 1908, part II, pp. 29 f.

8  Sèvres, inv. MNC (15 809).

9  Sèvres; the museum has not yet inventoried this part of its collections.

10  Albis and Romanet, 1980, p. 194.

11  *See* Lesur and Tardy, 1967.

12  Limoges, MAD, inv. ADL (3878).

13  Quoted in Du Pasquier, 1975–1976, p. 15.

14  Published in Bordeaux, 1852.

15  Quoted in Du Pasquier, 1975–1976, p. 16.

16  *See* H. Sarriau, 1900, pp. 193–196.

17  Albis and Romanet, 1980, p. 121, fig. 131 and p. 145, fig. 163.

18  Pelka, 1924, p. 69.

19  Quoted in Helsted, 1975, p. 37.

20  *Ibid.*, p. 50.

21  Cf. ills. 432–433. There are examples in many French collections but not, as far as I know, in the older German or Danish collections (*see* Hofmann, 2nd ed., 1980, ills. 293 a, b.).

22  Borrmann, [1902], ill. p. 81; originals lost since 1945.

23  Helsted, 1975, ills. 15 f.

24  According to the 'Berlin Protocol' (see p. 193), the committee of experts assembled in 1878 to advise the management of the Berlin factory also recommended greater exploitation of the possibilities of fire-proof decoration; quite obviously, however, as the reference to Meissen shows, they had in mind only the more saleable mass-produced lines such as onion-pattern ware.

25  *Sprechsaal*, XXI (1888): 671 f.

26  Garnier in Gonse and Lostalot, 1889, p. 489.

27  Helsted, 1975, fig. 10; Hofmann, 2nd ed., 1980, ill. 306. In the Copenhagen factory collection.

28  The most informative source on the various marks, model numbers, signatures, etc. is Cat., Bröhan, 1977, vol. II, part 2, p. 223.

29  For derivation from netsukes, *see* Woeckel, 1978, p. 36; the same source refers to the link with Japanese prints, proved by Leistikow-Duchardt, 1957, pls. IX, f.

30  Woeckel, 1978, p. 36.

31  Liisberg, in creating his first animals, was reminded of the procedure adopted by Bernard Palissy, who is known to have modelled small animals from nature. His works, however, with their highly stylized modelling and totally free painting, differ fundamentally from Palissy's veristic approach. Liisberg's remark is quoted in Leistikow-Duchardt, 1957, p. 97.

32  Far Eastern examples probably also underlay the stoneware work of Alexandre Bigot, who in 1897–1898 created bowls with lizards and frogs.

33  Krog's first and only service, the so-called Marguerite Service, dates from 1897. With its modelled flies and dragonflies, it is not a wholly successful piece of work (*see* Helsted, 1975, ill. 23).

34  The best source of illustrations are Lassen, 1978, and Cat., Bröhan, 1977, vol. II, part 2, pp. 195 ff.

35  In the other Scandinavian countries the factories of Porsgrund in Norway and Oy Arabia in Finland followed the new style from Denmark without achieving any artistic autonomy.

36  Borrmann, [1902], p. 97.

37  Just, typescript dissertation, 1972, p. 39.

38  In the Meissen exhibition room. *See* also Jedding, 1981, ill. 101, and Berling, reprint, 1972, figs. 309 f.

39  Berling, reprint, 1972, figs. 353 f.

40  Konrad (1872–1907) and Rudolf (1869–1951) Hentschel, sons of a Meissen figure painter, were the leading Art Nouveau artists actually employed by the factory. Their work and that of their contemporaries is described in monographs of Meissen artists contained in Just's typescript dissertation of 1972. The essential facts are reproduced in Jedding, 1981, index of persons, pp. 141 ff.

41  *See* note above.

42  All three services are illustrated in Jedding, 1981, pp. 100 f.

43  Established 1822. A page from an early nineteenth-century pattern catalogue is illustrated in Scherf, 1980, p. 398. On the factory's production programme, *see* Pelka, 1924, pp. 37–40.

44  Treskow, 1971, pp. 57 f.

45  Though not accepted for the wedding table, it was executed by the factory from 1908. For the intended arrangement of the centrepiece, *see* Treskow, 1971, ill. 188.

46  On the 'Schwarzburger Werkstätten', *see* Pelka, 1924, pp. 40 f. with ill., and Cat., Bröhan, 1977, vol. II, part 2, pp. 446 ff.

47  In 1978 Woeckel devoted a comprehensive publication specifically to Nymphenburg's animal sculpture; *see* Bibliography.

48  Hofmann, 2nd ed., 1980, ill. 313 b.

49  Cat., Bott and Heller, 'Jugendstil', 2nd ed., 1973, nos. 4, 5, 19, 27, 28, 30 ff., 62, 111.

50  On Selle in Burgau, see Fritz, *Keramos* XC (1980): 47–54.

51  Quoted in Just, 1972, p. 57.

52  The *Adressbuch der Keramischen Industrie...,* 5th ed., 1896, lists a firm in Krummnussbaum that had been producing pottery since 1865 and porcelain since 1875, including 'richly decorated luxury porcelains... vases, lamps... pots in fire-proof colours... Bünzli's enamel porcelain in gold cloisonné'. Factory mark: PB amalgamated.

53  *Sprechsaal* (1882): 191, 299, 466, 528; *Thonindustrie-Zeitung* (1881): 408 f. In his 1883 report Seger announced, in addition to the ox-blood glaze, a large number of monochrome coloured glazes that he used on Royal Factory porcelains. One of the most beautiful is a light-blue *clair de lune* shade. The other major factories also employed other coloured glazes in addition to *sang de bœuf,* one of the most spectacular being Copenhagen's 'tiger's-eye glaze' (*see* pl. 464).

54  *See* note above.

55  The 'Berlin Protocol', quoted in Treskow, 1971, p. 277.

56  Bodelsen, in Grandjean *et al.,* 1975, pp. 65 ff.

57  According to Just, 1972, note 102, this was probably a 'false' ox-blood glaze in which the reduction took place in the lighting-gas chamber subsequent to firing.

58  *Thonindustrie-Zeitung* (1883): 99 f.

59  Meissen was still producing very beautiful variants in the 1820s. Examples from the Pfeiffer period on show in the Meissen exhibition room.

60  In his 1972 dissertation on Meissen's Art Nouveau porcelains, Just is also critical of the factory's glazed porcelains, which strike him as 'inappropriate to the material'. His argument, which was of course on what led from muffle painting (which obscured the body) to underglaze painting, undoubtedly touches on a sore spot.

61  According to Ross, 1968, pp. 312 ff., Kornilov was a manufacturer of technically and artistically high-quality porcelains. From 1835 to 1885 the factory was managed by its founder, M. S. Kornilov, and subsequently by his sons, who traded as 'Kornilov Brothers'.

62  Again according to Ross, the technical quality of Kuznetsov's porcelains was superior to their artistic quality. On the Gardner mark: *see* Ross, 1968, p. 354.

63  Wolf, 1906, p. 364 (on the foregoing matter, *see* pp. 363 ff.).

64  On the history and marks of the Rozenburg factory and for illustrations, *see* Cat., Bröhan, 1977, vol. II, part 1, pp. 350 ff.

65  *Royal Crown Derby* (1976).

66  Twitchett and Bailey, 2nd ed., 1980, p. 59.

67  *Ibid.*, p. 61.

68  Eyles, 1980, p. 16.

# Catalogue of Porcelain Marks

The reference numbers in the captions refer to the numbers in this catalogue. Unless stated otherwise, the marks are in underglaze blue.

A great variety of marks were used on porcelain in the nineteenth century. Many factories changed their marks several times in the course of the century and were liable to continue using both old and new marks. Others applied an extremely complicated system of marks, the meaning of which can only be discovered by consulting the archives of the factory concerned. One example of this practice is the Vienna factory, which used the Habsburg shield as its mark between the end of the eighteenth century until its closure in 1864; in addition pieces from this factory were marked with a code letter indicating the date of the design, with the mark of the modeller or turner as well as that of the decorator, and with the sale price (see Neuwirth, 1979, p. 61). Marks on English porcelain had become especially complex by the end of the nineteenth century.

The Sèvres factory adopted a new mark at each change of ruler or political regime. Like Vienna, the French factory had a complicated system of codes that included incised marks often indicating the nature of the body and the date it was produced, painted marks used by the decorators and gilders, and the dates of manufacture and decoration. Collectors should consult books giving details of porcelain factory marks for further information; for example Marcelle Brunet has published a work entirely devoted to the marks used at the Sèvres factory (Paris, 1953) and see the Bibliography. However, it should be remembered that marks used by the major factories have frequently been copied with intent to deceive, and there are large number of pieces on the market 'in the style of' Sèvres, Meissen or Vienna with fake factory marks. A sound knowledge of the products of these factories is the only means of correctly identifying them, since this cannot be done on the basis of factory marks alone. There are few short cuts to identifying porcelain. Some of these 'rules of thumb' as applied to Sèvres are given below:

—The Sèvres factory *never* marked the inner surface of lids. Every piece with a mark inside the lid is therefore a fake. Sèvres porcelains are marked only on the base, or inside the neck in the case of large vases.

—Interlaced LLs (the monogram of Louis XV and later of Louis XVI) were used only on porcelains made during the eighteenth century. Pieces with this mark which are clearly nineteenth century in style are fakes. Pieces marked with interlaced LLs enclosing 'S' should be treated with special caution, since forgers have been particularly fond of using this mark. As a general rule fake pieces are in the style of a period later than that indicated by the mark they bear.

—Pieces bearing the mark of the royal residences and with dates between 1815 and 1845 should be regarded with extreme caution. Items with these marks *à la vignette* were in great demand and forgeries were therefore often made. However authentic pieces with these marks do exist.

Large factories such as Meissen and Sèvres sold undecorated blanks during the nineteenth century. These were purchased by outside decorators who painted them for resale. It is sometimes possible to identify such pieces as their factory marks may be partially ground away.

Finally, certain well-known factories (e.g. Herend in Hungary, Samson of Paris, Coalport in Great Britain) systematically copied pieces of an earlier period, at times producing porcelain of an extremely high quality.

As far as possible we have attempted to reproduce here the marks on—or under—the pieces illustrated in this book. However in some cases, particularly for Russia and Bohemia, the marks could not be ascertained.

## FRANCE

### Bayeaux

*Veuve Langlois*

1 painted in red
(under the cover)

painted
(on the base)

### Bordeaux

*J. Vieillard & Cie*

2 painted in green
(above the base)

### Bourg-la-Reine

*E. Chaplet studio*

3 incised

### Caen

*Aigmont-Desmares*

4 painted in gold

### Limoges

*Henri Ardant*

5 in relief with stamp
or blue biscuit
porcelain

*G.D.A. (Gérard,
Dufraisseix, and Abbot)*

6 printed in green
(factory mark)

7 printed in green
(mark of the
retailer, Samuel [or
Siegfried] Bing,
'Art Nouveau')

*G.D.M. (Gérard,
Dufraisseix, and Morel)*

8 printed in green

*Gibus & Cie*

9 printed in dark
green
(on the base of the
ewer)

10 printed

---

*Haviland & Co*

11 printed

12 impressed

printed in dark
green

printed in maroon

printed in maroon

13 printed in red

signature printed in
red
(in the decoration)

*Pouyat*

14 printed in dark
green

15 printed in green

### Mehun-sur-Yèvre

*Charles Pillivuyt & Cie*

16 printed in dark
green

### Paris

*Caron and Lefèbvre*

17 painted in gold

*Clauss*

18 in relief
(under the teapot,
sugar bowl, and
cream jug)

*Dagoty*

19 painted in gold
(under the cup)

20 painted in gold
(under the cup)

21 impressed

22 painted in gold
(under the cup)

---

*Darte*

23 printed in red

24 printed in red

*Denuelle*

25 painted
(under the cup)

painted in gold
(under the cup)

printed in red,
partially obliterated,
for rue de Crussol in
Paris
(under the saucer)

*Deroche*

26 printed in red

*Dihl and Guérhard*

27 printed in red

28 painted
(under the cup and
the saucer)

29 painted

*Faugeron [decorating
workshop]*

30 painted

*Honoré*

31 printed in red

32 printed in black

*Nast*

33 painted in gold

34 impressed

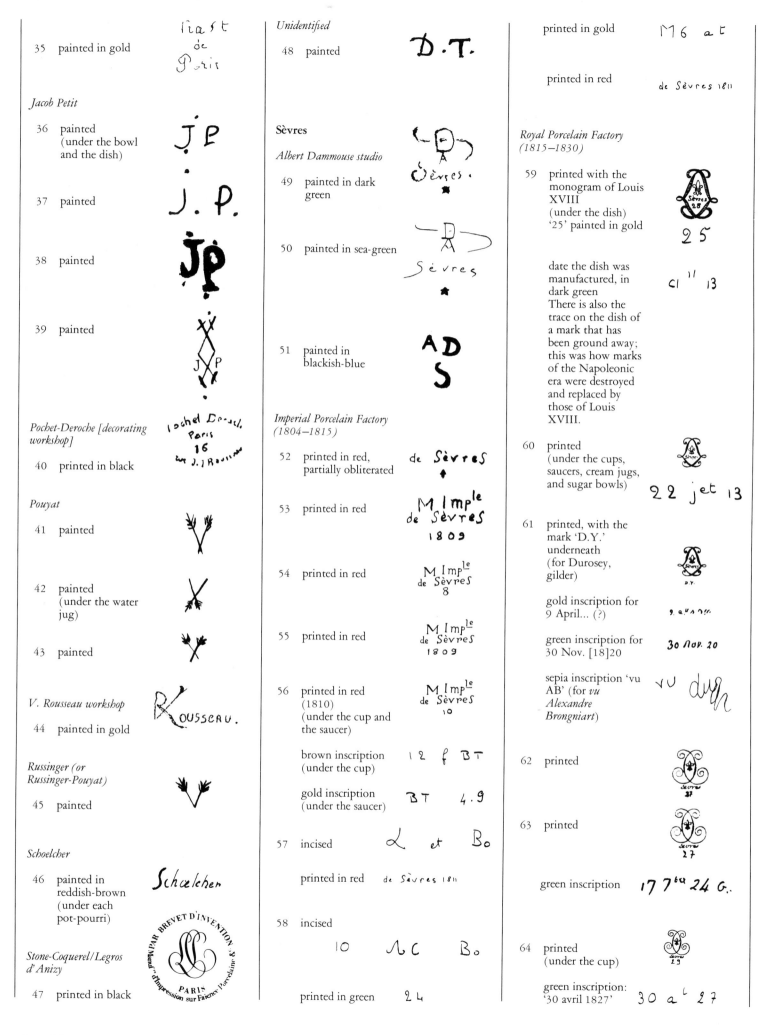

35  painted in gold  *Fiast de Paris*

### Jacob Petit

36  painted
(under the bowl
and the dish)  **J P**

37  painted  **J. P.**

38  painted  **JP**

39  painted  **JP**

### Pochet-Deroche [decorating workshop]

40  printed in black  *Pochet Deroch. Paris 16 en J. J Rousseau*

### Pouyat

41  painted

42  painted
(under the water
jug)

43  painted

### V. Rousseau workshop

44  painted in gold  *Rousseau.*

### Russinger (or Russinger-Pouyat)

45  painted

### Schoelcher

46  painted in
reddish-brown
(under each
pot-pourri)  *Schœlcher*

PAR BREVET D'INVENTION & Man.re d'Impression sur Faïence Porcelaine PARIS

### Stone-Coquerel / Legros d'Anizy

47  printed in black

---

### Unidentified

48  painted  **D.T.**

### Sèvres

#### Albert Dammouse studio

49  painted in dark
green  *Sèvres.*

50  painted in sea-green  *Sèvres*

51  painted in
blackish-blue  **A D S**

#### Imperial Porcelain Factory (1804–1815)

52  printed in red,
partially obliterated  *de Sèvres*

53  printed in red  *M Imp.le de Sèvres 1809*

54  printed in red  *M Imp.le de Sèvres 8*

55  printed in red  *M Imp.le de Sèvres 1809*

56  printed in red
(1810)
(under the cup and
the saucer)  *M Imp.le de Sèvres 10*

brown inscription
(under the cup)  *12 f BT*

gold inscription
(under the saucer)  *BT 4.9*

57  incised  *∝ et Bo*

printed in red  *de Sèvres 1811*

58  incised  *10 ∿C Bo*

printed in green  *24*

---

printed in gold  *M 6 at*

printed in red  *de Sèvres 1811*

### Royal Porcelain Factory (1815–1830)

59  printed with the
monogram of Louis
XVIII
(under the dish)
'25' painted in gold  *25*

date the dish was
manufactured, in
dark green
There is also the
trace on the dish of
a mark that has
been ground away;
this was how marks
of the Napoleonic
era were destroyed
and replaced by
those of Louis
XVIII.  *cl 11 13*

60  printed
(under the cups,
saucers, cream jugs,
and sugar bowls)  *22 jet 13*

61  printed, with the
mark 'D.Y.'
underneath
(for Durosey,
gilder)

gold inscription for
9 April... (?)

green inscription for
30 Nov. [18]20  *30 Nov. 20*

sepia inscription 'vu
AB' (for *vu
Alexandre
Brongniart*)  *vu dur*

62  printed

63  printed

green inscription  *177 bu 24 G..*

64  printed
(under the cup)

green inscription:
'30 avril 1827'  *30 a l 27*

gold inscription: 'D.Y.' (for Durosey, gilder)

65 printed (under the saucer)

green inscription: '15 décembre 1826'

gold inscription

*Royal Porcelain Factory (1830–1848)*

66 printed

green inscription

gold inscription

67 printed (under the tray)

68 printed (under the teapot)

printed

monogram painted in gold

69 printed (under the sugar bowl)

printed

green inscription

70 printed

71 inscription painted in green

*National Porcelain Factory under the Second Republic (1848–1852)*

72 decorator's mark printed in red (on the neck)

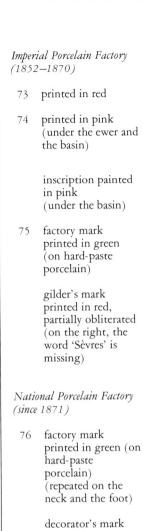

*Imperial Porcelain Factory (1852–1870)*

73 printed in red

74 printed in pink (under the ewer and the basin)

inscription painted in pink (under the basin)

75 factory mark printed in green (on hard-paste porcelain)

gilder's mark printed in red, partially obliterated (on the right, the word 'Sèvres' is missing)

*National Porcelain Factory (since 1871)*

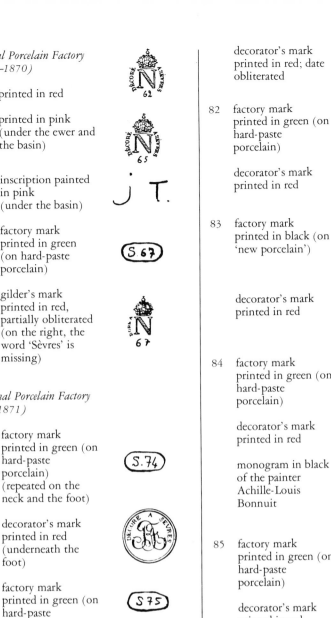

76 factory mark printed in green (on hard-paste porcelain) (repeated on the neck and the foot)

decorator's mark printed in red (underneath the foot)

77 factory mark printed in green (on hard-paste porcelain)

decorator's mark printed in red

78 factory mark printed in green (on hard-paste porcelain) (on the foot and the neck)

decorators' marks printed in red

79 printed (Lauth-Vogt porcelain)

80 factory mark printed in green (on hard-paste porcelain)

decorator's mark printed in red (on the neck and the foot)

81 factory mark printed in green (on hard-paste porcelain)

decorator's mark printed in red; date obliterated

82 factory mark printed in green (on hard-paste porcelain)

decorator's mark printed in red

83 factory mark printed in black (on 'new porcelain')

decorator's mark printed in red

84 factory mark printed in green (on hard-paste porcelain)

decorator's mark printed in red

monogram in black of the painter Achille-Louis Bonnuit

85 factory mark printed in green (on hard-paste porcelain)

decorator's mark printed in red

monogram in gold of the painter Louis Trager

86 printed in black (on 'new porcelain')

87 printed in black (on 'new porcelain')

88 printed in black (on 'new porcelain')

89 printed in black (on 'new porcelain')

90 incised (in the pleats of the robe) DN = 'new hard-paste porcelain'

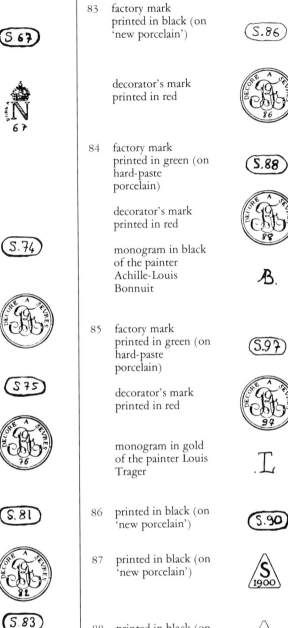

initials of Charles Villion, caster-repairer

$CV$

SEVRES

91  incised
(in the pleats of the robe)

S
1914
DN

mark of the caster-repairer (?)

$C$

SEVRES

92  incised

S
1914
DN

initials of Charles Robert, caster-repairer

$C$ $R$

SEVRES

93  two marks superimposed; on the inside, the factory mark 'S 1900', printed under the glaze in light blue; on the outside, the decorator's mark 'DECORE A SEVRES R 1901 F', printed under the glaze in light blue. The light blue signifies that the piece was made in soft-paste porcelain.

monogram in grey of the gilder Henri Uhlrich

$\mathcal{HU}.$

94  printed in black (on 'new porcelain')

(?) Forger

95  painted in two different blues (under the tray) The double L mark seems to be a forgery; the S probably stands for Soiron, who decorated this *déjeuner*.

*Optat Milet studio*

96  incised

*André Thesmar*

97  gold and black enamels by Thesmar. Thesmar decorated Sèvres porcelain at his own workshop on the factory premises.

1895

## BELGIUM

### Brussels (Liège)

*Van Marcke*

98  painted in gold (under the teapot)

C.E.C. Van Marcke.

## SWITZERLAND

### Nyon

*Dortu & Cie (or Bonnard, Veret & Cie, or Dortu, Soulier, Veret & Cie)*

99  painted fish mark, (several variations)

## ITALY

### Doccia

*Ginori (Lorenzo Ginori period)*

100  painted in gold

100a  printed

MANIFATTURA ✳ GINORI

### Milan

*Jules Richard*

101  incised

102  incised

### Naples

*Royal Naples Factory (1771–1806)*

103  incised

N  6

### Le Nove

*Antonibon (G. Baroni period)*

104  initials of Giovanni Baroni painted in the decoration

G.B. NOVE

## PORTUGAL

### Vista Alegre

*Ferreira Pinto & Filhos*

105  printed

VA

106  painted in gold

F.A.

## AUSTRIA

### Vienna

*Royal Imperial Porcelain Factory (1718–1864)*

marks with the Habsburg coat of arms in underglaze blue or impressed. Generally accompanied by embosser and white-thrower numbers, year (abbreviated), painter mark

107  pre-1824 and post-1860

108  c. 1790–1827

109  impressed 1827–1860

## BOHEMIA
(now Czechoslovakia)

### Elbogen
(now Loket nad Ohři)

*Haidinger Bros.*

110  painted 1815–1833

111  impressed 1833–1860

### Giesshübel
(now Struzná)

*Benedikt Knaute*

112  impressed 1815–1840

BK

### Klösterle
(now Klåštěrec nad Ohři)

*Count Thun's Porcelain Factory*

monogram marks

| 113 | impressed 1839–1870 |  |

### Pirkenhammer
(now Brezová)

*Fischer & Reichenbach (1810–1845), J.M. Fischer (1845–1853) and Fischer & Mieg (1853–1918)*
various monograms, painted or impressed; also crossed hammers in the second half of the century

| 114 | 1810–1853 |  |
| 115 | post-1853 |  |

### Schlaggenwald
(now Slavkov)

*Lippert & Haas (1808–1847), Haas & Czižek (1867–1945)*

mark with Schlaggenwald S or owners' names and place name; occasionally date as well

| 116 | until 1830, impressed, coloured or gilt | |
| 117 | impressed 1830–1870 | |
| 118 | c. 1830–1847 | |
| 119 | 1847–1867 | |
| 120 | from 1867 |  |

---

GERMANY

### Berlin

*Imperial Porcelain Factory (KPM) (1763–1919)*

marks with sceptres; from 1837 additional KPM or Prussian eagle; painter marks: pre-1832 stroke, post-1832 imperial orb

| 121 | 1780–1800 | |


| 122 | c. 1800, variants |  |
| 123 | c. 1815–1840, variants |  |
| 124 | c. 1837–1844 |  **KPM** |
| 125 | 1849–1870 |  |
| 126 | 1870–1945 |  |
| 127 | from 1882, special mark for Seger porcelain |  |
| 128 | from 1832, additional red mark for painted porcelain |  **KPM** |

*J.F.F. Schumann (1835–1869 ?)*

various marks designed to be confused with those of the KPM, Berlin, above

| 129 | c. 1835–1840 (?) |  |

### Fürstenberg

*The Duke of Brunswick's Porcelain Factory (est. 1747, 1807–1813 Royal, from 1876 the Fürstenberg Porcelain Factory)*

| 130 | 18th and 19th centuries | *F* |

### Gotha, Thuringia

*Private factory, with various owners*

R, G and Gotha variants as marks

| 131 | pre-1802 | R |

### Grossbreitenbach, Thuringia

*Greiner family and other owners*

| 132 | clover-leaf mark, as in all other Greiner factories (Ilmenau, later Rauenstein, Veilsdorf, etc.) |  |


### Lichte, Thuringia

*Heubach Bros.*

| 132a | from 1904 |  |

### Ilmenau, Thuringia

*Private factory*

marks with clover leaf or letter I

| 133 | 19th century |  |

### Meissen

*Royal Porcelain Factory (1710–1919, from 1919 National Factory, from 1945 VEB)*

In the 19th century all marks had the crossed swords, often with additional small painters' marks, etc.

| 134 | 1774–1814 under Marcolini |  |
| 135 | 1817–1823/1824 with paste-quality numbers I–III |  |
| 136 | c. 1814–1860 hand-painted, 1860–1924 stamped, usually, with recognizably enlarged pommels |  |

### Nymphenburg

*Royal Porcelain Factory (est. 1747 as Electoral, from 1806–1862 Royal)*

variants of the Bavarian coat of arms, pre-1921 as impressed marks

| 137 | 19th century, pre-1862 |   |
| 138 | 1862–1921 |  |

### Rauenstein, Thuringia

*Friedrich Christian Greiner & Sons*

R, R n variants and crossed flags, like the Gotha and Volkstedt marks

|  |  | |
| 139 | 140 | 141 |

## Selb

*Philip Rosenthal*

marks with monogram
or full name and crown;
many variants

142   *c.* 1900

## Sitzendorf, Thuringia

*Vogt Bros.*

variants of crossed straight
lines

143   second half of 19th
century

## Tiefenfurt, Silesia
(now Parowa, Poland)

mark imitating the initials of the KPM,
Berlin

143a   19th century

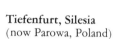

---

## DENMARK

### Copenhagen

*Bing & Grøndahl*

B & G monogram, three-towered gateway,
variants of city and country names in blue or
other colours; additional painters' marks

144   1854–1864

145   from 1854

*Royal Danish Porcelain Factory*

mark with three wavy lines in many variants;
additionally a crown and the name of the city
and country

146   19th century

147   post-1889

---

### Gorbunovo
(Dmitrov District near
Moscow)

*Alexander Popov*

marks with whole name or monogram in
Cyrillic letters

148   1811–1875

### Novocharitonovo
(Korotkaia, Dulevo, etc.)

*Kuznetsov Bros.*

exceptionally large number
of different marks
with name, eagle, etc.

149   19th century

149a   19th century

### Rechitsa
(Gzhel' District)

*A.L. Kiselev*

marks with full name
or monogram in Cyrillic
letters, 1832–1860

150   mid-19th century

### St Petersburg
*Sergey Batenin*

marks with Cyrillic B

151   1812–1839

*Imperial Porcelain Factory
(1763–1917)*

marks with the monogram of the reigning
tsar and imperial crown

152   1801–1825
      (Alexander I)

153   1825–1855
      (Nicholas I)

154   1855–1881
      (Alexander II);
      variant in green

*Savin Vasilevich Kornilov (1835, 1893–1917
Kornilov Bros.)*

various marks with full name in Cyrillic
letters; for export pieces, Russian bear and
English designation; also eagle marks

---

155   19th century

### Verbilki
(near Moscow)

*Francis Gardner*

many different marks; the Gardner G in
various scripts

156   18th and 19th
      centuries

---

## HUNGARY

### Herend

*Moritz Fischer*

name of the town, owner and coat of arms,
variants

157   19th century

---

## SWEDEN

### Rörstrand/Lidköping

*Porslin Fabriker
(1797–present day)*

marks in 19th century with
full name and often crowns

158   late 19th century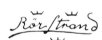

---

## NETHERLANDS

### Rozenburg

*Haagsche Plateelbakkerij, The Hague*

marks with the coat of arms of The Hague
(stork), crown, names of firm and city, and
always year, artist, and model marks

159   1899–1913

---

## GREAT BRITAIN

### Belleek (Ireland)

*D. McBirney & Co*

160   incised        BELLEEK

161   printed        BELLEEK
                     CO. FERMANAGH

---

162 printed

## Burslem

*Samuel Alcock & Co. Hill Pottery*

163 mark dating the registration of the motif: 20 February 1844

164 printed

165 printed

166 printed

S. A. & CO.

## Coalport

*John Rose & Co*

167 printed in red

168 printed

169 painted

170 painted in blue with 'C 204' in red

## Derby

*Duesbury & Kean—Robert Bloor & Co*

We are unable to reproduce here the marks of all the Derby pieces illustrated. Most of the marks were hand painted in the traditional 18th-century manner. They are all the same and yet all different, depending on the care taken in drawing them. For the period that interests us the marks were usually painted in red (before 1806 some were painted in blue or purple). We have assembled under no. 171 several examples taken from Barrett and Thorpe, 1971.

171

*Robert Bloor & Co*

172 printed in red

173 printed in red

174 printed in red

*Derby Crown Porcelain Company*

175 printed

## Etruria

*Josiah Wedgwood & Sons*

176 printed in red

**WEDGWOOD**

painted in red (on the cover and the base)

470

## Lane Delph

*Miles Mason*

MILES MASON

177 printed with an imitation-Chinese mark

## Liverpool

*Case, Mort & Co, Herculaneum Pottery*

178 printed in red

*Herculaneum Pottery Company*

179 incised

HERCULANEUM

## Longport/Burslem

*Davenport*

180 printed

181 printed in red

DAVENPORT LONGPORT

## Nantgarw (Wales)

*China Works*

182 incised (on one of the two plates, for Nantgarw China Works)

NANT GARW C. W.

## Shelton

*New Hall*

183 printed

## Shelton/Hanley

*Ridgway-Bates & Co*

184 printed

J RIDGWAY BATES & CO.

## Stoke-on-Trent

*Colin Minton Campbell (see also nos 209, 210)*

185 in relief

incised

MINTON

incised

inscription printed in black

*Minton and Co Modelled 1847 Manufactured 1865*

186 printed in red

incised

MINTON

incised sign for 1865

187 incised

MINTON

incised sign for 1868 (with a Minton mark and a retailer's mark printed in purple)

188 printed

189 printed in gold

| | | |
|---|---|---|
| 190 | printed in gold | *(Prince of Wales feathers with "PARIS EXHIBITION 1878" ribbon, MINTONS)* |
| | incised | MINTONS |
| | incised sign for 1878 | *(triangle mark)* |
| | Minton shape number 7348 | 7348 |
| 191 | printed in gold | *(crown and globe, MINTONS)* |
| | incised sign for 1888 (with the mark of the retailer, T. Goode & Co) | *(bow/infinity mark)* |
| 192 | printed in gold | *(crown and globe, MINTONS, ENGLAND)* |
| | incised | MINTONS |
| | incised sign for 1901 | *(circle with 1)* |
| 193 | printed | *(crown and globe, MINTONS)* |
| | incised | MINTONS |
| | incised sign for 1873 | *(cross/X mark)* |
| 194 | incised | MINTON |

*W.T. Copeland/Spode*

| | | |
|---|---|---|
| 195 | printed in green | COPELAND S CHINA ENGLAND |
| | painted in red | V125 S |

*W.T. Copeland & Garrett*

| | | |
|---|---|---|
| 196 | incised | COPELAND |

*W.T. Copeland & Sons*

| | | |
|---|---|---|
| 197 | printed in green | *(ornate monogram)* COPELAND |
| 198 | printed | COPELAND'S CHINA ENGLAND |
| 199 | printed in brown | COPELAND'S CHINA |

*W.T. Copeland, late Spode*

| | | |
|---|---|---|
| 200 | incised 'Beatrice' | COPELAND |
| 201 | incised | COPELAND A R. Monti |
| 202 | printed | *(ornate monogram)* COPELAND |
| 203 | printed in green | *(CC monogram)* COPELAND |

*Henry & Richard Daniel*

| | | |
|---|---|---|
| 204 | printed | *(royal arms, H. & R. DANIEL)* |

*Herbert Minton & Co*

| | | |
|---|---|---|
| 205 | incised (on the base) | **MINTON** |
| | incised sign for 1866 | X |
| | incised number of the figure and signature of Bell, who made the piece | 245 |
| | incised title of the work | MIRANDA |
| | incised, signifying that it was ordered by Felix Summerly | S |

*Minton*

| | | |
|---|---|---|
| 206 | painted (with pattern number) | *(ermine mark)* 85 |
| 207 | painted | *(ermine mark with M)* 816 |
| 208 | painted | *(ermine mark with M)* |

*Colin Minton Campbell (See also nos 185–194)*

| | | |
|---|---|---|
| 209 | printed | *(JOHN MORTLOCK, OXFORD STREET, LONDON 1880 circular mark)* |
| | incised | ( 18 MINTON 80 ) |

| | | |
|---|---|---|
| 210 | painted in gold | 10. 1. 1895 |
| | incised sign for 1893 | *(shield with 3)* |
| | incised | MINTONS |

*W.T. Copeland/Spode (see also no. 195)*

| | | |
|---|---|---|
| 211 | painted in red | *Spode* |
| 212 | printed in red (underneath THE LONDON, in a ribbon) | *(Spode Felspar Porcelain wreath)* |
| 213 | painted in brown | SPODE |
| 214 | painted in red | SPODE 1166 |
| 215 | painted | SPODE 2114 |
| 216 | printed in red (on the plate) | *(Spode Felspar Porcelain wreath)* |
| | painted (on the sugar bowl) | SPODE 4485 |
| | incised | *(circle with cross)* |
| 217 | painted in red | SPODE |

**Swansea (Wales)**

*Bevington & Co*

| | | |
|---|---|---|
| 218 | incised | BEVINGTON & CO. SWANSEA I. W. |

*Dillwyn & Co*

| | | |
|---|---|---|
| 219 | painted in red | *Swansea* |
| 220 | incised | SWANSEA |
| 221 | printed in red (on the tray) | SWANSEA |

**Swinton**

*Brameld & Co, Rockingham Works*

| | | |
|---|---|---|
| 222 | printed in purple | *(griffin, Rockingham Works Brameld)* |

| | | | |
|---|---|---|---|
| 223 | printed in red; date in gold: 1832 (on plate only) | | |

224 printed in purple

## Worcester

*Robert Chamberlain*

225 painted

*Chamberlains. Worcester*

226 painted in gold

*Chamberlains Worcester*

227 mark consisting of the Prince of Wales's feathers above the inscription (under the tureen and in the cover)

*Chamberlains Worcester Porcelain manufacturer to H. Ro. H. The Prince Regent*

228 with both marks and inscriptions (under the cups)

*Windsor new part Chamberlain's Worcester*

*Frogmore Chamberlain's Worcester*

---

*Flight*

229 painted

*Flight, Barr & Barr*

230 incised

231 painted

BARR FLIGHT . & BARR
ROYAL PORCELAIN WORKS
WORCESTER

LONDON HOUSE
Nº I COVENTRY STREET

incised

*James Hadley*

232 printed in mauve

incised   S C

painted   X 1

---

*Kerr & Binns*

233 printed

*Worcester Royal Porcelain Company (Royal Worcester)*

234 printed

235 printed

236 incised

237 printed

238 incised

# Nineteenth-Century Porcelain Factories

1   Sèvres
2   Paris
3   Sceaux
4   Bourg-la-Reine
5   Chantilly
6   Caen
7   Bayeux
8   Valognes
9   Limoges
10  Bordeaux
11  Toulouse
12  Niderviller
13  Tournai
14  Brussels
15  Nyon
16  Vinovo
17  Turin
18  Milan
19  Le Nove
20  Doccia
21  Rome
22  {Capodimonte
    {Naples

23  Madrid
24  Vista Alegre
25  Meissen
26  Vienna
27  Nymphenburg
28  Prague
29  Schlaggenwald
30  Klösterle
31  Giesshübel
32  Pirkenhammer
33  Herend (Hungary)
34  Gotha
35  Sitzendorf/Rudlstadt
36  Ilmenau
37  Grossbreitenbach
38  Lichte (near Neuhaus)
39  Rauenstein
40  Tiefenfurt (Silesia)
41  Fürstenberg
42  Berlin
43  Rörstrand
44  Copenhagen
45  The Hague

46  St Peterburg
47  {Verbilki
    {Novocharitonovo
    {Rechitsa
    {Gorbunovo
48  London
49  Derby
50  Worcester
51  Nantgarw (Wales)
52  Swansea (Wales)
53  Caughley-Coalport
54  Longton
55  Lane Delph
56  Stoke-on-Trent
57  Shelton
58  Etruria
59  Hanley
60  Burslem
61  Longport
62  Liverpool
63  Swinton
64  Belleek (Ireland)

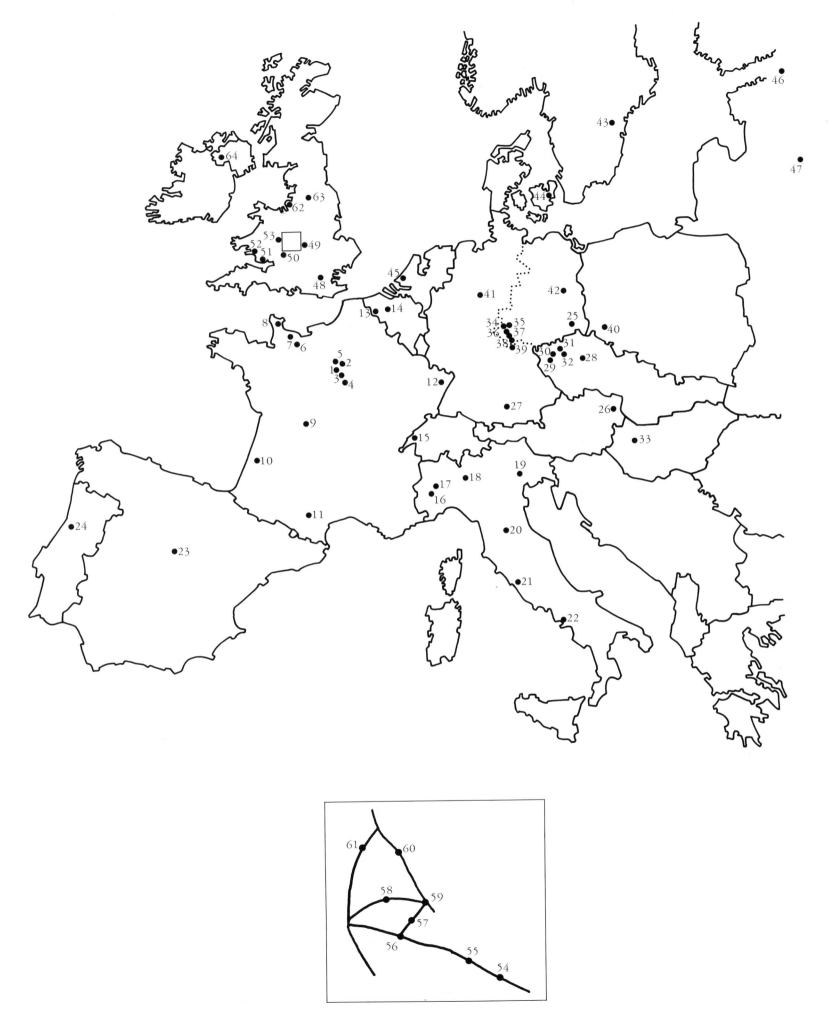

MAP 289

# Bibliography

GENERAL WORKS

Adressbuch der Keramischen Industrie... in Deutschland und Österreich-Ungarn. Ed. by Sprechsaal 8, 1883. 5th ed. Coburg, 1896.

Ainaud de Lasarte, Jean. Cerámica y vidro. Ars Hispaniae, vol. X. Madrid: Editorial Ultra, 1952.

Alfassa, Paul and Guérin, Jacques. Porcelaine française du XVII^ème au milieu du XIX^ème siècle. Paris: A. Lévy, 1931.

Arnaud, D. and Franche, Georges. Manuel de céramique industrielle. 1906. 2nd ed. Paris, 1922.

Auscher, Ernest-Simon. Les Céramiques cuisant à haute température. Paris, 1899.

Baer, W. 'Die Porzellankunst des Empire.' In Hofmann, Friedrich Hermann. Das Porzellan der europäischen Manufakturen. Propyläen-Kunstgeschichte, sp. vol. I. 2nd enlarged ed., rev. by V. E. Kemp. Frankfurt, Berlin, Vienna: Propyläen-Verlag, 1980, pp. 213–226.

Bastenaire-Daudenart, F. L'Art de fabriquer les poteries communes usuelles... Paris, 1835.

Bemrose, Geoffrey. Nineteenth Century English Pottery and Porcelain. London: Faber & Faber, 1952.

Blacker, J.F. The A.B.C. of English Ceramic Art: 19th Century. London: St. Paul, 1911.

Bladen, V.W. 'The Potteries in the Industrial Revolution.' Economic History I, 117 (1926).

Blondel, Nicole. 'L'Or de Limoges.' L'Estampille 100 (Sept., 1979): 40–49.

Borrmann, Richard. Moderne Keramik. Monographien des Kunstgewerbes, vol. 5. Leipzig, [1902].

Boyer. Manuel du porcelainier, du faïencier et du potier de terre, suivi de l'art de fabriquer les terres anglaises et de pipe. 2 vols. Paris, 1827.

Brongniart, Alexandre. Traité des arts céramiques ou des poteries considérées dans leur histoire, leur pratique et leur théorie... 3 vols. and 1 atlas. 1844; 2nd ed. rev., corrected and enlarged with notes by Alphonse Salvetat [in 1 vol.], 1854; 3rd ed. with notes by Alphonse Salvetat, 1877; 4th ed. Paris: Dessain & Tolra, 1977.

— and Riocreux, Denis Désiré. Description méthodique du musée céramique de la manufacture royale de porcelaine de Sèvres. 2 vols. Paris: Leleux, 1845.

Brosio, Valentino. Porcellane e maioliche italiane dell'Ottocento. Milan: A. Vallardi, 1960.

Chaffers, William. Marks and Monograms on Pottery and Porcelain.... 1863. 13th ed. rev. and augmented by Frederick Litchfield and Reeves S. Turner. London: J. Davy & Sons, 1930.

Charleston, Robert, J., ed. English Porcelain 1745–1850. London and Toronto: Ernest Benn, 1965.

—. ed. World Ceramics: An Illustrated History by John Ayers and Others. London, New York, Sydney, Toronto: Hamlyn and McGraw, 1968.

—. English Ceramics 1580–1830. London: Sotheby Parke Bernet, 1977.

Chavagnac, Xavier de and Grollier, Gaston de. Histoire des manufactures françaises de porcelaine. Paris: A. Picard, 1906.

Corona, G. L'Italia ceramica: Esposizione Industriale italiana del 1881 in Milano: Relazioni dei Giurati. Milan, 1885.

Cox, W.E. Book of Pottery and Porcelain. 3 vols. New York: Crown, 1947.

Cushion, John Patrick and Honey, William Bowyer. Handbook of Pottery and Porcelain Marks. London: Faber & Faber, 1956.

Dahlbäck Luttemann, Helena. Svenskt porslin: fajans, porslin och flint gods 1700–1900. Västeras: Ica-bokförl., 1980.

Danckert, Ludwig. Handbuch des europäischen Porzellans. 1954. 4th enlarged ed. Munich: Prestel, 1978.

—. Le nouveau Danckert: Manuel de la porcelaine européenne. Trans. by Tamara Préaud. 5th ed. augmented. Fribourg: Office du Livre, 1980.

Dodd, Arthur Edward. Dictionary of Ceramics: Pottery, Glass, Vitreous Enamels... London: Philosophical Library, 1964.

Dubreuil, Alfred. Encyclopédie chimique. Vol. 5: Applications de chimie inorganique: La Porcelaine. Paris, 1885.

Ehret, Gloria, ed. Porzellan: Battenberg Antiquitäten-Kataloge. Munich: Battenberg, 1979.

Ernould Gandouet, Marielle. La Céramique en France au XIX^e siècle. Paris: Gründ, 1969.

Fisher, Stanley William. English Ceramics: Earthenware, Delft, Stoneware, Creamware, Porcelain... London: Ward & Lock, 1966.

Godden, Geoffrey Arthur. 'English Pâte sur Pâte Porcelain'. The Connoisseur (June, 1954).

—. Victorian Porcelain. 1961. 2nd ed., London: Barrie & Jenkins, 1970.

—. British Pottery and Porcelain 1780–1850. London: Barker, 1964.

—. Encyclopaedia of British Pottery and Porcelain Marks. London: Barrie & Jenkins, 1964.

—. An Illustrated Encyclopedia of British Pottery and Porcelain. 1966. 2nd ed. London: Barrie & Jenkins, 1980.

—. The Handbook of British Pottery and Porcelain Marks. London: Barrie & Jenkins, 1968.

—. British Porcelain: An Illustrated Guide. 1974. 2nd ed. entitled Godden's Guide to English Porcelain. London: Granada, 1978.

Gonse, L. and Lostalot A. de, eds. Exposition Universelle de 1889—Les Beaux-Arts et les Arts Décoratifs. Paris, 1889.

Graesse, Johann G.T. and Jaennicke, E. Friedrich. Führer für Sammler von Porzellan und Fayence, Steinzeug, Steingut usw. Dresden, 1864. 23rd ed. Brunswick: Klinkhardt & Biermann, 1976.

Granger, Albert. La Céramique industrielle. Chimie. Technologie. 2 vols. Paris: Gauthier-Villars, 1929.

Grollier, Charles de. Manuel de l'amateur de porcelaines: Manufactures européennes (France exceptée). Paris: A. Picard, 1914.

Haggar, Reginald G. The Concise Encyclopaedia of Continental Pottery and Porcelain. London: André Deutsch, 1960.

Hannover, Emil. Pottery and Porcelain: A Handbook for Collectors.... Trans. by W.W. Worster. Ed. with notes by B. Rackham. London: Ernest Benn, 1925.

Havard, Henry. La Céramique (Histoire. Fabrication). 2 vols. Paris, 1894.

Hillier, Bevis. Pottery and Porcelain, 1700–1914: England, Europe and North America. London: Weidenfeld, 1968.

Hofmann, Friedrich Hermann. Das Porzellan der europäischen Manufakturen. Propyläen-Kunstgeschichte, sp. vol. I. 2nd ed. rev. by E. Kemp. Berlin: Propyläen-Verlag, 1980.

Honey, William Bowyer. Old English Porcelain: A Handbook for Collectors. 1928. 3rd ed. rev. by Franklin Allen Barrett. London: Faber & Faber, 1977.

—. English Pottery and Porcelain. 1933. 5th ed. rev. by Robert J. Charleston. London: Black, 1962.

—. European Ceramic Art from the End of the Middle Ages to about 1815. 2 vols. Vol 1: Illustrated Historical Survey; Vol. 2: A Dictionary of Factories, Artists, Technical Terms... London: Faber & Faber, 1949; 1952.

Hughes, George Bernard and Hughes, Therle. *English Porcelain and Bone China, 1743–1850.* London: Lutterworth Press, 1955.

Hunt, Leslie B. 'The Origin of English Silver Lustre.' *The Connoisseur,* CC, 805 (March, 1976): 185–190.

Jacquemart, Albert and Le Blant, Edmond. *Histoire artistique, industrielle et commerciale de la porcelaine...* [Lyons]: Perrin, 1861–1862.

Jacquemart, Albert. *Les Merveilles de la céramique.* 3 vols. Paris: Hachette, 1866–1869.

——. *Histoire de la céramique: Etude descriptive et raisonnée...* Paris: Hachette, 1873.

Jaennicke, Friedrich. *Grundriss der Keramik in Bezug auf das Kunstgewerbe: Eine historische Darstellung...* Stuttgart, 1879.

——. *Handbuch der Porzellan-, Steingut- und Fayence-Malerei über und unter Glasur in ihren verschiedenen älteren und neueren Abarten.* Stuttgart, 1898.

Jewitt, Llewellyn. *The Ceramic Art of Great Britain...* 2 vols. 1877. Rev. ed. by Geoffrey Arthur Godden, *Jewitt's Ceramic Art of Great Britain, 1800–1900.* London: Barrie & Jenkins, 1972.

*Keramos: Zeitschrift der Gesellschaft der Keramikfreunde e.V.* XIX (Cologne, 1958 ff.).

Kerl, Bruno. *Abriss der Thonwaarenindustrie.* 1871. 2nd ed. entitled *Handbuch der gesammten Thonwaarenindustrie.* 1879. 3rd ed. Brunswick, 1907.

Lane, Arthur. *Italian Porcelain: With a Note on Buen Retiro.* London: Faber & Faber, 1954.

Larchevêque, Marc. *Fabrication industrielle de la porcelaine dure.* Paris, 1898.

Lauth, Charles and Vogt, Georges. *Notes techniques sur la fabrication de la porcelaine nouvelle.* Paris, 1885.

Lehnert, Georg. *Das Porzellan.* Bielefeld, 1902.

Leistikow-Duchardt, Annelore. *Die Entwicklung eines neuen Stils im Porzellan: Eine Betrachtung über die neuzeitliche Porzellankunst in Europa seit 1860.* Heidelberger Kunstgeschichtliche Abhandlungen, new series, vol. 4. Heidelberg: Carl Winter-Universitätsverlag, 1957.

Lesur, Adrien and Tardy. *Les Porcelaines françaises.* Paris: Tardy, 1967.

Liebscher, Imfried and Willert, Franz. *Technologie der Keramik.* Dresden: VEB Verlag für Kunst, 1955.

Magnier, M. Désiré. *Nouveau manuel complet du porcelainier, faïencier, potier de terre...* 1864. 2nd ed. completely rev. by H. Bertran. Paris: Roret, 1898. 3rd ed. Paris: Laget, 1977.

Mallet, John. 'Panorama de la porcelaine anglaise.' *Les Cahiers de la Céramique, du Verre et des Arts du Feu* 59 (1977): 38 f.

Mankowitz, Wolf and Haggar, Reginald G. *The Concise Encyclopedia of English Pottery and Porcelain.* London: André Deutsch, 1957.

Martin, Alexis. *Art ancien: Faïences et porcelaines.* 1886. 2nd ed. Paris, 1890.

Morazzoni, Giuseppe. *Le Porcellane italiane.* 2 vols. Text by Saul Levy. Milan: G. G. Görlich, 1960.

Mottola Molfino, Alessandra. *L'Arte della porcellana in Italia.* 2 vols. Busto Arsizio, Bramante, 1976.

Mundt, Barbara. 'Vom Biedermeier bis zur neueren Zeit: 1830–1930.' In Hofmann, Friedrich Hermann. *Das Porzellan der europäischen Manufakturen.* Propyläen-Kunstgeschichte, sp. vol. I. 2nd enlarged ed. Berlin: Propyläen-Verlag, 1980, pp. 225 ff.

——. *Historismus: Kunstgewerbe zwischen Biedermeier und Jugendstil.* Munich: Keyser, 1981.

Neuwirth, Waltraud. *Porzellan aus Wien: Von Du Paquier zur Manufaktur im Augarten.* Vienna, Munich: privately published, 1974.

——. *Porzellanmaler-Lexikon. 1840–1914.* 2 vols. Brunswick: Klinkhardt & Biermann, 1976.

——. *Das Bindenschild als Porzellanmarke: Original, Imitation, Verfälschung, Fälschung.* Vienna: privately published, 1977.

——. *Meissner Marken und Wiener Bindenschild: Original, Imitation, Verfälschung, Fälschung.* Vienna: privately published, 1977.

——. *Wiener Porzellan: Original, Kopie, Verfälschung, Fälschung.* Vienna: privately published, 1979.

Olivar Daydi, Marçal. *La Porcelana en Europa desde sus origines hasta principios del siglo.* 2 vols. Barcelona: Seix Barrel, 1952.

Pelka, Otto. *Keramik der Neuzeit.* Leipzig: Klinkhardt & Biermann, 1924.

Picard, Mathurin. *Nouveau Traité de peinture sur porcelaine et sur faïence....* Paris, 1893.

Plinval-Salgues, Régine de. 'La Céramique française aux expositions industrielles de la première moitié du XIXème siècle.' *Les Cahiers de la Céramique* XXII (1961): 84–103. [*see also* Plinval de Guillebon]

Rada, Pravoslav. *Techniken der Kunsttöpferei.* Trans. from the Czech by C. and F. Kirschner. Berlin, 1960.

Rayner, Philip M. *Thomas Goode of London, 1827–1977.* n.p., 1977.

Ris-Paquot, Oscar Edmond. *Traité pratique de peinture sur faïence et porcelaine à l'usage des débutants.* Paris, 1886.

Rontgen, Robert E. *Marks on German, Bohemian and Austrian Porcelain: 1710 to the Present.* Exton, PA: Schiffer, 1981.

Sarasino, Ernesto [Mauri, L. de]. *L'Amatore di maioliche e porcellane.* 1899. 3rd. ed. Milan: Ubrico Hoepli, 1924.

Savage, George. *English Ceramics.* 1961. 2nd ed., New York: Alpine, 1981.

Schertel, Wilhelm. *Die deutsche Porzellanindustrie.* Leipzig, 1926.

Schnorr von Carolsfeld, Ludwig. *Porzellan der europäischen Fabriken.* 1912. 5th ed. completely rev. by E. Köllmann. Brunswick: Klinkhardt & Biermann, 1956.

Shinn, Charles and Dorrie. *The Illustrated Guide to Victorian Parian China.* London: Barrie & Jenkins, 1971.

*Sprechsaal: Organ der Porzellan-, Glas- und Thonwarenindustrie* (Coburg, 1876 ff).

Strele, Karl and Tscheuschner, Emil. *Handbuch der Porzellan- und Glasmalerei.* 4th ed. Weimar: Voigt, 1883.

Thieme, Ulrich and Becker, Felix. *Allgemeines Lexikon der bildenden Künstler von der Antike bis zur Gegenwart.* Ed. by V. Hans Vollmer. Leipzig: E. A. Seemann, 1907–1947.

*Thonindustrie-Zeitung: Wochenschrift für die Interessen der Ziegel-, Terracotten-, Töpferwaaren-, Steingut-, Porzellan-, Cement- und Kalkindustrie* (Berlin, 1877–1882).

Vogt, Georges. *La Porcelaine.* Paris, 1892.

Ware, George W. *German and Austrian Porcelain.* Frankfurt: Lothar Woeller Press, 1951.

Weiss, G. *Ullstein-Porzellanbuch: Eine Stilkunde und Technikgeschichte des Porzellans mit Marken-Verzeichnis.* 1964. 6th rev. ed. Berlin, Frankfurt, Vienna: Ullstein, 1975.

Wills, Geoffrey. *English Pottery and Porcelain.* London: Guiness Superlatives, 1969.

Wittwer, Elisabeth. *La Peinture sur porcelaine.* Lausanne: Payot, 1965.

## Austria

Bergmann, Alois. *Egerländer Porzellan und Steingut: 1789–1945; Ein Bildband aus Sammlungen in der Bundesrepublik Deutschland.* Amberg: Vereinigte Oberpfälzer Drück- und Verlags-Anstalt, 1975.

Ernst, Richard. *Wiener Porzellan des Klassizismus: Katalog der Sammlung Bloch-Bauer.* Vienna: Amalthea, 1925.

Falke, J. von. *Die K. K. Wiener Porzellanfabrik: Ihre Geschichte und die Sammlungen ihrer Arbeiten im K. K. österreichischen Museum für Kunst und Industrie.* Vienna: Gerold, 1887.

Folnesics, Josef and Braun, E. W. *Geschichte der K. K. Wiener Porzellan-Manufaktur.* Vienna, 1907.

Just, R. 'Karlsbader Sprudelbecher.' *Keramos* XVII (1962): 3–17.

Maué, C. 'Angelika Kauffmann invenit—Bildvorlagen für Wiener Porzellane.' *Keramos,* Fasc. 90 (1980): 9–38.

Mrazek, Wilhelm. 'Josef Nigg: Ein Wiener Blumenmaler.' *Alte und moderne Kunst* series 1, IV (1956): 2–5.

——. 'Anton Grassi.' *Alte und moderne Kunst* series 1, IV (1956): 15–20.

——. 'Das grosse Service für den Herzog von Wellington aus der Wiener Porzellanmanufaktur.' *Alte und moderne Kunst* series 11, LXXXI (1965): 22–24.

Neuwirth, Waltraud. *Wiener Porzellan: Original, Kopie, Verfälschung, Fälschung.* Vienna: privately published, 1979.

——. 'Weisse Ware Wien.' *Antiquitäten-Zeitung* XV (1980): Suppl. I–XXVII.

## Austria-Hungary

Boncz, C. and Gink, K. *Herender Porzellan.* Budapest, 1962.

Csány, K. *Geschichte der ungarischen Keramik, des Porzellans und ihrer Marken.* Budapest: Verlag für bildende Kunst, 1954.

Ruziscka, I. *Herender Porzellan.* Budapest: Officina, 1950.

## Belgium

Demeuldre-Coché, Henri. 'Windish-Cristophe.' In *Biographie nationale.* Vol. 41, fasc. 2. Brussels, 1980.

Jottrand, Mireille. 'La Porcelaine de Tournai.' *L'Œil* 282–283 (Jan.–Feb., 1979): 16–23.

## Bohemia

Meyer, Hans. *Böhmisches Porzellan und Steingut.* Leipzig: Hiersemann, 1927.

Poche, E. *Böhmisches Porzellan.* Prague: Artia, 1956.

## France

Albis, Jean d'. 'Le Japonisme et les céramiques de Bracquemond.' *Plaisir de France* 401 (July–Aug., 1972): 42–46.

—. 'Limoges: Bing et l'art nouveau.' *Connaissance des Arts* 320 (Oct., 1978): 125–132

— and Romanet, Céleste. *La Porcelaine de Limoges*. Paris: Sous le Vent, 1980.

Banès and Destenay. 'Les Manufactures de céramique à Toulouse et à Valentine.' *Bulletin municipal de la ville de Toulouse* 43rd year, V (May, 1939): 308–318.

Baumgart, Emile. 'La Manufacture de Sèvres en 1903.' *Le Figaro illustré* (Sept., 1903): 2–24.

Bloit, Michel. 'Une Porcelaine de Paris, Locré.' *Connaissance des Arts* 327 (May, 1979): 1–5.

Bourgeois, Emile and Lechevallier-Chevignard, Georges. *Le Biscuit de Sèvres: Recueil de modèles de la manufacture de Sèvres au XVIIIᵉ siècle*. Paris: Lafitte, 1913.

Brunet, Marcelle. 'L'Œuvre de Jean-Charles Develly à la Manufacture de Sèvres, 1813–1848.' Unpublished thesis, Ecole du Louvre, Paris, 1947.

—. *Les Marques de Sèvres*. Paris: Gérard Le Prat, 1953.

— and Préaud, Tamara. *Sèvres des origines à nos jours*. Fribourg: Office du Livre, 1978.

Chevallier, Bernard. 'Sèvres sous le Second Empire.' *L'Estampille* CXII (Aug., 1979): 28–39.

—. 'Les Marques en creux de la porcelaine de Sèvres (1801–1871).' *Bulletin des Amis Suisses de la Céramique* XCIV (Dec., 1980): 5–23.

Du Pasquier, Jacqueline. *Céramiques bordelaises du XIXᵉᵐᵉ siècle: Collection Doumézy*. Bordeaux, 1975. [Published by the city of Bordeaux.]

Faÿ-Hallé, Antoinette. 'De l'esprit dans les formes: Production de la Manufacture de Sèvres dans la seconde moitié du XIXᵉᵐᵉ siècle.' *Plaisir de France* 435 (Jan., 1976): 64–69.

Gaulejac, Bernard de. 'Les Manufactures de porcelaine de la Nièvre.' In *Mémoires de la Société académique du Nivernais,* vol. 53. Nevers, 1965.

Gauthier, Serge. 'Les Pouyat et leurs "blancs".' *Les Cahiers de la Céramique* XIII (1959): 35–39.

Giacomotti, Jeanne and Verlet, Pierre. *Le Musée National Adrien Dubouché à Limoges*. Paris: Editions des Musées nationaux, 1965.

Grellier, Camille. 'L'Industrie de la porcelaine en Limousin: Ses origines. Son évolution.' Thesis, Paris, 1908.

Hosotte-Reynaud, Manon. 'Aperçus inédits sur une manufacture de porcelaine de Paris La Courtille: De Locré à Pouyat, 1773–1823.' *Les Cahiers de la Céramique XXXV* (1964): 156–172.

Lechevallier-Chevignard, Georges. *La Manufacture de porcelaine de Sèvres....* 2 parts. Paris: Laurens, 1908.

Ledoux-Lebard, Denise. *Inventaire général du Musée national de Versailles et des Trianons*. Published under the direction of Gérald Van Der Kemp. Vol. 1: *Le Grand Trianon: Meubles et objets d'art*. Paris: F. de Nobele, 1975 ff.

Le Jeune, Jean. *Les Anciennes Manufactures de porcelaine de Basse-Normandie*. Coutances: Editions Nôtre-Dame, 1962.

Leroux, Alfred. *Histoire de la porcelaine de Limoges*. Published under the auspices of the Musée national Adrien Dubouché and the Musée national de Limoges. Limoges: Ducourtieux et Gout, 1904.

Leymaire, Camille. 'Essai de classification des anciennes porcelaines de Limoges, Saint-Yrieix et Solignac.' *Bulletin de la Société archéologique et historique du Limousin*. XXXVII (1890); XXXVIII (1891); XL (1893); XLI and XLII (1894); XLIX (1901).

—. 'La porcelaine artistique de Limoges pendant le premier tiers du XIXᵉᵐᵉ siècle.' *Réunion des Sociétés des Beaux-Arts des départements* (1901): 456–470.

—. 'Notes sur l'histoire du biscuit à Limoges.' *Réunion des Sociétés des Beaux-Arts des départements* (1904): 353–371.

*Les Œuvres de la Manufacture Nationale de Sèvres de 1798 à 1932*. 5 vols. Vol. 1: *La Sculpture de 1738 à 1815*. Vol. 2: *La Sculpture moderne*. Paris, [1932].

Plinval de Guillebon, Régine de [*see also* Plinval-Salgues]. *Paris Porcelain 1770–1850*. Trans. by Robin R. Charleston. London: Barrie & Jenkins, 1972. [Published in New York: Walker and Co. as *Porcelain of Paris*.]

Plinval-Salgues, Régine de. 'Les Schoelcher et la porcelaine de Paris, 1798–1834.' *Les Cahiers de la Céramique* VI (Spring, 1957): 52–60.

—. 'L'Exotisme de Jacob Petit.' *Art de France* III (1963): 195–200.

— and Lasserre, Charles. 'La Production de la manufacture de la Courtille, XVIIIᵉ et XIXᵉ siècles.' *Les Cahiers de la Céramique* XXXVIII (1966): 102–118.

—. 'Les Porcelaines de Jacob Petit.' *Plaisir de France* 365 (Mar., 1969): 2–20.

Tocqueville, Hélène de. 'La Porcelaine de Valognes 1792–1812.' *L'Estampille* LXXI (Nov., 1975): 21–29.

Verlet, Pierre; Grandjean, Serge and Brunet, Marcelle. *La Porcelaine de Sèvres:*

*XVIIᵉ, XVIIIᵉ, XIXᵉ et XXᵉ*. Paris: Gérard Le Prat, 1953.

Weisberg, Gabriel P. 'Gérard, Dufraisseix and Abbot: The Manufactory of Art Nouveau Bing Porcelain in Limoges, France.' *The Connoisseur* 792 (Feb., 1978): 125–129.

## Germany

Berling, Karl. *Das Meissner Porzellan und seine Geschichte*. Leipzig: Brockhaus, 1900.

—. ed. *Meissen China: An Illustrated History*. 1910. Facsimile reprint of 1st ed. of this trans. New York: Dover Publications, and London: Constable, 1972.

Braun-Ronsdorf, Margarete. *200 Jahre Nymphenburger Tafelgeschirr*. Darmstadt: Schneekluth, 1954.

Bublitz, E. *Die Königliche Porzellan-Manufaktur Berlin 1763–1913*. Berlin: Hausrath-Verlagsgesellschaft, 1913.

Deubner, Ludwig, ed. *Staatliche Porzellan-Manufaktur Nymphenburg, Ihre Entwicklung von der Gründung bis zur Gegenwart*. Munich: Bayerland, 1942.

Ducret, Siegfried. *Fürstenberger Porzellan*. 3 vols. Brunswick, 1965.

—. 'Das Schicksal des grossen Keramikers Louis Victor Gerverot.' *Keramos* XXVIII (1965): 29–39.

Erzgraber, J. *'Königlich Berlin' 1763–1913: Gedenkblatt zum 150 jährigen Jubiläum der königlichen Porzellan-Manufaktur*. Berlin, 1913.

Fritz, B. 'Die Porzellanmanufaktur Burgau 1901–1929: Ein thüringisches Unternehmen der Werkstättenbewegung des Jugendstils.' *Keramos* XC (1980): 88–154.

Hofmann, Friedrich Hermann. *Geschichte der Bayerischen Porzellan-Manufaktur Nymphenburg*. 3 vols. Leipzig: Hiersemann, 1921–1923.

Jedding, Hermann. *Meissener Porzellan des 19. und 20. Jahrhundert: 1800–1933*. Munich: Keyser, 1981.

Just, J. 'Marken und Markierungen auf Meissner Porzellan ab 1775.' *Keramos* LI (1971): 22–26 and LIV (1971): 113 f.

—. 'Der künstlerische Erneuerungsprozess der Porzellanmanufaktur Meissen um 1900.' Typescript dissertation, Halle: Martin-Luther-Universität, 1972.

Kolbe, G. *Geschichte der königlichen Porzellanmanufactur zu Berlin nebst einer einleitenden Übersicht der geschichtlichen Entwickelung der ceramischen Kunst*. Berlin: Decker, 1863.

Köllmann, E. 'Die Porzellanservice des Herzogs von Wellington.' *Keramos* X (1960): 86 ff.

—. *Berliner Porzellan (1763–1963)*. 2 vols. Brunswick and Berlin: Klinkhardt & Biermann, 1963.

König, W. von. 'Berliner Porzellaneier.' *Keramos* XLVIII (1970): 59–65.

Krause, H.J. 'Zur Geschichte der Regensburger Porzellan- und Steingutfabrik.' *Keramos* LXXXVI (1979): 79.

Kunze, J. 'Beitrag zur Geschichte der Porzellanmanufaktur Meissen in der Biedermeierzeit.' *Keramos* LXXXVI (1979): 59–64.

—. 'Lithophanien der Meissner Porzellanmanufaktur.' *Keramos* XCII (1981): 3–10.

Leichter, H. 'Berliner Lithophanien: Eine fast vergessene grafische Technik des Biedermeier.' In *idem. Der Bär von Berlin: Jahrbuch des Vereins für die Geschichte Berlins*, vol. 23. Berlin: Westkreuz Verlag, 1974, pp. 1–20.

Liers, L. and Neumeister, J. *Die Gothaer Porzellanmanufaktur*. Gotha: Museen der Stadt, 1975.

Pfeiffer, Max Adolf. *Schwarzburger Werkstätten für Porzellankunst, Max Adolf Pfeiffer GmbH*. Unterweisbach, 1912–1913.

Rückert, R. 'Wittelsbacher Porzellane: Tassen und Vasen des frühen 19. Jahrhunderts (aus Nymphenburg).' *Kunst & Antiquitäten* I–III (1980): I, 30–39; II, 24–32.

Schade, Günter. *Berliner Porzellan: Zur Kunst und Kulturgeschichte der Berliner Porzellanmanufakturen*. Leipzig: Koehler & Amelang, 1978.

Scheffler, Wolfgang. *Berlin im Porzellanbild seiner Manufaktur*. Schriften zur Berliner Kunst- und Kulturgeschichte, vol. 4. Berlin: Hessling, 1963.

Scherer, Christian. *Das Fürstenberger Porzellan*. Berlin, 1909.

Scherf, Helmut. *Thüringer Porzellan: Unter besonderer Berücksichtigung der Erzeugnisse des 18. und frühen 19. Jahrhunderts*. Leipzig: VEB E.A. Seemann, 1980.

Treskow, Irene von. *Die Jugendstil-Porzellane der KPM: Bestandskatalog der Königlichen Porzellan-Manufaktur Berlin 1896–1914*. Munich: Prestel, 1971.

Vershofen, Wilhelm. *Figurine und Fadenführer: Der Werkstoff Porzellan in der 180jährigen Geschichte der Porzellanfabrik zu Kloster Veilsdorf 1760–1940*. Bamberg, 1940.

Walcha, Otto. 'Der Meissner Porzellanmaler Christian Gottlieb Hottewitzsch.' *Keramos* XV (1962): 3–17.

—. 'Die Marcolini-Zeit der Meissner Manufaktur.' *Keramos* XL (1968): 13–38.

—. *Meissner Porzellan.* Ed. by H. Reibig. Dresden: Verlag der Kunst, 1973; 2nd ed., Gütersloh, Berlin, Munich, Vienna, 1975. [English trans. *Meissan Porcelain,* London: Trefoil; New York: Putnam, 1981].

Woeckel, Gerhard P. *Die Tierplastik der Nymphenburger Porzellan-Manufaktur: Bestandskatalog 1905–1920.* Forschungshefte/Bayerisches Nationalmuseum, no. 5. Munich and Berlin: Zentralinstitut für Kunstgeschichte, 1978.

Wolff Metternich, Beatrix von. *Fürstenberger Porzellan: Ein Brevier.* Brunswick: Klinkhardt und Biermann, 1976.

Windorf, Hermann. *Die thüringische Porzellanindustrie in Vergangenheit und Gegenwart: Eine historische, volkswirtschaftliche, statistische Studie.* Leipzig: W. Schunke, 1912.

Zimmermann, Ernst. *Meissner Porzellan.* Leipzig: Hiersemann, 1926.


## Great Britain and Ireland

Atterbury, Paul. *The Story of Minton from 1793 to the Present Day.* n. p., 1978.

— and Irvine, Louise. *The Doulton Story.* Stoke-on-Trent, 1979.

Barrett, Franklin Allen. *Worcester Porcelain.* London: Faber & Faber, 1953.

—. *Worcester Porcelain and Lund's Bristol.* London: Faber & Faber, 1966.
and Thorpe, Arthur L. *Derby Porcelain, 1750–1848.* London: Faber & Faber, 1971.

Cox, Alwyn and Angela. 'The Rockingham Dessert Service for William IV: A Royal Extravaganza…' *The Connoisseur* 756 (Feb., 1975): 90–97.

Exley, Clifford Landseer. *The Pinxton China Factory.* Ed. by Franklin A. Barrett and Arthur L. Thrope. Sutton-on-the-Hill: Mr. & Mrs. Coke-Steel, Trusley Old Hall, Derby 1963.

Eyles, Desmond. *Royal Doulton 1815–1962, the Doulton Lambeth Wares.* London: Hutchinson 1965.

—. *The Doulton Burslem Wares.* London: Barrie & Jenkins for Royal Doulton Tableware Ltd, 1980.

Gilhespy, Frank Brayshaw. *Crown Derby Porcelain.* Leigh-on-Sea: F. Lewis, 1951.

—. *Derby Porcelain.* London: MacGibbon & Kee, 1961.

Godden, Geoffrey Arthur. *Minton Pottery and Porcelain of the First Period, 1793–1850.* London: Barrie & Jenkins, 1968.

—. *Coalport and Coalbrookdale Porcelains.* London: Barrie & Jenkins, 1970.

—. *The Illustrated Guide to Ridgway Porcelains.* London: Barrie & Jenkins, 1972.

Haggar, Reginald George and Adams, Elizabeth. *Mason Porcelain and Ironstone, 1796–1853: Miles Mason and the Mason Manufacturies.* London: Faber & Faber, 1977.

Haslem, John. *The Old Derby China Factory: The Workmen and Their Productions.* London: George Bell & Sons, 1876.

Hayden, Arthur. *Spode and His Successors. A History of the Pottery, Stoke-on-Trent from 1765–1865.* London: Cassel, 1925.

Hobson, Robert Lockhart. *Worcester Porcelain. A Description of the Ware from the Wall Period to the Present Day.* London: Quaritch, 1910.

Holgate, David. *New Hall and its Imitators.* Faber monographs on Pottery and Porcelain. London: Faber & Faber, 1971.

Honey, William Bowyer. *Wedgwood Ware.* Faber monographs on Pottery and Porcelain. London: Faber & Faber, 1948.

Hurlbutt, Frank. *Old Derby Porcelain and its Artist-Workmen.* London: T. Werner Laurie, 1925.

John, William David. *Nantgarw Porcelain.* Assisted by S. John and B. A. Williams. Newport: R. H. Johns, 1948. Supplement, 1956.

—. *William Billingsley (1758–1828): His Outstanding Achievements as an Artist and Porcelain Maker.* Assisted by Anne and Jacqueline Simcox. Newport: Ceramic Book Co, 1968.

Lockett, Terence Anthony. *Davenport Pottery and and Porcelain, 1794–1887.* Newton Abbot: David and Charles, 1972.

Mackenna, F. Severne. *Worcester Porcelain: The Wall Period and its Antecedents.* Leigh-on-Sea: F. Lewis, 1950.

Nance, E. Morton. *The Pottery and Porcelain of Swansea and Nantgarw.* London: Batsford, 1943.

Rice, Dennis George. *Rockingham Ornamental Porcelain.* London: Adam, 1966.

—. *The Illustrated Guide to Rockingham Pottery and Porcelain.* London: Barrie & Jenkins, 1971.

Sandon, Henry. *The Illustrated Guide to Worcester Porcelain.* London: Barrie & Jenkins, 1969.

—. *Royal Worcester Porcelain from 1862 to the Present Day.* London: Barrie & Jenkins, 1973.

—. *Flight and Barr Worcester Porcelain 1783–1840.* Woodbridge: Antique Collectors' Club, 1978.

Smith, Alan Gilbert. *The Illustrated Guide to Liverpool Herculaneum Pottery, 1796–1840.* London: Barrie & Jenkins, 1970.

Smith, G. M. *Belleek Porcelain and Pottery: A Handbook for the Collector.* St Peter Port, Guernsey: Toucan Press, 1979.

Turner, W. *The Ceramics of Swansea and Nantgarw: History.* London: Bemrose, 1897.

Twitchett, John and Bailey, Betty. *Royal Crown Derby.* 1976. 2nd ed. London: Barrie & Jenkins, 1980.

Twitchett, John. *Derby Porcelain.* London: Barrie & Jenkins, 1980.

Whiter, Leonard. *Spode: A History of the Family, Factory and Wares from 1733 to 1833.* 1970. 2nd ed. London: Barrie & Jenkins, 1978.


## Italy

Baroni, Costantino. *Le Ceramiche di Nove di Bassano.* Venice, 1932.

Brosio, Valentino. 'La Céramique en Italie au XIX^ème siècle: Les Dortu, Richard et Cie à Turin.' *Les Cahiers de la Céramique, du Verre et des Arts du Feu,* no. 52 (1973): 34–39.

Caròla Perrotti, Angela. *La Porcellana della Real fabrica ferdinandea (1771–1806).* [Naples]: Banco di Napoli, 1978.

Ginori Lisci, Leonardo. *La Porcellana di Doccia.* Intro. by Arthur Lane. Milan: Electa, 1964.

Liverani, Giuseppe. *Il Museo delle porcellane di Doccia.* Preface by Bruno Molaioli. [Sesto Fiorentino]: Società ceramica italiane Richard-Ginori (Milan: A. Pizzi), 1967.

Mauri, L. de. *Vinovo and its Porcelain: A Page of the History in Piedmont.* London: Batsford, 1925.


## The Netherlands

Singelenberg-van der Meer, M. *Nederlandse keramiek- en glasmerken 1880–1940.* Lochem: De Tijdstroom, 1980.


## Portugal

Plinval-Salgues, Régine de. 'La Contribution française à la porcelaine portugaise.' *Museu,* series 2, no. 2 (May, 1961): 5–14.

Queirós, José. *Ceramica Portugueza.* 1907. 2nd rev. ed. entitled *Cerâmica portuguesa.* 2 vols. Lisbon, 1948.

Valente, Vasco. *Porcelana artistica portuguesa.* Porto, 1949.


## Russia

Lansere, A. K. *[Russian Porcelain: The Art of the First Porcelain Factories in Russia.]* Leningrad, 1968. [In Russian with summaries in English, German and French.]

Lukomskij, G. *Russisches Porzellan 1744–1924.* Berlin: Wasmuth, 1924.

Popov, A. 'Russian Imperial Porcelains.' *The Connoisseur* XCV (1935): 322 ff.

—. 'The Francis Gardner and Other Russian Porcelain Factories.' *The Connoisseur* XCVI (1935): 68 ff.

Ross, M. C. *Russian Porcelain: The Collections of Marjorie Merriweather Post, Hillwood, Washington, D.C.* Norman, OK: Oklahoma Press, 1968.

Rozembergh, A. *Les Marques de la porcelaine russe, période impériale.* Paris: H. Champion, 1926.

Wolf, Baron. *Imperatorski Farforovi Savod 1744–1904 [The Imperial Porcelain Manufactory at St Petersburg].* St Petersburg: Imperatorszi Savod, 1906. [In Russian with French summary.]


## Scandinavia

Arnö-Berg, Inga. *Serviser från Gustavsberg.* Västerås: Ica-bokförl., 1971.

Baeckstrøm, A. *Rørstrand och dess tillverkningar 1726–1926.* Stockholm: Nordiska Museet, 1930.

Bing, J. H.; Engelstoft, P.; Hendriksen, F.; and Simonsen, P. *Festskrift Bing & Grøndahls porcelaensfabrik 1853–1928.* Copenhagen: Nielsen & Lydiche, 1928.

Bodelsen, Merete. 'Sèvres–Copenhagen. Crystal Glazes and Stoneware at the Turn of the Century.' In Grändjean, Bredo L. *et al. The Royal Copenhagen Porcelain Manufactory, 1775–1975.* Copenhagen, 1975, pp. 58–88.

Bøe, Alf. *Porsgrunds porselaensbavrik 1885–1965. Bedrift og produksjon gjennom åtti år. 1885–1965.* Oslo: Hos Johan Grundt Tanums Forlag, 1967.

Grandjean, Bredo L. *Flora Danica Stellet.* Copenhagen, 1950. [English and Danish text.]

—. *Kongelig dansk porcelæn, 1775–1884.* Copenhagen, 1962.

—; Helsted, Dyveke; and Bodelsen, Merete. *The Royal Copenhagen Porcelain Manufactory, 1775–1975.* Trans. by David Hohnen. Copenhagen: Royal Copenhagen Porcelain Manufactory, 1975.

Grandjean, Bredo L. *Biscuit efter Thorvaldsen.* Copenhagen: Thorvaldsen Museum, 1978.

Hayden, Ritter Arthur. *Kopenhagener Porzellan (Royal Copenhagen Porcelain): Entwicklungsgeschichte der Königlichen Porzellanmanufaktur in Kopenhagen vom 18. Jahrhundert bis zur Gegenwart.* Trans. by C. F. Einhold. 2nd ed. Leipzig: Hiersemann, 1924.

Helsted, Dyveke. 'Arnold Krog and Porcelain.' In Grandjean, Bredo L. *et al. The Royal Copenhagen Porcelain Manufactory, 1775–1975.* Copenhagen, 1975, pp. 28–57.

Lassen, Erik. *En københavnsk porcelænsfabriks historie: Bing & Grøndahl 1853–1978.* Copenhagen: Nyt Nordisk Forlag, 1978.

Zahle, E. *Bing & Grøndahl 1853–1953.* Copenhagen, 1953.

### Spain

Conde de Casal, M. Escriva de Romani y de la Quintana. *Historia de la Ceramica de Alcora.* Madrid: Aldus, 1919.

### Switzerland

Martinet, Aimé. *Guide de l'amateur de porcelaine de Nyon (1781–1813).* Geneva, 1911.

Molin, Aloys de. *Histoire documentaire de la Manufacture de Porcelaine de Nyon: 1781–1813.* Lausanne: Georges Bridel & Co, 1904.

Pelichet, Edgar. *Merveilleuse porcelaine de Nyon.* Lausanne: Editions du Grand-Pont, 1973.

## CATALOGUES

### Austria

'Amtlicher Bericht über die Wiener Weltausstellung im Jahr 1873.' Fasc. 1–20. Brunswick, 1874–1875.

Griessmaier, Viktor *et al.* '100 Jahre Österreichisches Museum für angewandte Kunst, Katalog des Museums.' Vienna, 1964–1965.

Mrazek, Wilhelm and Neuwirth, Waltraud. 'Wiener Porzellan. 1718–1864.' Vienna: Österreichisches Museum für angewandte Kunst, 1970.

Neuwirth, Waltraud. 'Österreichische Keramik des Jugendstils: Katalog der Sammlung des Österreichischen Museums für angewandte Kunst.' Munich: Prestel, 1974.

### Belgium

Deroubaix, Christiane. 'Catalogue des porcelaines de Tournai du Musée de Mariemont.' Brussels, 1958.

### Bohemia

Brožová, Jamilla. 'Historismus umelecké remeslo 1860–1900 [Arts and Crafts in History].' Prague: Umeleckoprùmyslové Muzeum, 1975–1976.

Poche, E. 'Starý český porcelán [Old Czech Porcelain].' Prague: Umeleckoprùmyslové Muzeum, 1951.

Vresová, L. 'Český porcelán (Klášterec nad Ohři) [Czech Porcelain (Klösterle)].' Prague: Umeleckoprùmyslové Muzeum, 1959.

### France

'Amtlicher Bericht über die Weltausstellung zu Paris im Jahre 1867.' Vienna, 1867–1869.

Du Pasquier, Jacqueline. 'Exposition de céramiques bordelaises du XIXème siècle.' Paris: Musée des Arts décoratifs. Dec. 1975–Mar. 1976.

Faÿ-Hallé, Antoinette and Préaud, Tamara. 'Porcelaines de Sèvres au XIXème siècle.' Preface by Henry-Pierre Fourest. Paris: Editions des Musées nationaux, 1975. [Exhibition held at Sèvres: Musée National de Céramique.]

Gauthier, Serge. 'Porcelaine de Limoges des origines à 1880.' Preface by Henry-Pierre Fourest. Limoges: Musée municipal, 15 May–15 Oct. 1949.

Grandjean, Serge and Brunet, Marcelle. 'Les Grands Services de Sèvres.' Preface by Pierre Verlet. Sèvres: Musée National de Céramique, 1951.

### Germany

*Amtlicher Bericht über die Allgemeine Deutsche Gewerbe-Ausstellung in Berlin.* Vol. 3. Berlin, 1844.

Arenhövel, Willmuth, ed. 'Berlin und die Antike, Katalog.' Berlin: independently organized, 1979.

Baer, W. 'Berliner Porzellan vom Rokoko zum Biedermeier: Ständige Ausstellung im Belvedere des Charlottenburger Schlossparks.' Berlin, [1971].

— and Lack, H. W. 'Pflanzen auf Porzellan. Katalog zum 300jährigen Bestehen des Botanischen Gartens.' Berlin, 1979.

Beaucamp-Markowsky, B. *Europäisches Porzellan und ostasiatisches Exportporzellan. Geschirr und Ziergerät.* Kataloge des Kunstgewerbemuseums der Stadt Köln, vol. 4. Cologne, 1980.

Bott, Gerhard and Heller, Carl B. *Jugendstil. Vom Beitrag Darmstadts zur internationalen Kunstbewegung um 1900.* Katalog des Hessischen Landesmuseums. 2nd ed. Darmstadt, 1973.

Bröhan, Karl H. *Kunst der Jahrhundertwende und der zwanziger Jahre.* Sammlung Karl H. Bröhan, Berlin, vol. 2. Part II: *Metall-Porzellan.* Berlin, 1977.

'Carl Thieme, Potschappel: Katalog.' n.p., 1966.

Erichsen-Firle, U. *Figürliches Porzellan.* Kataloge des Kunstgewerbemuseums der Stadt Köln, vol. 5. Cologne, 1975.

Glaser, Hubert, ed. *Krone und Verfassung: König Max I. Joseph und der neue Staat. Katalog Wittelsbach und Bayern.* 3 vols. Munich, 1980. [Particularly the article by R. Rückert, pp. 651 ff. of vol. 3, part 2.]

Hakenjos, B. and Klinge, E. 'Europäische Kunst des Jugendstils: Ausstellungskatalog Düsseldorf.' Düsseldorf: Hetjens-Museum, 1976.

Hofmann, Friedrich Hermann. *Das europäische Porzellan des bayerischen Nationalmuseums.* Kataloge des bayerischen Nationalmuseums in München, vol. 10. Munich, 1908.

Klein, Adalbert. *Europäisches Porzellan im Hetjens-Museum.* Kataloge des Kunstmuseums Düsseldorf II. Vol. 1: *Keramik.* Düsseldorf, 1966.

Mundt, Barbara. *Historismus. Kunsthandwerk und Industrie im Zeitalter der Weltausstellungen.* Kataloge des Kunstgewerbemuseums Berlin, vol. 7. Berlin: Kunstgewerbemuseum, 1973.

Scherf, Helmut. 'Thüringer Porzellan. Geschichte, Fabriken und Erzeugnisse: Katalogheft Museum Leuchtenberg.' [Thuringia], 1978.

Spies, Gerd. 'Fürstenberger Porzellan. Empire–Gegenwart, Ausstellungskatalog Braunschweig.' Brunswick: Städtisches Museum, 1972.

### Great Britain

Aslin, Elisabeth and Atterbury Paul. 'Minton 1798–1910.' London: Victoria and Albert Museum, Thomas Goode & Co Ltd, 1976.

Holdway, H. and Whiter L. '200 Years of Spode.' Intro. by W. T. Monnington. London: Royal Academy of Arts, 1970.

Messenger, Michael Frederick. *Caughley and Coalport Porcelain in the Collection of Clive House, Shrewsbury: A Catalogue (Clive House Museum).* London: Remploy, 1976.

Mountford, A.; Holgate, D.; Haggar, R. G.; and Lockett, T. A. 'Staffordshire Porcelain, 1740–1851.' Foreword by R. A. Mountford. Hanley/Stoke-on-Trent: City Museum and Art Gallery, 1979.

'Official Descriptive and Illustrated Catalogue: Great Exhibition of the Works of Industry of All Nations.' London, 1851.

Rackham, Bernard. *Catalogue of the Schreiber Collection of English Pottery and Porcelain.* Vol. 1: *Porcelain.* London: Victoria & Albert Museum, 1928.

'Spode-Copeland 1765–1965.' Intro. by Robert Copeland. Copenhagen: Det Danske Kunstindustrimuseum, 1966.

'The Wedgwood Museum Barlaston.' [Barlaston], 1974.

## Italy

Barbantini, N. 'Le Porcellane di Venezia e delle Nove.' Venice; Ca' Rezzonico, 1936.

Pettenati, Silvana. *Cultura figurativa e architettonica negli Stati del Re di Sardegna 1773–1861.* 3 vols. Turin: Palazzo Reale, 1980. [Especially vol. 1, pp. 120–146; vol. 2, pp. 597–628; vol. 3, pp. 745–768.]

## The Netherlands

Haase, Heinz-Wilhelm. 'Rozenburg-Keramik, Sonderausstellung.' Fasc. 46. Bremen: Focke-Museum, 1976.

## Russia

Nikiforowa, L. R. 'Russian Porcelain in the Hermitage Collection: Catalogue.' Leningrad: Hermitage Museum, 1973.

## Scandinavia

Erichsen, J. 'Københavnske prospekter pa kongelig porcelain: Katalog.' Copenhagen: Københavns Bymuseum, 1975.

Lutteman, H., ed. 'Gustavsberg 150 år, Ausstellungskatalog.' Stockholm: Nationalmuseum, 1975.

Simonsen, E., ed. 'Bing & Grøndahl 125 år, Ausstellungskatalog.' Copenhagen: Det Danske Kunstindustrimuseum, 1978.

## Switzerland

Pettenati, Silvana. *Cultura figurativa a architettonica negli Stati del Re di Sardegna 1773–1861.* 3 vols. Turin: Palazzo Reale, 1980. [Especially vol. 1, pp. 120–146.]

# Acknowledgments

Antoinette Faÿ-Halle wishes to thank her colleagues in the French national ceramic museums for their constant and invaluable help: H.-P. Fourest, E. Fontan, G. Le Duc, G. Sarrauste de Menthière, J. Lafargue, P. Gossart and C. Albert. She owes a debt of gratitude to all those abroad who have helped her, in particular R. Copeland, A. Dawson and J. Mallet as well as N. Ballu-Loureiro, and would also like to thank the following for their assistance: D. Alcouffe, A. and J. d'Albis, B. Bailey, Miss Blake-Roberts, G. de Bellaigue, Y. Brunhammer, M.-T. Coulery, G. Godden, H. Guerreiro, J. Harland, J. Jones, A. Linscott, D. Ménager, A. Mountford, Prince Murat, R. de Plinval de Guillebon, T. Préaud, H. Sandon, and J. Twitchett.

Barbara Mundt is grateful to her colleagues and friends in Berlin, Stefan Bursche and Winifried Baer, for their untiring help and support, and also thanks those other colleagues who have provided invaluable assistance: A. Bergman, Nittenau; B. Grandjean and E. Lassen, Copenhagen; J. Horschik, Dresden-Pillnitz (†); H. Jedding, Hamburg; Rainer Rückert, Munich and W. Neuwirth, Vienna.

# Photo Credits

The authors and the publisher wish to thank the photographers who took the photographs as well as the private collectors, museums and institutions that aided in assembling the photographic material. The photo research for this book was done by Ingrid de Kalbermatten. The numbers refer to plate numbers.

Amsterdam, Rijksmuseum   452
Barlaston, Stoke-on-Trent, Josiah Wedgwood & Sons   174–6
Bayeux, Musée Baron-Gérard   66
Berlin, Hans-Joachim Bartsch   254
—Berlin-Museum   97, 244, 253 (photos: Hans-Joachim Bartsch, Berlin)
—Bröhan Coll.   446–7, 450, 457, 459 (photos: J. Littkemann, Berlin)
—Kunstgewerbemuseum, Staatliche Museen Preussischer Kulturbesitz 93, 104, 231, 234, 242, 445, 449, 453–6, 461, 464–5, 471 (photos: Hans-Joachim Bartsch, Berlin); 243 (photo: Arne Psille); 335 (photo: Funke); 325, 451
—Staatliche Schlösser und Gärten   92 (photo: Hans-Joachim Bartsch, Berlin); 469
Berlin (East), Kunstgewerbemuseum   90–1, 245–6, 334
Caen, Musée des Beaux-Arts   65
Cardiff, National Museum of Wales   151
Christiansborg Castle   266, 350 (photos: Royal Copenhagen Porcelain Manufactory)
Cologne, Kunstgewerbemuseum   81, 107, 257, 349 (photos: Rheinisches Bildarchiv, Cologne)
Copenhagen, Bing & Grøndahl   351–4 (photos: Ole Woldbye, Copenhagen); 441–2
—Coll. of the Royal Copenhagen Porcelain Manufactory   268–70 (photos: Ole Woldbye, Copenhagen); 436, 438
—Det Danske Kunstindustrimuseum   113, 439–40 (photos: Ole Woldbye, Copenhagen)
Darmstadt, Grossherzogliche Sammlung   96 (photo: Heilmann, Messel)
—Hessisches Landesmuseum   458
Derby, City Museum and Art Gallery   123–4, 126–7, 130, 134–8
—The Royal Crown Derby Museum   120–1, 128, 131–2, 472, 474
Dresden, Porzellansammlung   252 (photo: Institut für Denkmalpflege, Berlin)
Düsseldorf, Hetjens-Museum   82, 468 (photos: Landesbildstelle Rheinland, Düsseldorf)
Eisenach, Thüringer Museum   106, 256, 258 (photos: Ursula Holzapfel, Eisenach)
Frankfort on the Main, Museum für Kunsthandwerk   89
Frederiksberg, Naturhistorisk Museum   115 (photo: Lennart Larsen)
Fürstenberg, Werksmuseum   100
Geneva, Coll. of the Musée d'art et d'histoire, Musée de l'Ariana   69–70 (photos: P. A. Ferrazzini, Geneva)
Hamburg, Museum für Kunst und Gewerbe   255, 332, 444
Leningrad, Hermitage Museum   95, 118, 228, 230, 233, 247, 470
Limoges, Bibliothèque de l'Ecole des Arts décoratifs   212–13 (photos: Georges Routhier, Paris); 214 (photo: Pierre Feuillade, Limoges)
—Coll. of Haviland & Co   310 (photo: J. A. Lajudie, Limoges)
—Musée National Adrien-Dubouché   38, 40–1, 52, 63–4, 201, 207–9, 215, 217–22, 304–9, 311–14, 373, 379, 391, 414, 416–17, 419–24, 427–8, 430–1, 434 (photos: Georges Routhier, Paris); 216, 303 (photos: Pierre Feuillade, Limoges); 302
Liverpool, Merseyside County Museum   188
London, Coll. of Her Majesty the Queen   277, 366 (photos: Lord Chamberlain's Office, London)
—Thomas Goode & Co, Ltd   381, 484
—Sotheby's Belgravia   338, 340, 342
—Victoria and Albert Museum   99, 156–7, 364, 367 (photos: Eileen Tweedy, London); 26, 73, 94, 125, 129, 133, 142, 148–9, 152–5, 159, 166, 170, 173, 178–9, 184–5, 271–5, 278–80, 283, 285–8, 291, 293, 295, 336–7, 355, 357–59, 361–63, 369, 371, 393–4, 475

Madrid, Museo Arqueologico Nacional   70, 224 (photos: Oronoz, Madrid)
Meissen, VEB Staatliche Porzellanmanufaktur   105, 250–1, 324, 327, 329–31, 333, 448
Munich, Bayerisches Nationalmuseum   108–9, 111
—Bayerische Verwaltung der staatlichen Schlösser, Gärten und Seen   326
—Residenzmuseum   110, 112, 241 (photos: Bayerische Verwaltung der staatlichen Schlösser, Gärten und Seen, Munich)
Neuilly, Pierre-Yves Guillemain Coll.   191
Paris, Michel Bloit Coll.   48, 51, 53, 426 (photos: Georges Routhier, Paris)
—Madeleine Castaing Coll.   49, 200 (photos: Georges Routhier, Paris)
—Coll. of His Excellency Prince Murat   12–13 (photos: Georges Routhier, Paris)
—Nicolier Coll.   46
—Conservatoire national des Arts et Métiers   294, 360 (photos: Musée des Techniques—CNAM, Paris)
—Musée des Arts décoratifs   33, 50, 199, 298, 405–6, 418–19, 437, 463 (photos: Musée des Arts décoratifs, Laurent Sully Jaulmes, Paris)
Pilsen, District Museum   87
Prague, Uméleckoprùmyslové Muzeum   85–6, 88, 259–62, 264–5, 267, 328, 343–5, 347; 346 (photo: Gabriel Urbanek, Prague)
Rueil-Malmaison, Musée National du Château de Malmaison   14, 28, 42, 44–5 (photos: Georges Routhier, Paris); 32 (photo: Musées Nationaux, Paris)
Sesto Fiorentino, Museo delle porcellane di Doccia   74, 315–17
Sèvres, Musée National de Céramique   1–9, 15, 17–19, 21–5, 27, 29–31, 34–7, 39, 43, 47, 55–62, 67–8, 72, 75, 98, 192, 194–8, 202–6, 210–11, 223, 232, 235–6, 263, 297, 299–300, 318–21, 348, 395–401, 403–4, 407–12, 413, 415, 425, 429, 432–3, 435 (photos: Georges Routhier, Paris); 102–3, 114, 117, 227, 229, 240, 248–9, 296, 341, 402, 443, 467 (photos: Musées Nationaux, Paris)
Stoke-on-Trent, City Museum and Art Gallery   182, 282
—Minton Museum, Royal Doulton Tableware Ltd   11, 289, 292, 365, 370, 372, 374–5, 485 (photos: Norman Jones, Stoke-on-Trent); 477, 483
—Spode Ltd Archives   10, 158
—Spode Ltd Museum   160, 377, 476 (photos: Norman Jones, Stoke-on-Trent); 163–5, 167–9, 171–2, 376, 378, 481
Stuttgart, Württembergisches Landesmuseum   101 (photo: Landesgewerbeamt, Baden-Württemberg); 339
Troyes, Musée des Beaux-Arts   301 (photo: Jean Bienaimé, Troyes)
Versailles, Grand Trianon   16, 20, 54, 193 (photos: Musées Nationaux, Paris)
Vienna, Ehemalige Hoftafel- und Silberkammer   79–80, 83–4 (photos: Marianne Haller, Südstadt)
—Österreichisches Museum für angewandte Kunst   77–8, 252–3, 255, 322–3; 466 (photo: Ingrid Schindler, Vienna)
Vista Alegre, Museu da Fabrica   76, 226
Washington, D.C., Hillwood Museum   116, 119, 356 (photos: James R. Dunlop, Washington, D.C.)
Weiden, Manufaktur Bauscher   460 (photo: S. Korn, Krefeld)
Windsor Castle, Coll. of Her Majesty the Queen   143, 145, 150, 274, 482 (photos: A. C. Cooper, London)
Worcester, The Dyson Perrins Museum   140–1, 368 (photos: J. M. Beckerley, Hanley Swan); 139, 144, 146, 383–90, 478–80
Worthing, Geoffrey Godden Coll.   177, 180–1, 183, 186–7, 189–90 (photos: Walter Gardiner, Worthing)
—Godden of Worthing Ltd   122, 147, 161, 281, 284, 290, 392, 473 (photos: Walter Gardiner, Worthing)
Zurich, Museum Bellerive   462 (photo: Marlen Perez, Hochfelden)

# Index

This book was printed in September, 1983 by
Grafische Betriebe NZZ Fretz AG, Zurich.
Setting: Febel AG, Basle.
Photolithography (coulour): Eurocrom 4, Treviso;
(black and white): Litho Kläusler AG, Kloten.
Binding: Burkhardt AG, Zurich.
Design and production: Emma Staffelbach.
Index: Christiane Gäumann-Gignoux.

Printed in Switzerland